Reading *Capital*'s Materialist Dialectic

Historical Materialism Book Series

The Historical Materialism Book Series is a major publishing initiative of the radical left. The capitalist crisis of the twenty-first century has been met by a resurgence of interest in critical Marxist theory. At the same time, the publishing institutions committed to Marxism have contracted markedly since the high point of the 1970s. The Historical Materialism Book Series is dedicated to addressing this situation by making available important works of Marxist theory. The aim of the series is to publish important theoretical contributions as the basis for vigorous intellectual debate and exchange on the left.

The peer-reviewed series publishes original monographs, translated texts, and reprints of classics across the bounds of academic disciplinary agendas and across the divisions of the left. The series is particularly concerned to encourage the internationalization of Marxist debate and aims to translate significant studies from beyond the English-speaking world.

For a full list of titles in the Historical Materialism Book Series available in paperback from Haymarket Books, visit: www.haymarketbooks.org/series_collections/1-historical-materialism.

Reading *Capital*'s Materialist Dialectic

Marx, Spinoza, and the Althusserians

Nick Nesbitt

Haymarket Books
Chicago, IL

First published in 2024 by Brill Academic Publishers, The Netherlands
© 2024 Koninklijke Brill NV, Leiden, The Netherlands

Published in paperback in 2025 by
Haymarket Books
P.O. Box 180165
Chicago, IL 60618
773-583-7884
www.haymarketbooks.org

ISBN: 979-8-88890-356-8

Distributed to the trade in the US through Consortium Book Sales and Distribution (www.cbsd.com) and internationally through Ingram Publisher Services International (www.ingramcontent.com).

This book was published with the generous support of Lannan Foundation, Wallace Action Fund, and the Marguerite Casey Foundation.

Special discounts are available for bulk purchases by organizations and institutions. Please call 773-583-7884 or email info@haymarketbooks.org for more information.

Cover art and design by David Mabb. Cover art is a monochrome detail of *Construct 35, Morris & Co. Medway / Rodchenko, untitled textile design*, pen on wallpaper mounted on canvas (2006).

Printed in the United States.

Library of Congress Cataloging-in-Publication data is available.

Contents

Preface: The Limits of Capital   VII
Acknowledgements   XIX
Abbreviations   XX

1 Introduction: *Reading Capital* Beyond Its Limits   1
   1   The Limits of *Reading Capital*   5
   2   An Act of Theoretical Repression   17
   3   *For Marx* in Its Limits   21
   4   Reading *Capital*'s Process of Exposition   28
   5   Hallucinatory Empiricism   35
   6   Reading *Capital*'s Apodictic Structure   38
   7   The Topography of the Attributes   42
   8   The Theoretical Danger of Monism   48
   9   Against Monism, the Return of Substance   53
  10   The Theoretical Basis of Theoreticism   57

2 What Is Materialist Analysis? Pierre Macherey's Spinozist Epistemology   62
   1   *Reading Capital*'s Materialist Dialectic   62
   2   A Theoretical Prolegomenon to the Materialist Analysis of Texts   68
   3   Textual Production in a Materialist Mode   69
   4   On the Inadequacy of the Structuralist Combinatory   72
   5   Toward a Materialist Analysis of Form   75
   6   Against Materialism, *en matérialiste*   76
   7   Reading Capital as a Theory of Literary Production   77
   8   Materialism in a Spinozist Way   80
   9   On Telling Stories   84
  10   The Persistent Problem of the Attributes   89
  11   Reading *Capital* in a Materialist Way   100

3 The Positive Logics of *Capital*: On Spinoza and the Elimination of the Negative Dialectic of Totality from Marx's Revisions to *Capital*, 1857–1875   107
   1   The Discontinuity of the Attributes   109
   2   Totality, Negation, Contradiction   112
   3   Totality   114
   4   The Imaginary Presuppositions of Systematic Dialectics   119

- 5 The Problem with Totality 126
- 6 The Systematic Dissonance of *Capital* 136
- 7 Negation and Contradiction 144
- 8 Constituting the Commodity 149
- 9 From Dialectical Contradiction to Additive Synthesis 153
- 10 Toward an Additive Demonstration, Without Contradiction 157
- 11 When Does Socially Necessary Labour Exist? 176
- 12 The Raw Materials of Marx's Additive Synthetic Method 189
- 13 On Ignorance and Common Notions 193
- 14 Marx's Spinozist Theory of Knowledge 198

4 Toward an Axiomatic Analysis of the Commodity in Badiou and Marx 209
- 1 1968: Logical Materialism 213
- 2 Bolzano and the Formalisation of Axiomatic Thought 217
- 3 Ontological Materialism in Its Limits 223
- 4 The Displacement of *Capital* 228
- 5 A Materialist Axiomatic 229

5 Capital, Logic of the World 232
- 1 Badiou's Lacan, Badiou's (Marx) 235
- 2 'Qu'en est-il de la logique?': Reading *Logics of Worlds* After *Capital* 242
- 3 Logics of (Capitalist) Worlds 247
- 4 Reading *Capital* as the Logic of a World 257

Conclusion: Theory and Practice Today 261

References 267
Index 281

PREFACE

The Limits of Capital

Is capitalism dead?[1] If corporate persons like McDonald's or Walmart – nodal points for the global enclosure and commodification of working class food, the most basic necessity – could reveal their thoughts in a language with which we are familiar, they would surely shrug their shoulders and reply with a hearty laugh that such reports of the death of capitalism have been greatly exaggerated.[2] This book proceeds from the contrary presupposition that we still do, in fact, live in the capitalist social form as Marx defined it over a century and a half ago. This is so despite the many real and consequential transformations to its functioning since that time. It may well be the case, for example, that social domination is no longer primarily determined through ownership of the means of production, but instead via the control of information. It is most certainly the case that there now exist novel, technological procedures for the extraction of surplus information from individual workers and consumers, procedures that may allow for the tendential subsumption of all activity within an information-based political economy.[3]

However much importance one grants to such increasingly-familiar claims, the insufficiency of trying prove this assertion with the criteria inherited from traditional, Stalinist Marxism – whether ownership of the means of production, the nature of class antagonism and the forces of production, or the dominant mode of production (as opposed to Marx's more capacious category of *social form*) – is patent.[4] Instead, the question of capitalism's continued existence and the specific limits governing this singular social form should simply be measured by the minimal, true idea of its nature that we always already possess.

We, subjects of capital across the planet, do indeed have a true – if minimal and inadequate – idea of what capitalism is, an idea Marx formulated as the starting point for his critique of political economy, a minimal, materialist definition of the form of appearance of the capitalist social form as 'an immense

---

1 Wark 2019.
2 Walmart made $11.68B profit and McDonalds $6.88B profit in 2023 (*Forbes* "The Global 2000", June 8, 2023).
3 Wark 2019, pp. 5, 11, 48.
4 Wark 2019, p. 41.

accumulation of commodities', as what I would rephrase as the general, tendential commodification of all things and relations of value.⁵

On the opening page of Jacques Stephen Alexis's magnificent proletarian novel *Compère Général Soleil*, his protagonist Hilarion wanders 'naked' in the night, possessing nothing but his bodily suffering and visions, driven 'crazy' from hunger.⁶ For a succulent breakfast of corn *boullie d'acassan*, he cries out, 'you'd cut off your finger!' Instead, lying in the dark, Hilarion has only his cutting hunger for company: 'His gut. His stomach where his guts were marching like a twisted knot of snakes'. This is the ravenous hunger that drives Hilarion to crime, to steal in the night, to end up in jail, the jail that will unexpectedly be his salvation from this misery, through his encounter with his cellmate Roumel, who holds out to him the promise of communism.

Among the questions Alexis's narrative of hunger and social injustice forces us to ask is this one: is it the case, in fact, that we no longer live in a social form in which it makes sense, when one is driven mad with starvation as is Hilarion, either to steal a wallet (which one cannot eat) or to set off in desperate search of a job that pays wages (which one also cannot eat)? The simple answer is that it makes sense only in a social form (which we call capitalism) in which the means of survival, food and shelter take the monetary form of commodities, and, captured by capitalist property relations, remain otherwise unavailable; a social form in which food, as a commodity, can only be obtained by those without accumulated wealth through monetary exchange for another commodity (labour power); a social form in which a dispossessed proletarian class remains subject to primitive accumulation, subject to the dispossession of the traditional property holdings of the rural *moun andeyò*, unable to respond to hunger in the most obvious way: to farm the land.⁷

Ellen Meiksins Wood argued compellingly that it is the general enclosure and commodification of biological necessities – above all food and shelter – that historically initiates the capitalist social form, in the sense that it is this transformation alone that forces formerly feudal subjects, on pain of death by exposure or starvation, to agree to the sale of their labour power to capital.⁸ While Marx's monetary labour theory of value presupposes the general, as opposed to specific and limited, commodification of all things and relations,

---

5 'The wealth of societies in which the capitalist mode of production prevails appears as an "immense collection of commodities"' (Marx 1976, p. 125).
6 Alexis 1955/1982, pp. 8, 10, 11, my translation. All further translations are my own unless otherwise indicated.
7 Nesbitt 2022, p. 265.
8 Wood 2002.

Wood argues that the commodification of food is nonetheless the crucial factor that forces the sale of labour power, the only commodity, Marx shows, that can produce and accumulate surplus value.[9]

We can, however, repurpose the historicist argument of Wood's Political Marxism to indicate as well a general limit of the capitalist social form, in the sense of its endpoint, beyond which some other social form would exist: when it is no longer the case that we require a general equivalent – whether paper, metal coin, or its onscreen cipher – to purchase commodified food and shelter and other commodities essential to life, then, and despite all the intervening, subsidiary modifications to its functioning, capital will be a thing of the past, and something else, whether communism or catastrophe, will have replaced it. The social production, distribution, and exchange of food and shelter, in this view, thus indicates more than a mere transhistorical human right; in addition, it constitutes a specific neuralgic point at which the capitalist social form finds both its weakest links and real limit.

To theorise such limits, this book remains faithful to Althusser's rejection of a general, even universal concept of *practice* as such, to investigate instead the singular category of Marx's *theoretical practice*, developing a position I will call political epistemology.[10] While the political stakes of the adequacy or inadequacy of knowledge are no doubt immediately familiar and compelling in this age of fake news, gaslighting, and Trumpist populism, to grasp the limits of capitalism more specifically, to know, in other words, when, how, and under what conditions we might exit from the capitalist social form, requires the

---

9 On *Capital* as a monetary labour theory of value, see Murray 2017.
10 The corollary being that this is not a book about political practice, Marxist or otherwise. Even less will the reader find a rehearsal of the debates over Althusserianism from the 1970s. So, for instance, the short-lived British journal *Theoretical Practice* (1971–73), which mounted one of the rare defences of Althusserian theoreticism, published virtually no articles on Marx's theoretical practice in *Capital* (the topic of this book). The sole exception to this disinterest in the journal's seven issues is Athar Hussain's 'Marx's "Notes on Adolph Wagner": An Introduction', which underscores the importance of this late text for Marx's method of demonstration in *Capital* (Hussain 1972). Otherwise, the journal focused almost exclusively on debates regarding the relation of Althusser and Balibar's theoretical practice to Marxist-Leninist politics, the editors insisting that the journal's 'philosophical practice is a political and partisan practice, [...a] political intervention in politics from the position of a politics, Marxism-Leninism' (*Theoretical Practice* 1971, p. 2). I will discuss in Chapter 1 the journal's spirited defence of Althusser's theory of theoretical practice against what its editors saw as the revisionism of Althusser's post-1967 redefinition of philosophy. Thanks to Panagiotis Sotiris for kindly sharing his manuscript 'The Strange Fate of British Althusserianism: The *Theoretical Practice* Group'. I discuss Althusser's concept of theoretical practice in this book's Conclusion.

deployment of a politics of epistemology in the specific sense in which French philosophy implemented the concept in the twentieth century.¹¹

Épistémologie must in this sense be defined in distinction from both the Kantianism of German *Erkenntnistheorie* and the English 'epistemology', the latter two indicating broadly general, psychologistic theories of knowledge and the processes governing the objectification of phenomena, including the acts of mental objectification and their transcendental conditions performed by a knowing subject.¹² In French, these are instead indicated by the more general term *gnoséologie*.¹³ In contrast, André Lalande's concise definition in the *Vocabulaire technique et critique de la philosophie* – not incidentally the reference work Althusser himself repeatedly turned to – defines *épistémologie* as the critique of the principles governing the sciences, which in the case of Marx would of course include the science of political economy.¹⁴

Lire le Capital was above all and most obviously such an epistemological intervention meant to change how we read Marx's *Capital*, in order more adequately to conceptualise the capitalist social form. Yet the secondary literature on *Reading Capital* has tended to address the many concepts Althusser introduced only in the context of Marxist philosophy in general, ignoring the specific object of the book's intervention. Kaplan and Sprinker's *The Althusserian Legacy*, for example, contains not a single reference to *Capital*; and while Diefenbach, Farris, Kirn, and Thomas's *Encountering Althusser* contains many passing nominal references to *Capital*, Michele Cangiani's chapter 'Althusser

---

11 In redeploying here Althusser's concept of theoretical practice, I am indebted to Alain Badiou's probing critique of the concept in his article 'The Althusserian Definition of Theory.' I agree in particular with his critique of the latent psychologism inherent in Althusser's text – theoretical practice as, in Althusser's words, 'a process that takes place entirely within thought' (cited at Nesbitt 2017: 26). The threat Badiou identifies of a return of idealism in Althusser's absolute distinction between thought and the Real is no doubt the price Althusser pays for refusing to identify Spinozist Substance as the materialist unity of the attributes of thought and extension, as I will discuss below.

12 This is the case for example with Sohn-Rethel's *Intellectual and Manual Labour*: though subtitled *A Critique of Epistemology* [*zur Epistemologie der abendländischen Geschichte*], it is explicitly a phenomenological critique of 'the socially necessary forms of thinking of an epoch' (2021, p. 4).

13 Cassin 2014, 'Epistemology', p. 274.

14 Here is Lalande: *L'Épistémologie* 'designates the philosophy of the sciences, but in a quite precise sense. It is neither the specific study of various scientific methods, which is the object of *la Méthodologie*, and pertains to Logic. Nor is it a synthesis or conjectural anticipation of scientific laws …. It is instead, essentially, the critical study of the principles, hypotheses, and results of the various sciences, destined to determine their logical (as opposed to psychological [i.e., as opposed to a theory of knowledge or *Erkenntnistheorie*]) origin, their value, and their objective scope'. Lalande 1996, p. 293.

and Political Economy' in that volume is the lone exception that, in its explicit engagement with Marx's critique of political economy, proves the rule of this general tendency. On a more personal note, when in 2017 I edited a volume dedicated to assessing the legacy of *Reading Capital*, I was quite surprised when not one of the distinguished contributions to that volume elected to discuss the reading of Marx's *Capital* after Althusser.[15] This is to say that while there continues to be no shortage of readers of both *Capital* and Althusser, few and far between are those who since 1965 have pursued the epistemological project of *Reading Capital*.

In contrast to this long-standing disregard for the specificity of *Reading Capital*'s object, when reading *Capital* with (and beyond) Althusser, epistemology becomes political in the preliminary but consequential sense that Marx's theoretical practice, in its capacity to produce adequate – as opposed to merely imaginary or ideological – knowledge of the real complexity of the capitalist social form, consequently produces subjects of that knowledge.[16]

To read *Capital* in the terms Althusser first proposed, refusing ontological guarantees, presuppositions, and imaginary assertions of monism and totality, is to assume only the single presupposition that initiates Marx's demonstration: that we, subjects of capital, always already have a true idea of the nature of capitalism – a minimal, raw, merely apparent idea, but a true one nonetheless: that the capitalist social form is characterised by the accumulation of commodities and the generalisation of their exchange.[17] From this single, immanent starting

---

15 Nesbitt 2017. Robert J.C. Young's chapter in that volume does briefly review the complex publication history of the first volume of *Capital* in its implications for the concept of symptomatic reading, but without engaging an explicit reading of Marx's text per se (Young 2017, pp. 36–9).

16 This is the general thesis Jean Matthys argues in *Althusser lecteur de Spinoza: Genèse et enjeux d'une éthico-politique de la théorie* (Matthys 2023, p. 343).

17 In the 1975 'Soutenance d'Amiens', Althusser underlines the crucial importance of the Spinozist presupposition *Habemus enim ideam veram* for the entirety of a theoretical position dedicated to the rejection of any and all a priori methodological guarantees: 'Que veut dire en substance Spinoza, quand il écrit la phrase célèbre : *"Habemus enim ideam veram* ?" ... C'est *en effet* parce que, et seulement parce que nous détenons une idée vraie, que nous pouvons en produire d'autres, selon sa norme. ... C'est un fait, que nous la détenons (*habemus*), et de quoi que ce soit que ce fait soit le résultat, il inscrit *d'avance* toute théorie de la connaissance ... sous la dépendance du *fait* de la connaissance détenue. Par là toutes questions d'Origine, de Sujet ou de Droit de la connaissance, qui soutiennent les théories de la connaissance sont récusées' (Althusser 1998a, p. 218). Althusser refers to the *Emendation of the Intellect*, where Spinoza writes: 'A true idea (for we do have a true idea) is something different from its object (ideatum). A circle is one thing, the idea of a circle another. For the idea of a circle is not something having a circumference and a centre, as is a circle, nor is the idea of a body itself a body'.

point, *in media res*, a beginning determined not ontologically, but in materialist fashion by Marx's previous analytical enquiry, *Capital* develops a demonstration of the real complexity of this social form as an open, general system of law-governed causality without totality, what Marx called the 'law of motion' of capitalism, and Althusser, its systemic structural causality.

To develop this political epistemology of the limits of capital, *Reading Capital's Materialist Dialectic: Marx, Spinoza, and the Althusserians* analyses the theory of a materialist dialectic as it is developed in the writings of Louis Althusser, Pierre Macherey, Etienne Balibar, and Alain Badiou, focusing on their singular analyses of Marx's process of demonstration in *Capital* and Spinoza's *Ethics*.[18] My argument flatly rejects the imaginary figure of *Reading Capital* as a 'theoreticist' relic, to focus attention precisely on the long-overlooked yet radically anti-Hegelian epistemological claims of *Reading Capital*: that, in Althusser's words, 'in *Capital* we find an apodictic [i.e., logically certain] arrangement of the concepts in the form of demonstrational discourse that Marx calls analysis'.[19] While artful readers to this day seek to extract a Hegelian, negative dialectical logical kernel from the core of *Capital* (as in the 'Systematic Dialectics' of Geert Reuten, Tony Smith, and Chris Arthur), furthermore presuming without demonstration that *Capital* constitutes a totality (whether real or merely logical), this book critically rejects this imaginary figuration. Instead, *Reading Capital's Materialist Dialectic* remains faithful to Althusser's essential identification of Marx's synthetic, materialist dialectic, a dialectic excluding totality, negation, and contradiction, its 'apodictic' demonstration deploying the Spinozist

---

18 The relative neglect of Etienne Balibar's writings in this book is not due to any disinterest in Marx's masterpiece following Balibar's initial contribution to *Reading Capital*. To the contrary, and in contrast to both Macherey and Badiou, Balibar has continued to reaffirm the necessity of reading *Capital* as an unending task: 'Are we still, will we always be, "reading *Capital*"? No doubt; and we are beginning to understand that, as with every truly great theoretical oeuvre (Hegel's, for example), our task is by its nature endless because the meaning we are looking for can only be found at the point where questions formulated on the basis of current events (or even current emergencies) encounter contradictions that, in latent fashion, haunt the writing of the text that we have to set back in motion'. That said, Balibar's interest in Marx remains primarily and explicitly political, to the neglect of the epistemological problems of reading *Capital* that this book will explore: 'The goal I am pursuing [in rereading *Capital*], however, is not (if it ever was) purely epistemological. I am trying to shed light on the thorny question of the various conceptions of politics, their irreducible plurality, and the choices they dictate'. Balibar 2015a, p. 205, translation modified. Thanks to Josef Fulka for reminding me of Balibar's masterful and penetrating analysis of the final section of *Capital* in the third chapter of *Violence and Civility*.

19 Althusser et al. 2015, p. 51 (henceforth RC).

creative power of the real in its immanent, 'structural' causality, whether that power is grasped in the attribute of thought or material extension.[20]

Never a systematic thinker, Althusser was instead a *semeur d'idées*, and it has been left to his readers to test and deploy those manifold ideas as to their degree of creative productivity. It is certainly the case that Althusser does not explicitly link Marx's 'apodictic' method to Spinoza in *Reading Capital*, nor even say the first word about what actually makes Marx's demonstration 'apodictic' (the latter task falling in part to Pierre Macherey in his long-forgotten chapter for *Reading Capital*). Instead, I will take him at his word – 'Nous étions spinoziste', he famously declared of the *Reading Capital* collective, and again, publicly declaring to colleagues in 1967, 'Je suis spinoziste'[21] – and follow Vittorio Morfino's injunction to 'go beyond Althusser, but *with* Althusser', to show that when systematically developed, Althusser's undemonstrated claim for the Spinozist 'apodicticity' of *Capital* is in fact correct.[22]

While a thinker of polemical genius, Althusser – unlike Spinoza, Marx, Macherey, or Badiou – never developed his countless insights into systematic, large-scale works on the model of *Ethica* or *Capital*, but instead sought continuously to refuse all reassuring guarantees of knowledge and desired to sustain theoretical practice in a state of perpetual enquiry, critique, and questioning. As such, his thought seems in hindsight destined never to have produced the affect Spinoza called *beatitude*, and instead fitfully to signify and elicit, *à ses risques et perils*, the distressing yet simultaneously exhilarating positions of both uncompromising desire and apprehension before the absence of the law that Lacan called *anxiety* (*l'angoisse*).[23]

---

20   Macherey has said of the Althusserian project in which he participated that 'Spinoza was that which, for us, bridged epistemology and politics: by returning to theoretical practice its consequential reality [*poids de réalité*], insofar as it made of it an order of reality unto itself. It seemed to us by that token to open perspectives for practical investment, the dynamic of thought simultaneously acting in reality' (Macherey 1999, p. 24).

21   Althusser 1974. In his correspondence with Franca Madonia, Althusser describes Spinoza as 'mon unique maître', and again as 'le plus grand [philosophe] de tous, à mes yeux'. Althusser 1998b, pp. 528, 579.

22   Morfino 2022, p. 86.

23   Lacan 2016. See McNulty 2009. Spinoza was the decisive formative thinker for Lacan, who discovered him at the age of 14, at which point 'he hung a diagram on the wall of his bedroom that depicted the structure of the *Ethics* with the aid of colored arrows' (Roudinesco 1995, p. 11). Spinoza then became the central conceptual reference for Lacan's 1932 thesis, at which point the *Ethics* offered him the means to formulate a monist materialist intervention in psychology based on the traditional 'parallelist' reading of the Spinozist attributes. Subsequently, for example in the 1962–63 seminar *Anxiety*, Lacan's position, while no longer explicitly citing Spinoza, would reject the monist phantasy of an episte-

If, as Tracey McNuty has suggested, 'anxiety is the affect that responds to the desire of the Other',[24] the aggressive resistance this uncompromising desire tends to provoke (think for example of Freud's Moses, Robespierre, or more recently Jean-Bertrand Aristide) can tell us much about the ongoing demonisation of Althusser. Equally, it can help to explain Althusser's own initial, uncompromising theoretical intervention (as the Other of Marxist philosophy) as well as his own subsequent theoretical anxiety to the point of self-destruction in his relation to the proletarian Other. Like Moses, Robespierre, and Freud before him, Althusser desired ruthlessly to destroy an existing god and clergy and to construct a new, impossible object for his people: in Althusser's case, these were the god that was 'Man' for Marxist humanism, along with the Party who represented Him; the object he sought to produce, a fully adequate construction of Marx's philosophy, shorn of all phantasmatic Hegelian guarantees of monist totality and the Absolute. The price he paid for this uncompromising intervention is well-known.

Althusser, intensive and singular reader of Spinoza and Marx, without reserve pushed Spinozist thought to its furthest limit, a point where substance is understood not as Absolute Subject, as an imaginary *Abwermechanism* (defence) against the anxiety of not knowing, nor as reified monism (Plekhanov), indeed, not as a thing at all. Instead, Althusser's esoteric, unpublished writings show that he decisively redefines substance as the infinite order of causal connection within a contingent historical field (the capitalist social form), an order *existing* only in the immanent immediacy of its situated effects – though I will argue that this order can be made to *nonexist* through acts of theoretical formalisation such as the modes of schematic formalisation Marx introduces into later drafts of *Capital*.

It is precisely here, I will argue, at this limit-reading of Spinoza, that Althusser's intuition of a Marx-Spinoza co-determination manifests its decisive originality: if the logic of capital is not a whole, not a substantial thing to be reified as an imaginary monist totality, it is nonetheless the case that this structure can be made to *nonexist*, produced in the attribute of thought, in other words, as what Spinoza calls a *nonexistent thing*.[25] This, then, is the ultimate tendency of Marx's original process of exposition in *Capital* that Althusser's intuition first began fitfully to construct in *Reading Capital* and that this book

---

mological whole in terms doubtless attractive for Althusser, to argue instead that 'logic henceforth has the essentially precarious function of condemning the real to eternally stumble [*trébucher*] within the impossible' (Lacan 2016, p. 78, translation modified).

24   McNulty 2009, p. 7.
25   EIIP8.

pursues: the theoretical production, as a science of causality, of the structure of capital as nonexistent, atemporal thing, as the eternal, formalisable laws of its tendencies.

Althusser's militant refusal to speculate on the ontological foundations of science in his published works, however, pushes his Spinozist thought, as a theory of contingent structural causality without (monist) substance, to the brink of relativist pluralism; the theoreticist position of *Reading Capital*, in other words, was not wrongheaded, as Althusser's admirers and detractors alike have so often claimed, but, on the contrary, *insufficiently theoreticist*. Remaining faithful to the Althusserian refusal to regress to a neo-Hegelian monism of the One, Pierre Macherey and Alain Badiou instead have proceeded in two directions in the wake of *Reading Capital*, to more adequately develop Althusserian theoreticism. Macherey, on the one hand, systematically demonstrates the coherence and accuracy to the letter of the Althusserian limit-conception of Spinozist substance as causality without monism in his massive, five-volume exposition, *Introduction à l'Ethique de Spinoza*. To read *Capital* with Macherey, then, will require demonstrating the fundamental nature of Marx's demonstration as a Spinozist science of ramified, systemic causality without totality.

Badiou, in contrast, develops in the three volumes of *Being and Event* an *axiomatic* epistemology, one that can rigorously initiate apodictic demonstrations of the logic of a given, purely immanent world (such as the capitalist social form) without recourse to imaginary, speculative foundations or the totality of the One. This orientation will require reading *Capital* as a science or logic of causes whose apodicticity arises not from a speculative foundation or guarantee, but from a minimally axiomatic beginning – a minimal yet absolutely true idea we already possess of the nature of capitalism – the necessity of which starting point arises from Marx's prior materialist enquiry into the critique of political economy.

To do so, I argue that while the explicit engagement of these Althusserian thinkers with Marx's process of exposition in *Capital* remained largely limited to the pages of *Reading Capital* (and in the case of Badiou's massive oeuvre is to this day virtually nonexistent), after 1968 this theoretical intervention remained insistent, to adopt instead the more abstract form of a general theory of positive, materialist dialectic. The movement of the book's argument is thus twofold: to follow the exposition of this theory of a materialist dialectic in the wake of *Reading Capital* across sites including Althusser's unpublished archive, Macherey's *Hegel or Spinoza* and five-volume exposition of Spinoza's *Ethics*, and Badiou's *Logics of Worlds*, on the one hand, while simultaneously, at each step, bringing this general theory of materialist dialectic to bear anew on the reading of *Capital* itself.

When Althusser asserted the 'apodictic' nature of Marx's demonstration in *Capital*, he was essentially asking what gives the capitalist social form its *binding* nature in the absence of all ontological presuppositions and epistemological guarantees of subject-object correspondence.[26] The Spinozist answer he suggested is that we are capable of apprehending one and the same capitalist social form via two attributes, thought and extension, without substance – when correctly understood not as thing but as the immanent, infinite order of a historically contingent causality – offering an extrinsic ground or guarantee to this knowledge, which instead comes to depend only upon the adequacy of its construction, *verum index sui et falsi*.

In the empirical attribute of temporal extension, that of our lived, sensuous experience of the capitalist real, that compulsion is immediately and violently apparent in the form of the lived, daily experience of commodity fetishism – as the compulsion of all subjects of capital to sell as a matter of survival the commodity that is our labour power; to then work for monetary remuneration, in order to realise continuous and unending increases in surplus value for capital, etc.

As such, however, as mere empirical, sensuous experience, the veiled, fetishistic nature of this compulsion is nonetheless not adequately *understood*, even by the classical political economists who were the object of Marx's critique. This would instead require that the binding nature of the capitalist social form be *demonstrated* in the attribute of thought, as an apodictic *logical* exposition; and this not as a mere formalist exercise, but as a science of causes in the mode of a materialist critique of political economy. This demonstration, in other words, must begin not from a *concept* such as value, or from some merely formal axiom, but from our initial, minimal, but nonetheless true idea of capitalism, which is to say from 'the simplest social form in which the product of labour presents itself in contemporary society[:] the commodity'.[27] Only then does Marx proceed to produce and deploy, from the first sentence of *Capital*, his world-historical array of original concepts that cohere to convey, in the attribute of thought, the logically binding nature of this necessity.

In the book's Introduction, I refuse the ideological dummy of so-called 'theoreticism' to argue for the crucial, long-overlooked importance of Althusser's uncompromising epistemological propositions in his introduction to *Reading Capital*. While upholding Althusser's intervention, this critique simultaneously identifies a series of theoretical impediments to the arguments of *For Marx* and

---

26 Thanks to Laurence Hemming for posing the question to me in this form.
27 'Wovon ich ausgehe, ist die einfachste gesellschaftliche Form, worin sich das Arbeitsprodukt in der jetzigen Gesellschaft darstellt, und dies ist die "Ware"'. Marx 1879.

Reading Capital (figurative nominalism, dualistic treatment of the attributes thought and the real), impediments that in fact are shown to dissolve when considered in light of Althusser's esoteric, unpublished writings. I then turn in Chapter 2 to Pierre Macherey's theory of materialist dialectic, first examining his little-discussed yet decisively original contribution to *Reading Capital* on Marx's process of exposition, to then engage his subsequent works (*Theory of Literary Production, Hegel or Spinoza*, 'En matérialiste', *Introduction à l'Ethique*). I show that each of these substantive contributions to a theory of materialist dialectic can serve to illuminate crucial aspects of Marx's process of demonstration in *Capital*, beyond the brief indications of Macherey's precocious 1965 contribution to *Reading Capital*.

In the book's central chapter, I redirect these theoretical materials to systematically investigate Marx's additive synthetic dialectic in the text of *Capital* itself. I demonstrate that Marx's cumulative revisions to *Capital* tend to eliminate the logical categories of totality (*Totalität*), the reflections of determination (*Reflexionsbestimmungen*), *aufhebung*, and contradiction from its exposition of the essential nature of capitalism. Instead, I show that Marx's modifications serve to increasingly develop and implement a positive, additive synthetic dialectic as the categorial demonstration of the necessary forms of appearance and relation of the capitalist social form, the real construction of this nonexistent thing, the idea of the laws of its tendencies. In contrast to previous analyses of Spinoza's influence on the young Marx that have uniformly addressed its *political* and *critical* content, through a close reading of Chapters 1 and 11 of the first volume of *Capital*, I argue for the decisive importance of Marx's 1841 reading of Spinoza for the *epistemological* project of *Capital*. This analysis confirms Althusser's proposition of Marx's objective, tendential development after 1857 (as an ongoing epistemological transition rather than evental 'break') of a non-Hegelian, additive synthetic dialectic – and this despite what Marx might consciously have continued to believe to the end of his days about his imaginary, lived relation to Hegel.

Chapters 4 and 5 turn to the philosophy of Alain Badiou, to argue that despite his non-engagement with Marx's *Capital*, the development of an *axiomatic* philosophy in *Being and Event*, and of a 'science of appearance' in *Logics of Worlds* can and should be brought to bear on *Capital* itself, toward the construction of a theoretically consistent understanding of the capitalist social form as an object of thought. In Chapter 3 I thus turn to Badiou's theory of the necessity of an axiomatic theoretical foundation for apodictic discourse – underscoring in the process the crucial importance of Bernard Bolzano for Badiou's argument – to interpret Marx and Spinoza's starting points in *Capital* and *Ethics*. In Chapter 4, I argue that Badiou has in fact fulfilled to some real extent the project Althusser first called for in his 1947 thesis, i.e., to read *Capital* as a theory of the 'transcendental' structural determinations of the capitalist social form, Badiou objectively displacing and refiguring Althusser's initial, undeveloped claim that '*Capital* is our transcendental analytic'.[28] I thus take Badiou's 'science of appearance' to indicate, in Marx's terms, the science of the necessary forms of appearance of all things of value (commodities) in the capitalist social form, the logic, that is to say, of our world.

---

28 Cited in Estop 2021, p. 113.

Acknowledgements

It would not have been possible to complete this project without the inestimable support of Etienne Balibar, Rok Benčin, Nathan Brown, Harrison Fluss, Landon Frim, Josef Fulka, Peter Hallward, Roman Kanda, Ivan Landa, Jean Matthys, Warren Montag, Vittorio Morfino, Charlie Post, and Panagiotis Sotiris, and at Brill HM, Danny Hayward and Marlou Meems. At the IMEC, discussions with François Bordes crucially helped test and develop these arguments, and Allison Demailly offered invaluable assistance obtaining manuscripts from Althusser's archive. In Prague, my colleagues at the Philosophical Institute – including Ivan Landa, Petr Kužel, Jana Berankova, Michael Hauser, and Joe Grim Feinberg – continue to offer invaluable intellectual inspiration, as well as critical perspectives on my arguments on Marx, Althusser, Badiou, and Bolzano. Others for whose assistance, insights, and support I am grateful include Emily Apter, Alain Badiou, Banu Bargu, Riccardo Bellofiore, Yann Moulier Boutang, Svenja Bromberg, Rebecca Comay, Chad Córdova, Sam Diiorio, Maxfield Evers, Jackson Smith, Ruo Jia, Elena Louisa Lange, Philippe Le Goff, Rob Lehman, Jacques Lezra, Tracey McNulty, Gregor Moder, Donald Moerdijk, Alberto Moreiras, Bertrand Ogilvie, Knox Peden, Seth Rogoff, Max Tomba, Gabriel Tupinambá, McKenzie Wark, Audrey Wasser, and Szymon Wróbel. Love and gratitude above all to Eva Cermanová.

Earlier versions of two of these chapters have previously appeared: Chapter 2 in the volume *Pierre Macherey and the Case of Literary Production* (Warren Montag and Audrey Wasser, eds., copyright © 2022 by Northwestern University), and Chapter 5 as 'Capital, Logic of the World' (*Filosovski Vestnik* FV XLII 2).

This book was written as part of the grant project GA19–20319S 'From Bolzano to Badiou. An Investigation of the Foundations of Historical Epistemology and Modern European Philosophy', supported by the Czech Science Foundation and coordinated by the Institute of Philosophy of the Czech Academy of Sciences in Prague, and benefitted as well from the support of Princeton University.

I dedicate this book to our beautiful, beloved son Rafael:

> Mens nostra, quatenus intelligit, aeternus cogitandi modus fit. … In hac vita igitur apprime conamur, ut Corpus infantiae in aliud eique conduci, mutetur, quod ad plurima aptum fit, quedque ad Mentem referatur, quae fui, et Dei, et rerum plurimum fit conscia.
>
> EVP39S

Abbreviations

RC *Reading Capital: The Complete Edition*, by Louis Althusser, Etienne Balibar, Roger Establet, Pierre Macherey, and Jacques Rancière. Translated by Ben Brewster and David Fernbach, New York: Verso, 2015.
LC *Lire le Capital*, by Louis Althusser, Etienne Balibar, Roger Establet, Pierre Macherey, and Jacques Rancière, Paris: PUF, 1996 [1965].

References to Spinoza's *Ethics* will take the standard form: E, followed by section, proposition, and subdivision of the proposition: appendix (A), corollary (C), demonstration (D), definition (Def), lemma (L), proposition (P), scholium (S). E vP39S, for instance, refers to *Ethics*, section 5, proposition 39, scholium.

CHAPTER 1

Introduction: *Reading Capital* Beyond Its Limits

The publication of *Reading Capital* in 1965 by François Maspero remains today a momentous theoretical event in the fullest sense of the word: the founding and preliminary construction of a novel theoretical project and domain, the idea of the idea of Marx's *Capital* itself. An event: in the history of the production, analysis and reception of Marx's *Capital* since the publication in 1867 of its first volume; in its consummate break with the theoretically problematic traditions of Marxist thought after Marx – whether economistic, humanist, productionist, or teleological – all generally united (with important exceptions to be sure) in their superficial, tendential, or even flatly ignorant acquaintance with Marx's systematic analysis of the capitalist social form; above all, in the unfinished project *Reading Capital* initiated, to construct Marx's philosophy as an object of thought, its method of presentation rightly grasped for the first time as an additive synthetic, materialist dialectic without negation. The striking fact from which this book begins, then, is how rarely this Althusserian reading of *Capital* – surely one of the two or three most original and influential readings in the history of Marxist thought, however one may judge its propositions – has been relayed and developed, whether by former students of Althusser themselves or across the vast literature on Althusserianism, all while volume after volume continues to assert the negative dialectical nature of Marx's process of exposition.[1]

---

1 The most notable exception to this striking neglect is perhaps Jacques Bidet's *Exploring Marx's Capital* (2006). While authors such as Chris Arthur continue to assert the Hegelian negative dialectical nature of Marx's demonstrations, generally with only highly selective citation of the text, it is striking how Michael Heinrich's *How to Read Marx's Capital* (2021), in closely reading the first seven chapters of *Capital* line by line, actually concludes – without ever mentioning Althusser or *Reading Capital* – that Marx's process of exposition is in fact an additive synthetic one without negative dialectical sublation of the categories, precisely as Althusser and Pierre Macherey first claimed in 1965. The Althusserian tenor of Heinrich's argument is hardly surprising, as Vittorio Morfino has shown that Heinrich's debt to Althusser is much greater than the handful of citations – both positive and negative – to be found in *The Science of Value* (2022 [1999]). In fact, Morfino shows that Althusserian categories are crucial to Heinrich's argument in his principal work: 'Si infatti il nome "Althusser" appare con parsimonia e sempre con misura critica, lo stesso non si può dire di tre concetti althusseriani che hanno una presenza ubiqua all'interno del testo: ... *Bruch* (rottura), ... *theoretisches Feld* (campo teorico), ... e *Problematik* (problematica)'. Morfino 2023, p. 121. Heinrich's analysis will prove crucial to the post-Althusserian reading of *Capital* I will develop in Chapter 3. Thanks to Vittorio Morfino for sharing his text ahead of its publication.

Etienne Balibar has repeatedly testified to this event, arguing that *Reading Capital* 'inscribed Marxism within the history of French philosophy in the ... 20th century', its intervention forcing the human sciences more generally to 'take Marxism seriously [as] a horizon and challenge for contemporary thought'.[2] In addition to this crucial historical accomplishment, however, this book argues that *Reading Capital* marked a commanding, situated theoretical intervention, an intervention on the Kampfplatz of the absolute, as it promulgated a Spinozist project of political epistemology, seeking at once to relegate all (Hegelian) forms of negative dialectic and contradiction to their rightful domain – existence – and to grasp the demonstration of the essential nature of the capitalist real as a singular world in its eternal, infinite nature.

This book argues that the core epistemological[3] claim of *Reading Capital* ('In *Capital* we find ... an apodictic arrangement of the concepts in the ... demonstrational discourse that Marx calls analysis') did not disappear as an object of post-Althusserian theory, but instead shifted terrain: from an initial attention in *Reading Capital* devoted to the literal text of *Capital* itself, this claim became instead a more abstract theoretical object of investigation. No longer situated and nominally defined as a non-Hegelian mode of reading Marx's text itself, the Althusserians, and above all Pierre Macherey and Alain Badiou, nonetheless objectively sustained the theoretical project initiated by *Reading Capital* at a higher level of abstraction, henceforth defined as the theoretical imperative to produce the concept of a positive *materialist dialectic*. Crucial texts such as Badiou's *Logics of Worlds* or Macherey's essay 'En matérialiste' (both to be discussed in subsequent chapters) explicitly develop this notion of a *materialist dialectic* in opposition as much to the Stalinist notion of dialectical materialism as to Hegelian negative dialectics.

This book will track this concept of a positive, materialist dialectic across various facets and moments in the writings of Spinoza, Marx, Althusser, Macherey, and Badiou, to construct this thought object, as Althusser famously enjoined, as the overdetermined, dynamic complexity of a theoretical force field or constellation, a conceptual structure whose reality exists in the discursive effects produced by the heterogeneous deployments it has received. I do so in the conviction that these varying epistemological interventions con-

---

2 Balibar 2018, p. 6.
3 Taking into account Althusser's warning, in the *Eléments d'autocritique*, against a speculative, idealist tendency inherent to the notion of *epistemology* (1974, p. 176n30). Jean Matthys notes that Althusser tends to prefer the phrase 'théorie de la pratique théorique' to 'epistemology' due to the dominant associations of the latter with traditional theories of knowledge (Matthys 2023, p. 237).

stitute always singular, yet faithful elaborations of Althusser and Macherey's initial reading of Marx's *Capital* as a positive, apodictic dialectic, a project of political epistemology dedicated to the displacement and dismantling of all ideological, imaginary guarantees – of *Capital* as logical or monist totality – to read *Capital* instead as an untotalised, open and incomplete science of the causal complexity governing the capitalist social form.

If Marx's process of exposition does in fact take the form of an 'apodictic' demonstration, as Althusser suggests, and if this process is furthermore to be understood in Spinozist terms, as Althusser retrospectively informed his readers ('we [the *Reading Capital* collective] were Spinozist'),[4] this immediately implies a series of radical epistemological protocols to be kept in mind across the following chapters, provisos that Vittorio Morfino succinctly summarises:

1. For Spinoza, infinite substance must be thought simultaneously as immanent within the finite, a position that eliminates the logical distinction between the *possible* and the *actual*.
2. Rejecting the Aristotelean and Cartesian plurality of substances, the Spinozist real is indivisible; it can be apprehended through an infinity of attributes (of which humans implement thought and extension); within the attribute of thought, Spinoza distinguishes in turn three forms of knowledge: the imaginary, common notions, and 'intuitive' knowledge.
3. Spinoza regularly adopts traditional and scholastic philosophical terminology, yet radically reworks its meanings in ways that must constantly be kept in mind. A case in point is the distinction essence/appearance. Morfino observes that for Spinoza, 'There are no essences – that is complete concepts of individuals that subsist before their worldly existence. Rather, the essence of an individual emerges after the fact – after the individuality already exists – from its power of acting and its ability to enter into relations with other individuals'.
4. Above all, the development of knowledge takes non-traditional forms. The domain of the law of non-contradiction is not so much 'eliminated', as Morfino suggests, but put in its measured place within Spinoza's process of exposition.[5] Similarly, Spinoza continues to deploy subject-predicate

---

4 'Nous avons été Spinozistes' (Althusser 1974, p. 29).
5 A great many of Spinoza's demonstrations in *Ethics* depend upon the law of non-contradiction, which Spinoza deploys in a specific subset of cases that Macherey clearly defines: 'Spinoza does not hesitate to use [the method reasoning via non-contradiction] on occasion, when it is a matter of questions that are not susceptible to direct consideration [*d'un abord direct*], as for example the fact that the existence of God is a necessary existence (a question treated in Proposition 11 of *de Deo*). Despite its negative character', Macherey observes,

forms of judgement and logical implication within and between the increments of his demonstration, but as an infinitely open, 'structured complexity ... that unfolds within the aleatory and material realm of duration, without center or end', an uncountable whole without totality, 'an open system that constructs the object of knowledge through a process of transforming the imagination'.[6]

5. This ethics of the intellect as an open, infinite process, though necessarily articulated as the discursive, linear passage from one proposition to the next, additively forms a highly, even infinitely complex and open *network* of references, implications, and consequences without totality, such that Spinozist substance, as Althusser displaces it within his own theoretical framework, is neither reified thing (as in monist readings of Spinoza), nor ontological guarantee, but *structural causality* understood as the necessity governing a given form of social relations: the finite, contingent, historically limited, yet fully determinate causality of the capitalist social form.[7]

The chapters that follow develop this argument neither as a linear *history of ideas* (from Spinoza and Marx to the post-Althusserian present) nor by reducing various theories to the status of mere determinate *expressions* of a single text (whether *Capital*, *Ethics*, or *Reading Capital*). Instead, my argument strives to proceed topologically, seeking to construct a complex, overdetermined network of theoretical articulations, its object a *materialist dialectic* of the capitalist social form structurally determined, in the last instance, by Marx's unfinished masterwork, his critique of capitalist political economy.

'this form of reasoning is perfectly integrated within the geometric method, and is particularly apt when it is a question of treating objects that – due to their absolute nature which completely contains [*renferme*] their reality within themselves – seem to refuse a demonstrational approach that considers causes [since these] would as such be given within themselves [*données en eux-mêmes*]' (Macherey 2001 [1998], p. 246).

6 Morfino 2022, pp. 87–8.

7 In the case of Spinozist substance, Macherey takes extraordinary care to indicate this transversal, ramified network of the demonstration of general causality at every moment in his five-volume analysis, a concern that culminates in his highly complex schematic representation of this rhizomatic logical system in the appendix to volume one of his *Introduction*, 'The Demonstrative Network of the *Ethics*'. Macherey 2001 [1998], pp. 277–359. For every definition, axiom, postulate, proposition, corollary and scholium in the five books of the *Ethics*, Macherey carefully indicates both the anterior sequences by which each is justified, as well as the ensuing claims that will depend upon it in turn for their own justification.

1 The Limits of *Reading Capital*

Decades of reflexive, ideological criticism have continued to disavow the crucial originality and power of *Reading Capital* and have successfully produced in its place the imaginary figure of a wrong-headed relic of a bygone theoretical and political era. The stridently proclaimed sin of 'theoreticism' long served to summarise this dismissal, judging *Reading Capital* to have committed an act of dogmatic, idealist hubris that rightfully would have relegated its intervention to the dustbin of history.[8] This book argues against this received commonplace, from the position that we must look not merely to more familiar and readily accepted Althusserian concepts like 'symptomatic reading' or the 'continent of history', but precisely to the uncompromising, categorical epistemological claims of *Reading Capital*, in order to (re)discover, follow through, and fully reactivate the infinite productivity Althusser and his virtuoso students initially

---

[8] The most famous of these blanket condemnations is undoubtedly E.P. Thompson's 1978 fulminating historicist polemic *The Poverty of Theory*, in which Thompson sees fit to dismiss Althusser's thought as a 'freak' dedicated to an 'ahistorical theoreticism, ... a structuralism of stasis', although Thompson begins by freely admitting that 'I don't understand Althusser's propositions as to the relation between the "real world" and "knowledge"', which is to say, the entire basis of Althusser's epistemological position (Thompson 1987, pp. 17, 20, 21). While in retrospect Thompson's historicist diatribe is surprising mainly in its length and vehemence ('starting moderately and ending in a gale of fury', Perry Anderson observes [1980, p. 4]), even insightful and sympathetic studies of Althusser have tended to sustain this condemnation of the 'theoreticism' of *Reading Capital*. Anderson's own famous response to Thompson, his 1980 essay *Arguments within English Marxism*, in fact begins by endorsing Thompson's empiricist condemnation of theoreticism, to conclude, without analysis, that Althusser's 'theory of knowledge, dissociated from the controls of evidence, is untenably internalist' (Anderson 1980, p. 7). Similarly, in his groundbreaking 1987 book *Althusser, The Detour of Theory*, Gregory Elliott proposes that 'the cause defended by Althusser some twenty years ago [i.e., in *For Marx* and *Reading Capital*] – the axiomatic scientificity of Marxism – cannot be championed today' (Elliott 1987, p. 45). Why is this the case, the reader might ask? Elliott provides no theoretical reasons relating to the adequacy, or not, of this axiomatic position in relation to the object of Marx's analysis in *Capital* (the capitalist social form), but instead argues that 'the vicissitudes of contemporary history [circa 1987]' have shown that 'Marxism has proven fallible' (1987, p. xxii). The correctness of a theoretical position, in other words, is to be judged based on its ability to read the tea leaves of the future, or, as Engels famously put the matter in *Socialism: Scientific and Utopian*, 'The proof of the pudding is in the eating'. Althusser's Spinozist position in *Reading Capital* (*Verum index sui et falsi*) might instead take the alternate form: 'The proof of the pudding is in ... the pudding'. All three of these quite different and famous studies of Althusserianism share this focus on the materialist *historiography* of capitalism (historical materialism), while tending to ignore the theoretical status of *Capital* as the abstract analysis and exposition of the theoretical categories determining the capitalist social form (on the latter, see Heinrich 2021, p. 39).

produced: the idea of Marx's positive, materialist dialectic, a dialectic without negation that deploys the Spinozist creative power of the real (substance) not as ontological, monist guarantee, but as the sheer immanence of structural causality, whether that power is grasped in the attribute of thought or material extension.[9]

'Nothing positive contained in a false idea can be annulled by the presence of what is true';[10] never was Spinoza's epistemological politics of the adequate idea and the ongoing struggle it requires to instantiate itself better exemplified than in the endless flow into the present of books and articles that seek to reduce *Capital* to a palimpsest of Hegel's *Logic*, readings that, for all their often ingenious complexity, should, this book will argue, rightfully have been short-circuited by the demonstrations of *Reading Capital* five decades ago.[11] Unfortunately, both for *Capital* and the adequacy of its reception, *Reading Capital* itself could muster only a very limited power to impose the concept of Marx's positive dialectic it rightfully proclaimed. Its chapters, consisting of oral presentations written up from Althusser's seminar at the Rue d'Ulm from January–April 1965, could attain, as Althusser himself candidly proclaimed, no more than the status of 'incomplete texts, the mere beginnings of readings ... [marked by] hesitations and uncertain steps ... no more than a sketch'.[12]

To these inherent limitations of texts necessarily situated and constrained by the context and moment of their iteration, must be added the impediment of the hobbled editions of *Reading Capital* following its initial publication: its second, 1968 abridged edition amputating, to constitute a handy 'pocket' edition, not only Jacques Rancière's rich and probing initial chapter, but, even more problematically for the argument I wish to develop here, Pierre Macherey's brief, long-overlooked but positively dazzling and unprecedented analysis of Marx's process of exposition in the initial pages of *Capital*; that is to say, precisely the text in which Althusser's core proposition of 'the apodictic

---

9   It was only in the final phases of revising this manuscript that I discovered Jean Matthys' brilliant study *Althusser lecteur de Spinoza*, perhaps the only other monograph in the literature on Althusser to affirm the fundamental validity of the 'theoreticist' epistemological positions of *For Marx* and *Reading Capital*. Thanks to Jean Matthys for sharing the prepublication manuscript of his book.
10 EIVP1.
11 For recent, thoughtful examples, see *Hegel's Logic and Marx's Capital: A Reconsideration* (Moseley and Smith 2014); Chris Arthur's *The New Dialectic and Marx's Capital* (2002) and *The Spectre of Capital: Idea and Reality* (2022).
12 RC, pp. 2, 11.

[i.e., logically certain] character of the order of [Marx's] theoretical discourse' found its minimally adequate demonstration.[13]

To this self-inflicted blow was added the contingent historical encounter that was Mai-68, bringing in its wake the anti-intellectual categorical imperative of 'practicism', the caricatural positive valence of a henceforth proscribed 'theoreticism'.[14] The 1970s Siren song of *practicism* – whose forceful interpellation drove Althusser himself to recant the putative 'theoreticism' of *Reading Capital* (i.e., what *Reading Capital* had assuredly called 'theoretical practice') in the name of the revisionist *mot d'ordre* of 'class struggle in theory' – declared open season on the daunting theoretical complexity of *Reading Capital*. In response, Althusser found himself interpellated by the empiricist demand to reflect 'proletarian experience'.[15] This abandonment of the autonomy of 'theoretical practice' (rebaptised 'theoreticism' after 1968) for a position in which 'philosophy represents the class struggle in theory',[16] this theoretical regression from Spinoza's *verum index sui et falsi* to a theory of knowledge as the adequacy of its representation of an empirical object,[17] marks a moment of epistemological break in Althusser's thought, at least in published texts such as *Lenin and Philosophy* and *Éléments d'autocritique*.[18]

---

13   RC, p. 50.
14   Balibar 2018, p. 6. It was of course Althusser himself who identified in his autocritique the 'deviation' of a 'theoreticist tendency' in *For Marx* and *Reading Capital*, noting that the majority of critics had instead wrongly seen these as works of 'structuralism' (Althusser 1998a, pp. 177–81).
15   Althusser 1974. Althusser's revisionist position was first articulated in 1967 in the lectures collected as 'Philosophy and the Spontaneous Philosophy of the Scientists' (2012).
16   Althusser 1968, p. 5.
17   Ironically, Althusser's slogan is a perfect and explicit example of precisely the 'traditional theory of knowledge' he repeatedly condemned, a mode of thought universally dependent upon the principle of reason as the demand that the theoretical object adequately represent or reflect the empirical. Althusser would in turn vehemently critique this very theoretical orientation in *Etre marxiste en philosophie* in 1977 (to be discussed below). Both Vincent Descombes (1980, pp. 134–5) and Gregory Elliott (1987, pp. 194, 222) analyse Althusser's turn to the position of 'class struggle in theory' as a theoretical regression from the radically novel propositions of *For Marx* and *Reading Capital*. Jean Matthys calls for readers of Althusser to 'nuance' the epistemologically extreme positions of *Reading Capital* with a 'more "politicist" conception in which political practice serves as prior and posterior determination [fait office d'amont et d'aval] for Marxist science', whereas I wish to argue that the position of 'class struggle in theory' constitutes an unambiguous regression from the political epistemology of *Reading Capital* that Matthys elsewhere champions without reserve (2023, p. 292).
18   This in contrast to recent studies that have tended to emphasise the often-subterranean continuity of thought across the arc of Althusser's intellectual production. See for example Goshgarian 2006; Bruschi 2021; and for a critique of this recent trend in Althusser studies, Thomas 2013, pp. 145–6.

G.M. Goshgarian succinctly summarises the problem of theoreticism as an incapacity of theoretical practice to account for the *political* necessity of its conclusions:

> The theory of philosophy this philosophy proposed [in *Reading Capital*] did not allow for an accounting of what it did. Proclaiming itself a science – and even a science of the sciences – the proper task of which, according to Althusser, is to work on a [thought] object distinct from its real object, it proved itself incapable of being transformed by the world that it theorised, or to transform it [in turn]: it could only know it.[19]

Goshgarian, however, arguably conflates what must necessarily remain two distinct problems or processes: A) the production of the adequate knowledge of the capitalist social form (such as Marx constructs in *Capital*) and B) the political problem of how that adequate knowledge, as a political epistemology, can be militantly brought to bear upon an existing world and its subjects toward the aim of its and their transformation.

In abandoning *Reading Capital*'s claims for the autonomy of theoretical practice as *index sui et falsi* in favour of the empiricist methodology of 'class struggle in theory', Althusser arguably conflated or inversed the necessary order of these two processes via the demand that the lived experience of class struggle (pre-)determine the adequacy of theory itself.[20] Marx himself proceeded

---

19   Althusser 2015, p. 26.
20   Along with Matthys' book, the only text that makes a similar defence of theoretical practice, to my knowledge, is Antony Cutler and Michael Gane's 'Statement: On the Question of Philosophy – for a Theory of Theoretical Practice', which appeared in the final issue of the British journal *Theoretical Practice*. Breaking with the journal's initial support for Althusser's 1967 'new definition of philosophy' (as the representation of class struggle in theory), Cutler and Gane interestingly emphasise the co-dependency of concepts such as conjuncture and symptomatic reading with the theory of theoretical practice articulated in *For Marx* and *Reading Capital*. In Althusser's new definition of philosophy, they argue, 'the significance of the elements of any theoretical problematic "encountered" in the intervention derives not from the structure of that problematic itself [as in the theory of theoretical practice] but on the contrary from the demands of the theoretical conjuncture', resulting, they conclude, in a return to a classic subject-object, representation-based theory of knowledge (1973, p. 39). Their position differs from that which I am defending here, however, in its extreme theoreticism (in the pejorative sense), arguing as they do that 'The modes of production exist only within thought as does history' (1973, p. 46). This is, Panagiotis Sotiris observes, 'a version of anti-empiricism that turns into a complete distancing between theoretical conceptual transformations, defined in a strict intra-theoretical manner, and any possible linking between historical political dynamics, conflicts and struggles and the terrain of philosophy' (Sotiris nd, p. 10). Neither Spinoza, Marx, nor Althusser

INTRODUCTION: READING CAPITAL BEYOND ITS LIMITS   9

differently, strictly maintaining the purely theoreticist focus of *Capital*, the results of which demonstration could then be powerfully brought to bear in the militant interventions of his activity after 1867, for example in *Civil War in France* (1871) and the (unpublished) 1875 *Critique of the Gotha Program*.

While in 1969 flower children pelted Adorno to the point of infarct, Althusser, following his confrontation with Garaudy over theoretical orthodoxy and the humanism debate – for infinitely overdetermined reasons on which it would be pointless to speculate – took it upon himself to offer up in sacrifice the theoretical adequacy and power of *Reading Capital* to the Big Other's demand for practice.[21] In doing so, he arguably abandoned his initial categorical critique and rejection of all forms of empiricism and idealism in a proclamation of resentful bad faith that Etienne Balibar has identified as a veritable 'revenge of practice'.[22] Balibar has described how in the aftermath of May '68, Althusser himself sought to 'destroy' the theoretical position he had previously occupied, 'as though constrained by a merciless authority [*comme contraint par une force impitoyable*]'.[23] These wilful acts of theoretical self-immolation ('I will destroy what I have done' Balibar recalls Althusser telling him at one point) constituted the sabotaging of the very theoretical claims that had animated *For Marx* and *Reading Capital*.[24] While Balibar has denied that this position implied an

would ever claim that circles exist only in thought (and strictly speaking, Spinoza argues, they do not 'exist' in thought at all, but only in space-time extension); the same holds for modes of production and the other categories of the capitalist social form Marx constructs, aspects of which are perfectly perceptible, if inadequately understood, in lived, sensuous experience. The thought object and the real object are not two different things one can compare for their correspondence, but one and the same thing, perceived alternately via the absolutely distinct attributes of thought and extension.

21   Althusser 2003. On Adorno's last months, see Müller-Doohm 2004.
22   Balibar 2018, p. 10.
23   Ibid. Similarly, François Matheron has argued that in this period, 'Althusser progressively destroyed the theses he had constructed' (cited in Thomas 2013, p. 145).
24   Balibar has succinctly distilled the terms of this shift in Althusser's theoretical orientation: 'Au bout du compte, [Althusser in his writings of 1976–78] pointait le symptôme majeur de la crise et de son inconscience propre dans l'énoncé de Lénine : "La théorie de Marx est toute-puissante parce qu'elle est vraie." Or, [Balibar continues,] à quelques variantes près, c'est lui-même qui avait le plus hautement revendiqué cet énoncé, de 1965 à 1975, comme l'expression provocatrice et risquée de l'objectivité du marxisme, dont les critères de vérification (succès, échecs politiques) présupposent toujours une théorie explicative de la lutte des classes (bien loin de pouvoir l'engendrer). Désormais il y voyait l'expression la moins équivoque de l'illusion d'autonomie de la théorie, entretenue par son propre jeu conceptuel (la logique formelle de son "ordre d'exposition")' (Balibar 1978, p. 61). Balibar has more recently sought to nuance the vehement critique of his 1978 essay, in 'L'objet d'Althusser' (2015b, pp. 85–116).

abandonment of Althusser's insistence on the autonomy of theoretical production,[25] he is clearly over-generous to his intellectual mentor: Althusser's post-1975 position, as Balibar himself points out, was no mere 'inscription of non-theoretical practice in the definition of objectivity' (Balibar), a truly necessary imperative for any materialist theoretical practice. Instead, I wish to argue, Althusser's position constituted a far stronger, eminently empiricist insistence that theory must, in Balibar's words, '"listen" to what [the masses] say of their experiences and their struggles'.

This theoretical self-sabotage manifested in particular via Althusser's messianic, historico-theological faith in the possibility a 'fusion' between the workers' movement and Marxist theory, perhaps most explicitly and grandiloquently stated in a 1968 interview with *L'Unità*: 'The fusion of Marxist theory and the workers' Movement is the greatest event in the history of class struggle, which is to say, practically in the whole of human history'.[26] It would only be with the recognition of the collapse of this myth – polemically announced in

---

25 'Insistons bien sur le fait qu'il ne s'agit en aucune manière de renoncer à l'idée de connaissance scientifique ou "par concepts", et a fortiori de rabattre celle-ci sur un empirisme, un pragmatisme ou un subjectivisme. L'objectivité de la connaissance fait partie (comme l'existence de la lutte des classes) des thèses sur lesquelles, à travers quelque autocritique que ce soit, Althusser n'a pas cédé. Mais la référence à la pratique non théorique doit être inscrite dans la définition même de l'objectivité, comme sa condition' (Balibar 1978, 64).

26 Interview with *L'Unità*, 1 February 1968, cited in Estop 2021, p. 205. Estop goes on to incisively critique the messianic, theological tenor of Althusser's faith in this 'fusion' in the period 1968–77, reminiscent of nothing less than Lukács's humanist faith in the proletariat: '"Man", who had been expelled from theory [in *For Marx* and *Reading Capital*] seems here to rediscover a history, and, moreover, a "human" history bestowed by Marxism. The event of this fusion implies the self-transparency of the workers' movement, insofar as it possesses the science of its own history and that of humanity as a whole, a fusion of the subject and object of knowledge. ... This indistinction between science and ideology appears to regress to a form of historicism or Hegelian absolute knowledge in which the proletariat would be transparent to itself, not by virtue of its class consciousness [as Lukács had claimed], but through its science' (Estop 2021, p. 206, my translation). Althusser similarly invokes the actuality of this 'fusion' in his unpublished 1967 'Book Project on *Capital* Vol. 1': 'La situation du travail théorique a changé depuis Marx: très précisément depuis que s'est réalisé la "fusion" du Mouvement ouvrier et de la théorie marxiste. Cette "fusion" a produit une pratique absolument nouvelle'. IMEC, 20ALT 16.11, p. 36. Jean Matthys discusses the initial form of this Althusserian faith in the redeeming force of the proletariat in his 1947 thesis: 'Pour l'Althusser de 1947, ... le prolétariat nomme le lieu virtuel-réel, à la fois inscrit *dans* le contenu existant et *contre* lui, où pourra se réaliser véritablement la circularité absolue d'une humanité réconciliée ...: "L'action révolutionnaire peut concevoir, au moins formellement, l'avènement de la totalité humaine réconciliée avec sa propre structure"' (Matthys 2023, p. 96).

Althusser's 1977 speech 'Enfin la crise du Marxisme!' – that Althusser would come to affirm that 'for the masses, there no longer exists a "realised ideal" [in the USSR] or living reference for socialism'.[27] The concept of *fusion* in this sense functioned for Althusser after 1968 as an ideological guarantee, both for the teleological destiny of socialism and for the truth of its historical claims; in its absence after 1977 at the latest, the promise of socialism was reduced for Althusser to the status of a historical *déchet*.[28]

The call for 'philosophy to represent the class struggle in theory' and the attendant faith in the 'fusion' of proletarian lived experience with Marxist theory thus formulated the protocol of a regressive theoretical position. In the same February 1968 interview with *L'Unità*, Althusser publicly broke with the Spinozist theory of knowledge of *Reading Capital*, asserting instead a representation-based model in which 'world outlooks [such as that of the working class or "idealist bourgeois"] are *represented* in theory ... by philosophy. Philosophy represents the class struggle in theory'.[29] In this interview, Althusser publicly silences the aim of *Reading Capital* to understand Marx's critique of political economy and the capitalist social form as an object of thought that finds the measure of its truth (and falsity) immanently from its own construction, and instead reduces the hollow affirmation that 'Yes, it is essential to read and study *Capital*' to a utilitarian political imperative, the object of which is merely to grasp 'the revolutionary character of Marxist theory'.[30] Althusser furthermore claims to base this reductive protocol on the sorry, meagre platform of a politicised identity politics: 'Proletarians', he claims, 'have a "class instinct" which helps them on the way to proletarian "class positions". Intellectuals, on the contrary, have a petty-bourgeois class instinct which fiercely resists this transition'.[31]

To be sure, one might sustain a weak view of this dogmatic, empiricist position, i.e., that an infinite variety of external factors (the lived experience

---

27 Cited in Estop 2021, p. 208, my translation.
28 Estop 2021, p. 209. The result of this final *kehre*, in Althusser's post-1980 writings, was his turn to an 'aleatory' materialism, focused principally on neither the epistemological concerns of *Reading Capital*, nor the directly militant political imperatives of 'the class struggle in theory', but instead engaging a Spinozist critique of ontological foundations via the concept of the void.
29 Althusser 1968, p. 5, emphasis in original. Althusser repeats this claim on the following page: 'Marxist-Leninist philosophy, or dialectical materialism, represents the proletarian class struggle *in theory*' (Althusser 1968, p. 7, emphasis in original).
30 Althusser 1968, p. 7.
31 Althusser 1968, p. 2.

of working-class exploitation, the encounter with Engels, political militancy, the failed revolutions of 1848, Marx's intellectual temperament and 'genius', etc.) were indeed necessary external *conditions* for the orientation and vehemency of *Capital*'s 'critique of political economy'.[32] Althusser, however, summarises this position in far stronger, psychologistic and epistemologically absolute terms in the Preface to *Lenin and Philosophy*, stating categorically that 'it is only from the point of view of class exploitation that it is possible to see and analyse the mechanisms of a class society and therefore to produce a scientific knowledge of it'.[33]

This position must be rejected categorically on the very Spinozist grounds that animate the claims of *Reading Capital*, arguing as it does from imaginary lived experience ('the point of view of class exploitation') backward to impute its imaginary causes. *Capital* must instead be understood as the systematic demonstration of the necessary forms of appearance and relation in *any* society, past, present, or future, real or imagined, of any and all 'societies in which the capitalist mode of production prevails'.[34] Marx shows, among his countless propositions, that in *any* society in which all things of value tend to take the form of commodities and commodified relations (the form of appearance of which is 'an immense collection of commodities'), the basic 'cell form' of that society is, necessarily, the commodity; that the commodity as such, at its most abstract, simply has, as a given fact, two principal aspects or attributes: its use-

---

32   In the sense that Alain Badiou has theorised the 'conditions' of philosophy (*Conditions*). Panagiotis Sotiris writes similarly that 'In Spinoza's terms, freedom is a consequence of intelligible necessity, and in Marx's terms it is knowledge of the objective conditions of the class struggle that makes possible the political direction of the class struggle'. Sotiris 2013, p. 37.

33   Althusser 1968, p. xvi.

34   Marx 1976, p. 125. Michael Heinrich shows that the received notion of *Capital* as a work of the history of capitalism, derived from Kautsky, 'baldly contradicts Marx's claims in the Preface to the first volume. There, he emphasises that the work deals with "theoretical developments" (1976: 90), and that the text makes reference to conditions in England only as an "illustration" of such developments. Marx makes it clear that he is by no means offering a historical depiction: "Intrinsically, it is not a question of the higher or lower degree of development of the social antagonisms that spring from the natural laws of capitalist production. It is a question of these laws themselves" (90). In keeping with this perspective, Marx emphasises at the end of Volume 3 that he wants to present "the internal organisation of the capitalist mode of production, its ideal average, as it were" (970). This way of defining the object of *Capital* is not arbitrary, nor does it exclude historical developments from the account. On the contrary, the presentation of this "ideal average" is what makes possible an approach to history that is not based on mere anecdotes but rather on scientific analysis' (Heinrich 2021, p. 397).

value and its exchange-value, which coexist as positive facts without contradiction;[35] that the substance of value of such commodities is abstract labour, etc.

Marx's propositions and their demonstration in *Capital* are not derived from 'the point of view of class exploitation', as Althusser would demand in 1968 (though, again, this 'point of view' certainly constitutes one of their indirect *conditions*), but instead from Marx's painstaking critique of the theories of classical political economy, working at his desk and in the British Library.[36] This theoretical revisionism on Althusser's part should be rejected as forcefully as the conclusion that because Marx's later unfinished manuscripts and study notes demonstrate his concerted engagement with empirical research and historical analysis (which is certainly the case), that the argument of *Capital* itself bears an 'empiricist' dimension.[37] The laws of the tendencies of capitalism that Marx demonstrates, are, in their materialist necessity, eternal, their truth or falsity, their adequacy or inadequacy determinable purely from their own construction (Spinoza's *index sui*). What Marx calls for example 'the law of the mass of surplus value',[38] in Chapter 11 of *Capital*, constitutes an abstract formalisation of an aspect of the capitalist social form, grasped in thought and derived not from workers' lived experience of exploitation, but as a necessary and summary consequence of the categories and relations he has demonstrated to that point in his argument.

The opposite as well is true: insofar as they have a real theoretical content, Marx's essays such as 'The Eighteenth Brumaire' and *The Civil War in France* might rightly be said to depend directly upon, and be necessarily limited by, empirical, historical experience, as Althusser demands. Marx's historical essays and journalism, for all their brilliance and flashes of insight, however, remain just that, pieces linked to a particular historical situation and do not possess

---

35 'En quoi la "valeur d'usage" qui est dite "porteur" – "Träger" – de "valeur", peut-elle bien être dite contradictoire à la valeur qu'elle porte? Mystère'. Althusser 1998, p. 253. I will argue this point systematically in Chapter 3.

36 Althusser would assert precisely the opposite in a series of unpublished 1967 notes for a 'Book Project on *Capital* Vol. 1', i.e., that *Capital* is the result of Marx's 'experiments'. There, Althusser claims that Marx's various enquiries to Engels on the actual process of running a capitalist enterprise (regarding the calculation of amortisation, for example), constitute an empiricist 'experimental usage [*l'usage expérimental*] that Marx made of the given facts [*données*] of Engels's practical experience'. IMEC, 20ALT 16.11, p. 38.

37 Musto 2020, p. 151n86.

38 'The masses of value and of surplus-value produced by different capitals – the value of labour-power being given and its degree of exploitation being equal – vary directly as the amounts of the variable components of these capitals' (Marx 1976, p. 421). I develop my argument about the apodictic, non-empirical nature of Marx's argument in light of this crucial chapter of *Capital* below in Chapter 3.

the same degree of 'scientific value' Marx vaunted in his 1875 Postface to the French edition of *Capital*.[39] The case of a journalistic piece such as *The Civil War in France* is just the opposite of the scientific apodicticity of *Capital*: if the latter can rightly be said to have depended upon Marx (and Engels's) direct experience of class exploitation and political militancy as a condition of its urgency and critical orientation, but *not* for the scientific rigour of its insights into the capitalist social form, *The Civil War in France* can conversely be said to depend upon Marx's prior, painstakingly acquired theoretical understanding of capitalism and its *limits*, but merely as an extrinsic *condition* that allowed Marx accurately to judge in the heat of the historical moment a chaotic and overwhelmingly complex empirical situation as 'the great harbinger of a new [communist] society'.[40]

Even the famous penultimate concluding chapter of *Capital*, Volume I, 'The Historical Tendency of Capitalist Accumulation', the moment in *Capital* at which Marx actually describes the 'transformation of capitalist private prop-

---

[39] In the sense that 'a scientific analysis of [the forms of appearance of capital such as] competition is possible only if we can grasp the inner nature of capital, just as the apparent motions of the heavenly bodies are intelligible only to someone who is acquainted with their real motions, which are not perceptible to the senses' (Marx 1976, pp. 105, 433).

[40] *The Civil War in France*. Available at: https://www.marxists.org/archive/marx/works/1871/civil-war-france/index.htm. It should be obvious that the problem of the material, biographical, and historical determination of Marx's critique of political economy vastly exceeds the scope of the problem this book addresses, the Althusserian analysis of Marx's process of apodictic exposition in *Capital*. Alain Badiou's concept of the materialist *conditions* of philosophy that I invoke here can do no more than serve as a placeholder for future work in that direction that would remain faithful to Althusser's critique of empiricism and the rigorous, Spinozist distinction between theory and the capitalist real. The outstanding existing example of such an orientation (devoid, to be sure, of any reference to Althusser) is Michael Heinrich's biography of Marx (Heinrich 2019). Flatly rejecting the inadequacy of existing biographies of Marx, Heinrich combines a deep and broad knowledge of Marx's relation to his contemporary society and thought with an unequaled familiarity with Marx's theoretical project, insight richly informed, in a way no other biographer of Marx in English can even remotely claim, by Heinrich's intimate familiarity with Marx's many drafts and notes for *Capital* across the MEGA^2 project. This knowledge, along with a critical approach to Marx's biography that explicitly distinguishes documented archival facts from the many myths and legends that have long been propounded from one biography to another, leads Heinrich to argue against the imaginary figure of the biographical subject as *totality*, and to propose instead that 'a biography contains mediations, breaking points, and contingencies [that] dispute the idea of an unmediated access to the subject. Biography should not aim to reveal the "essence" of the person Marx; rather, it is about the permanent, contradictory, and often ruptured process that characterises the constitution of a particular person under particular social conditions and conflicts' (Heinrich 2020, 478).

erty ... into social property', does not contradict this position, but rather stands as its negative confirmation.[41] As its title and adjunct position indicate, the chapter's seven paragraphs constitute a brief, rhetorically powerful but analytically meagre addition to the immediately preceding historical chapters on primitive accumulation.[42] As such, this entire concluding section comprises an exterior supplement to Marx's systematic, apodictic *demonstration* of the capitalist social form in chapters 1–25. It is no coincidence that its handful of famous predictions,[43] in the absence of any and all demonstration, articulate a theoretically enfeebled and imaginary teleology, one that continues to rely on the theoretical rump of a Hegelian vocabulary that demonstrates nothing: 'Capitalist production begets, with the inexorability of a natural process, its own negation. This is the negation of the negation'.[44]

Marx will renounce this teleology of historical necessity (as the necessity that the communist social form be preceded by developed, industrial capitalism), a regressive, Hegelian moment of 'writing recipes for the cook-shops of the future', not only by the time of his famous 1872 Postface (in which the latter phrase appears), but above all in his late turn to an aleatory position on the problem of transition in the 1881 letters with Vera Zasulich.[45]

To continue to think beyond Althusser, with Althusser, we should radicalise his famous assertion that philosophy has no object ('Philosophy has no object, it has *its* objects'), to assert more generally that *critique has no object*, in the sense of a preconstituted empirical object that it analyses, subsequently to represent in thought.[46] Critique – and this includes above all Marx's critique of

---

41 Marx 1976, p. 929.
42 Marx 1976, chs. 26–31.
43 'The centralisation of the means of production and the socialisation of labour reach a point at which they become incompatible with their capitalist integument. This integument is burst asunder. The knell of capitalist private property sounds. The expropriators are expropriated' (Marx 1976, p. 929).
44 Marx 1976, p. 929. In *The New Dialectic and Marx's* Capital, Chris Arthur takes a very different position on this chapter of *Capital*, to construct a highly complex Hegelian interpretation of its political logic. I will discuss Arthur's interpretation in Chapter 3.
45 Marx 1976, p. 99. See Musto 2020, pp. 63–70. Marx had already articulated this refusal of historical teleology in his 1877 unsent draft letter to the Russian journal *Patriotic Notes* [*Otechestvennye Zapiski*] in which he flatly affirmed that history shows only that 'events of striking similarity, taking place in different historical contexts, [lead] to totally disparate results'. The structural theory of the capitalist social form that Marx articulates in the body of *Capital* can under no circumstances, he writes, serve as 'the master-key of a general historico-philosophical theory, whose supreme virtue [as a highly abstract theory] consists in being super-historical'. Cited in Musto 2020, p. 64.
46 Althusser 1974, p. 66.

political economy – instead constructs its object, in the attribute of thought, as a composite, materialist intervention itself situated within a forcefield of tensions and positions. While both Althusser and Macherey, unlike Marx, limit this position to address the academic institution of 'philosophy' and the history of thought, Macherey has further argued that the materialist position constitutes 'an attitude of thought that initially possesses no objective contents'. Extended to include materialist critique in general (such as Marx's critique of political economy),[47] we necessarily arrive at the position that having no predetermined, empirical content, materialist critique cannot claim to knowledge of an empirical object, and thus remains 'dispossessed of its aspiration theoretically to apprehend a real content'.[48] Instead, this anti-empiricist materialist critique, strictly remaining within the attribute of thought, 'does not apply outside of itself, [yet] produces distinct effects [as] a process invested in the real'.[49]

Rather than the adequate representation of an object as its truth [*vérité*], Macherey argues that materialist critique, as a determinate intervention in a discursive field, stakes out an unstable, dynamic position of *justesse* or exactitude within divided and contradictory situations that possess 'adverse lines of force', to arrive at always precarious positions of equilibrium.[50] To read *Capital* as such a materialist intervention, one that possesses no pre-existing object, is to distinguish a text that instead actively constructs, in the attribute of thought, the real nature of the multifarious capitalist social form: as 'a discursive *dispositif*, itself a material process that develops specific effects [in this case, as the century and a half of effects of the reception of *Capital*] in the problematic space opened by the development of its own contradictions …. [Materialist critique] is real movement [*mouvement réel*], the objective process that discovers, in inventing them step by step, the overdetermined forms of its materiality'.[51]

Keeping due measure, the writing of this book subjectively confirms to me the correctness of Macherey's anti-empiricist position: prior to its composition, there existed no empirical object 'the materialist critique of Marx, Spinoza, and the Althusserians' for me to analyse, but only a series of disparate texts, with their contradictions and often incomplete discursive powers, a sundry set including manifold abandoned intentions and unpublished fragments, and,

---

47 Macherey himself seems to encourage such a position, observing in his 1997 commentary that his 1991 essay 'could be interpreted as the resurgence of a critical conception of philosophy' (Macherey 1999, p. 110).
48 Macherey 1999, p. 109.
49 Macherey 1999, p. 96. I will follow Macherey's further development of this position in the next chapter.
50 Macherey 1999, p. 97.
51 Macherey 1999, p. 98.

above all, a succession of silences, all of which I have sought to articulate – not to reveal a truth – but instead as the exact and exacting composition of a force-field of discursive relations that constitute *Capital*'s materialist dialectic.

2 An Act of Theoretical Repression

In contrast to the slogan of 'class struggle in theory', the 'theoreticist' object of *For Marx* and *Reading Capital* that Althusser's retrograde call to arms sought to terminate was arguably never openly engaged with in theoretical struggle, but dutifully repressed, the theoretical object that is Marx's philosophical 'thought-concrete' [*Gedankenkonkretum*] seemingly forgotten even by those who remained faithful to the project of *Reading Capital*. Simply put, nowhere in all the literature on Althusser and *Reading Capital* did there occur a sustained engagement with and interrogation of what is arguably the central claim of Althusser's famous introductory text: the claim that in the place of a (Hegelian) negative dialectic, 'in *Capital* we find [instead] a systematic presentation, an apodictic arrangement of the concepts in the form of that type of demonstrational discourse that Marx calls analysis'.[52]

The correlate of this claim is Althusser's unadulterated Spinozist statement of the 'theoreticist' position, i.e., that 'theoretical practice is indeed its own criterion, and contains in itself definite protocols with which to validate the quality of its product'.[53] In opposition to all forms of empiricism, Althusser's assertion in *Reading Capital* redeploys Spinoza's famous axiom 'verum index sui et falsi', uncompromisingly to assert the absolute autonomy of Marx's materialist

---

52   RC, p. 51. In his discussion of the dialectical method Marx progressively developed in *Capital*, Michael Heinrich's *Science of Value* makes a similar claim with distinctly Althusserian overtones (such as the focus on the 'placement' of concepts): Marx, Heinrich writes, 'sie in eine bestimmte Ordnung bringt, die ihnen aber nicht äußerlich ist und lediglich den Gesamtzusammenhang herstellt, sondern die zur Bestimmung der Kategorien selbst noch wesentlich ist: eine Ordnung, die wesentliche Beziehungen der Kategorien ausdrückt.' (Marx 'places them [concepts] in a certain order, one that is not external to them to merely establish an overall context, but [an order that] is essential for determining the categories themselves: an order that expresses the essential relationships between the categories') (Heinrich 2022 [1999], p. 172; 2023, p. 268, my translation). Where Heinrich differs from Althusser is in his quite traditional, empiricist theory of knowledge, one in which, for Heinrich, Marx's dialectical demonstration attends to 'den Zusammenhang von Begriffen (Plural) geht, die empirisches Material verarbeiten' ('the context of concepts (plural) that process empirical material', ibid.).

53   RC, p. 61.

thought-concrete, refusing empiricist theories of knowledge, and consequentially rejecting all subject-object, representational and correspondence-based models of truth:

> The criterion of the 'truth' of the knowledges produced by Marx's theoretical practice is provided by his theoretical practice itself, i.e., by the proof-value, by the scientific status of the forms which ensured the production of those knowledges.[54] Marx's theoretical practice is the criterion of the 'truth' of the knowledges that Marx produced; and only because it was really a matter of knowledge, and not of chance hypotheses, have these knowledges given the famous results.[55]

This epistemological claim, which it is the aim of this book to sustain and amplify, has, despite its theoretical daring, remained almost without exception *lettre morte* in the literature on *Reading Capital*; even among the Althusserians themselves, only Pierre Macherey's precocious, all-too-brief 1965 analysis attends systematically to the process of exposition and demonstration Marx deployed in *Capital*.

Among the results of Althusser's theoretically self-destructive turn after 1968 is the surprising fact in question here: his general failure to extend and develop the innovative and henceforth world-famous reading of Marx's *Capital* initiated by *For Marx* and *Reading Capital* itself. To my knowledge, Althusser would reiterate the theoreticist position of *Reading Capital* on only three occasions. Above all, in his inflection of the positions of *Reading Capital* in the single published instance of this return, his 1977 'Avant-propos du livre de G. Duménil, *Le concept de loi économique dans* Le capital'. There, Althusser: 1. warns against the temptation of erecting a concept of a 'methode dialectique' in general (whether Hegelian, Marxian, or otherwise) as well as that of 'method' *tout court*; 2. argues for a process of exposition in *Capital* by the 'positioning' of concepts rather than their idealist deduction as an 'autoproduction'; 3. argues against any ide-

---

54　Here, as at so many other points in his Introduction, Althusser redeploys a fundamental notion from Cavaillès' *On Logic and the Theory of Science*, i.e., that of what Jacques Bouveresse calls the 'effective construction [*construction effective*]' of a theoretical object, to illuminate Marx's conceptual realism (Bouveresse, IMEC 20 ALT 51.7, p. 30). Cavaillès points out in his critique of Kant that 'there must be a substratum or substance in order for subject and predicate to be distinguished, or for the act of judgement to be recognised as an act that can be accomplished as such and linked to the act of reasoning. But a direct description presupposes knowledge, which is to say *the construction of the object of the concept*' (Cavaillès 2021, p. 30, emphasis added).

55　RC, p. 62.

ological understanding of the 'axiomatic' nature of Marx's demonstration; and 4. identifies a *multiplicity* of orders of exposition in *Capital*.⁵⁶

In his 1967 notes for a 'Book Project on *Capital* Vol. I', Althusser writes that 'Formally the beginning of *Capital* resembles the order of exposition of a mathematically *formalised* system. ... In mathematics the order of exposition holding to the criteria of the formalisation begin with the *most abstract concepts* (*the definitions*), which are indispensable for the ensuing development [of the demonstration], and subsequently, according to the demands of the theoretical development, one proceeds via the "injection" of new concepts. *This is exactly what Marx does in the beginning of Book I* [of *Capital*]'.⁵⁷

Subsequently, in a 1978 text (in the wake, that is, of the antithetical position of 'class struggle in theory'), composed of 23 meticulously drafted and typewritten pages and bearing the archival title 'Cours sur le mode d'exposition chez Marx', Althusser would reaffirm that

> *Capital* [is a] work that belongs to the register of a presentation (*Darstellung*) of truth according to the order of reasons [*l'ordre des raisons*]. Truth does not take the form in it of presence, but that of the production of presentation, of deduction in a system dominated by the order of reasons or method. ... There is an order of reasons, a method, an order for the linking of things [*un ordre d'enchainement des choses*] that is *par excellence* that of the *Darstellung* of truth. Truth can only be presented, which is to say, in the strongest of terms, rendered present, visible to the eyes in its presentation, in the form of a *Denkprozess* that conforms to this norm and takes no other form.⁵⁸

For the reader hoping for some further specification, a demonstration, even a citation from *Capital* to bolster this claim, not a word, any more than in *Reading Capital*. This would be Althusser's last written statement on the logic of *Capital*.

---

56 Althusser 1998a, pp. 247–66. Althusser's interest in apodictic demonstration in general (and not only in its deployment by Marx) persisted at least until 1968: there exists, for example, an unsigned document in the IMEC Althusser archive entitled 'Cours sur Frege, Carnap, et Bolzano'. Shortly before his passing, Jacques Bouveresse confirmed (in an email to Etienne Balibar et al., 9 November 2020) that this is the (incomplete) text of a seminar he offered at Ulm in 1967, the typescript of which Althusser explicitly requested from him in that year ('Althusser l'avait fait dactylographier' JB), the same year as he (Althusser) made the above comments on Marx and mathematical formalisation. 'Cours sur Frege, Carnap, et Bolsano [*sic*]'. IMEC 20ALT 28.5, pp. 1, 3.
57 IMEC 20ALT 16.12, pp. 54–5, emphases in original.
58 IMEC 20ALT 28.5, pp. 1, 3.

In the case of Althusser's *Reading Capital* collaborators, Jacques Rancière has never returned to the study of *Capital*, a disinterest made eminently manifest in his very public 1974 denunciation of Althusser's 'theoreticism' (*La Leçon d'Althusser*). Indeed, only Etienne Balibar has explicitly developed the Althusserian idea of Marx's philosophy (*La philosophie de Marx*), but even here, the majority of that book addresses Marx's thought prior to the elaboration of *Capital* beginning in 1857. The case of Alain Badiou is even clearer. While not an original contributor to *Reading Capital* itself, he in fact remained closely aligned with the Althusserians as a member of the so-called *groupe Spinoza* in the years 1965–67.[59] Nonetheless, and despite both his frequent invocations of Marx's political writings and his consistent critiques of capitalism in the name of the 'Idea of Communism', Badiou has never written a study engaging Marx's *Capital* in any fashion, let alone to address the specific epistemological claims *Reading Capital* put forward.

Pierre Macherey's writings since 1965 constitute in many ways the most complex and fascinating case in this regard, and much of this book is devoted to investigating his thought. While he as well has never published further analyses of *Capital* since his brief, long-overlooked study of Marx's process of exposition that constituted the third chapter of the first edition of *Reading Capital*, he nonetheless intended, but then abandoned, a 1967 project for a thesis on Marx's philosophy, a project that would presumably have extended and developed his avowedly Spinozist reading of *Capital*.[60] Instead, the object of Macherey's sustained philosophical attention has remained Spinoza himself, the theorist whose thought had initially inspired the most radical epistemological positions of *Reading Capital*. In this vein, Macherey has produced an original and compelling understanding of Spinoza's thought as a positive, materialist dialectic, first in his celebrated 1979 book *Hegel or Spinoza*, and, above all, in his masterful five-volume, line by line exposition and analysis of Spinoza's *Ethics*.

In fact, Macherey's post-'68 turn from Marx to Spinoza can be said to structure the argument of this book as a whole.[61] On the surface, the epistemological claims of *Reading Capital* appear to have been largely if not entirely abandoned by the Althusserians in the wake of May '68. This occurred in the context of a more general theoretical turn, a movement away from the notion of *theoretical practice* that had guided *For Marx* and *Reading Capital*, toward the immediate imperative of political action at the level of theory: ready examples from the

---

59 Althusser 1994.
60 Macherey 2021.
61 Peter Thomas has called into question the adequacy of Spinozist philosophy to that of Althusser. See Thomas 2002 and Sotiris 2021, p. 180.

1970s in addition to Althusser's writings on the 'class struggle in theory' include Badiou's so-called 'Red Years' texts, Balibar's *La Dictature du prolétariat*, and Rancière's *Proletarian Nights*.

That said, in the remainder of this Introduction, I wish to leave aside Althusser's dubious programme of 'class struggle in theory' and to return to address in detail his initial epistemological critique in the arguments of *For Marx* and *Reading Capital*. To do so, it will be essential to indicate the originality of that intervention in Marxist theory, as well as the real ambiguities and limitations of Althusser's incipient propositions. These initial theoretical impediments will then find further, conclusive development when read in light of the esoteric, unpublished writings of Althusser and, in the subsequent chapters of this book, in the writings of these 'Althusserians' – Spinoza and Marx, Macherey, and Badiou – as the shared pursuit of a theory of the materialist dialectic.

3 *For Marx* in Its Limits

Already in the essays collected in *For Marx*, Althusser articulates the core epistemological proposition of his rereading of Marx, but in an initial form marked by various deficiencies that will find subsequent (if still problematic) development in the essays of *Reading Capital*. The 1962 essay 'Contradiction and Overdetermination' sounds an opening salvo in Althusser's theoretical intervention, in its steadfast refusal to take Marx's word on Hegel at face value. This is the Marx who famously asserted in the 1873 Postface to the second edition of *Capital* that 'With [Hegel the dialectic] is standing on its head. It must be inverted, in order to discover the rational kernel within the mystical shell'. Althusser flatly rejects the idea that Marx simply 'overturned' Hegel, as Marx himself claimed. Instead of a mere overturning that would leave the structures of his dialectic unchanged but only inverted, Althusser famously affirms an epistemological break between the 'Marxist' and the 'Hegelian' dialectic, as two radically heterogeneous philosophical practices:[62]

---

[62] In the *Eléments d'autocritique*, Althusser will reaffirm the correctness of this proposition ('Cette these, qui n'a pas éte épargné par les critiques, je la maintiens'), with the crucial proviso that it be understood as an *event* ('surgit quelque chose comme un événement sans précédent') in precisely the sense Badiou has given the concept: as a punctual break 'à partir de *L'idéologie allemande*', but one that required Marx's ongoing fidelity as a perpetual struggle to realise, step by step, to the end of his days, its full theoretical implications (Althusser 1974, pp. 165, 164).

> If the Marxist dialectic is 'in its principal' fully the opposite of the Hegelian dialectic, ... this radical difference must manifest itself in its essence, which is to say in its determinations and its own structures. To speak clearly, this implies that the fundamental structures of the Hegelian dialectic, such as negation, the negation of the negation, the identity of opposites, 'sublation', the transformation of quality into quantity, contradiction, etc., possess for Marx (in so far as he takes them up, which is not always the case!) a different structure from that which they possess for Hegel.[63]

On the one hand, Althusser here rightly refuses simply to take Marx at his word, as though Marx's declared, imaginary relation to Hegel's thought were sufficient in itself to resolve the complex question of the nature of the epistemology deployed in *Capital*. Marx, for all his genius, was necessarily a subject of ideology like anyone else, even in a text as authoritative as the 1873 Postface to the Second Edition of *Capital* in which he makes his famous claim 'to discover the rational kernel within the mystical shell'. Instead, Althusser rightly proposes that the difference between these two forms of dialectic can only be determined immanently, through an analysis of the 'determinations and structures' of Marx's logical demonstration itself, that is to say, through a critical analysis of the actual dialectical method deployed in the pages of *Capital*.[64]

At the same time, Althusser's initial formulation of his proposition suffers from several inadequacies. Althusser appears hesitant and anxious at the very thought that Marx might in fact have constructed a dialectic based upon entirely different principles than those of Hegel's negative dialectic. It remains a tentative suggestion, merely hinting that the categories of the 'Marxist dialectic' might possess 'a different structure' than the 'Hegelian dialectic', offering no more than a summary list of the principal characteristics of the latter ('negation, ... contradiction, etc.') without substantiating this claim through even a minimal concrete investigation or example.

Even more problematically, Althusser immediately abandons the distinction he indicates between the Marxist and Hegelian dialectics as a question of

---

63 Althusser 1974, p. 165, my translation.
64 This is the procedure I seek to follow throughout this book, above all in Chapter 3. Victor Béguin, in contrast, takes Marx's declarations on his relation to Hegel at face value, and finds in *Capital* the intentional working-through of Marx's initial, 1843 critique of Hegel, and this on three registers, which Béguin terms *genetic*, *empirical-historical*, and *dialectical* (Béguin 2021, p. 109).

thought at the level of the 'determinations and self-same structures' of a dialectical demonstration, as what Pierre Macherey will call, in his contribution to *Reading Capital*, Marx's 'process of exposition'. Instead of pursuing this insight, he quickly shifts his analysis to the temporal, worldly domain of existing things, to engage a discussion of 'the Marxist concept of contradiction' via Lenin's analysis of the historical conditions governing the phenomenal unfolding of the Bolshevik revolution. It is in this discussion, which occupies the remainder of the essay, that Althusser first develops his famous concept of historical overdetermination and deploys it to offer a penetrating critique of traditional and Hegelian philosophies of history; that said, in doing so he completely abandons his initial proposition to investigate the 'Hegelian' and 'Marxist' dialectics at the level of a logic of apodictic demonstration rather than historical existence.

While Pierre Macherey's contribution to *Reading Capital* will redress this shortcoming, to focus precisely on the dialectical logic of Marx's initial process of exposition in *Capital*, 'Contradiction and Overdetermination' is marked by a further weakness, one that will only be more adequately addressed when Althusser's students Macherey and Badiou shift the object of their critique from the analysis of *Capital* itself to the more abstract determinations of the concept of a materialist dialectic as such. Althusser's argument in fact suffers from a *nominalist deficiency*, in its repeated assertion that the proper names 'Marxist' and 'Hegelian' in fact suffice to indicate the essential, universal nature of two forms of dialectic. I will argue throughout this book that these attributes ('Hegelian' and 'Marxist' dialectics) should rightfully be replaced, as Macherey and Badiou will not hesitate to do, with the functional attributes 'positive' or additive synthetic vs. 'negative' or contradiction-based, to indicate more adequately the essential distinction governing the dynamic impulse of dialectical development in each case.

The reason Althusser's nominal distinction (Marxist vs. Hegelian) remains problematic is immediately familiar, since Althusser's claim that Marx made a clean and absolute epistemological break from Hegel has long constituted one of the principal sites of the rejection of Althusserian thought. Marx himself, as is often pointed out in response to Althusser's famous proposition of the epistemological break, continued to assert to the very end of his life that he remained 'the pupil of that mighty thinker [Hegel]'.[65] Taken in itself, however,

---

65   Marx 1976, p. 103, 1873 Postface. This late position from Marx's 'Postface' to the second, 1872 edition of *Capital*, reiterated earlier statements by Marx, for example, in his correspondence with Lassalle, where Marx already asserted that: 'This [Hegelian] dialectic is, to be sure, the ultimate word in philosophy' (cited in Fluss 2022, p. 481).

such a statement, while suggestive, cannot resolve the question of whether and in what ways what Marx calls the 'method of presentation' he deploys in *Capital* differs from that of Hegel. Marx's own subjective point of view both reduces the rich complexity of Hegel's development and deployment of his dialectical method across a lifetime of work to a single nominal cipher (the 'Hegelian … dialectical method'), as well as presupposing precisely what would need to be ascertained once those two methods were conceptualised: the determination through textual analysis of the precise factors that differentiate these two 'methods of presentation'.

Had Marx written his projected study of dialectical method,[66] he might well have found, as Althusser repeatedly suggested, that the actual method of exposition he had developed in the decades he spent writing *Capital* in fact differed far more fundamentally from that of Hegel than he had realised. Marx might have found that in fact Hegel had not been 'the first to present its [the dialectic's] general forms of motion in a comprehensive manner',[67] but had in fact only identified the forms of motion of a specific, negative dialectic, one that Marx himself gradually abandoned after 1857, to develop instead a positive dialectic of additive synthesis for his exposition in *Capital*, as Macherey demonstrates in his brief contribution to *Reading Capital* (to be discussed in the next chapter), a dialectic that finds antecedents in thinkers including Aristotle and Spinoza (both of whom Marx read intensively), and Bernard Bolzano (whom he did not).

A final limitation of what I am calling Althusser's nominalist deficiency encompasses the further reference – beyond that which Althusser makes to 'Hegelian' and 'Marxist' dialectics in 'Contradiction and Overdetermination' – to a putative 'Spinozist' method of exposition, an attribution that Althusser and Macherey will identify in both *Reading Capital* as well as in subsequent works that focus explicitly on Spinoza's method of exposition, such as Macherey's *Hegel or Spinoza*.[68] The problem is not that Spinoza lacked a coherent notion of an additive synthetic dialectic *more geometrico* (he did), but rather the impossibility of contrasting this with a so-called 'Hegelian' dialectic. Althusser's initial references in 'Contradiction and Overdetermination' to a 'Hegelian' dialectic

---

66 Marx famously intended, but never managed, to write a treatise on dialectics, as he wrote on various occasions to Engels and Joseph Dietzgen (Fluss 2022, p. 482).
67 Marx 1976, p. 103.
68 'With Marx, [there occurs] the emergence of a new science … rather in the way that Spinoza takes up the *more geometrico* only to give it a new and original meaning' (RC, p. 182).

remain vague and theoretically inadequate, lacking a formal identification that would enable more precise determination of the dialectical form or practice of a thinker in whatever variety and at whatever moment in the spectrum of their writings.

Hegel himself did not develop a single, antagonistic (mis-)reading of Spinoza, but in fact developed at least two conflicting readings of Spinoza in his early and later works, the first positive, the second (as Macherey shows) impoverished, critical, and tendential.[69] This general neglect of Hegel's early reading of Spinoza on the part of Althusser and Macherey is problematic in the present context because in texts such *Faith and Knowledge* (1802), the young Hegel in fact resolutely defended Spinoza's philosophy and his dialectical method in particular against its critique by Jacobi.[70] While it may well be the case, as Macherey has shown in his many studies of Spinoza, that the latter develops across the entirety of his thought a precise and coherent philosophy of a positive, materialist dialectic that one might well term 'Spinozist', the same coherency cannot be attributed to Hegel, whose own philosophy, while always acknowledging a real debt to Spinoza, moved from an initial appreciation in which Hegel unreservedly claimed Spinoza as 'a dialectical thinker' fully consonant with his own evolving thought, to then subsequently betray this initial position in the *Logic* 'in descriptions of Spinozism and pantheism so caricatured that they had very little in common with the defence Hegel gave of Spinoza in opposition to Jacobi decades before'.[71]

This initial imprecision in Althusser's many references to a 'Hegelian' dialectic remained hobbled by a further impediment, an obstacle related to the very notion of the 'dialectic' itself. Althusser's references to 'Hegelian' and 'Marxist' dialectics in 'Contradiction and Overdetermination' implies a formal, generic multiplicity of 'dialectics', as do subsequent references by Althusser, Balibar, Macherey and Badiou to 'materialist' and 'positive' dialectics. Post-Kantian and Marxist readers, however, have become all-too-accustomed to thinking of the

---

69 Macherey himself has in fact criticised his 1979 book on the grounds that it focuses on Hegel's later works and the *Logic* in particular, neglecting Hegel's engagement with Spinoza in his early writings (1999, p. 146).

70 Harrison Fluss has argued that 'Hegel's later understanding [of Spinoza] represented not so much an advance but a regression towards the very same anti-Spinozist positions he had already refuted in the early Jena period. In reverting back to old characterisations of Spinozistic substance as a-cosmic in his later work, Hegel obfuscated his own deeper connections with Spinoza, who had formerly represented for him a genuine philosopher of the absolute Idea' (Fluss 2016, p. 2).

71 Fluss 2016, p. 7.

'dialectic' as limited to the Hegelian metaphysics of totality, contradiction, and sublation, as the negation of the negation, and/or as traditional Marxism's understanding of the materialist 'inversion' of this contradiction-based logic.[72]

It is too often forgotten, however, that the principal meaning of *dialectic* in English, according to the OED, is simply 'logical argument', and in French (from which the English derives), 'the art of reasoning in general'.[73] Anterior to these

---

[72] This reductive position perhaps originates with Engels's famous assertion, in *Anti-Duhring*, that dialectics, as the science of nature, can be reduced to three laws: the transformation of quantity into quality; the interpenetration of opposites; and the negation of the negation (Bhaskar 1983, p. 126).

[73] A key moment in this forgetting of the plurality of dialectical methods is surely to found in Abram Deborin's crucial contributions to the theoretical foundations of Soviet philosophy in the pages of the journal he edited from 1922–30, *Pod Znamenem Marksizma* (Under the Banner of Marxism). In a 1927 article on the occasion of the 250th anniversary of Spinoza's death, Deborin neatly divided the forces of Soviet theory into 'the Hegelian front and the Spinozist front', in which reference to Hegel (and his constitutive negative dialectic) is judged relevant for 'the foundation of our *method*' and Spinoza for 'our world view' (cited at Oittinen 2022, p. 5). At the stroke of a pen, Deborin disappears the latter's positive dialectic as a viable methodology for dialectical materialism. More recently, Harrison Fluss, in an otherwise insightful and informed presentation, from his first sentence radically limits his definition of 'Dialectics' to its post-Hegelian, negative dialectical form, when he writes: '*As the logic of contradiction*, dialectics has a long pre-history before Marx' (Fluss 2022, p. 474, my emphasis). Similarly, in her article on 'Dialectics' for the *Bloomsbury Companion to Marx*, Carolyn Lesjak presents the topic of her article as the 'imperative for thought to expose and work through the contradictions and tensions that underlie all conceptual coherence …. This critique proceeds by the route of negation, a path whereby the contradictions of capitalism are made apparent' (Lesjak 2021, p. 463). Andrew Cole, in his brilliant analysis of the Medieval origins of Hegelian dialectic, focuses almost entirely on the concept as 'the dialectic of identity and difference' and underscores the originality of Hegel's 'recuperation of the concept of contradiction' (Cole 2014, p. 34). Roy Bhaskar, in the Harvard *Dictionary of Marxist Thought*, identifies three predominant meanings of the term 'dialectics' in the Marxist tradition: 'as (a) a method, most usually scientific method, instancing *epistemological* dialectics [i.e., the general usage Althusser invokes in *For Marx* and *Reading Capital*]; (b) a set of laws or principles, governing some sector of the whole of reality, *ontological* dialectics; and (c) the movement of history, *relational* dialectics'. Yet for all this real subtlety, Bhaskar too ultimately reverts to a contradiction-based understanding of Marx's epistemology: 'Marx's dialectics is scientific, [Bhaskar summarises], because it explains the contradictions in thought and the crises of socio-economic life in terms of the particular contradictory essential relations which generate them' (Bhaskar 1983, pp. 122, 124, 125). Patrick Murray is the only reader of *Capital* as far as I am aware who underlines the generic, non-Hegelian meaning of *dialectic* for Marx as the art of logical demonstration per se. Murray 2017, p. 131.

various definitions,[74] for Aristotle, *dialectic* [διαλεκτική] indicates quite simply, in the words of E.S. Forster, 'the application of logical methods to argument'.[75]

André Lalande, in his classic *Vocabulaire technique et critique de la philosophie* – which has served as the standard theoretical reference for generations of French thinkers since its initial publication in 1923 and which Althusser himself refers to for his initial definition of 'political economy' in *Reading Capital*[76] – follows this degree of generality in defining *la dialectique* as '*toute suite de pensées ... qui dépendent logiquement l'un de l'autre*' [any sequence of thoughts that depend logically upon one another].[77]

Althusser, Macherey, and Badiou's use of 'dialectics' in the plural (whether Hegelian, Marxist, Spinozist, negative, positive, or materialist) follows this etymological plurality and refers to various modes of 'logical argument' or demonstration in this capacious sense. Althusser, in *For Marx*, initially indicates this generic plurality of processes of logical demonstration via the bare nominal distinction between 'Hegelian' and 'Marxist' dialectics, without substantially developing this distinction at the level of Marx's method of demonstration. *Reading Capital*, in contrast, would attend far more fully to the formal and functional differences between these two modes of exposition.

---

74 In Latin, from which these derive, *dialectica* is defined as simply 'the art of methodical reasoning' (*Le Robert historique*). In German the *Historisches Wörterbuch der Philosophie* defines *Dialektik* as 'der Art einer Disziplin mit der Analyse und Synthese von Begriffen und dient vornehmlich der Erkenntnis des Seienden, um die Ideen zu begreifen' [a discipline in which the analysis and synthesis of concepts primarily addresses the knowledge of being in order to comprehend Ideas]. On the multifarious interpretations of the concept of *dialectic* in *Capital*, see Heinrich 1999, pp. 164–79; 2023, pp. 259–75.

75 Aristotle, *Posterior Analytics*, 25, note *b*.

76 'I can take as my elementary theoretical guide the definitions proposed in A. Lalande's *Dictionnaire philosophique* .... They can be taken as so many indices not only of a common theoretical background, but also of the possible resonances and inflexions of sense this background provides' (RC, p. 312, LC, p. 366).

77 Lalande 2010 [1923], p. 227. Lalande furthermore notes that 'This word [*la dialectique*] has received such diverse meanings that it can only be usefully employed by indicating precisely in what sense it is taken' (ibid.). Throughout this book, I will follow Althusser's lead and repeatedly refer to Lalande's definitions from his magisterial 1923 work of erudition, currently in its eighteenth edition, a reference work that Jacques Fallon described on its 1993 reedition with PUF as 'the most famous philosophical dictionary in the French language .... Still today, no other dictionary in our language can claim to rival either in quality or scope this monument of French erudition'. Fallon 1993, p. 512.

4   Reading *Capital*'s Process of Exposition

This further development of the initial claims of 'Contradiction and Overdetermination' occurs in *Reading Capital* in three stages: 1) an initial critique of empiricist epistemologies in Althusser's introductory essay 'From *Capital* to Marx's Philosophy', followed by 2) the crucial and rarely discussed affirmation in that same essay's section 14, which argues that 'in *Capital* we find ... an apodictic arrangement of the concepts in the form of [... a] demonstrational discourse',[78] a proposition that Althusser nonetheless leaves to Macherey actually to demonstrate in 3) the latter's analysis and demonstration in Chapter Three, 'The Process of Exposition of *Capital*'.

Althusser initiates his determination of Marx's epistemological method in 'From *Capital* to Marx's Philosophy' through a general critique of empiricism. He refuses to limit the notion of empiricism to the bare dictionary definition, as the assertion that all knowledge arises from sensuous experience, whether classically for Hume or as the 'vulgar empiricism' that 'takes the objects of scientific practice to be pure phenomena that have not undergone a process of either ideological or theoretical transformation'.[79]

If in his Introduction to *Reading Capital*, Althusser seeks to develop an encompassing and unyielding critique of empiricism, its articulation is nonetheless surprising: one would expect Althusser simply to have based his critique on Spinoza's familiar claim, in the Appendix to *Ethics* Book 1, for the radical inadequacy of all thought derived from sensory impressions, in its necessary movement from observed effects backward to their imaginary, ideological causes.[80] Instead, Althusser identifies an entirely different criterion that he will

---

78   RC, p. 51.
79   RC, p. 243.
80   Spinoza's critique of empiricism in Book II of *Ethica* is absolute: 'Insofar as the human mind imagines an external body, to that extent it does not have an adequate knowledge of it' (*quatenus mens humana corpus externum imaginatur aetenus adaequatam ejus cognitionem non habet*) EIIP26C, and again, the corollary to Proposition II29, 'Whenever the human mind perceives things after the common order of nature, it does not have an adequate knowledge of itself, nor of its body, nor of external bodies, but only a confused and fragmentary knowledge' (*mens humana quoties ex communi naturae ordine res percipit nec sui ipsius nec sui corporis nec corporum externorum adaequatam habet cognitionem*) EIIP29C. Spinoza once more: 'When we gaze at the sun, we see it as some two hundred feet distant from us. The error does not consist in simply seeing the sun in this way but in the fact that while we do so we are not aware of the true distance and the cause of our seeing it so. For although we may later become aware that the sun is more than six hundred times the diameter of the earth distant from us, we shall nevertheless continue to see it as close at hand. For it is not our ignorance of its true distance that causes us to see the sun

contrast with Marx's materialist method of exposition in *Capital*. Althusser pointedly claims that 'The whole empiricist process of knowledge lies in fact in an operation of the subject called abstraction. To know is to abstract from the real object its essence, the possession of which by the subject is then called knowledge'.[81] This initial formulation already casts empiricism, in all its variants, as a dualist relation of subject to object, a conception of knowledge production that Althusser will then contrast with Marx's Spinozist 'thought-concrete' that *reproduces* (as opposed to merely representing) the material, extensive real of the capitalist social form, capitalism itself, that is to say, in the attribute of thought.[82]

Althusser then takes a further step in this general critique of empiricism, to draw a necessary implication of the empiricist extraction the essential truth from an object.[83] In all empiricist operations, Althusser asserts, encompassing both its sensualist and rationalist variants, the 'sole function [of knowledge] is to separate, in the object, the two parts which exist in it, the essential and the inessential, ... the gold [from] the dross – by special procedures whose aim is *to eliminate the inessential real*'.[84]

In the case of Marx's *Capital*, Althusser makes a very compelling claim indeed. For a real distinction should be drawn between the empiricist methods of Adam Smith, for example, and Marx's Spinozist materialism in *Capital*. Smith, to take a famous example, begins *The Wealth of Nations* with the assertion of a universal notion inductively abstracted from the observed regularities of human communities in general. Transhistorically, these constitute the basic anthropological features that need only, in this view, naturally come to flourish once the historical impediments to trade of previous social forms (agrarian, feudal, etc.) were lifted. There exists, Smith writes in the first paragraph of *The Wealth of Nations*, 'a certain propensity in human nature, ... the propensity to truck, barter, and exchange one thing for another. ... It is common to all men, and to be found in no other race of animals'.[85]

---

to be so near; it is that the affection of our body involves the essence of the sun only to the extent that the body is affected by it'. Spinoza, EIIP35S.

81   RC, p. 35.
82   RC, p. 41.
83   RC, p. 36.
84   Ibid.
85   Adam Smith 1999, p. 11. I take this example from the analysis of Marx's 1857 methodology by Juan Iñigo Carrera (2013). The same point could be made of Hegel and capitalism: none of the various categories that Hegel develops in his social logic (*Elements of the Philosophy of Right*), from the family to the free association of individuals in civil society, to political community and the relation of states, can be properly comprehended in abstraction from

Althusser's point is well taken, since not only does Smith appear to derive this universal notion from empirical abstraction, but he furthermore deploys it to distinguish an essential characteristic of human behaviour from other inessential qualities common to human and other animal species ('passions', 'acting in concert'). Marx, in contrast, does not merely demystify the illusory nature of the various phenomenal features of capitalism, such as commodity fetishism, money, profit, the 'freedom' of the wage labour contract, the illusions of a supposedly virtuous and benevolent primitive accumulation, and of the Trinity Formula of profit, land-rent, and wages, as well as many others. In every case, Marx does not simply dismiss these as inessential features of capitalism, in contrast to the more 'essential' categories he discovers such as abstract labour, labour power, or surplus value. In addition, in Spinozist fashion, he rigorously demonstrates in every case the systematic necessity that governs each category of the capitalist social form, including its superficial forms of appearance.[86] In addition to mere negative *critique*, Althusser emphasises *Capital*'s production of a positive *theory* of ideology and its forms of appearance as a science of causes.

Rather than an extraction of truth from an empirical object, Marx asked a more fundamental question in *Capital*: *what are the laws of the tendencies governing these empirical, quantitative fluctuations?* In contrast, the 'empiricist' dimension of the initial enquiries for *Capital* (the *Grundrisse*) and the decades of painstaking drafting and revision from 1859 to just before his death in 1883 is arguably limited to Marx's tired eyes scouring the markings across thousands, even millions of sheets of paper.[87]

---

their subordination to what Marx calls the objective 'social form' of compulsion that is *valorisation* under the general social predominance of capital; in contrast, these remain for Hegel (highly-developed) empirical analytical categories arguably drawn from the forms of appearance of capitalist society, like those of Smith before him. See Tony Smith 2014, p. 28.

86   Jacques Bidet develops this Althusserian argument in *Exploring Marx's Capital: Philosophical, Economic, and Political Aspects* (2009 [1985]). While Bidet's work richly and productively pursues the Althusserian reading of *Capital*, in this book I refer to his writings only intermittently, focusing instead on the first generation of Althusserians, Macherey, Badiou, Balibar, and Althusser himself.

87   Althusser in fact tries to argue along these lines at one point in his introduction, in contradiction, I think, with the entire thrust of his general critique of empiricism: 'Taking Marx as an example, we know that his most personally significant practical experiences (his experience as a polemicist of 'the embarrassment of having to take part in discussions on so-called material interests' in the *Rheinische Zeitung*; his direct experience of the earliest struggle organisations of the Paris proletariat; his revolutionary experience in the 1848 period) intervened in his theoretical practice, and in the upheaval which led

Essentially, empiricism, in the strong, Spinozist sense in which Althusser rightly understands the term in 1965 in *Reading Capital*, refers not to the varied nature of the texts Marx studied, from the abstract theories of classical political economy or socialism to histories of the British workers' struggle over wages and letters from Engels. Empiricism is not a matter of what one sees (or hears or touches), whether words on a page, a slide through a microscope, or living workers on an assembly line. It is certainly the case that Marx, among countless examples, undertook an intensive study of world history in 1881–82, filling four large notebooks with details and critical observations on events from the Roman Empire to the beginnings of capitalism in Renaissance Italy and the Reformation.[88] These readings no more make Marx's method of scientific analysis 'empiricist' than does his reading letters from Engels on the capitalist management of production.

The mode of demonstration of *Capital* categorically repudiates empiricism because Marx systematically deploys what Althusser calls an 'apodictic' argument to construct his critique of political economy. *Capital* articulates this systematic exposition of the materials of Marx's research via the narrative deployment of an initial materialist axiom ('The wealth of societies in which the capitalist mode of production prevails appears as an "immense collection of commodities"'),[89] propositions ('the individual commodity appears as its elementary form'), and their demonstration, in radical distinction (on the model of Spinoza's non-identity of the attributes) from all lived, sensuous experience, whether that of words read on a page or the street battles of 1848 and the Paris Commune.[90]

---

    him from ideological theoretical practice to scientific theoretical practice; but they intervened in his theoretical practice in the form of objects of experience, or even experiment, i.e., in the form of new thought objects, 'ideas' and the concepts, whose emergence contributed, in their combination (*Verbindung*) with other conceptual results (originating in German philosophy and English political economy), to the overthrow of the still ideological theoretical base on which he had lived (i.e., thought) until then' (RC, p. 63). The entire argument of an epistemological break is undermined by such a claim. Rather, the theoretical break occurs, as an ongoing transitional process till Marx's death, through the ceaseless development of his theoretical practice.

88   Musto 2020, pp. 99–102.
89   While warning against any idealist or ideological understanding of the axiomatic nature of Marx's method of demonstration and reaffirming instead its materialist determination by Marx's preliminary enquiries (*Grundrisse*, etc.), Althusser nonetheless admits that 'il faut bien reconnaître [in *Capital* ...] un mode de pensée très proche d'une pensée axiomatique'. Althusser 1998, p. 259.
90   Marx 1976, p. 125. It is precisely in such Spinozist terms that Lalande formulates a general definition of *empirisme* in the *Vocabulaire technique de la philosophie*, as 'the generic name

Here is Marx's famous definition of this anti-empiricist method, from the 1873 Postface: 'The method of presentation must differ in form from that of inquiry. The latter has to appropriate the material in detail, to analyse its different forms of development and to track down their inner connection. Only after this work has been done can the real movement be appropriately presented'.[91] Marx's method (in *Capital*) is anti-empiricist because the apodictic mode of exposition or 'presentation' of the materials of his various 'inquiries' (of which the *Grundrisse* is the best-known example[92]) presupposes a fundamental epistemological distinction between his systematic, category-based demonstration and the muddled (empirical) indistinctness of his theoretical sources of all kinds (Aristotle, Smith, Ricardo, Bastiat, the notes on Darimon with which *Grundrisse* contingently begins in media res) as well as, a fortiori, that of temporal lived, subjectively experienced events. In distinction to the infinite variety and obscure nature of these lived, empirical experiences, were capitalism never to have existed, Marx's analysis and demonstration, insofar as it is adequate (and it must not be forgotten that *Capital* is an unfinished work made largely of incomplete and tentative drafts, with even Volume I existing in multiple versions, none of which can be called definitive or final)[93] would remain apodictically true (or false, insofar as its demonstrations remain inadequate), albeit lacking its materialist grounding in the capitalist real.

Althusser's critique of empiricism is decisively indebted to the 'philosophy of the concept' that Jean Cavaillès famously proposed in his posthumous *On Logic and the Philosophy of Science*.[94] In contrast to Bachelard's experimental-

---

of all philosophical doctrines that deny the existence of axioms as principals of knowledge logically distinct from experience' (Lalande 2010 [1923], p. 281).

91 Marx 1976, p. 102.

92 On the *Grundrisse*'s status as a preliminary inquiry into the nature of the capitalist social form, as opposed to constituting a 'first draft' of *Capital*, see Nesbitt 2019.

93 See Heinrich 2021, p. 15; Musto 2020, pp. 85–93.

94 The thought of Cavaillès, legible in palimpsest in many of the most decisive passages of Althusser's introduction to *Reading Capital*, constitutes an emphatic rejection of all empiricist understandings of the scientific experimental apparatus (see Nesbitt 2017, pp. 4–8). Althusser problematically in fact proposes such an empiricist conflation in the 1966 lecture 'The Philosophical Conjuncture and Marxist Research' (Brown 2021, p. 14). Althusser's two positions from 1965 and 1966 are theoretically incoherent: the Introduction to *Reading Capital* finds Althusser at the peak of his theoretical powers of insight in pages of genius, cast with Rimbaldian clairvoyance, while in the latter Althusser – constitutionally weakened and theoretically ambivalent, embroiled in the debates with Garaudy and Aragon on theory and practice, under attack by the PCF for the so-called 'theoreticism' of *Reading Capital*–weakly asserts the reductive conflation of a line of thought he names 'rationalist empiricism' (Brown 2021, p. 6). While Althusser is clearly making a broadly

ist empiricism, Cavaillès there initiated a philosophical orientation attentive to the historical determinations of the criteria governing adequate demonstration, in which the formal signs or marks of logic are taken to constitute an (asubjective) history of mathematics, precisely, that is to say, what Althusser will call 'the history of the theoretical as such'.[95] It is in this Cavaillèsian sense that empiricism should be defined as any doctrine that denies the existence of axiomatic principals as logically distinct from sensuous experience.

In *On Logic* – a text that Althusser read intensively after its initial publication in 1947 – Cavaillès called for a notion of mathematics, and scientific development more generally, that follows the *internal* development of its concepts rather than a dualist model of the adequation of an empirical object to its mathematical formalisation. Cavaillès invoked in this manner an apodictic philosophy of the concept, a dialectic that displaces the philosophy of consciousness to demonstrate the 'internal necessity' determining the necessary development of a science.[96] Though Cavailles' debt to Spinoza is as decisive as it is elusive,[97] and the object of his writings remained devoted entirely to the philosophy of mathematics (in which domain this 'internal necessity' governs most evidently), Althusser, in the Introduction to *Reading Capital*, simultaneously brings together the thought of Spinoza and Cavaillès, while expanding their materialist propositions to encompass the non-mathematical science of Marx's critique of political economy.[98]

---

inclusive point about the history of French epistemology, to place as he does the name of Jean Cavaillès next to that of Bachelard in this brief essay obscures the anti-empiricist intervention that Cavaillès initiates in *On Logic and the Theory of Science*: 'Even in the natural sciences, this increase [in the system of concepts] takes place without any input from the outside world [*l'exterieur*]: there is a rupture between sensation or right thinking [*opinion droite*] and science. Far from being an involvement in nature, the experiment is, on the contrary, the incorporation of the world into the scientific universe'. Cavaillès 2021 [1942], p. 41. See also Cavaillès 1994.

95 'The question of the form of order required at a given moment in the history of knowledge by the existing type of scientificity, or, if you prefer, by the norms of theoretical validity recognised by science, in its own practice, as scientific' (RC, p. 50).

96 Cassou-Noguès, 2017, 12. 'Science', Cavaillès writes, 'is no longer considered as a mere intermediary between the human mind [*esprit*] and being in itself, equally dependent upon both and lacking its own reality, but rather as an object sui generis, original in its essence and autonomous in its movement' (2021, p. 40).

97 Cavaillès' sole surviving reference to Spinoza comes from a personal remark to Raymond Aron: 'I am Spinozist. I believe in necessity. The necessity of mathematical inferences, the necessity of the history of mathematics, the necessity also of the struggle [against fascism] in which we are engaged'. Cited at Cassou-Noguès 2017, p. 13.

98 While Althusser only mentions Cavaillès in passing, many of his formulations on the historicity of science should be read as direct refigurations of the latter's positions in *On*

This Spinozist materialist critique, which Althusser in his Introduction argues governs Marx's 1957 methodological Introduction, refuses the dualist empiricist logic of the representational adequation of an object to its concept, to assert instead a single order and connection of all things (including ideas), differentially grasped under the attributes of extension or thought (or any other).[99] The conclusion to be drawn from Althusser's Spinozist epistemology is that the material thought-concrete (*Gedankenkonkretum*) that Marx constructs, the unfinished book that is *Capital*, that is to say, is not analytically or inductively *extracted* from any supposed experimental observations of capitalism, but simply *is* capitalism, grasped under the attribute of thought rather than in its physical extension.

Spinoza, in the Scolium to EIIP7, refuses any notion of the adequation of the object to the idea as the index of its truth, to assert instead the epistemological position that so influenced Althusser in *Reading Capital*, i.e., that adequate knowledge of a thing, as knowledge, can be demonstrated only from within the attribute of thought itself rather than as an abstraction from observed empirical extension. 'Theoretical practice', Althusser observes, 'is indeed its own criterion, and contains in itself definite protocols with which to validate the quality of its product'.[100] Marx's *Capital*, in this view, is exactly what its subtitle names,

---

Logic: 'To pose this question [of the history of the theoretical] is obviously to pose the question of the form of order required at a given moment in the history of knowledge by the existing type of scientificity, or, if you prefer, by the norms of theoretical validity recognised by science, in its own practice, as scientific. ... The essential problem presupposed by the question of the existing type of demonstrativity is the problem of the history of the production of the different forms in which theoretical practice (producing knowledges, whether "ideological" or "scientific") recognises the validating norms it demands. ... This history [is] the history of the theoretical as such, or the history of the production (and transformation) of what at a given moment in the history of knowledge constitutes the theoretical problematic to which are related all the existing validating criteria, and hence the forms required to give the order of theoretical discourse the force and value of a proof. This history of the theoretical, of the structures of theoreticity and of the forms of theoretical apodicticity, has yet to be constituted' (RC, p. 50).

99 'The idea of the circle, which is the object of knowledge, must not be confused with the circle, which is the real object. In the third section of the 1857 Introduction, Marx took up this principle as forcefully as possible' (RC, p. 40).

100 RC, p. 61. Here is Spinoza: 'The formal being of the idea of a circle can be perceived only through another mode of thinking as its proximate cause, and that mode through another, and so on ad infinitum, with the result that as long as things are considered as modes of thought, we must explicate the order of the whole of Nature, or the connection of causes, through the attribute of Thought alone; and insofar as things are considered as modes of Extension, again the order of the whole of Nature must be explicated through the attribute of Extension only' (EIIP7S). See Pierre Macherey's meticulous, materialist explication of

a critique of political economy: a radical reworking of the substantial ideas forged by the tradition of thought from the Physiocrats, Smith, and Ricardo onward (ideas of value, of money, of labour, etc.). In *Reading Capital*, Althusser puts the matter in decisively and unapologetically theoreticist terms: 'No mathematician in the world waits until physics has verified a theorem to declare it proved, although whole areas of mathematics are applied in physics; the truth of his theorem is a hundred per cent provided by criteria purely *internal to the practice of mathematical proof*, hence by the criterion of mathematical practice'.[101]

5   Hallucinatory Empiricism

In his critique of empiricism, Althusser argues that *Capital* must be read not as a history, but instead as a *logic*. Not, Althusser quickly points out, as 'logicians [would, which] would have meant posing it the question of its methods of exposition and proof',[102] in other words as a mere discursive, logical positivist word game, but as the Spinozist, materialist logic of the necessary forms of appearance of things in the capitalist social form. While Althusser's critique of empiricism is encompassing and unyielding, it is not always clear on what grounds he rejects the empiricist processes of, for example, the abstraction of a kernel of truth from the empirical object, or the 'scouring' of material. Why, one might ask, are these *necessarily* inadequate procedures? Spinoza, in contrast, offers in EIIP14–24 clear and simple terms for his own rejection of empirical, sensory-derived truth.[103] Macherey will interpret and develop Spinoza's cri-

---

Proposition EIIP7 in volume II of his *Introduction à l'Ethique de Spinoza: La réalité mentale* (1997, pp. 70–81), which I discuss below in Chapter 2.

101   RC, p. 61, my emphasis.
102   RC, p. 12. Of course, it is precisely the object of Macherey's contribution to *Reading Capital* to analyse what he calls the 'Process [Macherey avoids the term "method"] of Exposition of Capital', but to do so in terms other than those of traditional logic, and instead to begin to construct the concept of Marx's exposition as a Spinozist positive, materialist dialectic. I return to Macherey's argument in the next chapter.
103   While Spinoza's conception of adequate, scientific knowledge and the processes governing its development are radically original, the Spinozist rejection of empiricism is already a shibboleth for Aristotle's conception of scientific knowledge in the *Posterior Analytics*, where he states categorically: 'Scientific knowledge cannot be acquired by sense-perception. … A universal term of general application cannot be perceived by the senses, because it is not a particular thing or at a given time; if it were, it would not be universal; for we describe as universal only that which obtains always and everywhere. Therefore, since demonstrations are universal, and universals cannot be perceived by the senses, obviously

tique in a series of comments on these passages that I wish here to bring to bear as a further specification of Althusser's initial rejection of empiricism in *Reading Capital*.[104]

In the second book of the *Ethics*, Spinoza, as Macherey reads him, rejects sense-perception as a basis for adequate knowledge due to the provisional, mutable nature of the composition of any body:

> Composed bodies [writes Macherey,] possess no other reality than a purely circumstantial one given by their configuration [*figure*, from Spinoza's Latin *figura*], the provisional stability of which is never definitively guaranteed. ... Corporeal nature in its entirety, in the sense of the set [*ensemble*] of things existing in the category of extension [is] fluidified by the application of the universal law of movement ... without any of these configurations defined by the dynamic of its global system arriving at a definitive stability.[105]

While physical bodies, in this view, are determined by a necessary instability, this inherent volatility need not universally invalidate the sensory derivation of knowledge. In contrast, the fundamental deficiency of empirically derived knowledge, Spinoza argues in EIIP14–23, lies in its overwhelming *complexity*, inherently at odds with the scientific demand for *abstraction* from empirical convolution.[106] In sensory perception, Macherey argues,

> Perceptions, insofar as they are ideas, are related to the fundamental activity of the psyche [*âme*] that is knowledge, but under conditions such that this knowledge is simultaneously that of the psyche itself, the body of which is an idea, and the other things of which it has knowledge through the intermediary of the idea it has of the body. ... In this sense, one could say that the deficit that ideas of the imagination present from the point of

---

knowledge cannot be obtained through sense-perception. Again, it is obvious that even if we were able to perceive by the senses that the sum of the angles of a triangle is equal to two right angles, we should still require a proof of this; we should not *know* that it is so. ... The value of the universal is that it exhibits the cause.' (Aristotle, *Posterior Analytics*, pp. 157–9).

104   I will show in the next chapter that Althusser's rejection of empiricism is a constant for Macherey as well, from *Theory of Literary Production* to his studies on Spinoza.
105   Macherey 1997, p. 150.
106   Recall Marx's invocation of the necessity of abstraction for scientific understanding: 'In the analysis of economic forms, neither microscopes nor chemical reagents are of assistance. The power of abstraction must replace both' (1976, p. 90).

> view of rational knowledge corresponds, in their economy itself, not to a lack but to an *excess* of reality, an excess linked to their natural complexity. These ideas, which simultaneously bear upon too many things, are themselves made up of too many ideas; they are not simple enough, and this is precisely what renders them inadequate by reason of their constitutionally confused character. ... The life of the psyche begins with the most complicated forms [from experience], the most muddled [*embrouillés*], and it is only at the price of a considerable work upon itself that it can move to simpler forms, such as those that correspond to the production of clear and distinct ideas.[107]

Sense-perception is inherently inadequate, Macherey argues, insofar as it presents itself 'in the form of an unanalysable perceptual complex', one that is at once partial and an instantaneous bodily perception.[108] Inherently and necessarily absent from this perception, as Macherey reads Spinoza, is an adequate understanding of the essential nature governing that body, since the sensory perception of a body is impossible to distinguish from the idea of its nature and thus the causes that govern its sensory manifestation. This amounts to the presentation to sense-perception of a knowledge of certain effects without a clear understanding of the causes upon which these effects depend.

The result of this necessary imprecision is what Macherey terms the 'hallucinatory character' of all sense-perception, since we do not perceive things themselves, in their essential nature, but only, Macherey observes, corporeal 'images of things [*rerum imagines*]'.[109] In other words, the psyche's immediate *representation* of the sensuous things it perceives is necessarily imaginary, since ultimately this representation must remain ignorant of the real nature of things, and instead can only indicate an imaginary representation of the body it perceives.[110] Now to be sure, Spinoza argues in EIIP17 that the formation of imaginary representations (such as our inadequate sense-perception of the distance of the sun from the earth) inherently depends upon necessary causes; the inadequacy of such representations, however, lies in their obscure nature, in their necessary deficit of knowledge (such as the scientific determination of

---

107 Macherey 1997, pp. 165–6. I cite here and the following chapters passages from Macherey's 1997 commentary on *Ethics* II not only for their power of insight, but because none of these five volumes of extraordinary analyses of Spinoza's materialist dialectic have yet to be translated, and what is in my view the most important of these, Book II, is no longer in print even in its original French edition.
108 Macherey 1997, p. 171.
109 Macherey 1997, p. 182.
110 Macherey 1997, p. 184.

the distance of the earth from the sun).[111] It is in this sense, precisely, that the representation-based model of knowledge that Althusser rightly condemns in his Introduction, but with little justification, can be said, in light of Macherey's subsequent comments on EIIP13–24, to indicate the purely 'indicative' function of perception, in which a thing is perceived without being understood.[112]

Knowledge, for Spinoza, instead of indicating the adequacy of an empirical object and its representation, constitutes the adequacy of an idea to its inherent degree of clarity and power within the attribute of thought alone. The empiricist model of knowledge thus constitutes in contrast, Althusser argues, a secular 'transcription' of revelation, a 'religious reading' compromised by its inherent circularity, the presupposition that its truth occurs not in the constructed thought object, but lies hidden in the real object itself.[113] This implies in consequence that empiricist knowledge cannot inquire into the real conditions of the production of an adequate idea, since this (empiricist) truth is claimed to lie dormant, always-already present in the real object itself, awaiting its mere extraction.

Eventually, after the compromised theoretical interlude of 'class struggle in theory', Althusser would – in his late, posthumously published texts *Etre marxiste en philosophie* and *Sur la philosophie* – return to further specify this initial critique of the representational nature of empiricist knowledge. In this late thought, Althusser reformulated his initial critique of empiricism based on a reference to the Heideggerian critique of the *principal of reason*. This is the principle shared by idealism and materialism alike that, in Althusser's words, 'every existing thing, whether ideal or material, [must] submit to a questioning of the *reason* for its existence', that any existing thing, in other words, must uphold the exactness of its *representation* of the real object.[114]

6 Reading *Capital*'s Apodictic Structure

In *Reading Capital*, however, Althusser's condensed critique of empiricist knowledge already sets the ground for that volume's principal positive epistemological claim, that 'In *Capital* we find ... an apodictic arrangement of the concepts in the form of that type of demonstrational discourse that Marx

---

111   Macherey 1997, p. 185.
112   Macherey 1997, p. 173n1.
113   RC, p. 34.
114   Althusser 1994, p. 57, cited in Estop 2021, p. 251, my emphasis.

calls analysis'.[115] This unassuming proposition for reading Marx's method of exposition in *Capital* as a positive (Spinozist) dialectic has, for all its radical implications, gone virtually unheeded in the literature on both Althusser and *Capital* itself in the intervening decades, the latter in particular continuing to suffer from an unrelenting allegiance to the conviction that *Capital* should be read as a palimpsest of the negative dialectic Hegel expounded in the *Logic*.[116]

Althusser unfolds this epistemological proposition in the two central sections (13–14) of his Introduction. There he articulates, in opposition to the empiricist representational model of knowledge he has just rejected, a properly Spinozist affirmation of the strict heterogeneity of the attributes of thought and the material, extensive reality of the real, actually existing object (in this case, the capitalist social form), stating categorically that 'the order which governs the categories of thought in the process of knowledge does not coincide with the order which governs the real categories in the process of real historical genesis'.[117]

Here in his Introduction Althusser strategically torques the literal words of Marx's own famous 1857 'Introduction' in order to rout the otherwise still-Hegelian, negative dialectical argument of the *Grundrisse*. Althusser's rhetorical strategy here seeks to displace and invalidate the traditional Marxist reading (an 'empiricist' and 'Hegelian' problematic) of Marx's assertion in that 1857 text, i.e., which Althusser summarises as the claim that

---

115   RC, p. 51.
116   Chris Arthur's *New Dialectic*, which I discuss in chapter three, is surely the most extensive and notable example of this continued dedication to reading *Capital* as a palimpsest of Hegel's *Logic*. Examples abound of this neglect of the epistemological dimension of *Reading Capital* in Althusser studies: in what is otherwise one of the most rigorous, original, and stimulating books on Althusser in recent decades, Juan Domingo Sanchez Estop summarises the three innovations of *Reading Capital* in comparison to the essays of *For Marx* as: 1. Its initiation of a close reading of *Capital* in the wake of its neglect in traditional Marxism and French Marxism in particular; 2. Its theory of a practice of symptomatic reading; and 3. Its elaboration of theory of philosophy as a practice of reading. As such, Estop entirely disregards the book's call to determine the positive, materialist dialectic deployed in *Capital*'s mode of exposition (2021, p. 81). Similarly, while many contributors discuss Marx's *Capital* in the outstanding edited volume *Encountering Althusser: Politics and Materialism in Contemporary Radical Thought* (2013), none mentions Althusser's central epistemological proposition that *Capital* is characterised by an 'apodictic' mode of analysis.
117   RC, p. 47.

the 'logical' order, being identical in essence with the real order and existing in the reality of the real order as its essence itself, can only follow the real order; [and furthermore] that the real order being identical in essence with the 'logical' order, the real order, which is then merely the existence of the logical order, must follow the logical order.[118]

This traditional reading of Marx's distinction between the real object and the thought object [*Gedankenkonkretum*] thus follows precisely the empiricist model Althusser has rejected a moment before in the abstract: both that the order of thought 'follows' the real order of capitalism in the form of its *representation*, and, furthermore, that what presents itself, in traditional Marxism, as a materialist argument is in fact eminently idealist, since the order of the real object (capitalism) is then said not to have priority, but instead merely to 'follow the logical order'. Each of these positions, Althusser maintains, 'does violence' to Marx's actual argument.[119]

While 'Contradiction and Overdetermination', as we have seen, quickly abandoned its epistemological propositions regarding Marx's method of demonstration to pursue a politico-historical discussion of Lenin and the Bolshevik Revolution, in *Reading Capital* Althusser insists on staying with and pursuing this methodological terrain as a strictly 'theoretical problematic'.[120] The force of Althusser's argument – lacking as it does any explicit analysis of Marx's mode of analysis (he leaves this to Macherey's contribution) – has rarely been registered as anything but dogmatic polemic. To take the position Althusser adopts, following Marx's own literal suggestion, that there exists not a *relation* but 'a radical *distinction* between the order in which [conceptual] "categories" appear in knowledge, on the one hand, and in historical reality on the other',[121] is quite simply to relegate the traditional, empiricist inquiry into the correspondence of the thought object and the real object, along with various monist idealist readings of Spinoza, to the status of a nonexistent problem.

---

118   Ibid.
119   Though both Alain Badiou and Jean Matthys read Althusser as here *rejecting* the Spinozist principle of the 'parallelism' of the attributes, I will argue in the next chapter against these interpretations that Althusser's position constitutes a *radicalisation* of Spinoza in his own terms, and that, in line with Macherey's critique of this philosophical commonplace, the so-called 'parallelism' of the attributes (a term Spinoza never used, by which Leibniz (mis)represented his thought) is simply a monist misreading of Spinoza, one that Althusser overcomes by theorising substance not as a reified (monist) thing, but as structural causality.
120   RC, p. 47.
121   RC, p. 48, my emphasis.

While this correspondence-based position certainly exists in traditional Marxist understanding, it is nonetheless a perfectly 'imaginary', inadequately conceived problematic, one that Althusser summarises as 'the ideological (empiricist or absolute-idealist) myth of a one-to-one correspondence between the terms of these two orders'.[122]

In section 11 of his Introduction, Althusser briefly and schematically, if unequivocally, specifies the Spinozist basis of this assertion of the absolute heterogeneity of the thought- and real-objects in this reading of Marx: 'Spinoza warned us that the object of knowledge or essence was in itself absolutely distinct and different from the real object. ... In the third section of the 1857 Introduction, Marx took up this principle as forcefully as possible'.[123] The precise nature of this claim nonetheless remains unclear: is Althusser ascribing to Marx an explicitly Spinozist understanding of the thought and real objects, precisely as the *Ethics* presents the concept of the Attributes thought and extension, in their so-called parallelism, or is this merely Althusser's interpretation of Marx's comment? Ignoring the question of Marx's subjective intentions, I will argue in chapter three that traditional, political interpretations of Marx's relation to Spinoza have in fact entirely ignored the *epistemological* dimension of his 1841 reading of Spinoza and the *Ethics* specifically. Marx's method of exposition as he actually deploys it in *Capital* after 1867 (whatever he subjectively continued to believe about his relation to Hegel), as Althusser first suggested but never demonstrated, does in fact gradually eliminate the various 'Hegelian', negative dialectical epistemological impediments overwhelmingly predominant in the *Grundrisse*, to produce an additive synthetic, materialist dialectic, this no matter what Marx thought of his lived relation to his theoretical predecessor.[124]

---

122 RC, p. 48.
123 RC, p. 41.
124 My argument thus refuses the commonplace that Marx 'popularised' and essentially dumbed-down the presentation of the first chapter of *Capital* at Engel's urging. While the addition of a simplified Appendix to the 1867 edition undoubtedly accorded with Engels's request to that effect, when Marx subsequently combined and rewrote the two to constitute a single, unified first chapter for the 1872 German and 1875 French editions, he carefully chose which aspects of his presentation to retain and which to modify or eliminate. In chapter three, I will argue that at this point he systematically, though not entirely, eliminated (Hegelian) negative dialectical forms of presentation – i.e., *Reflexionsbestimmungen* (determinations of reflection) – in favour of a positive dialectic of his own fashioning. Heinrich points out that Backhaus and Reichelt's support for the 'popularisation' argument (in their 1995 critique of Heinrich 'Wie ist der Wertbegriff in der Ökonomie konzipieren?') implies that given this position, 'an authentic understanding of [Marx's] method would only be possible via the *Grundrisse*' and the 1859 *Urtext* (Heinrich 2022

The result is in fact to have produced in *Capital* a positive, materialist dialectic of decisively Spinozist character, as Althusser first suggested in these paragraphs of his 1965 Introduction. To point ahead to my argument in Chapter 3, this process of exposition in *Capital* tends, above all in its crucial and theoretically arduous first chapter, to displace the 'Hegelian' figures of totality, negation and contradiction to the domain of *existence* rather than *essence* (themselves traditional scholastic terms that Marx ambiguously retains despite this shift). Marx, furthermore, explicitly signals (in Chapter 11 on the 'laws' governing the rate of surplus value production) the correlation of what he calls the 'laws of the tendencies' of the capitalist social form to Spinoza's concept of *common notions*. All of this can serve to sustain and prove Althusser's claim that Marx's distinction between the thought and real objects is in fact a distinction of the attributes of thought and extension as Spinoza conceived them.

7   The Topography of the Attributes

Althusser's distinction in *Reading Capital* between the object of thought and the real object operates a decisive and original refiguration of Spinoza's concept of the attributes.[125] Never explicitly developed or even posited in *Reading Capital*, Althusser's position on the attributes instead reveals its explicitly Spinozist tenor across the expanse of Althusser's unpublished texts, from his earliest notes on Spinoza in 1948[126] through the now-famous 1980s essays on aleatory materialism and the 'rain' of the infinite attributes.[127] Althusser's understanding of the concept, while evolving and always highly original, derives directly from the argument of the *Ethics* to inform this distinction between the thought and real object in *Reading Capital*.

In his 1965 essay 'A propos de la rupture', Macherey further specified the Spinozist character of the Althusserian distinction between thought and the real, noting that 'Althusser should have further developed the allusions he

---

[1999], p. 171). Marx's 1867 Appendix can be found at Marx 1983, MEGA² II/5 'Anhang zu Kapitel I, 1. Die Wertform' 626–55.

125 I agree with Jean Matthys that 'Behind every great Althusserian conceptual innovation, ... there lurks the figure of Spinoza. ... The multiplicity of Spinozist figures in Althusser's [thought] is no heteroclite assemblage, ... but articulates in a relatively coherent fashion a true Spinozist "plane of consistency" or "problematic"' (2023, pp. 192, 43).

126 IMEC 20ALT/32/10. See Matthys 2023, Chapter 2.

127 Estop 2021, pp. 226–32.

made to Spinoza [in *Reading Capital*]'.[128] For Macherey, science takes on its fundamental character as a materialist inquiry into the real 'from the moment it gives form to reality'.[129] Science is not the representation, classification, or explication of the real; instead, 'the thought real [is] the real transformed'. Macherey even seems to distinguish between the real [*le réel*] and reality [*la réalité*], such that the former would occupy the theoretical position of the (infinite, untotalisable) set of all things – both nonexistent idealities and actually existing things – in their infinite relations, and the latter that of substance: 'The rupture between the real [le réel] and thought is the difference between two forms of reality [la réalité] ... the science of the real [le réel] is the institution of a new form of reality [la réalité]'.[130] Macherey's distinction between the real and reality seems to address, without truly explicating, this point of ambiguity or obscurity in Althusser's thought, without, on the other hand, explicitly reverting to Spinoza's scholastic terminology.[131] In other words, if Althusser is a self-proclaimed 'spinoziste', and the theory of substance, the attributes, and modes the foundation of Spinozist thought, how does Althusser parse and critically reconfigure these crucial concepts? In the absence of explicit elaboration on Althusser's part, this must ultimately remain a speculative reconstruction elaborated from materials across the expanse of his published and unpublished works.[132]

Simply to distinguish between thought and the real, as does Althusser in *Reading Capital*, or even between thought, the real, and reality, as Macherey will inflect this pair in 'En matérialiste', constitutes a point of ambiguity in the conceptual apparatus of *Reading Capital*.[133] Provisionally, and I will address aspects of this problem at different points below, I wish to indicate a series

---

128   Macherey 1999, p. 16.
129   Macherey 1999, p. 15.
130   Macherey 1999, p. 16.
131   Macherey seems to encourage such an interpretation in his 1997 commentary on this essay in *Histoires de dinosaure*, noting that 'In affirming that "the rupture between thought and the real is the difference between two forms of reality" ... I tried to develop, in the spirit of the Spinozist doctrine of the attributes, the thesis according to which thought being also of the real [du réel], ideas are things unto themselves'. Macherey 1999, p. 23.
132   My own reconstruction is decisively informed by the two most recent treatments of this problem, Estop's *Althusser et Spinoza* (2021) and Matthys' *Althusser lecteur de Spinoza* (2023).
133   Althusser initially takes the concept of the 'real' [*das Reale*] in its opposition to thought from Marx himself. 'Hegel fell into the illusion of conceiving the real (das Reale) as the product of thought concentrating itself' (Marx, cited in RC, p. 41; LC, p. 40). See also Althusser 1998, p. 255.

of Spinozist concepts that can more adequately parse Althusser's flat, binary distinction between thought and the real. Substance, the most basic and fundamental of Spinozist terms, is one that Althusser publicly and polemically refuses in its reified form, through his critique of Marxist-Hegelian philosophies of monism (while tentatively affirming its necessity in private discussion with the Groupe Spinoza).[134]

Instead, through attention to Althusser's archive, it becomes clear, above all in his 1948 notes on Spinoza, that Althusser refigures the concept of substance, rejecting the reifying implications of the word itself as well as its status as ontological guarantee, instead to conceive of substance as the finite structural causality of a social form, a causality that exists only in its effects.[135] This is the famous concept Althusser develops in the final sections of *Reading Capital*:

> Structure is not an essence outside economic phenomena. ... The absence of the cause in the structure's 'metonymic causality' on its effects ... is the very form of the interiority of the structure, as a structure, in its effects. This implies therefore that the effects are not outside the structure, are not a pre-existent [reified] object, element or space upon which the structure arrives to imprint its mark: on the contrary, ... the structure is immanent in its effects, a cause immanent in its effects in the Spinozist sense of the term, that *the whole existence of the structure consists of its effects.*[136]

While Althusser nowhere indicates in his published writings that his concept of structural causality is a materialist, anti-monist refiguration of Spinozist substance, Jean Matthys has shown that this operation, which remains a constant in Althusser's thought, finds explicit articulation as early as Althusser's first notes on Spinoza from 1948. Though these notes cannot be interpreted unilaterally, it is here that Althusser asserts that Spinoza should not be understood 'from the identification God = Substance but [from the position that] substance = attribute, which is the foundation of structure'.[137] Althusser further indicates that this 'problem' must be understood not 'ontologically', as 'the identity of

---

134 I will discuss Althusser's critique of Marxist monism below in this chapter.
135 IMEC 20ALT/32/10, 'Notes sur Spinoza (1948)'. I take this crucial insight for my argument from Matthys 2023, pp. 123–8.
136 RC, p. 344, translation modified, emphasis in original.
137 Cited at Matthys 2023, p. 123.

INTRODUCTION: READING CAPITAL BEYOND ITS LIMITS 45

an essence', but rather as the finite 'identity of causal structure'.[138] Substance, in this view, is not what Althusser terms 'a unity prior to [all] differences', but constitutes instead finite causality itself, understood as the productive power that *exists* only in the infinite plurality of the attributes and their modes. It is substance decisively recast as materialist social form, the means to think the structure of causality that governs an actually existing systemic complex, in which the heterogeneity of substructures and their production does not, cannot constitute a closed, ontological totality.[139]

Macherey, in his analysis of the first book of *The Ethics*, will pursue this conception, to develop a rich and original reading of substance as uncountable and not a thing at all, but rather as just what Spinoza indicates, what is in itself (*quod in se est*), that is, *causa sui*. In his 1998 *Introduction* to Book 1 of the *Ethics*, Macherey develops this materialist understanding of Spinozist substance as pure immanence through an attentive, literal reading of Spinoza's initial definitions and propositions. Macherey stresses that in adopting this crucial philosophical concept, inherited from Aristotle, Descartes, and Scholastic thought more generally, Spinoza reinvents the notion of Substance to indicate not a thing, in the sense of an individually existing, and thus numerically countable thing (as monist One), nor a mode of the apprehension of a thing (this is the role of the attributes), but Being as such, 'the fact of being in itself. ... Forcing syntax, one could say that [substance] *"s'est"* ["be's itself"]'.[140] If 'the existence of substance coincides with its essence, to which it adheres immediately [*étroitement*], [... substance] is not at all 'an' existence, ... but existence itself, thought in the absolute'.[141]

The attributes thought and extension, as Spinoza defines them, are no more existing things, however, than is Substance. Althusser's binary distinction between thought and the real would thus seem from Spinoza's perspective

---

138 Matthys 2023, p. 124. Matthys' commentary on this note is revealing: 'Dans le but d'éviter que cette identité soit fondée sur une essence ontologique qui réduirait les attributs (et *a fortiori* les modes) au statut d'apparences phénoménales dénuées de toute forme d'autonomie et de diversité réelles, mais en cherchant tout autant à éviter l'écueil symétrique d'une pure et simple juxtaposition des attributs, Spinoza invite, selon Althusser ... à penser une "identité de *structure causale*. ... La substance n'est pas le lieu d'une identification ou d'une réduction "essentielle" entre les attributs, où ceux-ci seraient réduits à de simples formes secondaires et épiphénoménales réductibles à une essence commune que serait la substance. L'identité des attributs dans la substance, et donc l'uni(ci)té de celle-ci, réside dans l'identité de l'*acte causal* "naturant" qui constitue "un seul et même ordre, autrement dit un seul et même enchaînement des causes'. Matthys 2023, pp. 127, 128.
139 Matthys 2023, pp. 127, 117.
140 Macherey 1998, p. 39.
141 Macherey 1998, p. 86.

to constitute a category mistake: the former clearly an attribute, it makes no sense to understand 'the real' as the *attribute* of extension. This categorial confusion occurs in the sense that thought and extension, as attributes, indicate for Spinoza 'what the intellect perceives [quod intellectus de substantia percipit] of a substance as constituting its essence',[142] which is to say, Macherey observes, what the intellect *apprehends* as 'a constitutive form of substance', rather than, as with Descartes, qualities inherent in things themselves. The attribute, in Macherey's reading of Spinoza, is 'not a property or a *propre* (proprium) attached to a substance, but an intrinsic determination of the being of substance as it can be known by the intellect'.[143] In contrast, to refer to 'the real' in distinction from thought, as Althusser does in *Reading Capital*, is arguably to confuse categories: thought, for both Spinoza and Althusser, refers to a form in which the intellect apprehends being. In contrast, Althusser's 'real', unlike Spinozist 'extension', remains indeterminate.

The immediate object Marx constructs in *Capital* is not an ontological theory, in any case, but an analysis of actually existing things, such as the capitalist social form, commodities, social classes, and the like, beginning from the single dogmatic presupposition that we always already have a true idea of the nature of capitalism (as general commodification). Althusser's 'real', then, might best be defined simply as does Lalande: what is 'real' [*réel, Wirklich*, actual] is 'that which is a thing, ... that which constitutes a definite, logical, permanent object having a certain autonomy', and 'the real' as such, therefore, as the set of actually existing things along with their infinite and untotalisable relations of composition.[144] Such a definition of the real would have the advantage of invoking two other crucial, yet less familiar Spinozist categories, the idea of 'singular things existing in act' (*idea rei singularis actu existentis*) and the corresponding idea of 'Anything whatsoever that can be conceived as nonexistent' (*quicquod ut non existens potest concipi*).[145]

---

142 EID4.
143 Macherey 1998, p. 43.
144 Lalande 2010, 'Réel', pp. 900, 902. In *For Marx*, Althusser writes that 'Pour nous, le "réel" n'est pas un *mot d'ordre théorique*: le réel est l'objet réel, existant, indépendamment de sa connaissance, – mais qui ne peut être défini que par sa connaissance'. Althusser 2005, p. 257.
145 EIIP8 and 9. In Chapter 2, I will offer a critique of Alain Badiou's assertion that Althusser's term 'the real' refers to Spinozist substance, to argue instead that it would be more coherent to take it as the infinite set of all things. In Chapter 3, I will follow Macherey's exposition of the Spinozist distinction between nonexistent and actually existing things, to argue that Marx's schematic formalisation of the law of the rate and mass of surplus value in Chapter 11 of *Capital* should rightly be understood as distinguishing between actually

In the case of Althusser, among the key documents that can serve to clarify his properly Spinozist understanding of the attributes of thought and extension is an unpublished manuscript from 16 June 1967.[146] Here Althusser summarises a discussion with Stanislas Breton on the nature of structural causality and the attributes. Althusser emphatically rejects Breton's assertion that in Spinoza the attributes can be understood to *emanate* from substance, as an *expressive* form of causality in which a reified substance retains its transcendence to the attributes and modal expressions of being.[147] Instead, Althusser affirms the 'discontinuity' and 'cut' [*coupure*] between Spinoza's various orders or topoi of being (substance, attributes, infinite and finite modes): 'Though one may have the illusion of a continuity of "emanation" between the "orders" [in fact] there is a non-preinscription of these cuts in the concept of substance and in the concept of immanent causality'.

The various Spinozist orders of being do not derive or emanate from substance, Althusser continues in his notes to their discussion, they are not 'inscribed in advance', but simply exist, as a given 'Faktum', as the 'immanent (not eminent) cause of the structuration of these regions in their efficacity, regions structured insofar as they are separated by "cuts"'.[148] These various dimensions of being thus determine the Spinozist orders of substance as what Althusser calls a *topography* [*topique*] of 'defined regions', a decentred structure of causality without a transcendent subject, a position strictly analogous to the Freudian topographic model of the psyche.[149]

The point to be taken here in relation to the theoretical position of *Reading Capital* is that the elliptical nature of Althusser's presentation of the absolute distinction between the orders or attributes of thought and the real as he reads Marx's 1857 'Introduction' in his own 'Introduction' to *Reading Capital*

---

existing things (such as the 'bakers' and 'spinners' Marx invokes) and atemporal, nonexistent things such as the generic formula for this law that he introduces to the 1875 French translation of *Capital*.

146 Juan Domingo Estop is the first to have discussed this fascinating document, and to have reproduced it in its entirety as an Appendix to his *Althusser et Spinoza* (2021).

147 This position from 1967 might be brought to bear on Althusser's later, autocritique of his 'theoreticism' as a putative neglect of the 'primat de la théorie sur la pratique' (1974, p. 176). Althusser's later practicist position should be rejected in favour of the Spinozist one articulated in these private notes on the discussion with Breton: for a Spinozist materialist critique, there is a primacy of neither theory nor practice, as though theory emanates from practice (as 'class struggle in theory'), or the converse. Instead, thought (theory) and extension (practice) must be conceived in their sheer immanence within a structure of causality.

148 Cited at Estop 2021, p. 286.

149 Estop 2021, p. 288. On the latter, see Laplanche and Pontalis 2018, pp. 448–453.

can and should be seconded by reference to Althusser's explicit invocations of the Spinozist concept of the attributes in unpublished texts such as his 1948 notes and this discussion with Breton. In this view, Althusser remained committed from beginning to the end, with varying turns of interpretation, to the Spinozist understanding of the heterogeneous attributes of thought and extension.[150]

That said, it is this same distinction – between Althusser's at times suggestively enigmatic exoteric (published) writings and his often more explicitly Spinozist unpublished texts – that points to a final epistemological obstacle of *Reading Capital*.[151] This refusal to discuss Spinoza in Althusser's published works as anything more than a nominal cipher for a highly original epistemological position forms a final epistemological impediment in *Reading Capital*, one that will lead directly to my subsequent chapters' investigations of the materialist dialectic. In the case of the absolute distinction Althusser draws in *Reading Capital* between thought and the real, to adequately grasp the theoretical intent of this claim requires following up on Althusser's own passing indication of the Spinozist origins of this distinction, bringing to bear a selection of Althusser's unpublished writings on Spinoza and the attributes such as these notes to his discussion with Stanislas Breton, all set alongside his explicit and public rejection of substance monism in Marxist thought.

8   The Theoretical Danger of Monism

Given that Althusser categorically identified Spinoza as 'in my view the greatest philosopher of all time',[152] and publicly asserted in 1968 (in response to Paul Ricœur's invocations of Kantian and Hegelian positions) that 'I am a Spinozist',[153] it is quite surprising that one has to search through his archives to find obscure suggestions of the link between Spinoza's most basic, founding principle and one of Althusser's most famous and original concepts. This absence of explicit reference to Spinozist substance is no doubt due to Althusser's allergy to grandiose metaphysical pronouncements and guarantees, a position he maintained from *For Marx* through late texts such as *Philoso-*

---

150   In Chapter 2, I will discuss Pierre Macherey's penetrating critique and rejection of the philosophical commonplace of the 'parallelism' of the Spinozist attributes.
151   For a different parsing of the distinction between an exoteric and esoteric Althusser, see Thomas 2013, pp. 144–5.
152   Althusser 2015, p. 76.
153   Althusser 1969.

phy for Non-philosophers, where he observes that 'It is inordinately pretentious of idealist philosophy to claim to ... "think" the whole, or aspire to "totalisation".'[154]

In the absence of any explicit development of the concept in his published texts, however, this nominalism of actually existing singular things radicalises Althusser's Spinozism to the limit position of a relativist pluralism.[155] Althusser's critique of the concept of substance as reified thing, in the sense of Hegelian monism, indicates a rejection of monist, ontological understandings of substance and the 'parallelist' (mis)readings of Spinoza that have predominated since Leibniz. What then is the problem with monism with which Althusser takes such vehement, polemical issue?

In the first footnote to Section v of 'Contradiction and Overdetermination' in *Pour Marx*, in reference to Plekhanov's Spinozist 'monism' and its appropriation by Garaudy and Gilbert Mury, Althusser unambiguously affirms that 'this concept [of Substance monism] has no positive theoretical use in Marxism, and is even theoretically dangerous'.[156] The polemical nature of Althusser's position is eminently clear. Monism, the position that the set of all things is reducible to a unity, whether of matter or idea,[157] consistently represents in Althusser's thought not just the monisms of Hegelian expressive causality and Cartesian mechanistic causality, but also, and at least as crucially, the vulgar determinism of traditional Marxist dialectical materialism.[158] Such fan-

---

154 Althusser 2017, 68.
155 Jean Matthys argues that this pluralist position indicates not a radicalisation, but a break with Spinozist monism and the 'parallelism' of the attributes. I will argue against this reading, which is substantially identical to that of Alain Badiou, in Chapter 2. See Matthys 2023, p. 244.
156 Althusser 2005, 300.
157 Lalande defines *monisme* as any 'philosophical system that considers the set of things as reducible to a unity. ... From the point of view of substance, Wolff, who created the term, applied it to the ontological doctrine that reduces all things either to matter or mind [*l'esprit*]. ... Monism itself [thus] divides into 'materialist' monism and 'idealist' monism'. Lalande 2010, p. 648. Interestingly, in light of Althusser's anti-Hegelianism, Lalande's substantial 1923 article – seemingly unaware of the ongoing Russian debates on Spinozist monism since the 1890s – never mentions Spinoza in its history of the concept, but instead links the term above all to 'the Hegelian conception of the universe'.
158 In *Etre marxiste en philosophie*, Althusser will explicitly reconfirm the condemnation of monist materialism first articulated in *For Marx*, when he observes that 'dire que ... le Sujet et l'Objet sont une seule et même chose, ce qui est la position moniste, ... peut être aussi bien spiritualiste (si cette seule et même chose est l'esprit) que matérialiste (si cette seule et même chose est la matière)' (Althusser 2015, §12). In his 1984 discussion with Fernanda Navarro, Althusser again reaffirms this position in even stronger terms: 'Navarro: Why do you criticise dialectical materialism? Althusser: Because I have to destroy the material-

tasmatic closure of a speculative totality consistently represents for Althusser the zenith of imaginary, ideological fantasy [*Phantasie*], a theoretical *kyblík* that he opposes to the interminable scientific production of knowledge of the real.[159]

It is the Stalinist doctrine Dialectical Materialism that forms the actual substance of Althusser's topical condemnation of the monism of Ernst Haeckel, Plekhanov, and Roger Garaudy in 'Contradiction and Overdetermination'.[160] The source of Althusser's rejection of this Marxist monism lies in the crudely codified materialism promulgated to generations of Marxists in Stalin's influential and didactic philosophical summum *Dialectical Materialism and Historical Materialism*.[161] Drawing on Plekhanov's reductive interpretation of Spinozism as a deterministic dialectic of *matter*, Stalin's breviary presents dialectical materialism as the general science of motive matter, such that 'the multiple phenomena of the universe are the different aspects of matter in movement'.[162] In Stalin's reductive materialism, matter as such is imperiously stated to possess a general essence that founds and guarantees the universal consistency of the lawful behaviour of phenomena in their necessary determinations.

---

ism of monism, with its universal dialectics. Materialist dialectics is an erroneous theory invented by the Soviet Academy of Sciences. It just replaces Hegel's "spirit" or "absolute idea" with "matter"'. See also Vargas 2008, p. 162.

159 'What Freud means in the first place by '*Phantasien*' are … fictions which the subject creates and recounts to himself in the waking state' (Laplanche and Pontalis 2018, p. 315). Althusser's definition of materialist analysis as 'not telling oneself stories' invokes precisely this Freudian topos of phantasy (Althusser 1994, p. 221). I discuss Althusser's definition in chapter 2. As Althusser constantly reasserted, ideology takes real material forms: in Central Europe, infants are often bathed in an upright bucket or *kyblík* that reassuringly supports and encases them in a facsimile of the intra-uterine experience. In contrast, Lacan would name the affective position of the interminable scientific production of knowledge *anxiety*: 'With anxiety, … it's a matter of going deeper into the function of the object in the analytic experience'. (Lacan 2016, p. 43). On the latter, see also Matthys 2023, p. 260.

160 On Plekhanov's reading of Spinoza as an empiricist materialism, see Matysik 2023, Chapter 6.

161 Stalin, *Dialectical and Historical Materialism* (1938), available online at https://www.marxists.org/reference/archive/stalin/works/1938/09.htm. See also Estop 2021, pp. 26–9; Elliott 1987, pp. 20, 127–9; Van Ree 2000; Thomas 2008; Oitinnen 2022. Plekhanov's monism was far exceeded in theoretical vulgarity by Vladimir Shulyatikov's farcical claims that 'Spinoza's conception of the world is the song triumphant of capital', his thought putatively the mere and direct reflection of the capitalistic organisation of the forces of production of his era. Cited in Oitinnen 2022, p. 3.

162 Stalin, cited in Estop 2021, p. 28.

An inherent teleology thus governs the Stalinist determination of the essence of matter and its movement, such that all phenomena are said to adhere to the principal of reason and universal necessity. In its ultimate consequence, the rudimentary determinism of Stalin's materialism reduces thought to the status of a sheer reflection of determining matter, with knowledge itself merely a relatively complex and developed form of matter. Matter itself remains always already the seat and emanant foundation of the meaning and essence of reality. In consequence of this universal, speculative determinism, *historical* materialism then constitutes for Stalin the science of the necessary laws of social organisation and movement, the knowledge of which, embodied in the Party, stands as the governing and determining epistemological instance, its discernment legitimated by a 'scientific' insight into this determinist teleology.[163]

The immediate context of Althusser's public and absolute rejection of substance monism lies in his exchange with Gilbert Mury in the pages of *La Pensée*, a polemic that he summarises in his unpublished 1976 memoir *Les vaches noires*. Following the theoretical disquiet his first articles in the journal introduced in the Marxist humanist consensus of the PCF, Roger Garaudy tasked Mury, at the time Garaudy's 'right hand man', with writing an article that would rebut Althusser's theoretical deviation, 'to execute me with a lightening rebuke in *La Pensée*'. Looking back on the event, Althusser does not mince words, qualifying Mury's indeed feeble article as 'long, confused, verbose, and peremptory'.[164]

Althusser's immediate response to Mury's meandering and tepid rebuke, a biting and summary three-page 'Annexe' attached to the essay 'Sur la dialectique matérialiste' (in other words, just what Garaudy had hoped Mury would produce, only with the inquisitor interrogated), was not included in *Pour Marx* ('to spare Mury', Althusser comments dryly in *Les vaches noires*), and must be consulted in the original 1963 text.[165] There, Althusser focuses on the place of the 'ideological' concept of monism in Mury's convoluted argument, as the concept, the 'unique essence' that 'seals the identity Hegel-Marx', a concept that, Althusser observes, might well have served its purpose, were it not 'foreign to Marxism'.[166] Marx, in turn, is said by Mury to be 'monist', in Althusser's reading, insofar as 'all the determinations of society (political, the State, ideolo-

---

163 Estop 2021, pp. 28–9.
164 Althusser 2016. See Mury 1963, pp. 38–51.
165 Althusser 1963, pp. 43–6.
166 Althusser 1963, p. 43.

gies ...) are mere *phenomena* of a *unique reality* that constitutes their *essence*'. Here, Althusser observes, Mury rejoins 'the latent substantialism' of Plekhanov: 'There is a unique mother-reality [*réalité-mère*], a sort of active substance, an essence-cause producing effects that are its proper phenomena .... [as a form of] of substantialism'.[167]

Flatly rejecting the speculative ontological dictates on the nature of reality of Mury and those of Plekhanov and Stalin behind him, Althusser seeks to rebut Mury by refusing all theoretical guarantees, asserting in reply that the example of 'the unity of a mode of production, in reality, has nothing "moniste" about it, because the mode of production, is, in itself, a highly complex totality, in which the forces of production, themselves complex, and the relations of production, attain their unity in this real complexity'.[168]

Reality, Althusser asserts, 'is not in the least materially constituted by a unique reality, substance, matter, etc.'.[169] Refusing all imaginary, specious guarantees of the nature of ontological totality, Althusser's reply to Mury is simply to note that 'the unity of society for Marx ... is not the unity of a substance or single reality, but that of a structured totality ...: nature, instruments of production (tools, machines, techniques), men, technical knowledge'.[170] Where Mury talks of speculative first principals, Althusser rejects monism by invoking the differential complexity of actually existing singular things. While Mury's essay lacks the clarity of Althusser's that might make it a coherent defence of substance monism rather than a mere polemical assertion,[171] Althusser's truncated rebuttal in *For Marx* articulates in turn only a polemical desire to suppress the 'theoretically harmful' ontological category of substance as flatly equivalent to monism, a theoretical acting-out, one that in its refusal explicitly to work through the problematic of a materialist reformulation of Spinozist substance as structural causality, leaves the impression of a mechanistic pluralism of heterogeneous existing singular things.

---

167 Althusser 1963, p. 44.
168 Ibid.
169 Ibid.
170 Ibid.
171 Composed of 'miraculous concepts', Althusser observes, Mury's claims 'are not scientific clarifications, but declarations of clarity; they are designed not to resolve a problem, but to declare it resolved' (ibid.).

9 Against Monism, the Return of Substance

What Althusser leaves in a state of theoretical underdevelopment, Pierre Macherey will subsequently develop as a coherent Spinozist critique. In the case of monism, Macherey addresses his critique at precisely the level Althusser invokes in his reply to Mury: not that of ontological first principals and presuppositions, but that of actually existing things such as the forces and instruments of production or the scientific and technical organisation of production (to repeat Althusser's examples against Mury). Macherey's critique of monism takes place in the context of his exposition of Spinoza, and so lacks any reference to Marx or Marxism, occurring in a note accompanying his analysis of Spinoza's distinction between nonexistent and actually existing things,[172] along with their corresponding scholastic referents *essence* and *appearance*, respectively, and so can be said to address the same problem as Althusser (that of the relation of monism to the heterogeneity of the real), albeit at a greater level of abstraction.[173]

In explicating two of the most 'obscure' propositions of the *Ethics*, Macherey stresses the absolute heterogeneity of these two categories in Spinoza's radical reformulation of the essence/appearance doublet.[174] To conceive nonexistent things (*res singulares non existentes*) is to grasp them, Macherey writes, 'from the point of view of essence', as 'idealities' [*idéalités*], precisely analogous to the idea of a (nonexistent, ideal) circle (Spinoza's illustration) and the properties that follow solely from this essence as its infinite, immediate modal determination, as opposed to the actually existing figure of a real circle and two intersecting lines actually drawn within it from among the infinite number that constitute one of its essential properties.[175]

---

172   EIIP8, 9.
173   Macherey 1997, pp. 81–97.
174   Macherey 1997, p. 85.
175   Macherey 1997, p. 87. In distinguishing between nonexistent and existent things, Spinoza is clearly reacting to Descartes' overtly psychologistic understanding of *essential*: '[B]y essence we understand the thing insofar as it is objectively in the intellect, by existence [existentia], this same thing insofar as it is outside the intellect [rem eandem prout est extra intellectum]' (Descartes, 'Correspondance, vol. 4,' cited in David, 2014: 194). In contrast to Descartes' psychologism, Spinoza's purely logical understanding of *res singulares non existentes* would await further theoretical development until Bolzano's concept of *Vorstellungen an sich* [Representations as such], the primary universal characteristic of which he formulates as "*Vorstellungen an sich haben kein Dasein*" ["Representations as such have no existence"] in the *Wissenschaftslehre* (Bolzano 1978: 75). I discuss Bolzano in Chapter four. Spinoza's emphasis on the *atemporality* of nonexistent things (vs. essence as a lack of *spatial extension*, as in the thereness of 'being there'), however, is quite unique in

The crucial corollary to the nature of nonexistent things, that which above all and absolutely distinguishes them from actually existing things (and here we return to the problem of monism and the heterogeneity of the real), is that they are, Macherey observes, 'by definition abstracted from all consideration of duration and deploy themselves in the perspective of eternity'. The idea of actually existing singular things, in contrast, necessarily 'implies', Spinoza writes, 'the existence by which they are said to endure' (*earum ideae etiam existentiam per quam durare dicuntur involvunt*). Macherey emphasises the radicality and absolute nature of this distinction, insofar as it precludes any understanding of existence as the actualisation of a (temporally) precedent essence, 'the temporal passage for singular things from essence to existence'. Essence and existence must instead be understood as 'completely distinct manners of being, equally real'.[176]

It is at this point, then, that Macherey inserts his rejection of monism as the consequent implication of this position. Here is Macherey:

> Spinoza's philosophy, then, is situated in complete opposition to an elementary monism [i.e., such as that of Plekhanov, Stalin, and Mury] that would conceive of reality as an undifferentiated set [*un ensemble indifférencié*] given once and for all in its massive globality. Whether considered from the point of view of essence or from the point of view of existence, ... reality declines itself [*se décline*] in completely different forms, forms so entirely distinct that it is impossible to compare them by interpreting them as levels of reality situated at differing positions on a single scale of judgement [*échelle d'appréciation*].[177]

Here, as Althusser had before him, Macherey limits the problem of monism to the domain of things (*les êtres* or 'beings' in Heideggerian jargon) rather than *Being qua Being* and the nature of substance. Considered alongside his materialist explication of Spinozist substance as uncountable *causa sui*, however, while certainly not accounting for the real diversity of Marxist theories of monism since Plekhanov, Macherey's Althusserian critique nonetheless constitutes a coherent and compelling critique of substance monism as such.

---

the complex history of the related concepts of the Latin *existentia*, the French and English 'existence,' and the German pseudo-synonyms *Existenz* and *Dasein* (David, 2014).

176 Macherey 1997, p. 91.
177 Ibid.

To return to Althusser's polemical position, however, absent a systematic critique of monism such as that of Macherey, the reductive determinism of traditional, Stalinist materialism such as that of Mury nonetheless readily explains Althusser's situated, polemical rejection of all expressions of substance monism, as well as his refusal explicitly to articulate an alternative materialist concept of substance in his published, exoteric works. To have done so would arguably have compromised with speculative guarantees the situated articulation of a polemical theoretical position, one that consistently, for all its variation, refused a metaphysics of emanant matter as another form of idealism, which in positing matter as universal causal determinacy, merely constitutes an alternative form of idealist transcendence: matter as subject, essence, substrate, and emanant cause.[178]

This univocal polemical position, however, grows decidedly more complex when one considers Althusser's unpublished writings on Spinoza. Althusser readily takes on Macherey's precocious, 1965 critique of Althusser's references to 'the whole' (*le tout*)[179] in the first edition of *Lire le Capital* as the theoretically superfluous introduction of a reified, transcendent *subjectum* to an otherwise materialist critique. At times, Althusser's notes go on to invoke a heterodox notion of Spinozist substance as the infinite, unmediated expression of a structure of causality in an infinity of registers and modes, a philosophy of pure immanence that *exists* only in its effects.[180] In these esoteric writings, the Althusserian concept of a structural causality, of a structure that exists only in the immediacy of its determinate effects, more explicitly deploys the

---

178 In his essay 'En matérialiste' (to be discussed in the following chapter), Pierre Macherey more consistently than Althusser (who continued to the end to speak positively of certain forms of materialism), generalises this rejection of all forms of material*ism*, to invoke instead a fidelity to a material*ist* dialectic, a commitment shared as well by Alain Badiou (see below Chapter 5).

179 Montag 2013, pp. 84–6; Estop 2021, pp. 138–44. I discuss Macherey's critique of the concept of totality in Chapter 3.

180 'Althusser', Estop insightfully writes in his analysis of Althusser's 1967 notes to the discussion with Stanislas Breton (discussed above), 'makes of Spinoza his fundamental philosophical reference for a theory of immanent causality. ... The different orders of being are not prefigured either positively or negatively [as a negative theology or the absent cause of *metonymic* causality] in the cause; their discontinuity is of the order of the *Faktum*, and not that of a necessary derivation from a [transcendent] essence. ... There is only a factual relation of substance to the attributes and these to the modes: a simple 'there is' [*il y a*] without guarantee and without justification. ... Substance [for the Althusser of these 1967 notes] is nothing but structure as such, the complexity of a plural infinity that [immediately] expresses and thus effectuates an infinite power [*puissance*]' (Estop 2021, pp. 154–5, my translation).

Spinozist notion of substance to indicate not the transcendent and countable ('monist') causal subject, but rather the complexity (as overdetermination) and immanence (as topology or *topique*) of purely intrinsic causality.[181] As early as his 1940s notebook on Spinoza, Althusser had already affirmed the necessity of thinking the attributes in their immediate articulation of immanent substance: 'In Spinoza, the famous parallelism is itself abstract: what is affirmed before parallelism is the unity and unicity of substance – it is this identity that resolves the problem of dualism'. Althusser's early commentary, however, articulates this unity in precisely the terms of the 'substance monism' that he would reject categorically in *Pour Marx* over a decade later: 'An epistemological dualism persists, but sustained [*soutenu*] by a radical ontological monism'.[182]

Following Althusser's public rejection of any and all substance monism in *For Marx* and the corresponding absence of any unifying, substantial materialist category in the arguments of *Reading Capital*, Althusser makes an implicit auto-critique of this silence in the founding, privately circulated document of the *Groupe de travail théorique* (aka 'Groupe Spinoza'), the 'Three Notes on Discourse' from October 1966.[183] In these working notes to his informed readers (Etienne Balibar, Pierre Macherey, Yves Duroux, and Alain Badiou), Althusser initially reiterates the seemingly dualistic terminology of *Reading Capital*, continuing to distinguish in the abstract between 'the object of knowledge' and 'the real object', as if these indicated two separate, directly comparable objects or things, as opposed to, in the case of the Spinozist attributes of substance, two modes of *apprehending* a singular existing thing, such as the capitalist social form (for Marx in *Reading Capital*), or the object of this 1966 text, the unconscious for Freud and Lacan.[184]

Toward the end of his first note, however, Althusser privately specifies for his circle the insufficiency of a position (such as that which Althusser had expressed in *Reading Capital*) that refuses to think the nature of the articulation of theoretical domains, such that 'we remain [merely at the abstract level] of the parallelism of the attributes'. The necessary supplement to the heterogeneity of the attributes, Althusser immediately adds, lies in the manner in which 'Spinoza tempers and corrects the parallelism of the attributes by the concept of substance: the different attributes are the attributes *of a single and same substance*. It is the concept of substance that plays the role of the concept

---

181   Estop 2021, p. 152. See also Matthys 2023, Chapter 4.
182   ALT 2. A 60–08, cited in Estop 2021, p. 229.
183   In *Ecrits sur la psychanalyse* (Althusser 1993, pp. 111–70). See also Williams 2013, pp. 157–8; and Sotiris 2021, p. 183.
184   Althusser 1993, p. 120.

of the articulation of the attributes. ... The *distinction* of the attributes is only possible under the condition of their articulation'.[185]

Althusser sustains and further specifies this necessity of a concept of purely immanent structural causality that would allow for the distinction between the object of thought and the real object in his 1976 text *Etre marxiste en philosophie* (first published in 2015). It is precisely Spinoza's concept of substance, Althusser argues there, that allows for the construction of 'a consequential form of materialism, one that annuls the difference between the object and its knowledge, all the while recognising ... the difference between the object and its knowledge'.[186] While the mechanism of this 'annulment' remains unspecified, in place of the identity of the object and its representation in traditional theories of knowledge, Althusser argues that a Spinozist epistemology moves, always within the attribute of thought, from inadequate (though necessary) imaginary forms of knowledge, to the contrasting adequacy of common notions and singular things, 'a dialectic', Althusser specifies, 'that passes, in three moments, from one to the other, across the diverse genres of knowledge'.[187] The essential Spinozist epistemological distinction between the real circle (which is round) and its concept (which is not) articulated in *Reading Capital* would merely constitute, in this view, an initial distinction that escapes the ideological constraints of traditional theories of knowledge whether as 'reflection or revelation', to found the adequate knowledge of any singular thing in which the circle and its adequate idea are not two objects of adequation, but rather 'one and the same [existing and nonexisting] thing in two different attributes'.[188]

10   The Theoretical Basis of Theoreticism

The suppression of any explicit reference to and/or rearticulation of the Spinozist concept of substance in Althusser's published writings, and its replacement by the untheorised dualism of thought and the real, articulated alongside the seemingly unrelated concept of structural causality, had disastrous consequences for the reception of Althusser's thought. These consequences resonate into the present, as a general agreement on all sides – from E.P. Thompson's historicist ravings to the manifest desire to save Althusser from

---

185   Althusser 1993, p. 150, emphases in original.
186   Althusser 2015, §12.
187   Althusser 2015, §12.
188   E2P7S, cited in Estop 2021, p. 195.

his 'theoreticism' shared by highly informed readers including Anderson, Elliot, and Goshgarian – that the epistemological positions articulated in *For Marx* and *Reading Capital* constituted a politically dysfunctional, hyper-rationalist idealism. From Thompson ('Althusser and his acolytes ... offer an a-historical theoreticism which, at the first examination, discloses itself as idealism'),[189] to Elliot (Althusser's proposition of a '*"knowledge effect"* ... remains unilluminated beyond cryptic, and in any case circular, allusions to the significance of the internal organisation and disposition of concepts'),[190] and Anderson, one finds general agreement: 'Althusser does indeed rely improperly on logico-mathematical protocols of proof as models of scientific procedure. His theory of knowledge, dissociated from the controls of evidence, is untenably internalist'.[191]

If the charge of theoreticism has any real basis, however, this is to be located not in a putative political deficit (Goshgarian, Anderson) or historiographic imprecision or idealism (Thompson, Elliot), but *at the theoretical level*, precisely as *a failure to be theoreticist enough*. To follow Althusser down the retrograde path from an initial repentance for 'theoreticism' toward the empiricist

---

[189] Thompson 1987, p. 18.
[190] Elliott 1987, p. 87, emphasis in original.
[191] Anderson 1980, p. 7. It is worth noting that Elliott, whose brief presentation of Spinoza's thought symptomatically disregards the category of substance (1987, p. 77), sees fit to draw a diametrically opposite conclusion to the Spinozist position I offer here, i.e., that Althusser's 'guilty silence' regarding the relation of thought and the real disavows the true nature of this theoreticist epistemology as 'a reprise of the diamat tradition' (1987, p. 88). Elliott does so by problematically reducing Spinoza and Althusser's appropriation of him to the reflection theory of Engels: '"The differential nature of scientific discourse" is assured [for Althusser] by its identity with the structure of reality, the "non-problematicity between an object and the knowledge of it" guaranteed by ontology ... Insofar as [Althusser's critique of empiricism] encompassed epistemologies which posit an identity between knowledge and the object of which it is knowledge, it would therefore not only include Althusser's own, but also – and crucially – Spinoza's' (1987, p. 89). This critique remains superficial – although consonant with Althusser's truncated dualism of thought and the Real – since Elliott first reimports the traditional epistemological criterion of the adequation of subject and object, to then assert that *Spinoza* posits the identity of thought and the real object. In contrast, Spinoza (and Althusser in his unpublished writings such as the notes on his discussion with Père Breton discussed above) rigorously maintains the *distinction* of the orders of the attributes, while at the same time rejecting any notion of substance as a transcendent *thing* (see note 96 above). Elliott's parallelist misreading of Spinoza should be measured against Macherey's more exacting analysis of *Ethics* IIP7, which I discuss in the following chapter. There Macherey argues that this proposition indicates not an identical order of thought and order of extension, but rather that the attributes differentially comprehend one and the same *thing*.

position of 'class struggle in theory' is to risk ending up, with no small irony, at precisely the Stalinist epistemology *For Marx* had rightly and so powerfully excoriated. At its most extreme, this position is nothing less than the regressive endorsement of a bureaucratic politicisation of science (Lysenkoism) such as that explicitly formulated for the PCF by Jacques Desanti in a 1950 editorial for *La nouvelle critique*: i.e., that 'taking a proletarian stance in science and adopting the criteria of proletarian science [are] preconditions for objectivity in scientific debate'.[192]

When Althusser made the political decision publicly to reject the ontological and epistemological guarantees of substance monism in *For Marx*, in order to categorically distinguish his theoretical intervention from the vulgar materialism of Plekhanov and Stalin, he suppressed the category of Spinozist Substance from his (public) discourse, developing the concept of structural causality as finite determination within a contingent (capitalist) social form. Though Macherey echoes Althusser's condemnation of substance monism in his five-volume commentary on the *Ethics*, he articulates in its place a rigorous, materialist understanding of Spinozist Substance as uncounted causality.

To count Spinozist substance as One (i.e., as a monism) is for Macherey to grasp substance from the standpoint of the imagination, which is to say, inadequately, 'by replacing [the concept of substance] in a network of exterior determinations in which it is made to figure as one thing existing alongside or above [in transcendence to] all others, which is to deny its absolute self-relation [*rapport à soi*] that excludes any relation to another thing than itself'.[193] Substance, in Macherey's reading of the *Ethics* as a materialist dialectic of pure immanence, cannot be 'considered as 'one' [*une*] substance, but as subsisting [*le subsister*], or existing [*l'exister*], considered as such'.[194]

For Macherey, if Proposition 1 of *Ethics* I emphasises the priority of substance to its modal *affections*, this implies not only the overarching Spinozist epistemological imperative to 'think the real in its totality according to [Spinoza's] synthetic procedure ... *from cause to effects*, and not the inverse', but also, and at least as importantly, the unstated corollary of this proposition as the Spinozist position of a radical immanence of the attributes: that, in other words, 'substance is [in contrast to its affectations] *not* first in nature in relation to its *attributes*. There is no more priority of substance in relation to

---

192   Cited in Elliot 1987, p. 69.
193   Macherey 1998, p. 87.
194   Macherey 1998, p. 90.

its attributes than there is a priority of the attributes in relation to substance, because they [substance and the attributes] neither can be nor can be conceived separately'.[195]

In place of Spinoza's rigorous distinction between Substance as 'that which is in itself and conceived through itself' and the attributes as 'that which the intellect perceives of substance as constituting its essence', Althusser's dualist invocation of thought and the real either makes a lopsided category error (if we take the real to indicate Spinozist substance) or seems to articulate an idealist dualism or even pluralism without materialist determination (if we take the real to indicate the attribute of extension). In either case, the reader of *For Marx* and *Reading Capital* is understandably left with the impression of a rationalist, idealist construction, a *Gedankenkonkretum* devoid of materialist necessity.

In his public writings, Althusser never invoked Spinoza as more than a spectral presence (in *Reading Capital*) or lapsus of theoreticist hubris (in *Essays in Self-Criticism*). By the time Macherey would supplement this lack through his exacting construction of a materialist theory of Spinozist substance and the attributes in *Hegel or Spinoza* and his *Introduction* to the *Ethics*, the self-inflicted, damaged reception of Althusser's thought had long become a fait accompli, and, in any case, Macherey's rearticulation – rigorously addressed neither to Marx nor Althusser, but to Spinoza alone – could only respond to a question no one had asked, nor seemed interested in asking, since all concerned, starting with Althusser himself, agreed on the nature of *Reading Capital*'s theoreticism as a politico-historicist, as opposed to epistemo-theoretical, inadequacy.

To grasp the true nature of Althusser's theoreticism as a failure to be theoreticist enough would in consequence require, as I seek to do in this book, the construction of a new object of thought, along with the incipient demonstration of its necessity, a theoretical object that would refuse to limit the thought of Althusser, Macherey, and Badiou to their nominal subjects (whether Spinoza, Hegel, or Marx), but which instead articulates the complex and overdetermined theoretical field these thinkers have constructed since 1960, interrogating its resonances and dead spots, its silences and invocations, in their attempt to formulate this common theoretical object: the materialist dialectic.

Althusser's published texts suppress the category of Substance to leave readers with the impression of a rationalist dualism, the inwardness of a thought construct without materialist purchase on an untheorised 'real'. In contrast, Althusser's unpublished writings point toward the necessary, Spinozist artic-

---

195 Macherey 1998, p. 72, my emphases.

ulation of *Reading Capital*'s merely dualist distinction between the capitalist social form distinguished as an object of thought and the real order or attribute of temporal extension: they do so through a reconceptualisation of substance as the immanence of a conjunctural structural causality without transcendence. While this Spinozist proviso provides an essential articulation to the principal proposition of that book – that in *Capital*, Marx 'really did invent a new form of order for axiomatic analysis, ... a new order in the theoretical, a new form of apodicticity or scientificity' – this as yet says nothing about the actual form of Marx's analysis.[196]

Althusser himself says little more about Marx's actual process of exposition and analysis in *Reading Capital*, and rarely returned to the topic after 1965.[197] To further elaborate this claim will require turning in the following chapter to Pierre Macherey's contribution to that volume, a text to be read as a prolegomenon to Macherey's elaboration of a Spinozist, materialist dialectic. Macherey's concept of a positive, materialist dialectic without negation can then (in chapter three) be returned and brought to bear anew on Marx's actual process of exposition in *Capital*, in essence extending Macherey's innovative initial reading of *Capital* from 1965 in light of his later readings of Hegel and Spinoza. This in turn will set the stage for the final chapters of this book, which will consider the concept of a materialist, axiomatic dialectic in Alain Badiou's thought, to show that all of these texts written in the wake of *Reading Capital*, texts that rarely if ever explicitly engage with or even mention Marx's *Capital*, nonetheless sustain the fidelity to a heterogeneous school of Althusserian theory, the insistent return to read and reread *Capital* as a materialist, apodictic analysis of the capitalist social form.

---

196   RC, p. 52.
197   See above, note 29.

CHAPTER 2

What Is Materialist Analysis? Pierre Macherey's Spinozist Epistemology

In this chapter, I turn to Pierre Macherey's theory of a materialist dialectic, a project that can be said to unite his work from his initial contribution to *Reading Capital* into the present. I will first discuss Macherey's reading of the first five pages of Marx's *Capital* in his brief but decisive contribution to *Reading Capital*. I will then turn to his 1966 book *A Theory of Literary Production*, to argue that it cogently summarises the materialist critique of *Reading Capital* as a general theory of the materialist production of the textual object in the form of thought as opposed to its extensive, empirical reality on the page. My discussion will then turn to Macherey's subsequent development of a theory of materialist dialectic in works such as *Hegel or Spinoza*, the essay 'En matérialiste', and Macherey's extraordinary, five-volume, line by line explication of Spinoza's *Ethics*. The latter, a major work that as of this writing remains untranslated into English, offers in my view not only a masterful explication of Spinoza's dauntingly complex and original philosophical masterpiece; its extensive commentary itself constitutes, I will argue, an original theoretical intervention that can serve systematically to articulate the theory of positive, materialist dialectic that Macherey initially proposes in his earlier works.

1   *Reading Capital*'s Materialist Dialectic

Pierre Macherey's brilliant and long-overlooked contribution to *Lire le Capital*, 'A propos du processus d'exposition du *Capital*', is a treasure of theoretical investigation revealed anew by the republication of the complete volume of *Reading Capital*.[1] Macherey's precocious genius in these pages pushes

---

1   To be sure, the second edition of *Lire le Capital* that appeared in two volumes in 1968, comprised only of Althusser and Balibar's texts (and which served for the various international translations of the book), was eventually completed in 1973 with a third and fourth volume, containing the original contributions of Rancière (Vol. III) and Macherey and Establet (Vol. IV). That said, even among Francophone readers, who save a few specialists can be said to have actually read that obscure fourth volume in the waning years of Althusserianism in the 1970s?

Althusser's Spinozist epistemology to its most extreme and rigorous formulation imaginable. The object of Macherey's brief chapter is to investigate Marx's conception and practice 'of the scientific exposition' of his principal concepts in the initial five pages of *Capital* Vol. 1, chapter 1, section 1.[2] In its modest pretensions to closely read these five pages of text, the essay expands on the form of the scholastic *explication de texte* that every French *normalien* is trained to master by the 'caïmans' such as Althusser who prepared them for the rigorous *agrégation*. Macherey's brief exposé nonetheless brings a discerning precision to bear upon the opening lines of *Capital*, to draw a series of analytical divisions between the concepts with which Marx begins his critique of political economy: wealth (*la richesse/Reichtum*), the commodity (*la marchandise/Ware*), the commodity's two essential aspects or attributes, its use-value and exchange-value, and, finally, value itself (*la valeur/Wert*).

If the first of these, wealth, is only fleetingly presented in the opening sentence of *Capital* ('The wealth of societies in which the capitalist mode of production prevails appears as an "immense collection of commodities"'), Macherey argues that this is due to its extreme conceptual poverty. Wealth, in this reading, is a reductively empirical category, the general form of appearance that any and all things take on as objects of value in any given social form whatsoever. This form of appearance of any object of wealth *per se* is 'the empirical mode of existence of the thing', says Macherey, 'its manner of appearing, showing itself, manifesting itself'.[3] In contrast to value, a much richer concept that, above all, 'does not show itself, does not appear', wealth is 'empirically very thin [*maigre*]: transparent'.[4]

The concept of wealth serves to initiate the conceptual analysis of *Capital* primarily, Macherey argues, as a 'reminder', in its capacity to refer back to the origins of classical economy, to its arbitrary and precritical status in Smith and Ricardo. Consequently, this implies for Macherey two key points that he will develop intensively. First, that the array of concepts Marx deploys in *Capital* are not equal: wealth is an impoverished, 'sterile', concept, referring merely to the empirical form of appearance of things, a form fully inadequate to its essen-

---

2 Macherey has offered a surprisingly modest, even resentful disavowal of his contribution to *Lire le Capital*: 'When, with fifty years' distance, I reread [my] contribution, I see all of its imperfections. ... When, subsequently, I was addressed as a 'coauthor' of *Reading Capital*, I could not prevent myself feeling a certain *malaise* .... In reality, *Reading Capital* has only one author: it is Althusser who, when he constructed this book on the basis of the working documents [we] provided him with, made a work unto itself, for which he himself bears responsibility' (Lasowski 2016, pp. 176–7).
3 RC, p. 191.
4 RC, p. 192.

tial nature as commodity.⁵ 'Wealth' is never anything more than the empirical definition Marx gives it: 'a mass of commodities'. In contrast, the endpoint of Macherey's exposition, value, is a rich concept, one that will require the entire, incomplete exposition of *Capital* volumes I–III to elaborate. Secondly, however, Macherey argues that wealth, for all its superficiality and brevity of appearance in Marx's analysis, is nonetheless purely a concept. Wealth can never be confused with any of its empirical manifestations; it is and remains purely a concept.

Macherey's analysis attends closely to the logical components and operators he identifies in the opening pages of *Capital*. These constitute what he terms 'intermediaries', the 'instruments of rationality' that allow for the construction of a rigorous demonstration. Macherey's assertion that the various concepts laid out in these opening lines of *Capital* are fundamentally and necessarily heterogeneous is a point his own demonstration will sustain and develop step by step; the notion of conceptual heterogeneity constitutes, moreover, 'one of the fundamental conditions of scientific rigour'. The system of Marx's concepts, and the system of rational operators more generally, in this view, consists of various components that do not coexist 'on one and the same level of intelligibility', but which instead inhabit multiple, incommensurable planes.⁶

This assertion next leads Macherey to consider the relations of heterogeneity between the four concepts under consideration: the 'empirical form' of wealth, the contradictory pair of 'factors' of the commodity that are use-value and exchange-value, and, finally, the purely relational concept of value. If use-value, like wealth, remains tied to the empirical, but grasped as 'the notion of a thing' rather than via its sensuous existence, exchange-value in contrast only exists as a relation between commodities.⁷ This dual nature of the commodity,

---

5   RC, p. 190.
6   RC, p. 188.
7   RC, p. 194. This key point, first elaborated by Macherey in 1965, will undergo intensive development by Michael Heinrich in his close reading of the first seven chapters of *Capital*: 'Why can't we grasp value-objectivity in a single commodity', Heinrich asks? 'This is due to the social character of the substance of value, which was emphasised in the first subsection [of *Capital*]. The substance of value, abstract labour, is not inherent to a single commodity, but rather held in common by two commodities that are exchanged. ... The table can only become an expression of equal human labour through exchange, when confronting other commodities. Then the various particular and individual acts of labour are reduced to equal human labour. From this "purely social" character of value-objectivity, Marx says that it follows "self-evidently" that "it can only appear in the social relation between commodity and commodity" (1976: 139). ... Commodities have value-objectivity only in the social relation of one commodity to another – which is why it first comes to light here. Prior to and outside of this relation, they are mere use-values: they are on the way to becoming commodities, but far

as both thing and relation, is for Macherey a primary contradiction or aporia of capital that is not 'resolved' in a Hegelian *Aufhebung*, but which is instead 'suppressed'.[8] This contradiction between use-value and exchange-value exists, furthermore, purely at the level of Marx's concepts, and leads to 'a break in the treatment of these concepts ... and in no way refers to a real process ... The concepts that sustain the scientific exposition are not of the same kind'.[9]

Adhering to Althusser's principled rejection of empiricism described in the previous chapter, Macherey's analysis furthermore rejects phenomenological experience as a basis for Marx's demonstration. Value, in this view, is a category invisible to immediate experience of the commodity in its phenomenological appearance. Value, in Macherey's reading, is to be located neither on the surface of phenomena (in their appearance as use-values), nor in their empirical relation to one another (as exchange-values); but for all that, nor can value be said to lie hidden within the depths of that relation, to stand revealed in a moment of Hegelian *Aufhebung*. Instead, the concept of value exists in a relation of 'rupture' to commodities given their dual aspects as use-values and exchange-values. 'The paradox of the analysis of exchange is that value is neither in the terms of exchange, nor in their relation. Value is not given, or revealed [*dégagée*], or displayed [*mise en évidence*]: it is constructed as concept'.[10] The object that is value 'is more hidden than revealed' in the act of exchange.

Thus the necessity for Marx's categorial, 'scientific' critique of political economy: 'Without the rigor of scientific exposition, which alone is able to produce knowledge, the concept of value would have no meaning: that is to say, it would not exist'.[11] The aporetic structure of the commodity, its dual nature, thus leads to the heart of Macherey's analysis. Macherey identifies in the relation between two equivalent commodities, in the system of market exchange, the determinant condition of a concept devoid of all empiricism. To approach value itself, he writes, 'the analysis must no longer be conducted in terms of experience'. Instead, the concept of a relation of exchange, Macherey provocatively asserts,

---

from being commodities. When Marx speaks of the value of a single commodity (or its magnitude of value), he always presupposes a value-relation to another commodity, of which the individual commodity is a part'. Heinrich 2021, pp. 93–5.

8   RC, p. 195.
9   RC, p. 196. In the next chapter I will argue against Macherey that Marx's presentation of the concepts of use-value and exchange-value is in no sense based upon a logic of contradiction [*Widerspruch*], but that the two are simply factual aspects or attributes of the commodity that coexist in 'opposition' [*Gegensatz*] without contradiction.
10 RC, p. 203, original emphasis.
11 RC, p. 205, translation modified, italics in original.

has no empirical content.¹² Unlike wealth or the commodity, value, the concept of the measure allowing for the exchange-based equality of empirically nonidentical commodities, is purely and only that, a concept. Like any other concept, it is real but nonexistent, a reality in the attribute of thought alone, rather than the empirical attribute of sensuous extension.

The conceptual relation that is value, Macherey continues, poses the equality of two commodities as a formula, a = b; it is, in other words, 'defined as a relation of expression'.¹³ Unlike the qualitative, empirical relation of two use-values standing side by side in the market, the relation of exchange-value is characterised by the extinction of all qualities. Fungibility is thus more precisely represented as a purely quantitative schematisation, as the expression of relative value: 'ax = by (a is so much of b)'.¹⁴

It is this schematic reduction of the commodity form to a purely quantitative relation that then definitively displaces Macherey's analysis in its final step, to enjoin the concept of value itself: Marx's 'new analysis [now addressing of the concept of value] begins with a decisive choice: the refusal to study the exchange relation as a qualitative relation, to only consider it in its quantitative content'.¹⁵ It is this pure conceptualisation, then, that will finally allow for the adequate (initial) construction of the concept of value, as 'the structure of the relation' of exchange itself.¹⁶

The heterogeneous, nondialectical series of logical steps Macherey identifies in Marx's exposition then suddenly culminates in a parenthetical gesture of pure conceptual abstraction, momentarily abstracting, that is, from Marx's exposition itself to articulate a purely axiomatic statement regarding the nature of conceptual formalisation. It is possible, Macherey provisionally concludes from this exposition, to 'formulate a general rule: ... to compare objects non-empirically, it is necessary as a preliminary to determine the general form of this measurement ... It is not possible to make a relation of

---

12 'In experience, it is possible to conceive that two things stand alongside the other, that they are juxtaposed (like commodities in wealth). But they do not explicitly tolerate any relation; from the standpoint of experience, between two things and one thing there is a quantitative difference, but absolutely no qualitative difference' (RC, p. 200).
13 Ibid.
14 I will present a more complex and developed version of this position first asserted by Macherey, in my analysis in the next chapter of Marx's introduction of a formula to schematise the Law of the Rate and Mass of Surplus Value that is the object of Chapter 11 in Roy's 1875 French translation of *Capital*.
15 RC, p. 200.
16 RC, p. 201.

expression say what it expresses if it is examined only in its empirical reality'.[17] The concept expressing the nature of any relation whatsoever is of a different nature, 'another kind', than empirical experience. 'To know what a relation expresses', Macherey concludes, 'it is also necessary, even first of all, to know what is expressing it'.[18]

Macherey's demonstration advances not via a logic of the negation of negation, but rather through a series of quantum-like leaps from one discrete, bounded concept to another, each shown to occupy a singular, heterogeneous orbital.[19] Macherey's analysis to this point has traced the systematic elimination of all empirical qualities (of wealth, and the use-value aspect of commodities) in the analytical passage to exchange-value and then value, arguing in Spinozist terms that just as 'the area of a triangle is not in itself triangular; in the same way too, the notion of value is not exchangeable'.[20]

At this culminating point in Macherey's demonstration, however, the previously abandoned notion of *quality* suddenly returns, now, however, residing in a state of pure nonempirical conceptuality, a state in which 'the notion of value qualifies commodities as the notion of area qualifies areas'. In contrast to the merely sensuous nature of wealth, it is abstract labour, a purely relational, nonempirical notion, that now constitutes 'a new quality', the substance of value itself.[21] As Macherey quotes Marx, to conclude his brief conceptual exposition of these pages from *Capital*, 'there remains only a quality', the abstract, nonquantifiable concept of the substance of value.[22] The logic is implacable and unyielding, the density of Macherey's argument in these seven pages formidable, brilliant, original, in itself as daunting as the five introduc-

---

17 RC, p. 201. Here too, I will argue in the next chapter that Marx rigorously and systematically adheres to this proposition of Macherey's above all in Chapter 11 of *Capital*.
18 RC, p. 201.
19 In this sense, Macherey's precociously original analysis already points forward in 1965 to Althusser's assertion in his late writings (described in the previous chapter) that Marx's process of exposition proceeds in its demonstration through the successive 'positioning' [*position*] of concepts, as opposed to their negative dialectical ('Hegelian') *aufhebung*. Instead, Althusser will argue, Marx's order of exposition is no mere (structuralist/formalist) combinatory, but in fact derives its materialist necessity from the priority of Marx's preliminary enquiries (*Grundrisse*, etc.) to the drafting of *Capital*.
20 RC, p. 205.
21 'As mere things', Macherey writes, 'objects are differentiated by their uses, i.e. their irreducibility. If this character is set aside then at the same time as their empirical qualities disappear, there appears, not their quantitative aspect, but *another quality* (of a quite different nature: not directly observable): ... It will be precisely value whose *substance* it will then be possible to determine' (RC, p. 206).
22 RC, p. 206.

tory pages of *Capital* it theorises, its Cavaillèsian rigour constituting a culminating and bravura theoretical gesture of *Lire le Capital* in its totality.

2   A Theoretical Prolegomenon to the Materialist Analysis of Texts

Pierre Macherey's next work, *A Theory of Literary Production*, might seem, to all appearances, a mere work of literary criticism, familiar in its genre, modest in its intentions, a study in which, after a somewhat lengthy methodological introduction, Macherey proceeds to offer a number of 'materialist' analyses of works ranging from Lenin's comments on Tolstoy to Jules Verne, Jorge Luis Borges, and Defoe's *Robinson Crusoe*. Such a view, however, would profoundly misrepresent the enormous scope and compass of the book's epistemological implications. Instead, the achievement of *A Theory of Literary Production* is far more sweeping than the analysis of a handful of classic novels; Macherey, in this, his first book, in point of fact puts forward a generic protocol for the materialist analysis of textual, symbolic objects of all types, a compellingly original analytical practice for the critique of discourse as such, a procedure that can then, in the next chapter, illuminate Marx's process of exposition in *Capital*, moving beyond Macherey's all-too-brief propositions in his contribution to *Reading Capital*.

It will surprise none of his readers that materialism in Macherey's understanding receives a comprehensively Spinozist inflection. While Macherey only mentions Spinoza nine times in *Theory of Literary Production*, and then only in passing, Warren Montag has shown the degree to which Spinoza's epistemology – inflected through a series of intensive exchanges with Althusser from 1961 onward – underwrites and founds an encompassing philosophico-critical project.[23] Indeed, it is now clear, given the trajectory of Macherey's research, that from his initial, precocious contribution to *Reading Capital* in 1965, through his explosive and highly influential critique of Hegel's misreadings of Spinoza in *Hegel or Spinoza* (1979), and culminating in his extraordinarily meticulous, systematic, and original interpretation of Spinoza's *Ethics* across five volumes and over a thousand pages, Macherey has synthetically redeployed Spinoza to articulate a comprehensive theory of materialist analysis, one that fully takes into account and builds upon the classic Althusserian critiques of empiricism, hermeneutics, totality, and negative-Hegelian dialectics.

---

23   Montag 2013; Montag 1998.

3   Textual Production in a Materialist Mode

A Theory of Literary Production initiates its materialist critique via a three-fold proscription: against empiricism, against hermeneutics, against expressive totality. Each of these protocols resonates in consonance with Althusser's critical introduction to *Reading Capital* published the year before (discussed in the previous chapter). Each of these proscriptions can in turn be traced to the subterranean influence of Spinoza on the thought of Althusser and his students, an influence to be explicated and further elaborated in Macherey's later works.

Against empiricism. If the study of literature traditionally attends to an empirically accessible domain or field, Macherey rejects this 'necessarily insufficient' orientation to argue instead that critical analysis, properly understood, entails in every case the novel *construction* of its object of analysis: 'Rational investigation bears directly upon objects that have no prior existence, but are instead *produced*'.[24] This is the materialist lesson Althusser had drawn from Marx's crucial 1857 methodological introduction to the *Grundrisse* notebooks, where Marx rejects Adam Smith's empiricist, representational method to assert instead a properly materialist, *productionist* epistemology.[25] If Smith famously asserts the universally observable nature of human economic comportment as a 'propensity to truck, barter, and exchange', such an assertion constitutes the abstract, merely conceptual *representation* and generalisation of an empirically observable series.[26] Against the inadequacy of Smith's method of mere empiricist representation, flawed in its derivation of general knowledge from immediate, sensuous impressions, Marx – and Althusser and Macherey in his wake – asserts the autonomy of conceptual production, the *reproduction* (as opposed to representation) of the real object as what Marx calls a 'thought-concrete' (*Gedankenkonkretum*).[27]

---

24   Macherey 2006, p. 6, translation modified, my emphasis.
25   'Marx defends the distinction between the real object (the real-concrete or the real totality, which "retains its autonomous existence outside the head (*Kopf*) just as before"), and the object of knowledge, a product of the thought which produces it in itself as a thought-concrete (*Gedankenkonkretum*), as a thought-totality (*Gedankentotalität*), i.e., as a thought-object, absolutely distinct from the real-object, the real-concrete'. RC, p. 41. See also Marx 1973, p. 101.
26   Adam Smith 1974, p. 11. See above, p. 29.
27   RC, p. 41. 'However far back we ascend, into the past of a branch of knowledge, we are never dealing with a "pure" sensuous intuition or mere "representation", but with an *always-already* complex raw material, a structure of "intuition" or "representation" which combines together in a peculiar "*Verbindung*" sensuous, technical, and ideological elements; that therefore knowledge never, as empiricism desperately demands it should, confronts a *pure object* which is then identical to the *real object* of which knowledge aimed to produce

Macherey redeploys this fundamental assertion of *Reading Capital* in the opening pages of *A Theory of Literary Production*. Never the mere exposition or translation of a latent, hidden meaning, adequate knowledge of a text requires the incipient production of an analytical discourse, an object necessarily distinct from that initial text itself.[28] This analysis will furthermore have as its content not the description of an authorial intention, but the presentation of the 'laws of production' of the text in question, the synthetic elaboration of the conditions of its situated necessity: 'To know the conditions of a process: this is the true programme of a theoretical investigation'.[29] Such an inquiry will refuse the mere description of a product (for transmission, for consumption); instead, it will formulate the universal and necessary 'laws of literary production', a general science of the causes governing textual fabrication, a process that is distinctly Spinozist in its affirmation of necessity and an adequate knowledge of the common, universal notions of textual production, that precede the further articulation of the singular essence of any given discursive object.[30]

Against textual hermeneutics. From the critique of empiricism necessarily follows a refusal of any hermeneutic that would seek to reveal the hidden truth lying latent within a text: 'It is not enough to unfold the line of the text to discover the message inscribed there, for this inscription would be that of an empirical fact'.[31] Textual interpretation – understood as the revelation of an immanent meaning (*sens*), as the true, concealed content of a text that would take form in critical discourse – inherently relies on an ideology of *depth*. Immanent critique constitutes, in this view, an empiricism of the factic text in its putative self-sufficiency; in its place, Macherey calls for adequate knowledge to be derived from the text, but as its analytic supplement: neither the translation of an immanent content nor its comprehension as a normative act of judgement indexified to an objectified truth, instead, 'analysis can hope to articulate the *necessity* determining the textual object'.[32]

Macherey associates such a procedure with a weakened form of analysis. If in so-called structural analysis (Macherey's example is Roland Barthes) there

---

precisely ... the knowledge'. RC, p. 43, emphasis in original. Similarly, in 'On the Materialist Dialectic', Althusser writes, in terms that directly invoke the epistemology of Jean Cavaillès and Gaston Bachelard, that 'a science never works on an existence whose essence is pure immediacy and singularity ("sensations" of "individuals") ... A science always works on existing concepts'. Althusser 2005, p. 184.

28 Macherey 2006, p. 6.
29 Macherey 2006, pp. 8, 10, translation modified.
30 Macherey 2006, p. 13.
31 Macherey 2006, p. 85, translation modified.
32 Macherey 2006, p. 87.

occurs a certain minimal fabrication of 'the object of an analysis', this nonetheless remains an empirically derived, immanent criticism, one that understands the text as the utilitarian carrier of an encoded message, 'its value lying in the specific information that it transmits'.[33] This interpretive rendering of a message encrypted within the depths of the text requires a mere act of translation to render its truth visible, *decoded* into the language of structuralism, *reduced* into the form of a totalised structure of meaning 'deposited in the interior of the work'.[34]

Warren Montag has argued that in place of this structuralist hermeneutic, the materialism of the textual object that Macherey calls for, on the model of Spinoza's critique in the *Tractatus Theologico-Politicus*, considers 'writing, as a part of nature in its materiality, as irreducible to anything outside of itself, no longer secondary in relation to that which it represents or expresses, a repetition of something posited as primary'.[35] This materialism of the textual object, rejecting the hermeneutics of depth, attends to the pure textual surface in its fully present materiality: 'The work hides nothing, it holds no secret: it is fully legible, offered to view, given up'.[36]

Any and every discursive text – and this emphatically includes *Capital*, as I will argue in the next chapter – is thus for Macherey fundamentally incomplete, contradictory, and devoid of a coherent totality, a given whole whose immanent meaning could be simply decoded and translated via the revelatory logos of the critical operation. Macherey rejects any notion of the consistent unity of a text, affirming instead its necessary 'incompleteness and informity'.[37] Analysis, in this view, consists not in revelation but in the production, as an object of thought, of the discursive object in its internal *décalage*, this uneven textual network of forces 'corresponding' to the work without constituting its mere reflection.[38] Criticism devoted to the work's specious totality remains in this view mere interpretation, the rendition of a principle that would conjure the coherence of any such totality, the nominal identity of its unity, the reason underwriting its harmony.[39]

---

33   Macherey 2006, p. 158, translation modified.
34   Macherey 2006, p. 159, translation modified.
35   Montag 1999, p. 5.
36   Macherey 2006, p. 111.
37   Macherey 2006, p. 88, translation modified.
38   Macherey 2006, p. 89.
39   Macherey 2006, p. 170.

4   On the Inadequacy of the Structuralist Combinatory

These critiques of empiricism, hermeneutics, and totality necessarily culminate in Macherey's comprehensive rejection of the notion of structure as totality.[40] In *A Theory of Literary Production*, Macherey systematically deploys the critique of Claude Lévi-Strauss's structuralism that had been patiently elaborated in Althusser's seminar and subsequent exchanges between the two since 1961. Warren Montag has described in revelatory detail the complex articulations of this critique, in which, most notably, it is Macherey, Althusser's astonishingly precocious student, who identifies the contradictions in the master's presentation of the concept of structure in *Reading Capital*.[41]

Elements of this critique of structuralism were first elaborated in Althusser's 1962–63 seminar on structuralism (in which Macherey participated), and in Althusser's 1963 essay 'On the Materialist Dialectic: On the Unevenness of Origins', collected in *For Marx*; there then ensued an exchange of letters between Althusser and Macherey at the moment of the publication of the *Reading Capital* seminar in 1965 and again in 1966; and Althusser returned to the problem in his essay 'On Feuerbach' from 1967. As Montag shows, the results of this discussion, marked by Althusser's self-contradictions, flashes of insight, backtracking, and self-censorship, never amounts to a coherent, totalised presentation of its object. After tracing an unpredictably inflected 'prehistory' of structuralism, from Edmund Husserl and Wilhelm Dilthey through Georges Canguilhem, Tran Duc Thao, and Jacques Derrida, Montag focuses in particular on Althusser's twofold rejection of Lévi-Strauss's structuralist method, as simultaneously comprising a *transcendental idealism* and *empiricist functionalism*.

For Lévi-Strauss, Althusser argues in the 1962 seminar, the universal ban on incest identified by structural anthropology functions as a transhistorical, transcendental category that grounds human identity in its singular manifestations across time and space, determining the various possible kinship combinations (thus its description as a 'combinatory'), in which the system of all possible kinship structures remains ultimately grounded by 'the structure of the human mind'.[42] Through the manifold historical variations of this combinatory, humans produce social forms in exhaustive divergence, but in accord with a limiting structural determination of which they are unaware. This amounts to the imputation on Lévi-Strauss's part of a social unconscious, one that remains,

---

40   Macherey's critique of totality will prove essential in my critique of Chris Arthur's reading of *Capital* in the following chapter.
41   Montag 2013, Chapters 3–5.
42   Lévi-Strauss, cited in Montag 2013, p. 68.

in Althusser's biting critique, 'still a form of subjectivism that endows 'society' with the form of existence of a subject having intentions and objectives'.[43] This unconscious structure, hidden beneath the manifest content of social comportments, requires Lévi-Strauss to decode hermeneutically its form of constraint as the identity of infinite variation across time.

Structural anthropology thus manages to articulate a *transcendental idealism* – the hidden nature of which requires hermeneutical elaboration – to which Lévi-Strauss appends in uneasy tension an even less satisfactory *empiricist functionalism*. The latter, wholly inadequate, functionalist explanation of the role of kinship becomes necessary for Lévi-Strauss, Althusser observes, insofar as the transcendental structural combinatory can only identify the admissibility of any given kinship combination within the compass of an ungrounded series of otherwise arbitrary combinations. What the combinatory remains unable to explain is the causal *necessity* governing any specific instantiation, 'why', in Althusser's summary rejection, 'it is that this reality and no other has become and therefore is real'.[44] To address this problem, Lévi-Strauss merely appends to the combinatory model a weak functionalism, referring the variety of empirical kinship systems to the putative survival needs of any given empirical group.[45]

In contrast to the Spinozist imperative to explain ends always by their necessary causes, kinship structures are thus for Lévi-Strauss to be comprehended and justified by the ends they serve. Althusser summarily rejects such an imaginary explanation of the unconscious structuration of society as the mere imputation of a spurious intentionality to a subject: in this case, neither God nor Man, but instead Structure.[46] The problem structural anthropology remains unable to address is precisely that to which Spinoza's epistemological undertaking addresses its labours: to know adequately what constitutes the necessity

---

43   Cited in Montag 2013, p. 69.
44   Cited in Montag 2013, p. 68.
45   Montag 2013, p. 69.
46   In the famous appendix to *Ethics* I (a key text, moreover, for Althusser's appropriation of Spinoza), Spinoza's example of such faulty reasoning from empirical effect backward to an imaginary cause is that of a tile falling from a roof, which, in striking a passerby, is (necessarily but inadequately) attributed to a vindictive deity by the imagination of the observer of this empirical event. 'Nature', Spinoza trenchantly retorts, 'has no end prescribed to it [*naturam finem nullum sibi praefixum habere*] and all final causes are but figments of the human imagination .... The doctrine of final causes turns Nature completely upside down, for it regards as an effect that which is in fact a cause, and vice versa'. Spinoza, *Ethics* I, App., translation modified. See also Macherey's insightfully detailed explication of this passage in the final section of his analysis of *Ethics* I in *Introduction à l'Éthique de Spinoza. La première partie: La nature des choses* (1998, pp. 205–70).

governing any singular essence, without recourse to a transcendental formalism of the combinatory.

To adequately grasp the necessity governing a text thus constitutes the challenge Pierre Macherey puts to a rightly conceived theory of literary production. Althusser was never able to fully articulate a theory of structural causality, but instead only managed to address his own theoretical hesitations and inconsistencies regarding the concept through the mere suppression of problematic passages in the second, 1968 edition of *Reading Capital*, passages that Macherey had initially brought to Althusser's attention in their correspondence of 1965–66.[47] In contrast, *A Theory of Literary Production* articulates a systematic critique of the concept of structure: rather than merely rejecting the term outright, Macherey distinguishes inadequate conceptions of structure – dependent upon notions of coherency, totality, functionalism, depth, and hermeneutic translation – from its more adequate conceptualisation.

This more adequate understanding of structure is for Macherey to be indexified to (1) the Spinozist distinction between the work as an object of theoretical (structural) knowledge and that same work understood empirically, under the attribute of its material extension (as a tangible book one takes in hand to read); (2) the necessary affirmation of structure qualified as the infinite incompletion of any set without totality;[48] (3) adequate understanding of such a notion of structure without recourse to a hermeneutics of revelation, affirming instead the immanent materiality of the text in its manifest articulations; and consequently, (4) an unremitting faithfulness to writing, taken in its immediate, necessary *materiality*, irreducible to any inherent, hidden meaning or intention.

Such are the propositions Macherey deploys in his discussion of structure in *A Theory of Literary Production*. If the concept of structure allows for comprehension of the 'type of necessity from which the work derives', this necessity can refer neither to a unity derived from the putative productive intention of an author nor the formalist unification of the work via a transcendental theory of totality.[49] Structure is not to be discovered, as a bounded totality latent within

---

47 Montag 2013, Chapter 5.
48 In *Hegel or Spinoza*, Macherey cites Gilles Deleuze's lapidary formulation of this key proposition of a Spinozist materialist dialectic without totality: 'Nature as the production of the diverse can only be an infinite sum, that is, a sum that does not totalise its own elements'. Macherey 2011, p. 195, quoted in Montag 2013, p. 187. Althusser will in fact take on (without explicit attribution) Macherey's critique of the notion of totality in the 1976 *Essays in Self-Criticism*, where he writes that 'Spinoza served us as a (sometimes direct, sometimes very indirect) reference: in his effort to grasp ... a Whole without closure, which is only the active relation between its parts'. Quoted in Morfino 2015, p. 93n11.
49 Macherey 2006, pp. 45, 55, translation modified.

the hidden depths of the work, but is instead constituted in the very absence of a coherent totality of meaning, in the productive *décalage* and 'real complexity' of the constructed thought object.[50] Analysis – truly adequate, *materialist analysis* of an object of knowledge – can in this view only refer to 'the constitution of a structure', the interpretive act of structuration (*structurer*) as the demonstrative deployment of elements, a process that paradoxically constructs the object of knowledge in its infinite incompletion, as an 'absence' (of the whole).[51] Such an absence will attend to this incoherence, to the gaps and contradictions of a text, as what Althusser had famously termed in *Reading Capital* a 'symptomatic [*symptomale*] reading'.[52]

5   Toward a Materialist Analysis of Form

In his 2006 afterword to the fortieth anniversary edition of *A Theory of Literary Production*, Macherey distils the question that, in hindsight, compelled the book's original intervention in 1966: 'How was it possible to be simultaneously a materialist and a formalist?'[53] To this point, I have largely attended to this question, addressing the book's critiques of empiricism, hermeneutics, and totality, culminating in Macherey's critical diremption of inadequate from adequate notions of structure, while leaving what is for me a key, unaddressed problem of materialism itself in suspense.

It can seem immediately, intuitively obvious that Macherey, in accord with Althusser and his fellow Althusserian Étienne Balibar, practices a 'materialist' form of analysis (in a materialist way, as the title of the 1998 Verso collection of Macherey's essays puts it), and that, moreover, this practice is in some way consonant with that of those thinkers Macherey has repeatedly addressed, those whom Althusser called 'the only materialist tradition': Lucretius, Spinoza, and Marx.[54] To be sure, Althusser famously asserted that in the texts composing *Reading Capital*, if 'we were never structuralists', this is because 'we were Spinozists', and in fact he further specifies that this entailed rejecting the 'relation of adequacy between mind and thing, in the Aristotelean tradition'.[55] In

---

50   Macherey 2006, p. 114.
51   Macherey 2006, p. 168.
52   See RC, p. 26. See also Young 2017, pp. 35–48.
53   Macherey 2006, p. 362.
54   See Althusser 1997, pp. 3–20. Macherey notes the crucial influence of Lucretius in Spinoza's elaboration of the appendix to *Ethics I*. Macherey 1997, p. 238.
55   Althusser 1976, pp. 132, 137, quoted in Morfino 2015, pp. 2, 4.

the absence of a more explicit critique of the concept of materialist analysis, however (and this is even more the case for Althusser himself), we are left to construct such a concept from the diverse (Spinozist, Marxian) materials of Macherey's many analyses addressed to other, related problems.[56] What then is the relation between materialist critique, and the Althusserian proscription of monist material*ism* (described in the previous chapter), in which imputation of motive matter, as Althusser argues in his unpublished notes on a conversation with Stanislas Breton, constitutes one more form of transcendental idealism? More specifically, how are we to conceive a properly materialist analysis, given the various Althusserian proscriptions described above against empiricism, idealism, functionalism, the hermeneutics of depth, and totality, critiques that, as we have seen, Macherey wholly subscribes to and even further clarifies in *A Theory of Literary Production*?

6   Against Materialism, *en matérialiste*

Macherey will in fact address this problem in his 1981 essay '*En matérialiste*', to distinguish categorically between the process of materialist critique as the science of causes and all forms of materialism.[57] There he argues that all materialisms, including the Marxist construct 'dialectical materialism', are 'theories of matter' to be rejected as such in their inherent idealism (in positing matter as transcendent prime mover). Macherey does not argue this point in sustained fashion, but instead punctually invokes Engels's attempt to elaborate a 'general theory of movement', the failure of which ('this path led him nowhere, … abandoning it in incompletion') serves to indicate in abbreviated fashion the impossibility of a coherent doctrine of materialism: 'Engels's aborted attempt has produced an essential consequence: it is henceforth no longer possible to be *a* materialist'.[58]

---

56   In *La philosophie de Marx* (2014, p. 98), Étienne Balibar observes in passing that in the 1845 *Theses on Feuerbach*, 'Marx's materialism has nothing to do with a reference to matter [but is instead] a strange "materialism without matter"'. Alberto Toscano has extrapolated on Balibar's suggestive comment in relation to Sohn-Rethel and I.I. Rubin's analysis of the value form, proposing that Marx's subsequent analysis of the capitalist social form of value constitutes precisely such a materialism, one in which, as Marx famously comments in *Capital*, 'not an atom of matter enters into the objectivity of commodities as values'. Toscano 2014. See Marx 1976, p. 138.
57   Macherey 1999, pp. 87–113.
58   Macherey 1999, p. 88.

In place of any and all doctrines of materialism, Macherey asserts in contrast the necessity of a properly 'materialist dialectic, which must necessarily culminate in a refutation of materialism as such'.[59] Materialist critique, then, necessarily takes the form not of the positive doctrine representing the object of philosophy – since for Macherey like Althusser, philosophy has no preexisting object – but instead takes the form of an intervention within a field of thought; not a representation of reality, materialist critique constructs instead a critical orientation within the attribute of thought: 'Neither doctrine, theory, nor knowledge [savoir], but a mode of intervention, ... the philosophical field apprehended in the concrete complexity of its internal conflicts'. Materialist critique, in this view, is materialist in the sense of a real intervention, an 'objective practice of intervention' within the domain or attribute in which it operates.[60] Macherey draws the full implications of this materialist position, in which the critique of the real as a science of necessity that intervenes to displace and weaken the hold of ideology, given sufficient force, can serve to produce a new disposition of *potentia*. It necessarily enacts this operation within the attribute of thought, 'without having to find beyond itself [*au-dehors*] the instruments and criteria that could allow it to test [*éprouver*] and measure its power, its capacity effectively to act in the terrain of reality which it has never left'.[61]

7   Reading Capital as a Theory of Literary Production

In the wake of his key contribution to *Reading Capital*, Macherey has in his published work only occasionally returned to the analysis of Marx's magnum opus, most notably and extensively in the talk he gave on 13 July 1967, at Cérisy-la-Salle during the conference 'Le centenaire du *Capital*'.[62] Macherey's discussion of the object of analysis in *Capital* in both these texts (as is the case in *A Theory of Literary Production*) closely follows the series of imperatives first presented in *Reading Capital* and reiterated in *Theory*: Macherey argues that Marx's epis-

---

59   Macherey 1999, p. 88.
60   Macherey 1999, p. 89.
61   Macherey 1999, p. 96.
62   Macherey 2012. Macherey's 13 July talk was followed immediately by that of Étienne Balibar, titled 'La Science du "Capital"', both of which are immediately followed in the published version of the proceedings by some thirty pages of rich and often polemical discussion with the other members of the colloquium. Thanks to Étienne Balibar for calling my attention to this volume.

temological procedure in *Capital* constitutes the refusal of empiricism, idealism, hermeneutics, communication, genesis, and transcendental notions of totality.

To read *Capital* adequately, 'to escape from the empiricist myth of reading', requires, Macherey reiterates, a 'theoretical reading, constructing at each step its novelty, elaborating its principles. Reading so conceived is a theoretical practice: it produces in effect an effect [*en effet un effet*] of knowledge'.[63] The result of such a reading of *Capital* will be, he argues, an adequate understanding of the 'systematic' nature of Marx's work, an 'organisation that depends upon the laws of theoretical rigor'. That said, the rigorous theoretical organisation of *Capital* that Macherey identifies in this talk, as he had in his earlier chapter from *Reading Capital*, by no means implies that *Capital* forms a coherent totality; on the contrary, *Capital*, like the literary works that constituted the object of *Theory*, is subject to 'a strict incompletion [*inachèvement*]', an incompletion that calls upon its reader to 'develop the logic proper to' *Capital*.[64] Macherey's critique of the notion of totality in *Capital* is uncompromising: 'We can even say', Macherey continues, 'that the enterprise of a total or 'totalising' reading is ideological in its essence: it lies at the root [*au principe*] of all revisionisms, which are absolute by vocation .... A scientific text can only be taken up on the condition of being continued: a closed, repetitive reading is itself an ideological reading'.[65] Macherey then continues in this vein to reiterate various subsidiary themes from *Theory of Literary Production*, here applied to the reading of *Capital*, including the critique of all *commentary*, and the mere aesthetic delectation of texts.[66]

As Althusser had before him in the passages of *Reading Capital* discussed above, Macherey reiterates the constructed, nonempiricist nature of the object of thought.[67] Macherey furthermore rigorously adheres to Althusser's primary distinction between the constructed object of analysis (Marx's *Gedankenkonkretum*) and reference to the 'real', substantial order of being. It is in this sense then that Macherey will assert that 'the real [*le réel*] subsists outside of thought and preexists it. This difference between the real and the thought [*le pensé*] must be understood so as to avoid expression in a new form of

---

63 Macherey 2012, p. 54.
64 Macherey 2012, p. 55.
65 Macherey 2012, pp. 57, 61.
66 Macherey 2012, p. 60.
67 'Scientific discourse has been produced as a new reality .... Knowledge is a reflection only of itself'. Macherey 2012, p. 61.

empiricism that would conclude that thought is the emanation or mechanical reproduction of the real'.[68]

While this last point constitutes a further reiteration of the anti-empiricism of *Theory of Literary Production* and *Reading Capital*, Macherey suddenly injects a properly Spinozist clarification of this critique, a point crucially missing, I argued in the previous chapter, from Althusser's dualist presentation in *Reading Capital*. Not only must an adequate reading of *Capital* reject all empiricism, Macherey reminds his listeners in terms that echo those of the 1965 essay 'A propos de la rupture' cited above, now addressed explicitly to *Capital* itself: it must further refuse all forms of neo-Cartesian dualism, drawn between thought and a material order of extension in the sense of two distinct substances: 'Nor can it [scientific discourse] constitute a dualism in which thought is exterior to the real, such that it would be necessary to think the coexistence of two independent orders'.

At the same time, it (scientific discourse) must bear some clear distinction from the material order. If 'science is the science of the real', it involves no mere 'transposition' or elaboration of a reflective, 'allegorical object'. Science involves 'the institution of another form of reality. It is the production of a new real that is the thought real [*le réel pensé*] ... The thought real is not the real considered from another point of view, the interpreted real; *it is the real transformed*'.[69] While Macherey here reiterates Spinoza's distinction between the real and the idea of the real, the terms of Macherey's rejection of Cartesian dualism already point forward to his further discussion of Spinoza's concept of the attributes in *Hegel or Spinoza*, along with its further development and interpretation in his systematic and powerful critique of so-called parallelism and the proper understanding of the famous proposition 7 of *Ethics* II, 'The order and connection of ideas is the same thing as the order and connection of things' (*Ordo et connexio idearum idem est, ac ordo, et connexio rerum*).

---

68   Macherey 2012, p. 55.
69   Macherey 2012, p. 64. my emphasis. Macherey is emphatic in his elaboration of this point in the ensuing discussion: 'A science is defined by an object that is constructed according to a definition – not [empirically] by an object given by reality [*la réalité*] – and by functional rules .... The object of *Capital* is an object constructed theoretically, and this is precisely why *Capital* is not a formal system. If we were to read it as a closed system, this would constitute an interpretive reading, a repetition and reprisal of a completed system .... Marx did not record [in *Capital*] the theoretical results spontaneously issued from a historical "experience"' (Macherey 2012, pp. 92, 93).

8 Materialism in a Spinozist Way

The initial Althusserian formulation of a materialist dialectic lies, I wish to argue, immediately at hand in the texts of esoteric texts of high 'Althusserianism' of 1965–67: the 'Notes on Discourse' (discussed in the previous chapter), and Macherey's lesser-known 'A propos de la rupture' and 'Lire *Le capital*'.[70] In essence, and to reiterate and further develop the position of the previous chapter, this is to claim that Althusser's famous general proposition in *Reading Capital* on the subterranean Spinozism of philosophy (Spinoza's 'radical revolution was the object of a massive historical repression. ... The history of philosophy's repressed Spinozism thus unfolded as a subterranean history') holds true for Althusserian epistemology itself, in which Spinozist thought functions as an occasionally acknowledged but never adequately explicated theoretical foundation.

In the wake of their combined Spinozist critiques of the subject-object logic of empiricism, of expressive totality, and of the functionalist combinatory of structuralism, for Althusser, Macherey, and Balibar and in contrast to the imprecision of many Hegelian readers of *Capital*, in the Spinozist epistemology that avowedly underlies their various analyses of *Capital*, there is in fact no substantial distinction to be made between the constructed, a posteriori 'object' of materialist analysis and that of analysis itself.[71]

---

70   Under this category of high Althusserianism I would include not only the published volumes *For Marx*, *Reading Capital*, *A Theory of Literary Production*, and Macherey and Balibar's contributions to the Cérisy colloquium '*Le centennaire du Capital*', but also the various exchanges of the Groupe Spinoza and related texts such as Althusser's 1966 'Sur Lévi-Strauss' in Althusser 1994. On the Groupe Spinoza, Alain Badiou has reflected: 'The Groupe Spinoza was a group composed by Althusser, with some friends of Althusser, all reading *Capital* practically, engaged in the project to write a sort of synthesis of our epistemological convictions. The idea was to produce a fundamental book concerning theory: concerning what theory is, what constitutes an epistemological rupture and so on; to propose something like an educational book concerning all these sorts of themes. All that was destroyed by 1968 and, after that, by very strong political differences and struggles'. Badiou 2017, p. 25.

71   As Althusser famously wrote in the 1972 *Essays in Self-Criticism*, 'If we were never structuralists, we can now explain why: ... we were guilty of an equally powerful and compromising passion: *we were Spinozists* [nous avons été spinozistes]'. Quoted in Morfino 2015, p. 2. Vittorio Morfino points to the decisive influence Spinoza brought to bear on Althusser's 1965 reading of *Capital*: 'The reference to Spinoza ... is fundamental with respect to three decisive questions in the Althusserian re-reading of Marxism: the process of knowledge, structural causality, and ideology'. Morfino 2015, pp. 2–3. For an outstanding, often critical and always informative recent example of the ongoing effort to read *Capital* as a palimpsest of Hegel's *Logic*, see Moseley and Smith 2015.

The pseudo-problem of an object that materialist analysis would represent is an inadequate, imaginary fabulation, once one accepts instead that substance is indivisible, that the infinite attributes constitute, immediately, the expression of substance and its infinite modes as the determinations of those attributes, and that, above all, the order of ideas is *one and the same thing* as the order of things ('Ordo, et connexio idearum idem est, ac ordo, et connexio rerum'). To conceive of materialist analysis in terms of a substantial distinction and representational correlation between analysis and its object is, from a Spinozist perspective, inadmissible; it is to reintroduce precisely the Cartesian dualism of substances (between extension and the intellect) that Spinoza systematically criticises.

Judging by his powerful (private) critiques of Althusser's presentation of the concept of structural causality in the first edition of *Reading Capital*, Macherey seems to have developed a reading of Spinoza even more rigorous and systematic than Althusser's by 1965 at the latest, a reading that clearly determines the theoretical propositions of *A Theory of Literary Production*.[72] It is only in his writings since *Hegel or Spinoza*, however, that Macherey has fully explicated the interpretation of Spinoza that can retrospectively be said to determine the epistemology of the high-Althusserian texts of 1965–67. In *Hegel or Spinoza*, and above all in the second volume of his explication of the *Ethics*, Macherey reads Spinoza's demonstration of the formal structure or order of the attributes to constitute the singular essence of a materialist critique of the real.

Rejecting point by point the Hegelian misreading of Spinoza in *Hegel or Spinoza*, Macherey affirms that, for Spinoza, the following propositions hold true:

1) The (infinite) attributes of substance cannot consist in a linear and countable or ordinal sequence (i.e., the attribute of thought, plus the attribute of extension, plus all the other infinite attributes). 'The unity of substance is thus not an arithmetic unity ..., an empty form of the One .... It is this infinitely diverse reality that comprises all its attributes and that expresses itself in their infinity .... One can no more count substance than one can count its attributes, at least if one renounces the point of view of imagination .... To say that there is a single substance is to speak from the imagination that can only consider the absolute negatively, from nothingness, that is, from the part of the possible, which it envelops'.[73]

---

72 Montag 2013, Chapter 5.
73 Macherey 2011, pp. 99, 104.

2) That the attributes do not coexist in ordinal relation implies in turn that they do not consist of elements defining one another as a totality through their negative relation. 'If all the attributes together belong to substance, constituting its being,[74] they do not coexist within it as parts that would adjust to each other to finally compose the total system. If this were so, the attributes would define themselves in relation to each other through their reciprocal lack'.[75]

3) This further implies that substance itself cannot be divided up into its various (infinite) attributes, but is instead indivisible. 'To think the infinite, whether it be in the attribute (in a kind) or in substance (absolutely), is to exclude any notion of divisibility; substance is entirely complete in each of its attributes (because it is identical to them), just as, moreover, all extension is in each drop of water or all thought is in each idea .... The infinite is not a number; this is why it evades all division. Indivisible substance is not the sum of all its attributes'.[76]

From these propositions Macherey then concludes that the relation of the attributes is one of unitary (rather than comparative, negative) identity: 'As an attribute of substance, thought is *identical* to everything and therefore has nothing above it, but the sequence through which it is realised poses, at the same time, its absolute equality with all other forms in which substance is also expressed, and these are infinite in number'.[77]

We then come to what must count among Macherey's most radical interventions in the field of thought, his seemingly scholastic reading of Spinoza's proposition EIIP7. The so-called parallelism of the attributes (a term that Spinoza never uses in any of his writings, and which Macherey attributes to Leibniz), Macherey shows conclusively, is quite simply 'inadmissible'. This must be the case, Macherey argues, if one reads the wording of proposition EII7 attentively: in the statement '*Ordo et connexio idearum idem est, ac ordo, et connexio rerum*', Spinoza identifies the order and connection of ideas as not the same as the order of physical *bodies in extension*, but rather the same as that of '*things*' (*rerum*), of all things without distinction, including, of course, ideas themselves: 'The word *things* [*res*] absolutely does not, in a restrictive way, designate the modes of the attribute of extension, but the modes of all the attributes, whatever they are, *including thought itself* .... This is one and the same order, one and the same connection'.[78]

---

74 E1P10S.
75 Macherey 2011, p. 100.
76 Ibid.
77 Macherey 2011, p. 74.
78 Macherey 2011, p. 106, emphasis in original.

Macherey will subsequently, in his magisterial explication of Book II of the *Ethics*, further develop and refine this absolutely decisive critique of the notion of 'parallelism', to affirm in its place the more adequate understanding of the relation of the order of the attributes as a complex unity.[79] To do so, Macherey first repeats his assertion from *Hegel or Spinoza* summarised above, to the effect that Ethics IIP7 must refer to the substantial *coherence* (as opposed to a parallel identity) of the order of ideas and the order of things, further specifying this assertion, based first on grammatical and then apodictic determinations.

Grammatically, in the phrase 'Ordo et connexio idearum idem est, ac ordo, et connexio rerum', the masculine/neutral adjective *idem* cannot be argued to apply to the feminine *connexio*. The phrase 'is the same as' (*idem est ac*) therefore cannot be said to apply to a ('parallel') relation *between* two 'independent sets [*ensembles*]', but instead qualifies *a single substantial order as identical to itself*. From this, Macherey concludes that the proper translation of Spinoza's proposition should be 'The order and connection of ideas *is the same thing as* the order and connection of things'.[80]

This assertion finds its immediate confirmation in the demonstration of proposition 7, which points to its axiomatic basis in the initial axiom 4 of *de Deo*, the meaning of which is eminently clear: ideas are subject to a single, identical order that holds for all things.[81] In sum, Macherey concludes,

> Proposition 7 of *de Mente* does not affirm the extrinsic identity between two systems of order and connection facing each other, one of which would be the order of ideas and the other that of things bestowing on these ideas their objects, these things being themselves identified unilaterally as bodies. Instead, proposition 7 proposes that the order and connection inheres in its proper, intrinsic constitution to that by which all things in general are governed [*soumises*], and from which nothing distinguishes it.[82]

---

79 Macherey 1997, pp. 71–81. I insist on this development in Macherey's 1997 volume, which as of this writing is, like the other four volumes in the series, unavailable in English translation. Not only does it constitute the most developed explication of Macherey's substantialist, Spinozist materialist critique, but, moreover, the 400-plus pages of this crucial second volume of his explication are currently out of print even in the French original. All translations from this volume are mine.

80 Macherey 1997, p. 71. Macherey's analysis of this famous proposition of the *Ethics* strongly resonates with that of Martial Gueroult. See Peden 2014, p. 158.

81 Macherey 1997, p. 72.

82 Macherey 1997, p. 73.

For Spinoza, in Macherey's reading, the order of causality of ideas is literally 'the same thing' as the order and causality of all things, including ideas; there is, in other words, only one order and causality of things, which can be *differentially* apprehended through an infinite number of attributes, insofar as those attributes are in fact *different* means by 'which the intellect perceives substance' (though humans only have access to two, thought and extension).[83] To argue otherwise in the sense of a 'parallelism', Macherey insists, would be to reinstate a Cartesian dualism of thought and extension taken as distinct substances (precisely as Althusser had done in *Reading Capital* via the imperfect distinction between thought and the real): 'The 'parallelist' reading of proposition 7 reinscribes the Spinozist doctrine in a dualist perspective, explaining all of nature through the relation of extended substance and thought substance'.[84]

9 On Telling Stories

In contrast to Macherey's minute attention to the letter of Spinoza's text, Althusser offers little concrete analysis of Spinoza's formulations, but instead proposes at various moments a number of laconic, even enigmatic, one-line definitions of materialism.[85] It is thus possible to orchestrate, in counterpoint to Macherey's attention to Spinoza's demonstrations, the suggestive promise of Althusser's allusive materialist critique. It would take a volume in itself to address Althusser's various reiterations and critiques of the related problems of historical and dialectical materialism, of the materialist turns in Marx's philosophy, of the relation of materials of production to the capitalist mode of production, and the like. The 'aleatory materialism' of Althusser's final period poses similarly complex problems of interpretation beyond the scope of this chapter, which we might sum up in saying that in turning to Lucretius and Democritus in his now-famous 1982 essay, Althusser distances himself on crucial points from the Spinozist materialism of the 1960s and 70s with which I am here

---

83 EID4. Read 2007, p. 511.
84 Macherey continues to drive his grammatical point home: 'For this [parallelist] reading to be possible would require that, in the enunciation of the proposition, not only would the neutral singular *idem* [thing] have to be replaced by the masculine plural *iidem sunt*, but also that the term *corporum* [bodies] be implicitly substituted for the term *rerum*'. Macherey 1997, p. 72.
85 As Vittorio Morfino notes, 'The works published in [Althusser's] lifetime include only a handful of brief references to Spinoza – none longer than a paragraph. And neither his extensive posthumous work nor his archived writings [with two exceptions Morfino notes] contain texts dedicated to Spinoza'. Morfino 2022, p. 82.

concerned, and even more decisively from Macherey's categorical rejection of all doctrines of materialism and corresponding attention to the explication of Spinozist text as a materialist critique.[86]

Leaving aside the circularity of the definition Althusser offers in lecture 3 of *Philosophy and the Spontaneous Philosophy of the Scientists* (the 'materialist character' of science is characterised, as to its object, by 'an external object with a material existence') along with other definitions that merely equate materialism with an adequate scientific practice,[87] in *The Future Lasts Forever*, Althusser offers the following definition of materialism: '"Not to indulge in storytelling" still remains for me the one and only definition of materialism'.[88] Though Althusser makes no mention of Spinoza in this passage, 'to resort to mere sto-

---

[86] One striking example of this incongruity is Althusser's assertion in 'The Underground Current of the Materialism of the Encounter' (1982) that 'for Spinoza, the object of philosophy is the void'. This is not simply a 'paradoxical thesis', as Althusser observes; it is quite simply antithetical to Spinoza's explicit and extensive critique of the concept of the void in Book I of the *Ethics*. The free-floating associations of Althusser's argument culminate weakly in the metaphorical (rather than ontological) conclusion that Spinoza asserted '*the void that is philosophy itself*'. Althusser 2006, p. 178, italics in original. In fact, Macherey shows that Spinoza, reaffirming Descartes's critique, decisively rejects the atomism of the Ancients as fully inadequate, imaginary representation, to explicitly affirm instead that 'matter is everywhere the same [*materia ubique eadem est*] in its substantial principle'. Macherey 1998, p. 124. 'Corporeal substance', Spinoza writes unambiguously, 'can be conceived only as infinite, one, and indivisible' (41 EIP15Sch). Macherey consequently reads these passages in proposition 15 of Book I and its Scholium as 'the affirmation of a plenitude [of substance] leaving no place for void, absence, or negativity .... Substance is thought reality in the intense intimacy of its self-relation ... such that nothing else, not even nothingness ... can disturb its infinite positivity .... To conceive of extension as constituted of distinct parts is to deny its infinity'. In contrast to the Ancients' imaginary depiction of atoms in a void, 'only the intellect', Macherey concludes, 'is apt [*en mesure*] to understand that the materiality of extended substance is given at once as an indivisible totality'. Macherey 1998, pp. 128, 129. Althusser's related, imagistic redeployment of the thesis of the parallelism of the attributes in 'Materialism of the Encounter' – which Althusser claims 'fall in the empty space of their determination' (Althusser 2006, p. 177) – repeats the philosophical commonplace of so-called parallelism that Macherey subjects to such extensive and compelling critique in both *Hegel or Spinoza* (ch. 3) and his analysis of proposition 7 of *Ethics II*, discussed above.

[87] Althusser 1990, p. 135. In *Reading Capital*, following Lenin, Althusser affirms that 'In the expression "historical materialism", "materialism" means no more than science, and the expression is strictly synonymous with that of "science of history"' (RC, p. 360). Althusser will reiterate this definition, for example in 'Lenin and Philosophy': 'Historical materialism thus means: science of history', and again, in modified form, in 'Lenin before Hegel', where he refers to 'the materialist thesis of the material existence and of the objectivity of scientific knowledge'. Althusser 2001, pp. 23, 83.

[88] Althusser 1993b, p. 221.

rytelling' neatly encapsulates the principal assertion of Spinoza's appendix to *Ethics 1*, upon which many of the arguments of this book are grounded: that reasoning inadequately from effects to causes is the basis of imaginary, ideological thinking. Materialism, in contrast, would thus implicitly seek always to argue from the adequate understanding of causes to the effects they produce.

In his 1985 text 'The Only Materialist Tradition', Althusser proposes another enigmatic yet even more auspicious definition of materialism: 'Nominalism is not the royal road to materialism but *the only possible materialism*'.[89] Here again, it lies far beyond the scope of this chapter to distinguish Althusser's flat assertion that nominalism is 'the only possible materialism' from the innumerable accreted historical senses of nominalism, from the diverse critiques of universals and abstract objects as well as corresponding assertions of the reality of particular objects and of concrete objects. Instead, I propose merely to summarise the Spinozist construct Althusser's assertion is meant to encapsulate.

In the third section of 'The Only Materialist Tradition', in which this definition of materialism appears, Althusser – in the course of a broad reflection on the centrality of Spinoza to his thinking – turns to his interpretation of Spinoza's third genre (*genus*) of knowledge, the 'intuitive science [*scientiam intiutivam*]' that Spinoza characterises as 'the adequate knowledge of the essence of things [*adaequatam cognitionem essentiae rerum*]'.[90] In Althusser's usage in this passage, the term 'nominalisms' (in the plural) refers precisely to such singular essences of things, things comprehended as 'singularities'. Such singularities are to be distinguished from Spinoza's second genre of mere common or abstract universal notions (*notiones communes*), such as motion and rest taken as universal characteristics of all bodies in extension; these are explicitly, for Althusser, 'generic and not "general" constants'. In Althusser's reading, Spinoza's invention of an adequate materialist ('nominalist') knowledge is thus held to encompass his discovery of 'generic constants or invariants ... which arise in the existence of singular "cases"'. Equally, it is their genericity as constants of any singular case that allows for what Althusser revealingly calls, in clinical terms with psychoanalytic resonance, their 'treatment', as distinct from any empirical or experimental verification.[91]

---

89 Althusser 1997b, p. 10.
90 EIIP40S2.
91 The constants diagnosed in any singularity 'do not constitute the object of a will to *verification* in an abstract renewable experimental *dispositive*, as in physics or chemistry, but whose repetitive insistence permits us to mark the form of singularity in presence and, therefore, its treatment'. Althusser 1997b, p. 8.

If a common notion or *law* would constitute an abstract or general universal, the *constant* arising in a given instance (a symptom in the analysand or patient, for example) allows for the adequate analysis and treatment of that case in its 'nominalist' singularity: no universal treatment is proper for the singularity of every case, and yet the analyst must construct an adequate knowledge of its causes and not be misled by mere surface impressions (the manifest content of the dream, say, or the visibility of bodily symptoms) that threaten to be inadequately attributed to imaginary causes. Such attention to *constants*, moreover, holds in Althusser's view for any singular being, for example a people (the Jews, in Spinoza's analysis in the *Tractatus Theologico-Politicus*) or what Althusser calls a 'social singularity' (the critique of the capitalist social form in Marx, or political revolution for Lenin).[92]

Following this elaboration, along with a brief excursus on the TTP and Spinoza's 'philosophical strategy' of 'taking over the chief stronghold of the adversary',[93] Althusser then concludes his presentation with the affirmation of Spinoza's materialist 'nominalism' quoted above. The attribute 'nominalist' thus redeploys the critique of transcendentals that Althusser and Macherey had articulated in their parsing of Lévi-Strauss's structuralism in the 1960s, discussed above: 'Without ever sketching a transcendental genesis of meaning, truth, or the conditions of possibility of every truth, ... [Spinoza] established himself within the factuality of a simple claim: "We have a true idea"'.[94] The 'nominalist' materialist thus passes beyond the universal generality of common notions, of transcendental guarantees (such as Lévi-Strauss's kinship order or discourse in Gilles Deleuze's problematic definition of structuralism) to articulate instead the generic necessity determining any singular essence.[95]

This final step then brings Althusser to define, in eminently clear and distinct terms, the fundamental Spinozist proposition that should be seen retrospectively to constitute the essential order of Althusser and Macherey's epistemology in their works from 1965–67: 'This *factual nominalism* was rediscovered – and with what genius! – in the famous distinction ... between the *ideatum* and the *idea*, between the thing and its concept, between the dog that barks and the concept of the dog, which does not bark, between the circle that is round, and the idea of the circle, which is not round, and so on'.[96]

---

92 Ibid.
93 Althusser 1997b, p. 10.
94 Althusser 1997b, pp. 10–11.
95 On Althusser and Macherey's critique of Deleuze's famous text, see Montag 2013, pp. 96–100.
96 Althusser 1997b, p. 11.

What Althusser names his 'nominalist' materialism in this late, 1985 text might indeed be more properly termed an *axiomatic, substantialist materialist critique*. For the proposition that the order of ideas and of things is the same thing is indeed an axiomatic proposition for Spinoza: its ground lies not in the apodictic, synthetic demonstration of proposition 7 in *Ethics* II, but instead in the initial axiomatic foundation of Spinoza's entire system. It is in precisely this sense that proposition EII7 explicitly refers the reader back to *Ethics* I, axiom 4.

It is axioms 4, 5, and 6 of *Ethics* I that together constitute the fundamental epistemological order of an inherent, necessary identity between the two orders or attributes of thought and extension. While axioms 3–5 of *Ethics* I affirm the necessary structure of causality under both the attributes of extension and the intellect, it is axiom 6 that draws these together to affirm that the true idea 'must be in conformity with its ideate [*debet cum suo ideato convenire*]'.[97] Macherey's interpretation of this key axiom bears citing in whole, as it is this statement that arguably should be taken to summarise the entire epistemological apparatus of Althusser's and Macherey's thought:

> This axiom [EIAx6] takes up in a new perspective the general teaching [*enseignement*] from the initial definitions and axioms [of *Ethics* I]: as the thing is, so it is conceived, as well as the inverse: as the thing is conceived, insofar as this is a true knowledge, so it is, necessarily. For every idea in the intellect, insofar as it is true, that is to say, ... well formed – since all ideas are true in the intellect that understands them, and at the same moment relates them to the ideate to which they are in a relation of conformity – there necessarily corresponds a content given in reality.[98]

This position founds for Macherey a substance-based materialist critique, in which the 'real' – an indeterminate, reflexively deployed category in Althusser's contribution to *Reading Capital*[99] – stands plainly revealed in Macherey's explication as neither mere sensuous materia*lity* (empiricist, imagination-based materia*lism*) nor transcendentally finite totality (idealism); materialist critique as the science of necessity constructs, in the attribute of thought, substance itself, the infinite dynamic of the *causa sui* as 'the process within which substance determines itself through the "essences" that constitute it'.[100] This substance-based materialist critique affirms that

---

97   EIAx6.
98   Macherey 1998, p. 61, my translation.
99   RC, p. 41.
100 Macherey 2012, p. 91.

thought reality and extended reality coincide in the absolute being of substance, where they are only distinguished by the intellect. ... There is just as much materiality, no more nor less, in reality envisaged from the perspective [*angle*] of the mental as when envisaged from the perspective of the bodily. ... Mental reality is a reality unto itself [*une réalité à part entière*], whose elements, ideas, are materially existing things, no less consistent, in their own order, than those that materially compose extended nature.[101]

10 The Persistent Problem of the Attributes

I have dwelled on Macherey's critique of the so-called 'parallelism' of the attributes in part because what Macherey calls the 'problem of the attributes' is perhaps as actual as ever. In a recent text on 'The Althusserian Definition of Theory', Alain Badiou identifies in Althusser's 'Introduction' to *Reading Capital* what he, Badiou, reads as an explicit reference to, and *rejection* by Althusser of a Spinozist 'parallelism' inhering between the thought-concrete [*Gedankenkonkretum*] and the real.[102] Jean Matthys has made the same claim – i.e., that 'Althusser goes so far as to oppose a central point of Spinozist doctrine: the 'parallelism' of the attributes' – arguing that this so-called 'parallelism', this supposedly 'central point' of Spinoza's thought which is claimed by Matthys to lie 'at the heart of the entire Spinozist doctrine', despite being a term he never uses (it being the invention of Leibniz), constitutes a 'resurgence of an idealist tendency in Spinoza'. This is the case, Matthys argues, insofar as the concept of the unity of substance, what Matthys calls 'this monism' (and 'parallelism' is indeed a monist concept), stands as the *guarantee* that assures the identity of the order and connection of the attributes.[103] I wish to argue, against both Badiou and Matthys, that when carefully read, Althusser's claim ('The production process of the object of knowledge takes place entirely in knowledge and is carried out according to a different order, in which the thought categories which 'reproduce' the real categories do not occupy the same place as they do in the order of real historical genesis')[104] is an eminently Spinozist position, one that implies not a rejection of Spinoza, but its clarification, as a theory of finite, contingent structural causality without a priori ontological guarantee.

---

101 Macherey 1997, p. 5.
102 Badiou 2017, pp. 21–34.
103 Matthys 2023, pp. 281–4.
104 RC, p. 41.

Initially, Badiou flatly and problematically affirms the identity of the Althusserian 'real' with Spinoza's substance: Althusser's is for Badiou 'a Spinozist vision' in which 'we have the real ... understood as the Spinozist substance, that is, the totality of what exists'. This seems a blatant misreading of both Spinoza and Althusser. There are in any world both actually existing singular things and nonexistent things (such as eternal, atemporal ideas), a distinction Spinoza clearly develops in Propositions 8 and 9 of *Ethics* II. Althusser's 'real', absent any definition, I am arguing, indicates not merely Badiou's 'totality of what *exists*' but the set of all things, existent and nonexistent, in a given world. To equate Spinoza's substance, however, with 'the totality of what exists' makes even less sense, since Spinoza defines substance not as an actually existing thing or even all things, but only as 'that which is in itself and is conceived through itself'; Althusser himself avoids the term 'substance', given the term's reifying, monist implication as an emanant source and guarantee of the order of being, and refers in its place only to 'structural causality'.

Immediately following this statement, moreover, Badiou appears to relapse into the very Hegelian dualist misreading of Spinoza that Macherey criticises in *Hegel or Spinoza*, referring not to an infinity of attributes in the Spinozist system, but only two: 'There exist two attributes within the totality: thinking and what is not thinking', which, in Althusser's case, Badiou figures as 'the knowledge-object, completely inside thinking, and the real-object, completely inside the real'. Badiou, as did Hegel, thus reverts to the Cartesian dualism that Spinoza was at such pains to reject.[105] Badiou immediately disqualifies this dualist position, however, asserting that these two attributes are in fact for Althusser 'not the reproduction of a metaphysical dualism, but simply two attributes of the same generality ... the expression of the same order'.[106] Badiou nonetheless seeks to make a distinction between Althusser and Spinoza, where none in fact exists: 'For Althusser [unlike Badiou's Spinoza,

---

105 In *The Lectures on the Philosophy of History*, Hegel, to ground his accusation of Cartesianism in the Spinozist system, voices an astounding misrepresentation. Here is Hegel: 'Spinoza's philosophy is the objectification of that of Descartes, in the form of absolute truth. The elemental thought of Spinoza's idealism is this. What is true is quite simply the one substance, whose attributes are thought and extension. ... What comes second after substance is the attributes. ... Substance has only two attributes, Thought and Extension' (Hegel, cited in Macherey 2011, pp. 82–3). Even the most casual reader of Spinoza must be shocked at this extraordinary omission by close readers such as Hegel and Badiou, since Spinoza affirms unambiguously and repeatedly that substance is comprised not of two but of an infinity of attributes (EIP11), of which humans perceive only two, thought and extension.

106 Badiou 2017, p. 32.

the reader is led to assume], there is no isomorphism, no parallelism, no relationship point by point between the two [attributes]'.[107] The problem here is double: Badiou wrongly adheres to the philosophical commonplace of Spinozist 'parallelism' of the attributes, and thus misinterprets Althusser's real and explicit rejection of parallelism as a rejection of Spinozism. This stands in contrast to Macherey's immanent and more authoritative reading, which rejects the commonplace of Spinozist 'parallelism' as both a literal misreading of Spinoza's text and the extraneous attribution of a term and concept, parallelism, that Spinoza himself never uses.[108]

Badiou's text thus becomes problematic in its specious *distinction* between Spinoza's solution to the relation of the attributes and that of Althusser in *Reading Capital*. Here is Badiou: '[For Spinoza] there is no difference [between the attributes], in some sense; they belong to the same order, but the same order is expressed, is symbolised in two different forms. So there is no real problem of the relationship between the idea and the thing: the idea and the thing are in the same general order'. The confusion thus arises from Badiou's assertion that Althusser refuses the 'Spinozist' solution of 'parallelism'.[109]

Badiou bases this claim for Althusser's rejection of 'parallelism' on a specific passage in *Reading Capital*, a passage Badiou cites with introjected commentary and in ellipsis: 'The production process of the object of knowledge takes place entirely in knowledge [and so, Badiou interjects, completely within thinking] and is *carried out according to a different order ... which is different from the real order of real genesis* [... that organises] the process of production of a given real object'.[110] This is a passage that comprises, Badiou affirms, 'a categorical refusal of the Spinozist solution in which the two attributes are attributes of the same order'.[111]

In Badiou's reading of Althusser, the latter rejects the Spinozist substantial identity of the order of the attributes: 'For Spinoza, this problem does not exist ... because there is in fact no relationship between the two, because they are of the same substance. But, for Althusser, the order is not the same, so there is

---

107 Ibid.
108 This is the case, with even less ambiguity, in the more recent *Immanance des vérités*: 'Pour Spinoza, ... les relations de causalité entre les choses matérielles immanentes à l'attribut étendue sont identiques – isomorphes – aux relations de causalité entre les choses idéelles immanentes à l'attribut pensée. ... On voit bien qu'ici la structure des attributs est ce qui atteste, par isomorphie, l'identité invariable et suprême de la Substance.' Badiou 2018b, p. 377.
109 Badiou 2017, p. 32.
110 Badiou 2017, p. 41, my emphasis.
111 Badiou 2017, p. 33.

in fact a real difficulty'.[112] Here the real question is whether or not for Spinoza, like Althusser, the 'order' of the attributes is nonidentical. Rather than pursuing an immanent critique of Spinoza's text,[113] Badiou's *deus ex machina* solution to this putative problem is surprising, to say the least: 'It is a difficulty, the solution of which is for Kant "schematism", ... precisely the mechanism by which the formal organisation of the categories of knowledge are related to the external existence, which we cannot know, of the world'.[114] Badiou proceeds to suggest an awkward admixture of Spinoza and Kant in his reading of Althusser to resolve a (nonexistent) problem: 'a mixture of the immanent Spinozist vision of two attributes of the same real with this Kantian schematism. There is only one real: it is not an ontological dualism, but instead we find two attributes of the same substance but without parallelism, without identity of the order'.[115]

What Badiou here speciously presents as Althusser's rejection of Spinoza's 'parallelist' position ('we find two attributes of the same substance but without parallelism, without identity of the order') is precisely that which Macherey's literal, grammatical reading of EIIP7 has shown to be its actual proposition: the attributes are not to be reified any more than substance. They are not two *things* that can be compared point by point for their isomorphism, but are 'that which the intellect perceives' of substance (causality), remaining purely and eternally heterogeneous: the concept of a circle is not round. How a neo-Kantian schematism would mediate 'two attributes of the same substance but without parallelism' remains unclear in this brief, ambiguous closing section of Badiou's (oral) text.[116] What is immediately striking, however, is that Badiou, in spontaneously reverting to a dualist understanding of the Spinozist attributes, suddenly requires a Kantian solution to a problem (the 'parallelist' dualism of the attributes) that Spinoza himself has criticised and superseded. The 'materialist schematism' that Badiou calls for is already rendered superfluous by Spinoza's own understanding of the attributes.

Analogous to his argument that Spinoza has already pre-empted Hegel's various critiques, Macherey himself appears already to have anticipated Badiou's recourse to Kant in *Hegel or Spinoza*. 'Through his critique of Cartesianism', Macherey writes in *Hegel or Spinoza*, 'Spinoza invalidates, in advance, a Kantian type of problematic of knowledge, posed in terms of the relationship of

---

112 Ibid.
113 EIIP7.
114 Badiou 2017, p. 33.
115 Ibid.
116 The text originates from a talk Badiou presented at Princeton University, 6 December 2013, at the conference '*Reading Capital* Today'.

subject and object or form and content', precisely the binary relationship that it is the conceptual mission of Kantian 'schematism' to mediate.[117] Badiou's importation of the Kantian schemata as *deus ex machina* in fact reintroduces the Cartesian dualism of subject and object – what Althusser had provocatively termed 'the latent dogmatic empiricism of Cartesian idealism' – that Spinoza's thought renders inoperative.[118]

Badiou takes Althusser at his word ('The production process of the object of knowledge takes place entirely in knowledge [... an order] which is different from the real order of real genesis') without questioning what the phrase 'the real order of real genesis' might mean. Judging from his initial claim (i.e., that Althusser's 'real [indicates] the Spinozist substance, that is, the totality of what exists'), Badiou appears to assume that for Althusser the *order of the real* indicates not the intellect's apprehension of things via the attribute of sensuous, temporal extension but substance itself, (mis)understood as a determinate thing: as 'the order of the real'.

It is worth citing Althusser's proposition in whole, rather than Badiou's truncated version, because Althusser clearly bases his assertion of the heterogeneity of order not on the causal order of being qua being, but rather on the historical, factual, sensuous existence of actually existing things, apprehended in temporally determined extension:

> While the production process of a given real object, *a given real-concrete totality (e.g., a given historical nation)* takes place entirely in the real and is carried out according to the real order of real genesis (*the order of succession of the moments of historical genesis*), the production process of the object of knowledge takes place entirely in knowledge and is carried out according to a different order, in which the thought categories which 'reproduce' the real categories do not occupy the same place as they do in *the order of real historical genesis*, but quite different places assigned them by their function in the production process of the object of knowledge.[119]

Althusser in this passage predominantly uses the adjectival form of 'real', such that the term 'real' here clearly refers to factual, temporal events sensuously

---

117 'If for Spinoza', Macherey continues, 'the attributes are forms or kinds of being, or natures, or even essences, they are certainly not forms in opposition to a content, any more than they are predicates in opposition to a subject, or abstract categories in opposition to a concrete reality that would remain outside them' (2011, p. 86).
118 RC, p. 40.
119 RC, p. 41, my emphasis of the passages Badiou suppresses.

apprehended (through what Spinoza calls the attribute of extension). The question is thus whether Spinoza, like Althusser, asserts that the intellect's apprehension of things through the attribute of sensuous extension indicates a different order (rather than an isomorphic, 'parallelism' of reified attributes) compared to its apprehension of the causal order of things via the attribute of thought. It is perfectly obvious that for Spinoza, as for Althusser, the adequacy, and thus the order of things will be utterly heterogeneous between the two attributes.

One immediately thinks of Spinoza's example of the falling tile in the Appendix to *Ethics* I: it is simply impossible, Spinoza asserts, for the finite human mind adequately to understand the causality that determines the temporal, historical crash (or miss) of a given stone on a given day on a given passer-by's head, simply because the chain of causes is infinite, even in this minimal, simplest example of a 'historical' event (and the 'production process' of, in Althusser's example, 'a given historical nation' would of course be infinitely more complex than that single tile). But why did the wind blow, and the stone fall that day, and the man pass at that time? 'And so they will go on and on, asking the causes of causes, until you take refuge in the will of God – that is, the sanctuary of ignorance'. Any and all causal explanations of historical, temporal real things, what Spinoza calls actually existing singular things,[120] are necessarily and inevitably *inadequate*, the attribution of imaginary causes and ends.

In contrast, the universal and eternal ideas the intellect can construct of *nonexistent things*,[121] for example the common notion of the laws of gravity, along with the singular idea the intellect can construct of the fall of that stone as singularity within the parameters of those general laws (its weight, speed, wind speed, angle of striking the passer-by's head, etc.) will not explain *why* that stone fell on that day on that head (one – inadequate and imaginary – causal sequence) but how that singular event conformed to the general laws of gravity, replacing the variables in the Newtonian formula with constants.

Badiou and Jean Matthys seem to assume that Althusser is making a general statement regarding the universal structure of causality, when in fact it is quite clear from his statement that he is contrasting the temporal forms of appearance of actually existing things ('the order of succession of the moments of historical genesis'), with a thought construct. The former, Spinoza argues, will always take an inadequate form due to the nature of empirical sense impres-

---

120   EIIP8.
121   EIIP9.

sions, while the latter can be constructed adequately, without this implying that this construction refer to the ontological, infinite nature of causality as such. In fact, and despite his initial lapses in *Reading Capital* into an invocation of the social 'whole' (which Macherey rightly criticised), Althusser almost entirely avoids grandiose ontological statements on the nature of being, categorically rejecting such idealism, for example in the unpublished text *Philosophy for Non-philosophers*: 'It is inordinately pretentious of idealist philosophy to claim to "see" the whole, "think" the whole, or aspire to "totalisation". What gives philosophy this superhuman power?'[122]

In his truncated citation, Badiou does not cite Althusser's key qualifying phrase that supports the interpretation that Althusser is limiting his claim to that of the order of actually existing singular things in their sensuous, temporal existence: it is precisely 'the order of real *historical* genesis' which is said by Althusser to bear a different order from that of the adequately constructed thought-concrete. Althusser's example of such a 'real historical genesis' – which again Badiou does not cite – is, precisely, 'a given real-concrete totality (e.g., a given historical nation)', in other words, a phenomenal, temporal actually existing, singular (historical) thing. In the passage Badiou (partially) cites, it seems clear enough that the term 'real' refers to the phenomenal order of appearance of historical events as the intellect grasps them via the attribute of extension, an order that is necessarily perceived in a manner limited and qualified not only by the finite nature of human experience but above all by the inadequacy of imaginary, ideological modes of thought.

This interpretation of Althusser's admittedly ambiguous text is nonetheless confirmed quite plainly in Althusser's critique of historicism. Only a few pages before the passage Badiou cites, Althusser argues that the order of 'historical genesis', necessarily suffers from the fetishistic inscription of 'the illusion of an immediate reading', a necessarily symptomatic and compromised reading of the fetishised document – whether the Bible, in Spinoza's critique that Althusser here refers to, or the fetishisation of the archival document in historicist discourse more generally. Althusser moreover explicitly indicates Spinoza as the originator of this critique of the fetishisation of the historical document: Spinoza was 'the first in the world to have proposed both a theory of history and a philosophy of the opacity of the immediate'.[123]

Spinoza's critique of representation – in the final proposition 49 of *Ethics* book II, *de Mente* – ultimately implicates, in Macherey's reading, the entire

---

122   Althusser 2016, p. 68.
123   RC, p. 15.

sensuous order of images and words (as diverse, arbitrary and conventional signifiers), an order necessarily subject to the confusion of the imagination. In contrast, the necessity of the idea remains defined by the materialist order of the intellect, in its necessity absolutely distinct from that of mere sonorous and imagistic extension. Here is Macherey:

> Ideas are themselves things, mental things, which ... are not a sort of doubling of reality, as are [for Spinoza] representations, images, signs, and words. ... By affirming that images and words are products of bodily extension, and nothing more, Spinoza does not wish to say that they have more reality or even materiality than ideas; rather ... *they are things of an entirely different order*. ... This is why ideas are not reducible to representations of things, as images and signs are, because, as ideas, they bear a potential for reality and activity *that is conditioned by the position they maintain in the order of thought*.[124]

In sum, historicist discourse, in its empiricist reference to the attribute of temporal extension, necessarily lacks the means to an adequate analysis of the 'structure of structures' determining the phenomenal events that documentary history merely registers. It must necessarily remain, in this view, inadequate to the presentation of the causal necessity determining these empirical events, no matter how finely rendered its representations of the archive.

Both Spinoza and Althusser assert the absolute heterogeneity of the attributes; the attribute indicates not a thing (the order of extension) that can be compared with another thing (the order of thought), but nonidentical ways the intellect apprehends a single causal order. As such, it is perfectly clear that for both Spinoza and Althusser, apprehension of the real via the attribute of extension will be eminently inferior (and thus nonidentical to) its adequate apprehension via the attribute of thought.

To take an example close to Marx's critique of capital, the causal, temporal narrative of an act of simple exchange, of, say, buying an apple at market, will take a radically different form whether apprehended via temporal, sensuous experience or common notions. The former, empirical apprehension provides only an overwhelming mashup of sense impressions: I see the apple on the stand; I automatically reach in my pocket for a coin; I touch and smell the apple and feel the coin in my hand; the seller gives me a look for handling his merchandise; I feel shame and anger and hunger and resentment; I reflexively hand

---

124   Macherey 1997, p. 392, emphasis added; see also Macherey 1994, p. 85.

over the coin and take the apple and bite into it, tasting its tartness, etc., etc., in an infinite complex of phenomenal impressions, causes, and affects that are factually real, but inadequately understood.

In contrast, Marx's analysis of the capitalist social form might tell me that at the level of common notions, in a society governed by general commodification, the coin in my pocket is the necessary general equivalent form of value that commands the exchange of things of value, adequately explaining how it comes to be the case that handing over a piece of metal causes the seller to hand me the apple; that the commodification of food and other necessities as ongoing primitive accumulation enforces via the threat of starvation the social command that all subjects of capital sell their labour power to capital in order to have that coin in their pocket in the first place; etc.

Furthermore, at the level of an intuitive science of the singularity of this situation, I might conclude that the cause of the seller's resentment is not my touching the apple but the socially enforced sale of his own labour power, which required him to arrive at the market in early morning freezing temperatures to pay for his own necessities in order not to starve, etc. The point again, is that a single, complex order of causality – substance as *ordo et connexio* – will be apprehended in radically heterogeneous forms depending on the attribute in question.

At the more abstract level of a grand historical narrative, Althusser argues that it is Marx who relays the Spinozist invention of ideology critique, bringing its force to bear upon the determinant social structure of modernity, capitalism:

> Only from history as thought, the *theory of history*, was it possible to account for the historical religion of reading: by discovering that the history of men, which survives in Books, is however not a text written on the pages of a Book, discovering that the truth of history cannot be read in its manifest discourse, because the text of history is not a text in which a voice (the Logos) speaks, but the inaudible and illegible notation of the effects of a structure of structures.[125]

To take an example from *Capital*, a temporal narrative representing the historical development of an entity such as the universal equivalent, money, no matter how detailed its discursive, archive-based representation, remains incapable of adequately conceptualising and presenting the categorial necessity governing this genesis, unlike Marx's logical, categorial presentation of its cru-

---

125 RC, p. 15, my emphasis.

cial function in a commodity-based society.[126] The point is that it is only when the object's categorial necessity is adequately understood that the phenomenal, historical forms that that category takes on (in the case of money, as wages, as prices, as profits, and all the subsidiary forms and instances of its appearance) can be adequately understood in their identity with the concept of that category.

In Part IV of *Reading Capital*, 'The Object of Capital', Althusser describes just such a distinction, that of 'the Marxist whole' as a complex of heterogeneous orders:

> the Marxist whole ... is a whole whose unity ... is constituted by a certain type of complexity, the unity of a structured whole containing what can be called levels or instances which are distinct and 'relatively autonomous', and co-exist within this complex structural unity, articulated with one another according to specific determinations.[127]

This is precisely the heterogeneity inhering between the subjective, sensuous perception of the flow of linear, homogenous time (what Althusser calls variously 'the historian's empiricist practice [and the] ideological conception of historical time'[128]) on the one hand, and the conceptual order of the categorial presentation of capital on the other, the very heterogeneity Spinoza criticises between the inadequacy of apprehension of phenomena via temporal extension and that of common notions and intuitive science.

My point is that this heterogeneity obtains only when considering actually existing things from the distinct perspectives or attributes of sensuous human perception and thought; understood from the materialist perspective of infinite substance, contra Badiou, there is only one single order of causes, for Althusser as for Spinoza. Althusser clearly summarises this conclusion (in a passage Badiou notably ignores):

---

126   Jacques Bidet shows more generally in this fashion how Marx's famous critique of the fetishism of commodities in Volume 1 is systematically deployed at the level of the various forms of appearance of capital in Volume 3, and that this development constitutes, in other words, not merely a *critique* of ideological illusions (though it is of course that too), but, in truly Spinozist fashion, a 'theory of ideology' that adequately renders the *necessity* of these very forms of appearance for the system itself: 'This is the very project of a *theory* of ideology: to show what forms of consciousness are implied in the practice of its agents, in relation to the function they occupy in the system that has been progressively defined' in the course of the first two volumes of *Capital* (2005, p. 198, emphasis in original).

127   RC, p. 244.

128   RC, pp. 242, 244.

The fact that each of these times and each of these histories is relatively autonomous does not make them so many domains which are independent of the whole: the specificity of each of these times and of each of these histories – in other words, their relative autonomy and independence – is based on a certain type of articulation in the whole, and therefore on a certain type of dependence with respect to the whole .... The synchronic is eternity in Spinoza's sense, or the adequate knowledge of a complex object by the adequate knowledge of its complexity.[129]

Lacking this ultimate identity of the order of the thought-object and the order of the real adequately understood as structural causality, the capitalist real as the necessity of its 'structure of structures', beyond its various ideological, heterogeneous forms of appearance – as Badiou reads Althusser, that is to say – there would be no point to Marx's project of a *materialist* critique of political economy, and the three volumes of *Capital* would constitute a mere idealist exercise in the imagining of a hypothetical form of social existence.[130]

The point, then, is that while the mere historical forms of appearance of social life under capitalism do indeed follow an entirely different order from the adequately developed thought-concrete that is *Capital*, as a materialist critique, Marx's analysis nonetheless ultimately allows for the comprehension of the essential nature of capitalism as a causal structure existing only in its effects, as one and the same order, one and the same thing, as a 'structure of structures', whether grasped conceptually or in the *necessity* of its historical

---

129 RC, pp. 247, 255. 'The structure of the whole is articulated as the structure of an organic hierarchised whole ... governed by the order of a dominant structure' (RC, p. 245; LC, p. 282). Macherey, as discussed above, will privately critique Althusser's references to the 'whole' as superfluous and misleading, in terms that he then systematically formulates, as noted above, in *A Theory of Literary Production*.

130 This is the mistaken empiricist/idealist position Engels adopts in his review of Marx's 1859 *A Contribution to the Critique of Political Economy*, where he writes that 'The logical method of approach ... is indeed nothing but the historical method, only *stripped of the historical form and of interfering contingencies*. ... Its further progress will be simply the *reflection*, in abstract and theoretically consistent form, of the course of history' (cited in van der Linden and Hubman 2019, p. 4, my emphasis). Althusser summarises Engels's empiricist epistemology in the following terms: 'Engels applies to the concepts of the theory of history a coefficient of mobility borrowed directly from the concrete empirical sequence (from the ideology of history), transposing the 'real-concrete' into the 'thought-concrete' and the historical as real change into the concept itself' (RC, p. 263; LC, p. 304). It should be noted that though Engels does not seem to have ever read the notebooks comprising the *Grundrisse*, including Marx's now-famous methodological introduction, Marx was elsewhere perfectly clear about this question in passages Engels knew intimately, such as the 1873 Postface to the second edition of Volume 1 (Marx 1976, p. 102).

manifestations. This is not to read a multiplicity of orders against the measure of 'a single ideological base time', nor necessarily to agree with Althusser that that structure need be hierarchically 'fixed in the last instance by the level or instance of the economy', nor especially that the capitalist social form constitutes a single whole or totality, but, rather, to hold those diverse attributes of Marx's categories to the measure of the atemporal presentation of the absolute, what Althusser rightly and unequivocally calls 'eternity in Spinoza's sense'.[131] Badiou's dualist reading of Althusser, in contrast, would return *Reading Capital* to the Cartesian, Kantian dualist idealism it categorically abhors.

11   Reading *Capital* in a Materialist Way

In anticipation of my analysis in the next chapter of Marx's process of exposition in *Capital* as a positive, materialist dialectic, I wish briefly to indicate in conclusion a few of the implications Macherey's Spinozist materialism continues to hold for a reading of Marx's *Capital* itself. To be sure, *Reading Capital* long ago brought to bear upon Marx's masterwork, both explicitly and silently, a multitude of the varied implications of the Spinozist critique; it must be said, however, that in its wake, Spinozist readings of *Capital* remain exceedingly rare. In light of Macherey's subsequent extensive and infinitesimal articulation of a Spinozist, materialist protocol for textual critique, a great many other implications of Spinozism nonetheless remain to be developed in contemporary readings of *Capital*, a field that remains, for all its insight and vibrancy, overwhelmingly determined by a negative dialectical and even Hegelian horizon. Let me briefly indicate just three of these possible paths for reading *Capital* in a Spinozist way, which will lead directly to the analysis of following chapter:

1. In his 1965 contribution to *Reading Capital*, Macherey already discerns in *Capital* what he will subsequently, in *Hegel or Spinoza*, name a 'positive [Spinozist] dialectic'. In this long-overlooked yet insightful treatment of Marx's initial exposition of his concepts, Macherey argues that the movement of Marx's demonstration is governed by a number of logical 'intermediaries', mediations that allow for a rigorous, apodictic demonstration of the initial characteristics of the value-form in a demonstration that develops *synthetically* rather than via dialectical *Aufhebung*.

Macherey argues in particular for the fundamental heterogeneity of concepts such as wealth, use-value, and value, a heterogeneity that itself consti-

---

131   RC, pp. 244, 252.

tutes 'one of the fundamental conditions of scientific rigor' (RC 188). The relations between what Marx calls the various 'factors' of the commodity and the movement of Marx's exposition occasion no procedure of dialectical *Aufhebung*, Macherey argues, but Marx's demonstration instead proceeds in a series of synthetic 'ruptures' or leaps from one order to the next following the analytical exhaustion of each concept.

It is only in 1979, however, that Macherey will explicitly theorise this dialectic without negation in the closing pages of *Hegel or Spinoza*. Macherey there identifies in Spinoza a dialectic without subject, teleology, or negation. This invocation of a positive, Spinozist dialectic puts in its place the logical subject and its function of grounding all true propositions: 'What Spinoza refuses to think is the dialectic in a subject, which is exactly what Hegel does. [Spinoza] poses the problem of a dialectic of substance, that is, a materialist dialectic that does not presuppose its completion in its initial conditions through the means of a necessarily ideal teleology'.[132] In this manner, Spinoza limits the principle of contradiction and its grounding in the subject to existences and not essences. As such, Macherey concludes, Spinoza's 'theory of the subject' pertains above all to the constitution of bodies in extension.[133] This limitation, moreover, holds for all bodies as such, not merely the human body, Spinoza's privileged example.

A Spinozist limitation of negative dialectic to existences can therefore serve to ground a materialist analysis of the (actually existing) body of capital, an analysis that starkly contrasts with all Hegelian idealism (*Capital* is no mere reorientation of the Hegelian dialectic placed 'on its feet'), an analysis in which contradiction is strictly limited to the phenomenal features of the social forms constituting the body of capital in its existence (in the form of actually existing contradictions, between given forces and means of production, in the struggle over the working day or the violent imposition of primitive accumulation, and the like), while the *essential* nature of this social form (including the crucial confrontational relation between capital and the proletarian owners of labour power) will be adequately known by the intellect only as a thought-concrete without negation.[134] In this view, human social relations bear no inner, essential drive toward their culmination in capitalism, as the imaginary

---

132 Macherey 2011, p. 170.
133 Macherey 2011, p. 175.
134 'In response to [Hegel's] finalist conception that abstractly summarises an infinite sequence of determinations in the fiction of a unique intention, we must substitute an integrally causal explanation, one that does not take into account anything but the external relations of bodies'. Macherey 2011, p. 177.

doctrines of liberalism and neoliberalism would have us believe. Instead, as Marx first argued in his presentation of so-called primitive accumulation, and Ellen Meiksins Wood has further insisted, the historical body of capitalism is composed through a fundamental and renewed system of constraint based upon the methodical dispossession of the means of production and reproduction of the working class, to form a proletariat in the precise sense Marx gives the term, through the existential, juridical, and regulated compulsion of human bodies to compose themselves, in real subsumption, as subjects of the valorisation of value under capitalism.[135]

2. A positive dialectic, such as Macherey already discerns in the opening pages of *Capital* in 1965 and subsequently articulates in *Hegel or Spinoza*, requires for its adequate conceptualisation the *synthetic* mode of presentation that Spinoza upholds (*more geometrico*) against the Cartesian defence and deployment of an *analytic* analysis. While Althusser defends Marx's 1857 epistemological distinction between the thought-concrete (*Gedankenkonkretum*) and the 'real' in Spinozist terms, a Spinozist *synthetic mode of presentation* arguably determines *Capital* to an even greater and unsuspected degree, and furthermore comes to displace the initial Hegelian negative dialectical formulations of the *Grundrisse* in the actual drafts of *Capital* after 1861, as I will argue in detail in the next chapter.

The Spinozist, positive dialectic that Macherey identifies in the most theoretically developed arguments in *Capital*[136] implies that Marx's increasing tendency to deployment of a 'positive' dialectic throughout his manuscripts tends to displace the less adequate, negative, contradiction-based Hegelian dialectical structure still visible in the earlier drafts of *Capital*.[137] A contradiction-based dialectic is in this view inherently inadequate for the comprehension of the essential nature of capital, and moreover tends, in traditional, Left Ricardian

---

135   'Each part of the [Spinozist] body', Macherey writes, 'belongs to this global form that is the body taken in its entirety, not according to its own essence, but in light of this external liaison, *whose transitive necessity is one of constraint, which holds together all the elements* …. The reason for this harmony is not found in an obscure predetermination of singular essences that inclines them to converge all together toward a unique essence (an ideal nature) but in *the transitive relationship of determination that constrains them, provisionally, to associate*'. Macherey 2011, p. 177, my emphasis. See Wood 2002 [1999]. On Marx's various definitions of the proletariat, see Nesbitt 2022.
136   Chapter 1 of Volume 1 is undoubtedly the section that Marx rewrote more than any other, from the closing pages of the *Grundrisse* through the various drafts and editions, to Marx's final 1881 notes on his further intended revisions to volume I. On the latter, see Heinrich 2012, pp. 92–3; and also Heinrich 2021.
137   See the following chapter, as well as Bidet 2005, pp. 132–95.

readings of Marx (on the model of Alexandre Kojève) to represent this nature in the humanist form of subject-based, Hegelian conflicts – the struggle between proletariat and capitalist, between forces and relations of production, or, as a philosophy of praxis, that of a productive, conscious human subject whose intentionality transforms and humanises nature.[138] Such a negative dialectic describes the development of the whole and its *Aufhebung* in a process guaranteed by the rationality of a subject, whether human, logical, or absolute. As Macherey first indicated in *Reading Capital*, Marx's *Gedankenkonkretum* – the unfinished work-in-progress we know as the three volumes of *Capital* – contains a fundamental, if largely invisible, synthetic mode of presentation of its claims.[139] The identification of various moments of a synthetic demonstration in Marx's argument remains crucial for more adequate construction of theoretical protocols for the reading of *Capital*.

3. *Capital* should be read in light of the Spinozist epistemology of the three forms of knowledge: (1) imaginary; (2) via general or common notions; and as Althusser reminds us, (3) in light of eternity, as 'the adequate knowledge of a complex object by the adequate knowledge of its complexity'.[140] Each of these modes of understanding has in turn its element of truth and necessity, though only the third is fully adequate to the comprehension of its object.

---

138 See Kojève 1980. Among the key theoretical distinctions Marx analyses in the opening pages of *Capital* (in pure abstraction from prices, capital, and the human owners of commodities themselves) is that between the production of wealth (in the form of use-values), exchange-value, and value itself (RC, pp. 188–93). These fundamental categorial determinations not only delineate Marx's decisive break with Ricardian value theory (Marx was not a Left Ricardian) but remained as well a distinction generally overlooked by the productivist orientation of traditional, Leninist Marxism. On the concept of Left Ricardianism – that is, the failure clearly to distinguish wealth from value and the consequent promotion of the redistribution of that wealth rather than the overcoming of the capitalist mode of production – see Murray 2002, pp. 250–2.

139 Jacques Bidet has insightfully identified crucial moments of what I am calling after Macherey a positive dialectic in *Capital*. Implicitly developing Macherey's precocious, Althusserian identification of various nondialectical conceptual leaps in the opening pages of *Capital*, Bidet points to the crucial movement from the concept of the commodity to that of capital in Marx's exposition (from part 1 to part 2, chs. 4–6) – a passage 'devoid of dialectical continuity, genesis, deduction, or transition – between the presentation, that is to say, of C–M–C and that of M–C–M.' Bidet describes this as an 'isolated intervention' at this crucial axial moment of Marx's argument, one in which contradiction (the apparent impossibility that the exchange of equal values can nonetheless produce surplus value) is not a matter of essence, but ideological existence, a merely apparent contradiction that in fact shrivels away in the face of Marx's synthetic presentation of the concept of surplus value and valorisation in chapter 6. Bidet 2006, pp. 160–2.

140 RC, p. 255.

An example of Marx's deployment of the *imaginary* occurs, for example, in his famous image of the 'language of commodities':

> Everything our analysis of the value of commodities previously told us is repeated by the linen itself, as soon as it enters into association with another commodity, the coat. Only it reveals its thoughts in a language with which it alone is familiar, the language of commodities. In order to tell us that labour creates its own value in its abstract quality of being human labour, it says that the coat, insofar as it counts as its equal, i.e. is value, consists of the same labour as it does itself'.[141]

Marx here supplements the synthetic analysis of the structure of capital as a social form (the object of chapter 1 prior to the appearance of this passage) with an imaginary figure, that of two animated commodities, a length of linen and a coat, in an image that bears its own measure of truth and even necessity. Marx seems to be telling his reader that the abstraction that is value must be thought not only as concept but also vividly imagined, in the form of an animated manifestation in the concrete materiality that is the human symbolic order. This dreamlike dimension of Marx's critique is indeed one necessary aspect of the object of Marx's materialist analysis. Fredric Jameson has in this sense identified the more general repetition of what he terms 'figural demonstration' as central to the stylistic apparatus of *Capital*, a rhetorical process to which Marx repeatedly resorts in the attempt to represent to his reader the immaterial, real substance of surplus value, abstract labour (in the above example), or in another example Jameson develops, in the sense of the figuration of 'separation' that occurs in Marx's analysis of primitive accumulation.[142]

A second order of demonstration inherent in *Capital*, the one that I will focus on in the next chapter, is its presentation of a structure of general notions or categories, as what Marx calls the 'value-form', an order that, grasped in the complexity of its general articulation, constitutes the 'structure' of capital in the Spinozist sense of the synchronic that Althusser indicates.[143] Marx's construction of this structure produces a general, universal exposition of the laws of the tendencies of capitalist valorisation, accumulation, and reproduction.

Finally, Macherey's thought demonstrates – with no contradiction in terms whatsoever – that an adequately materialist analysis requires above all that we learn to read *Capital* from the perspective of the eternity of the singular nature

---

141 Marx 1976, p. 143.
142 Jameson 2014, pp. 31, 81–93.
143 Marx 1976, Chapter 1.3, 'The Value-Form'; RC, p. 255.

of its object. Such a reading might take many forms; for this reader of *Capital*, it seems essential to take into account, for example, the full development of Marx's founding epistemological distinction between the production of surplus value as a total mass and its subsequent distribution among many individual capitals in the manifest form of profit via competition, such as Fred Moseley has systematically argued. While Marx famously defines abstract labour as the substance of surplus value ('The labour that forms the substance of value is equal human labour, the expenditure of identical human labour-power'), we might further say with Moseley that surplus value, as distinct from material wealth, itself forms the general substance of capital.[144]

In this view, Marx abstracts from the temporal existence of production and the phenomenology of individual labourers and capitalists, to present, at every level of the increasing degrees of concretion that characterise his analysis in *Capital*, a monetary analysis that might rightly be characterised via the eternity of the concept (in the sense that Spinoza speaks of the adequate concept of the triangle[145]): 'Money', Moseley writes, 'is derived in the very first chapter (Section 3) of Volume I, as the necessary form of appearance of abstract labour, and from then on Marx's theory is about quantities of money that represent, and thus are determined by, quantities of labour time'.[146]

This in turn entails – as Moseley demonstrates in detail across Marx's innumerable manuscripts – that *Capital* is constructed at two levels of determination: first, an initial determination of the production of a total mass of surplus volume (its 'substance'), and subsequently, in analytical terms, via the determination of the distribution of that mass of value among competing individual capitals.[147] Marx's presentation, repeatedly invoking individual processes and factors of production, is admittedly confusing on this point; Moseley convincingly argues, however, that 'Marx's theory in Volume I is about the total capital

---

144   Marx 1976, p. 129. 'The most essential common property of all capitals [i.e., its "substance"] ... is the production of surplus-value'. Moseley 2017, p. 43. I bring this theoretical perspective to bear upon the concept of capitalist slavery in Nesbitt 2022.

145   'From the nature of a triangle it follows from eternity to eternity that its three angles are equal to two right angles'. EIP17S. It should be noted in the context of this argument, that to indicate the movement of *Capital* from the abstract to the concrete is to grasp the 'concrete' not as the abandonment of an abstract conceptual order for that of an empiricist, sensuous concretion but to invoke instead the meaning of 'concrete' closest to the Latin *concrescere*, indicating the cohesion or growing together of parts into a complex mass, compound, or composite (always remaining in the attribute of thought). Compare Bidet 2005, p. 174.

146   Moseley 2017, p. 9.

147   'The total amount of surplus-value must be determined prior to its division into individual parts'. Marx, quoted in Moseley 2017, p. 46.

and the total surplus-value produced in the economy as a whole, [even though] the theory is [necessarily] illustrated in terms of an individual capital and even a single, solitary worker .... Individual capitals are not analysed as separate and distinct real capitals, but rather as representatives and 'aliquot parts' of the total social capital'.[148] As Marx himself writes, 'In capitalist production [i.e., in Volume I], *each capital is assumed to be a unit, an aliquot part of the total* capital'.[149] Here again, following Moseley's analysis, we see the necessary inherence of all three forms of knowledge in the adequate presentation of Marx's object, even including in his apodictic, synthetic analysis the imaginary figure of the 'single, solitary worker'.

Attention to the capacious brilliance of Pierre Macherey's thought, from *Reading Capital* and *A Theory of Literary Production* to his five-volume explication of Spinoza's *Ethics*, necessarily draws the reader onward to interrogate the general nature of materialist critique, such as Macherey has developed that notion across the broad expanse of a life of theoretical analysis. No mere didactic exposition of the Spinozist system, the writings of Pierre Macherey as a whole construct for contemporary thought the adequate notion of a veritably materialist analysis of the conceptual system of knowledge, both in its immediate forms of appearance as a symbolic system and in the eternity of its singular concepts. Such, one might rightfully conclude, is the nature of Macherey's theoretical project: to grasp the eternal *in a materialist way*. It is this imperative, in turn, that will in the next chapter guide my analysis of Marx's development of a positive dialectic adequate to his world-historical critique of the capitalist social form.

---

148   Moseley 2017, pp. 45–6.
149   Quoted in Moseley 2017, p. 46, Moseley's insertion.

CHAPTER 3

The Positive Logics of *Capital*: On Spinoza and the Elimination of the Negative Dialectic of Totality from Marx's Revisions to *Capital*, 1857–1875

> Pour savoir quelles étaient véritablement leurs opinions, je devais plutôt prendre garde à ce qu'ils pratiquaient qu'à ce qu'ils disaient ...; car l'action de la pensée par laquelle on croit une chose, étant différente de celle par laquelle on connaît qu'on la croit, elles sont souvent l'une sans l'autre.
>
> DESCARTES, *Discours de la méthode*

∴

The previous chapters' discussion of Althusser and Macherey's concept of a materialist dialectic – not only in *For Marx* and *Reading Capital*, but in many of their subsequent writings, published and unpublished, texts that at times explicitly address Marx's *Capital*, but more often do not – provides the means now to return this theoretical position back to bear upon the logics or what Macherey calls the 'process of exposition' of *Capital* itself.[1] The plural of my chapter title ('logics') already indicates a crucial claim of my argument: that as opposed to the still-dominant view that Marx's theoretical exposition of the capitalist social form deploys a single negation- and contradiction-

---

1 Needless to say, in the scope of this chapter there can be no question of addressing the huge volume of philological and genetic research into *Capital* since the 1960s. Here, I only hope to extend Althusser's and Macherey's original epistemological propositions in *Reading Capital* in the context of their later work and its reception, in particular in relation to the problem of a Spinozist reading of *Capital*. For a summary of this broader discussion, focusing on the Germanophone field and in particular the relation of Hegel's *Logic* to *Capital*, see Heinrich 2009, pp. 71–98 as well as the entire contents of that outstanding volume more generally; and Heinrich 2022 [1999], pp. 167–71; 2023, pp. 263–7. Heinrich summarises his own view on the relation of Hegelian logic to *Capital* in the following terms: 'For me, the most plausible conclusion is the following: from Hegel, Marx gained a precise *perception* of the difficulties of presentation ... but regarding Hegel's notions and lines of argumentation themselves, there is no *application*' (2009, p. 75).

based logic (i.e., a materialist version of 'Hegelian' logic), *Capital* instead implements a diverse multiplicity of logics.[2] These include, predominantly, a post-Aristotelean and Spinozist positive logic of implication that I will call *additive synthesis*, which coexists with others that range from the imaginary-literary and polemic invective, to the highly original materialist process that Althusser names the determinate 'positioning' (*la position*) of concepts, and the related procedure Macherey identifies in *Reading Capital* as the 'exhaustion' of concepts.

Alongside these logics, remaining instances of a 'Hegelian', negative, contradiction-based dialectic, while existing in marginal passages such as *Capital*'s supplementary, historical (as opposed to apodictic) Chapter 23, constitute no more than a conceptually meagre theoretical relic of Marx's intellectual formation and habitus.[3] Marx tendentially suppresses, in this view, the initially predominant negative dialectic of the *Grundrisse*, with only lingering remnants increasingly relegated to the margins of *Capital*'s demonstration. This occurs as a fundamental aspect of the ongoing process of revision that Marx undertakes from his initial enquiries of 1857 to the final 1881 notes on his intended, but never implemented, revisions for a third edition of *Capital*, Vol. I.

Textual analysis of the various logics of exposition in *Capital* reveals, I wish to argue, that the negation-based version of so-called 'Hegelian' logic that is still widely referred to as Marx's 'dialectic', is in fact the least significant of these logics of exposition. More specifically, I wish to argue that Marx's initial exposition of the concept of the commodity (in Chapter I of *Capital*) in terms of an internal, constitutive contradiction [*Widerspruch*] between use-value and exchange-value, and this even as late as the first, 1867 edition of *Capital*, proves an epistemological impediment,[4] one that Marx overcomes through

---

2 An extreme example of the former position is to be found in Jairus Banaji's essay 'From the Commodity to Capital: Hegel's Logic in Marx's *Capital*', in which Banaji presents Marx's method of exposition as both static and unitary. Unitary since for Banaji every methodological comment Marx made constitutes a moment of an expressive totality ('It is obvious that the methodological references express a consistent and internally unified conception') and static, since Banaji identifies examples of this univocal totality – among which Banaji freely translates into Hegelese as necessary – from the 1841 dissertation to Volume II of *Capital*, the final manuscript on which Marx worked. Banaji 2015, p. 20.
3 On Marx's complex appropriation of Hegelian thought from 1836–48, see Levine 2012.
4 I take the term epistemological impediment from Jacques Bidet, who makes an analogous argument regarding Marx's appropriation of Hegelian negative dialectic, but without specifically addressing this to the putative negative dialectical contradiction between use-value and exchange-value in the concept of the commodity (Bidet 2005).

the articulation of a positive, materialist dialectical exposition without (ontological, constitutive) contradiction.

My argument on this score is thus quite specific: it is certainly the case that Marx continues to the end to identify real and crucial *theoretical* contradictions in his predecessors, such as the conceptual inadequacies that mired the classical political economists' analysis of surplus value (i.e., as what he calls, in chapter 5, 'Contradictions in the General Formula [of Capital]'); it is also certainly the case that Marx identifies real *practical* contradictions that render capitalism as an actually existing entity *necessarily* prone, for example, to crisis, via the contradiction between the contradictory systemic demands to reduce variable capital costs while simultaneously assuring the realisation of surplus value through, in part, the consumption of commodities by the working class.[5] Instead, here I wish to argue that it is only the specific logic of Hegelian, *negative dialectical* contradiction that proves an impediment to Marx's analysis and exposition of the commodity and the capitalist social form more generally.

1   The Discontinuity of the Attributes

The position I present here crucially depends upon the fundamental Spinozist distinction Althusser and Macherey sustain (described in the previous chapters), between the attributes of thought and extension, attributes (along with the infinite others to which humans do not have access) that in Spinoza's view remain absolutely and infinitely distinct – without, that is to say, being subject to their sublation in the Hegelian Idea of the Absolute Subject.[6] Follow-

---

5   In a note Marx placed in his manuscript for *Capital*, Volume II, he gives an example of this *practical* form of contradiction: 'Contradiction in the capitalist mode of production. The workers are important for the market as buyers of commodities. But as sellers of their commodity – labour-power – capitalist society has the tendency to restrict them to their minimum price. Further contradiction: the periods in which capitalist production exerts all its forces regularly show themselves to be periods of over-production; because the limit to the application of the productive powers is not simply the production of value, but also its realisation. However the sale of commodities, the realisation of commodity capital, and thus of surplus-value as well, is restricted not by the consumer needs of society in general, but by the consumer needs of a society in which the great majority are always poor and must always remain poor'. I take this example as well as the three-way distinction between theoretical, practical, and (Hegelian) dialectical contradictions from Arash Abazari's article 'Marx's Conception of Dialectical Contradiction in Commodity' (2019, p. 181). I will return to Abazari's argument below.

6   'Each attribute of one substance must be conceived through itself' (EIP10). Spinoza goes on to develop this crucial point in the second section of *Ethica*: 'As long as things are considered

ing Althusser and Macherey, the theoretical object I seek to construct here adheres to this Spinozist distinction, and addresses not the historical existence and development of capitalism as a singular existing thing bearing real contradictions, but only the logics or processes of exposition to be found in *Capital*.

Marx famously never wrote his proposed treatise on his dialectical method,[7] and in its absence, the logics of *Capital* do not constitute an autonomous 'method', but exist only immanently, discernible through what Althusser called their 'structural causality'. This singular (as opposed to generalisable or even universal) 'method' exists nowhere else than in its real effects, which is to say, in this case, in the text of *Capital* itself, but in the state of a discursive practice as opposed to an explicit theory of a ramified apodictic demonstration. This implies that to determine the logics at work in *Capital*, as I seek to do here, requires constructing a theoretical object distinct from Marx's literal demonstration of the capitalist social form, yet simultaneously insisting that this object of analysis remains determined in its necessity by the material object that is the finite discourse of *Capital*.[8] This process, as what Macherey calls materialist *explication*, stands opposed to the alternative fabrication of an autonomous *interpretation*;[9] the latter tends in contrast to disregard the materi-

---

as modes of thought, we must explicate the order of the whole of nature, or the connection of causes, through the attribute of Thought alone; and insofar as things are considered as modes of Extension, again the order of the whole of Nature must be explicated through the attribute of Extension only. The same applies to the other attributes' EIIP7Sch. These assertions derive in turn from Spinoza's initial propositions EIP2–4, which together imply, Macherey comments, that 'the attributes of substance ... can be distinguished without maintaining [*entretenir*] relations between themselves'. Furthermore, Macherey continues, the attributes are precisely 'defined by the fact that they have nothing in common between them and therefore do not reciprocally limit one another .... There is a mental reality as there is a corporeal reality, each neither more nor less real than the other, and without reciprocal relations [existing] between them' (1998, pp. 75, 94, my translation).

7 Marx was quite clear that despite the decisive influence Hegel's thought had on his intellectual development, his own method was not Hegelian: 'My method of exposition is *not* Hegelian, since I am a materialist, and Hegel an idealist' (Letter to Ludwig Kugelmann, 6 March 1868). In consequence, Marx famously wrote to Joseph Dietzgen in 1868 that 'When I have cast off the burden of political economy, I shall write a "Dialectic"'.
8 'If knowledge is expressed in discourse, and is applied to discourse, this discourse must by its nature be different from the object which it animated in order to talk about it. Scientific discourse is rigorous because its chosen object is defined by a different order of strictness and coherence'. Macherey 2006, p. 7.
9 Crucial to Macherey's materialist analysis of texts, as discussed in the previous chapter, is his systematic attempt 'to replace interpretation (why is the work made?) by explication [*explication*] (which answers the question, how is the work made?)' (2006, p. 84, translation altered).

alist determination of Marx's actual text and to create in its place an (aesthetic idealist) theoretical object (this, I will argue, is the case of Chris Arthur's *interpretation* of the logic of *Capital*).

An example may help to clarify this distinction between the logics of *Capital* and capitalism as a historically existing, contradiction-prone singular thing. Just as the concept of the circle is not circular,[10] the concept of negation is not negative, nor is that of contradiction contradictory; both can easily be defined positively and without contradiction. Bolzano, for example, defines negation positively, as the formal statement 'Proposition A has no truth', while Lalande defines contradiction without contradiction, as 'The relation ... that exists between two propositions, in the form: "A is true" and "A is not true"'.[11] Though Marx explains how as a lived, historical phenomenon the capitalist social form produces a multitude of lived, practical and theoretical, i.e., merely apparent contradictions, the concept of surplus value, in the adequate, positive formulation it receives in Chapters 6 and 7, is not contradictory in the least. It is this Spinozist distinction, between the logical process of exposition that is the purely conceptual analysis of the capitalist social form in *Capital*, and the finite, sensuous temporality of the capitalist real, that constitutes the key epistemological proposition and militant theoretical intervention of *Reading Capital*.

At stake in this book, however, is not merely this straightforward epistemological distinction, albeit one to this day all too frequently ignored in Marxist criticism (including, ironically, by Althusser himself in 'Contradiction and Overdetermination', as I argued in my Introduction). As already noted, I wish

---

10 'Spinoza ... warned us that the object of knowledge or essence was in itself absolutely distinct and different from the real object, for, to repeat his famous aphorism, the two objects must not be confused: the idea of the circle, which is the object of knowledge, must not be confused with the circle, which is the real object. In the third section of the 1857 Introduction, Marx took up this principle as forcefully as possible' (RC, p. 41, translation modified; LC, p. 40).

11 Bolzano 2011 [1837], p. 299; Lalande 2010, p. 183. I cite Bolzano not only because of the elegant simplicity of his positive definition of negation, a definition as devoid of psychologism as it is of dependency on the concept (negation) it seeks to define (*petitio principii*), but also because, though Marx could not have known of his work, Bolzano has come to be recognised, since his rediscovery by Husserl after 1893, as the crucial innovator in the development of a positive and objective logic, a logic that he developed, moreover, via explicit critiques of both Kant and Hegel's positions. His relation to the theory of materialist dialectic I discuss in this book is, moreover, crucial yet still underappreciated, both in the explicit importance of his theory of apodictic demonstration for Jean Cavaillès, and through the latter, indirectly for Althusser and Badiou in particular. I discuss Bolzano's importance for Badiou in the following chapter.

furthermore to argue that Marx's *logical* analysis of the concept of the commodity tends to replace a negative dialectical logic of exposition with a positive one. This is to say that although Marx's initial analysis of the commodity as constituted by an internal, ontological contradiction (between use-value and exchange-value) might well have been demonstrated (as it largely was in the *Grundrisse* and the first edition of *Capital*) without contradiction, Marx furthermore, at the level of his categorial exposition, comes to replace this negative dialectical logic with a more adequate, positive logic without (ontological, constitutive) contradiction. The Hegelian logic of constitutive contradiction can certainly be presented without contradiction; for all that, it may well have proven inadequate to Marx for what Althusser calls his 'apodictic arrangement of the concepts [as] that type of demonstrational discourse that Marx calls analysis'.[12]

2 Totality, Negation, Contradiction

To develop this position, to reprise an argument initiated in this book's Introduction, it is important to move beyond the inadequate formulation of Marx's dialectical (apodictic) method of exposition as a question of 'Hegel or Spinoza', whether we take this conjunction in its differential sense, following Althusser – as the either/or choice between two distinct modes of logical demonstration – or, following Macherey's argument in his book of that title, also in its connective sense, to suggest as well as the variegated unity of two modes of thought indicated by these famous proper names. Hegel's relation to Spinoza, for all its real complexity, is no mere question of disavowal and misrepresentation. In crucial aspects, Hegel explicitly and unambiguously reaffirms crucial aspects of Spinoza's epistemology.

Tellingly, Hegel makes a point of concluding his 1827 Preface to the *Encyclopedia Logic* with the categorical statement that 'It has been rightly said of the true that it is *index sui et falsi*, but that the true is not known [*gewusst*] on the basis of the false'.[13] Repeating this ringing endorsement of the Spinozist position in the body of his text, Hegel simultaneously appends to it a condemnation of empiricist theories of knowledge dependent upon the adequation of subject and object:

---

12 RC, p. 51.
13 Hegel 2010a, p. 21.

> Usually we call truth the agreement of an object with our representation of it. Thus we have an object as a presupposition, and our representation is supposed to conform to it. – In the philosophical sense, by contrast, truth means in general the agreement of a content with itself, to put it abstractly.[14]

No less than for Spinoza and Althusser, for Hegel, the empiricist model of truth remains radically inadequate and subject to ideological distortions: 'From the fact that immediate knowing is supposed to be the criterion of truth, it follows that all kinds of superstition and idolatry are declared to be true'.[15] Aligning himself with the epistemological tradition from Aristotle to Spinoza, Hegel likewise sustains, in his own fashion, the necessity of adequate demonstration and apodictic judgements.[16]

While I argued in my Introduction that Althusser's initial presentation of Marx's theory in *For Marx* and *Reading Capital* sacrificed analytical clarity on multiple fronts to the demands of a situated theoretical polemic (i.e., slippage from the theoretical to the historical, the unqualified suppression of the concept of substance, etc.), the extreme theoretical density and interwoven complexity of Macherey's contrasting argument in *Hegel or Spinoza*, seeking to parse Hegel's various (mis)readings of Spinoza through Spinoza's own proleptic responses to such positions and misunderstandings, is unnecessary fully to rehearse here, since my object is neither Spinoza nor Hegel per se, but rather Marx's process of exposition in *Capital*. Instead, in the place of proper names, it is important to focus on the specific logical operations Marx deploys in this process. Thus, instead of vaguely contrasting 'Hegelian' and 'Spinozist' logics, I wish more precisely to interrogate Marx's process of exposition in *Capital* in relation to three categories, all of which are as central to Hegel's logic as they are tendentially suppressed from Marx's: totality, negation, and contradiction. I will proceed by confronting one of the most influential and comprehensive recent

---

14 Hegel 2010a, p. 62.
15 Hegel 2010a, p. 121. 'Truth in the deeper sense consists in this, that objectivity is identical with the concept'; 'Correctness generally affects merely the formal agreement of our representation with its content; however this content may be otherwise constituted. The truth consists, by contrast, in the agreement of the object with itself, i.e. with its concept' (Hegel 2010a, pp. 284, 246).
16 'In the apodictic judgement we have an individual that relates itself, thanks to its constitution, to its universal, i.e. its concept .... The truth has to prove [*bewähren*] itself precisely to be the truth, and here, within the logical sphere, the proof consists in the concept demonstrating itself to be mediated through and with itself and thereby also as what is truly immediate' (Hegel 2010a, pp. 134, 254).

defences of a Hegelian reading of *Capital* – Chris Arthur's *The New Dialectic and Marx's Capital* – with various moments of Pierre Macherey's critique of these Hegelian categories, at each step bringing this critique back to bear upon the text of *Capital* itself in the desire not merely to counter neo-Hegelian readings of *Capital* such as Arthur's, but to further the interrogation and articulation of Marx's positive, materialist dialectic as it is deployed in his magnum opus, in the wake of the Althusserians' relinquishing of this project after 1967.

3   Totality

Marx's *Capital* does not constitute an objective totality, whether we take the term in its material, demonstrative, or logical sense. Such a position, I wish to argue, follows imperatively both from *Reading Capital* as well as Pierre Macherey's general critique of the concept of totality in *For a Theory of Literary Production* (in which he does not discuss *Capital* explicitly). It also follows directly from a comparison of the *Grundrisse* with the revised versions of *Capital*, from which the term *Totalität* almost entirely disappears. In *Grundrisse*, the Hegelian concept of totality is vital and determinant, recurring nearly a hundred times in Marx's notebooks: 'The conclusion we reach is not that production, distribution, exchange, and consumption are identical, but that they all form members of a totality [*Totalität*], distinctions within a unity'.[17] By the time Marx drafts and subsequently revises *Capital* Volume one in 1872, the term totality only occurs twice, within a single citation from Hegel's *Philosophy of Right*, while in the 1875 French translation, the final version Marx oversaw, the term *totalité* occurs just once in reference to the figure of a given sum ('la totalité du capital employé').[18]

This claim, to be sure, stands in direct contrast to the Marxist humanist tradition since Lukács and Karel Kosík, as well as to the exponents of the so-called systematic Dialectical reading of *Capital* such as Chris Arthur's neo-Hegelian position in *The New Dialectic and Marx's Capital*.[19] In what follows,

---

17   'Das Resultat, wozu wir gelangen, ist nicht, dass Production, Distribution, Austausch, Consumtion identisch sind, sondern dass sie alle Glieder einer Totalität bilden, Unterschiede innerhalb einer Einheit'. Marx 1973, p. 99; MEGA II.1.1 [1857–58], p. 35.

18   Marx MEGA II.6 [1872], p. 184; Marx MEGA II.7 [1875], p. 529.

19   Riccardo Bellofiore remarks that 'A consensus among all the ISMT [International Symposium on Marxist Theory] authors is that Marx is a systematic dialectician, that is, he proposes *the articulation of categories to conceptualise an existent concrete whole*'. Bellofiore is referring to Arthur, Geert Reuten, Tony Smith, Roberto Fineschi, Patrick Murray, and Fred Moseley, along with himself. Though my own reading of *Capital* is heavily indebted to

I will develop this position as both a critique of Lukács's original affirmation and Arthur's book, as well as immanently within Marx's text. I do so in three moments: first, by briefly recalling the Hegelian affirmation of totality; next, through an equally brief critique of its Marxist inflection in Lukács's 1921 essay 'The Marxism of Rosa Luxemburg' followed by an examination of Arthur's application of this Hegelian doctrine of totality to Marx's *Capital*. This will then allow for a consideration of the specific case of *Capital* and totality, in the three senses just mentioned: as a material totality (whether *Capital* the book forms a totality); as a demonstrative totality (whether Marx's process of demonstration in *Capital* constitutes a totality); and finally, whether the categorial critique of *Capital* theorises a *logical* totality (in the sense Arthur affirms, that 'Capital [the social form, not Marx's book] is a closed totality only in form').[20]

The category of totality is central to Hegel's doctrine of logic, and constitutes one of the most familiar aspects of his systematic thought. The theme of totality is crucial to the systematicity of Hegelian logic, and Hegel strongly underscores this importance in the capstone of his thought, the *Encyclopedia Logic*.[21] Hegel

---

the work of the ISMT authors, this is obviously a shared position with which I take issue. Bellofiore 2014, p. 167, emphasis in original. Among these authors, my critique of totality is closest to that of Bellofiore, who stresses, like Macherey's Spinoza (see below), the perspectival, subjective nature of any actually existing totality: 'In the section on reproduction, Marx was *looking at* capital relations from a *point of view* [of] the whole of the capitalist class [and] the whole of the working class' at which point we 'abandon the *perspective* of the single capitalist and the single worker and *look* instead at the capitalist class and the working class' (Bellofiore 2018, pp. 379, 380, emphasis added). Another proponent of the systematic dialectic school is Norman Levine. His book *Marx's Discourse with Hegel*, taking account of both recent Hegel scholarship and the MEGA², offers a detailed and comprehensive examination of Marx's appropriation of Hegel's thought, drawing attention both to those texts Marx read, and others he either ignored or which only became available after his death, along with the diverse consequences of this complex *dispositif*. Unlike the work of Bellofiore, Arthur and Smith, however, Levine's probing analysis is strictly limited to the years 1836–48, and thus does not address the process of exposition in *Capital*. See Levine 2012. In general, the Systematic Dialectic position can be said to move backwards from the observed reality of *Capital* to fabricate its imaginary cause – the Hegelian logical categories to be found in *Grundrisse* – as opposed to moving forward from 1857 to follow Marx's general tendency as the necessary replacement of many of the logical categories and operations he took from Hegel with original, more adequate concepts of his own construction, as I seek to do in this chapter, following Althusser and Macherey's Spinozist protocol for a materialist science of causes.

20 Arthur 2009, p. 175.
21 I will focus here on the *Encyclopedia*, since, in contrast to the more widely discussed *Phenomenology*, *Logic*, and *Philosophy of Right*, each of which constitute only partial elements of this system, the *Encyclopedia* is the only site in which Hegel systematically (if schematically) develops his system of thought as a totality. See Stein and Wretzel 2022.

argued that a coherent and comprehensive philosophical doctrine required systematic form, in the sense of its apodicticity, i.e., that all propositions be rigorously derived one from another in a systematic and methodical demonstration. Furthermore, this systematicity necessarily implied for Hegel the culmination of this demonstration (and thus his presentation of that system in the *Encyclopedia* as the capstone of his life's work) as a single closed system, one that would comprehensively present the logical structures of the real (the Idea, in Hegel's jargon). As opposed to Spinoza's absolute separation of the attributes thought and extension, thought for Hegel *sublates* extensive reality ('Nature', in the terminology of the *Encyclopedia*), such that in conceptualising the real, thought is understood to think itself in schematising the determinations of the natural world.[22]

This moment of sublation occurs in the crucial, final paragraph of the *Encyclopedia Logic*, which engenders the passage from the presentation of the system of logic itself to that of the natural world as Idea: 'The idea, which is for itself, considered in terms of this, its unity with itself, is the process of intuiting [*Anschauen*] and *the idea insofar as it intuits is nature*'. The idea, Hegel continues, is not a separate attribute through which to grasp an aspect of being, but is 'released' from its containment in nature:

> Yet the absolute freedom of the idea is that it does not merely pass over into life or let life shine in itself as finite knowing [i.e., as mere logical systematicity], but instead, in the absolute truth of itself, resolves to release freely from itself the moment of its particularity or the first determining and otherness, the immediate idea, as its reflection [*Widerschein*], itself as nature ... This idea insofar as it is [*diese seiende Idee*], is nature.[23]

In Hegel's understanding, philosophy itself forms a totality,[24] its constructed and reflected unity constituting a whole: 'The science of [the absolute] is essentially a *system*, since the true insofar as it is *concrete* exists only through unfolding itself in itself, collecting and holding itself together in a unity, i.e. as a

---

22 For Hegel, the sublation of nature within the absolute idea necessarily maintains what he calls a 'real content', that consists 'only in its exhibition [*Darstellung*], an exhibition that it [the concept] provides for itself in the form of external existence [*Dasein*]'. Cited in Schülein 2022, p. 139.

23 Hegel 2010a, p. 303, emphasis added, translation modified.

24 'The history of philosophy presents only one philosophy at different stages of its unfolding throughout the various philosophies that make their appearance .... the specific principles each one of which formed the basis of a given system are merely branches of one and the same whole' (Hegel 2010a, p. 42).

totality [*Totalität*]'.[25] In this manner, Hegel's system depends upon the notion of totality at all three levels indicated above: the three-volume *Encyclopedia* constitutes a *material* totality, its pretension being to present the total system of absolute knowledge – from its most abstract initial moment, to the most concrete, the absolute idea – across the material expanse of its pages and the discourse they convey; a *demonstrative* totality, the sequence of its argument proceeding apodictically from each moment to that which it logically entails, to demonstrate in sum the systematic unity of being in its totality; and, *logically*, the *Encyclopedia* presents the absolute idea as the rational totality of its determinations.

More precisely, Hegel's entire philosophical system consists in not just one final totality (the absolute idea) in distinction to the contradictory inadequacy of all its prior moments, but through the articulation of its various sections, it articulates a sequence of totalities. This is to say that each determination of being – from the first, most abstract determination of being and nothingness as becoming, through to the complete and sufficient totality of the absolute idea, along with the many other forms of determination Hegel considers along the way (finitude, identity, etc.) – constitutes an aspect of the totality of being according to a specific, determinate form. Hegel famously visualises this as a system in which the totality of being, understood as absolute idea, 'presents itself as a circle of circles, each of which is a necessary moment, so that the system of its distinctive elements makes up the idea in its entirety. ... Each sphere of the logical idea proves to be a totality of determinations'.[26]

If each Hegelian determination of being, from the most abstract to the most concrete, forms a totality, each of these (prior to the absolute) must furthermore be understood as ontologically constituted by its inner negativity and inadequacy;[27] each determination of being, in other words, is not simply a totality, but stands as an inadequate or *illegitimate* totality, to adopt Michela Bordignon's terminology.[28] This is to say that each logical determination or cat-

---

25 Hegel 2010a, p. 43, emphasis in original. Though *Gesamtheit* and *Totalität* are synonymous in German, Hegel's preferred term is *Totalität*, which appears 153 times in the *Encyclopedia Logic*, while the former is used only once.
26 Hegel 2010a, pp. 43, 136.
27 'Everything actual contains within itself opposite determinations, and therefore knowing and, more specifically, comprehending [*Begreifen*] an object means nothing more or less than becoming conscious of it as a unity of opposite determinations'. Hegel 2010a, pp. 94–5.
28 Bordignon 2022, pp. 115–32.

egory of being through which Hegel articulates his system of logic defines a totality according to a certain form: being as it is perceived under the determination of quantity, of finitude, of identity, etc.

The key point, then, is that if Hegel's analysis of being under the attribute of identity, or any other determination, constitutes a totality (the totality of being grasped via the concept of identity), this totality must necessarily, insofar as it refers to the totality of being, refer as well to the definition of identity itself as an element of this totality.[29] If each logical totality constitutes a set, then the immediate consequence to be drawn is that each and every one of these sets (i.e., each of Hegel's logical determinations of being) is 'illegitimate' in the familiar sense of Russell's paradox: in Bordignon's terms, 'each logical determination denotes a set of which it is a member, and thus refers to itself'.[30]

Hegel's familiar example of the contradictory logic of identity makes this paradox apparent.[31] Being, when grasped under the attribute or determination of *identity*, constitutes a totality – and since the definition of the absolute as a determinate totality necessarily includes the definition of identity, this set refers to itself (the concept of identity) as well. That identity is identical to itself (necessarily, according to its definition), however, implies, as Hegel shows in the doctrine of essence, that it is different from, not identical to, what it is not, namely, *difference*. Its difference from *difference* is thus not merely external, but gives *identity* its self-identity, making it a member of the set of all being grasped under the determination of identity. And yet, since its difference from *difference* constitutes in this sense, ontologically, the very identity of *identity*, it can be said that the concept of identity necessarily, ontologically, contains *difference* within itself. If this is so, then it cannot be a member of the set of all being grasped as self-same, determinate *identity* without difference. Or in Bordignon's recapitulation: 'Insofar as identity is identical with itself, identity

---

29 'The determination of the finite is the logical form of all there is insofar as all there is, is finite. The determination of identity is a logical form of all there is, insofar as all there is, is identical to itself .... If each determination is [therefore] a way in which all there is, is defined, the determination has to define itself too. In this way, the content of each determination is a definition of all there is, including itself' (Bordignon 2022, p. 122).

30 'Since the content of the determination defines a totality – all there is and all that is thinkable – according to a certain form, the whole content of this totality turn out to be inside the totality and, at the same time, paradoxically, outside the totality itself' (Bordignon 2022, p. 125). Alain Badiou founds his anti-Hegelian claim that there is no total universe or world of worlds, but only purely multiple worlds each possessing its own logic, upon a version of Russell's paradox (2008, pp. 109–11). I discuss Badiou's *Logics of Worlds* in Chapter 5.

31 I take the example from Bordignon 2022, p. 124.

differs from difference and thus it involves difference in itself and transcends the limit of the totality that it is supposed to define and that it is a part of'.[32]

Now, the interesting conclusion Bordignon draws from this presentation, which simply translates the notion of Hegelian negative dialectic into the language of set theory and Russell's paradox, is that this 'illegitimacy' of all Hegelian set theoretic determinations of being leads not to their ruination (as it will for Badiou, for example), but rather constitutes the singular power and dynamic source of Hegelian logic. Hegel, she argues, while not anachronistically adopting set theoretical terminology, was nonetheless quite aware of the contradictions governing such logical totalities, but simply rejected their 'illegitimacy' as a symptom of a specific, inadequate form of rationality, precisely one that could not incorporate such contradictions within its compass.[33] Instead, Hegel affirmed such contradiction [*Widerspruch*], in its integral necessity to the totality of the absolute idea, as a new form of logic, one precisely able encompass such limited, determinate forms of totality, negation.

4 The Imaginary Presuppositions of Systematic Dialectics

At stake in this chapter cannot be a summary judgement of Hegelian logic as such, nor abstractly to claim its absolute distinction from Marx's various modes of demonstration in *Capital*. As will become clear below, at certain moments, Marx does depend upon precisely such a Hegelian logic of constitutive totality, negation and contradiction (for example in the presentation of the concept of the commodity in the *Grundrisse* and the first, 1867 edition of *Capital*). The question instead must be to determine the multiple modes of demonstration that Marx deploys in *Capital* through an explication of the text itself, without invoking a transcendent, reified totality of which each of these moments would be a determinate expression.[34] This Althusserian analytical protocol, as

---

32 Bordignon 2022, p. 125.
33 Hegel shows, Bordignon concludes, that 'Russell's verdict on the illegitimacy of such totalities is neither universal nor necessary. In effect, his verdict is based on a specific understanding of logic and, more generally, on a specific understanding of thought, which Hegel would relegate to the paradigm of understanding (*Verstand*)' (Bordignon 2022, p. 126).
34 It is obviously well beyond the scope of this chapter to undertake such an explication in its entirety, and I will focus here only on certain key passages: the opening paragraphs of *Capital*, the concept of the commodity developed in Section Three of Volume I, and the concept of the rate and mass of surplus value in Chapter 11. As I write, the standard for such a comprehensive textual explication is set by Michael Heinrich's 400-page, line by line analysis of the first seven chapters of *Capital* in *How to Read Marx's Capital*. Hein-

the general rejection of the category of expressive totality, finds analogous iteration in Macherey's programme in *Theory of Literary Production* (discussed in the previous chapter); at the same time, it stands in direct opposition to the neo-Hegelian reading of *Capital* to be found in Chris Arthur's *The New Dialectic and Marx's Capital*.

To confront these two influential readings of *Capital* then is at once to choose between a reconstructive *interpretation* of the (Hegelian, negative dialectical) logical form of *Capital* (Arthur) and the autonomous construction of an analytic theory of *Capital*'s modes of demonstration and the necessity governing their organisation. At the same time, it is to clarify the decision drawn between an understanding of *Capital* as a unified, totalised negative dialectical object, in which each moment incompletely expresses this totality, and *Capital* as a materialist structure of multiple logics and concatenated conceptual singularities without totality.[35] In rejecting the inadequate nominal abstraction of 'Hegelian' vs. 'Spinozist' (or Marxian) logics, I choose to focus instead on three aspects of Marx's apodictic demonstration: totality, negation, and contradiction. I begin with the problem of totality not only because it offers a stark and radical contrast between Arthur's and Macherey's understandings of the process of exposition in *Capital*, but even more because Arthur's analysis of the status of negation and contradiction in *Capital* crucially depends upon his initial assertion of the book's status as a formal totality.

Chris Arthur's influential 2002 book *The New Dialectic and Marx's Capital* offers a sustained reading of the logic of *Capital* as what Arthur calls a 'systematic dialectic'.[36] By this, Arthur rightly seeks to distinguish this form of

---

rich's analysis of *Capital* has been called into question by Fred Moseley in *Marx's Theory of Value in Chapter 1 of Capital: A Critique of Heinrich's Value-Form Interpretation* (2023). What I take above all from Heinrich's analysis in *How to Read Capital*, as will become evident below, is his demonstration of the additive, as opposed to negative dialectical nature of Marx's demonstration. Moseley's critique of Heinrich in contrast addresses a problem extraneous to the issue in question here, i.e., whether value is created by the exchange of commodities (as Moseley reads Heinrich), or entirely in production itself (as Moseley claims). I discuss this critique below.

35   The tendential fabrication of a mere *interpretation*, Macherey observes, seeks to reveal 'the apparent expression of the unity of an intention or model that permeates and animates the work, bestowing on it life and the status of an organism. Whether this unity is subjective (the result of an authorial choice, conscious or unconscious) or objective (the embodiment of an essential device – a key signature, frame or model [or, for Arthur, the ubiquitous logical device of the Hegelian negative dialectic]) the assumption remains that it is the whole that is determinant' (Macherey 2006, 45–6, translation modified).

36   Arthur has sustained and further specified his original analysis of the capitalist social form in his more recent book *The Spectre of Capital: Idea and Reality* (2022), as well as in the

analysis as the attempt *logically* 'to articulate the relations of a given social order, namely capitalism', from what he calls the 'Old Dialectic', the Soviet Stalinist 'school of "Diamat", rooted in vulgarised versions of Engels and Plekhanov', a tradition that, retaining Hegel's teleological philosophy of history, has read *Capital* as the historicist analysis of the origins and progression of capitalism from so-called primitive exchange to the fully developed industrial capitalist social form.[37]

In contrast, the process of exposition Arthur calls 'systematic dialectic' adopts Hegel's concern to demonstrate the *logical* form of its object, as for example that found in the *Logic* or the *Philosophy of Right*, arguing that Marx univocally adopted this Hegelian logical dialectic in *Capital*.[38] While I have argued above that the Spinozist distinction between the historical development of capitalism, in the attribute of temporal extension, and the exposition of its logical structure in that of thought forms the basis of Althusser's epistemology in *Reading Capital* – a theoretical reference that Arthur, in his anti-Althusserian Hegelianism unsurprisingly neglects to mention – this quasi-Althusserian distinction that Arthur draws constitutes little more than an opening prelude to his analysis.

Instead, Arthur's introductory exposition of his project confusingly – from the Althusserian position I am arguing in this book – conflates a salutary rejection of Diamat historicist readings of *Capital*, with the imaginary, unexamined, and undemonstrated presupposition that Marx's *Capital*, via what Arthur calls its 'systematic dialectic', presents the logic of capitalism as a unitary expressive totality ('the significance of each element is determined by its place in the totality', Arthur states categorically) via a negative, contradiction-based dialectic.[39]

---

article 'Contradiction and Abstraction: A Reply to Finelli' (2009). I focus here on his earlier book both because it has been the object of sustained interest and critique, and, more importantly, because in his most recent book he largely abandons any earlier pretense actually to read and explicate *Capital*'s dialectic and instead borrows freely from Hegel and Marx's conceptual toolbox such that 'what I present here [in *The Spectre of Capital*] should be understood as my own view, not as Hegel's or Marx's' (Arthur 2022, p. 1).

37   Arthur 2002, p. 3. Michael Heinrich articulates a similar critique of historicist readings of *Capital* in *Wissenschaft vom Wert* (2022 [1999], pp. 172–3; see also Heinrich 2023, pp. 260–1).

38   Macherey is unsparing in his critique of such a procedure: 'The worst defect of such logical formalism is that it tries to explain the work in relation to a single series of conditions: the model, by definition, is unique and self-sufficient. And here we have smuggled back the postulate of the unity and totality of the work; its real complexity has been abolished, dismantled, the better to be ignored' (2006, p. 55, translation modified).

39   Arthur 2002, p. 25. This commitment to capitalism as totality is shared by other representatives of the Systematic Dialectic school, for example Geert Reuten: 'The starting point [of

Arthur's undefended position implicitly invokes the authority of the entire Marxist humanist tradition, a position that originates in Marx's early writings,[40] to find its definitive and most influential formulation in Lukács's 1921 essay 'The Marxism of Rosa Luxemburg': 'The decisive difference between Marxism and bourgeois thought [is] the point of view of totality'.[41] In Lukács's famous treatment, the category of totality constitutes 'the essence of the method that Marx took over from Hegel'.[42] This position necessarily implies, Lukács argues, the mediated unity of both subject and object as totality, such that 'only classes can represent this total point of view'. For Marx, abandoning the initial political sloganeering of the *Communist Manifesto*, the category of *class* would come to represent in *Capital*'s science of causes the terminal *explanandum* of its thousands of pages of analysis (in the form of the four, incomplete paragraphs of Volume III, chapter 52, 'Classes'), with the science of value in the capitalist social form its *explanans*. For Lukács, in contrast, the subjective point of view of totality, which is to say, that of the proletariat, miraculously explains the teleology it presupposes, the faith-based theodicy of revolution: 'Revolution', writes Lukács, 'is the product of a point of view in which the category of totality is predominant .... As doubt develops into certainty the petty bourgeois and reactionary elements disappear without a trace: doubt turns to optimism and to the theoretical certainty of the coming revolution'.[43] This assertion culminates in Lukács's dogmatic certainty of the historical necessity of revolution, as if the imputed, merely imagined proletarian standpoint of totality could predict the fall of paving stones on the collective head of the capitalist class: 'This certitude [of proletarian revolution] can be guaranteed methodologically – by the dialectical method ... as the certitude that the ... historical process will come to fruition'.[44]

Systematic Dialectics] is an all-encompassing conception of some object-totality (capitalism) that abstractly captures the essence of that object-totality (compare the "commodity" for Marx's *Capital*)' (Reuten 2014, p. 244).

40 We thus read in the entry on 'Totality' in the Harvard *Dictionary of Marxist Thought* that 'World history becomes decipherable only when the totalising interconnections *objectively* arise out of the conditions of capitalist development and competition "which produced world history for the first time insofar as it made all civilised nations and every individual member of them dependent for the satisfaction of the wants on *the whole world* [via] the productive forces, which have been developed to a totality"' (Marx, cited in Bottomore 1983, p. 480, emphasis in original).

41 Lukács 1968, p. 27.
42 Ibid.
43 Lukács 1968, pp. 29, 37.
44 Lukács 1968, p. 43.

Proletarian revolution having weathered the vicissitudes of the twentieth century, in Arthur's case, unlike that of Lukács, the 'standpoint of totality' remains strictly limited to that of a *logical* presupposition devoid of any explicit political teleology.[45] 'Ontologically', Arthur summarises, systematic dialectic 'addresses itself to *totalities* and thus to their comprehension through systematically connected categories'.[46] While, as we have seen, Hegel explicitly understands the object of his various analyses to be totalities, whether this is true for Marx remains uncertain in the absence of some degree of textual analysis on Arthur's part that would support this fundamental claim. Instead, Arthur simply begs the question regarding this shibboleth of the Systematic Dialectic school, and directly proceeds to draw his own original conclusions from a position that may or may not correspond to Marx's argument in *Capital*.[47]

Arthur thus rightly underlines the specificity of Marx's logical – as opposed to historical – form of demonstration, stressing its discontinuity with the order of historical events ('The expositional order of [the] categories does not have to coincide with the order of their appearance in history'), while in the very same sentence presupposing without demonstration that the categories of capitalism serve to 'conceptualise an existent, concrete whole'.[48]

Macherey, in contrast, decisively rejects a vision of critical interpretation as the revelation of the consonant unity of the work, 'the postulate of harmony or totality: the work is perfect, completed, and constitutes a finished entity'.[49] While in this view its constitutive dissonance subtracts the work from the category of totality, it is nonetheless a singular, existing thing.[50] Whether,

---

45 'Capital is closed in *form*, hence the relevance of Hegel's totalising logic' (Arthur 2009, p. 172, emphasis in original).

46 Arthur 2009, p. 5, emphasis added. Arthur goes on to repeat this undemonstrated presupposition in *The New Dialectic* (2002), for example pp. 17, 25, 26, 64.

47 Chris Arthur does not define his own understanding of totality, but simply deploys the term immediately from the beginning of *New Dialectic*: 'My own view starts from the premise that theory faces an existent totality [and] hence transitions in the argument spring from the effort to *reconstruct* the whole' (2002, p. 6).

48 Arthur 2009, p. 4.

49 Macherey 2006, p. 90, translation modified. See also Bellofiore's contrasting distinction between the reading, interpretation, and reconstruction of *Das Kapital*. Bellofiore 2018, pp. 358–60.

50 'What begs to be explained in the work is not that false simplicity that derives from the apparent unity of its meaning, but *the presence of a relation, or an opposition, between elements of the exposition or levels of the composition*, those disparities that point to a conflict of meaning. This conflict is not the sign of an imperfection; it reveals the inscription of an otherness in the work, through which it maintains a relationship with that which it is not, that which happens at its margins. To explain the work is to show that, contrary

like Marx's *Capital*, it remains a radically unfinished and incomplete work in progress, or nominally complete, like Spinoza's *Ethics* or Proust's *A la recherche*, the work, despite and even because of its infinite determinations, remains a finite thing, and, consequently, emphatically not a totality: 'If the work does not produce or contain the principle of its own closure, it is nevertheless definitively enclosed within its own limits (though they may not be self-appointed limits). The work is finite because it is incomplete'.[51]

Readers of *The New Dialectic* have tended to focus on the inadequacies of Arthur's liberal reconstruction of the capitalist social form, taking issue for example with Arthur's 'random selection of categories of Hegel's *Logic* ... applied to a selection of more or less random categories of the first five chapters of *Capital*', as well as with Arthur's reconstructivist claim that Marx prematurely introduces abstract labour as the substance of value in the first chapter of *Capital*.[52] Here, I wish to focus not on Arthur's interpretive reconstruction of the capitalist social form, but instead on the adequacy of categories such as totality and constitutive negation for understanding *Capital*'s process of exposition. On this score, Jacques Bidet's is to my mind the most relevant critique of *The New Dialectic*, for he asserts (without actually developing this argument) the basic inadequacy of the categories of totality[53] and the expressive determination that totality would bestow on each determination.[54]

---

  to appearances, it is not independent, but bears in its material substance the imprint of a determinate absence which is also the principle of its identity' (Macherey 2006, p. 89, translation modified, emphasis added).

51 Macherey 2006, p. 90.

52 Both of these critiques find eloquent elaboration in Elena Louisa Lange's article 'The Critique of Political Economy and the "New Dialectic": Marx, Hegel, and the Problem of Christopher J. Arthur's "Homology Thesis"' (2016).

53 'The mistake, to my mind, lies in the attempt to represent capitalism as a "system", whereas it can only be conceived in fact as a "structure"' (Bidet 2006, p. 132).

54 In contrast to Arthur, who argues that 'the significance of each element is determined by its place in the totality' (2002, p. 26), Bidet rightly reads Marx as presenting each conceptual category 'as a moment possessing its own coherence and completion .... And this is incompatible with the Hegelian concept of system .... It is not the concept that changes [in its negative dialectical determination through the progression of Marx's argument]; rather, there is a change of concept .... The "theory of value" is in no way transformed by the [subsequently introduced] theory of surplus-value, which, on the contrary, expressly presupposes it, unchanged, in the pure and perfect form that Marx has given it in his exposition in Part One' (Bidet 2006, p. 132). Bidet's position precisely develops Althusser's schematic proposition, in his 1977 'Avant-propos', that Marx proceeds by the positive dialectical 'positioning' of concepts, to be discussed below, as well as echoing Heinrich's exhaustively detailed analysis of the additive logic of the first seven chapters of *Capital* in *How to Read*.

The initial presentation of *The New Dialectic* is predetermined by a significant silence, in the form of its unquestioned presupposition that the concept of 'dialectic' refers to Hegelian, negative contradiction-based demonstration. Here too, Arthur simply presupposes what needs to be shown: if *dialectic* refers to the notion of logical reasoning in general,[55] and Hegel's dialectic based on constitutive negation and contradiction constitutes only one variety of this process, could it be that Marx deploys other modes of demonstration across the thousands of pages of *Capital*? Never actually addressing this possibility, one striking aspect of *The New Dialectic* is Arthur's general willingness to forgo analysis of Marx's actual modes of logical analysis and demonstration, and instead liberally to 'reconstruct' his own understanding of the (negative) dialectic of capitalism. With the important exception of his chapter 6, where Arthur analyses 'The Negation of the Negation in Marx's *Capital*' (discussed below), *The New Dialectic* never develops its claim for *Capital*'s 'systematic dialectic' via a systematic analysis of *Capital*'s dialectic (in the general sense of its modes of demonstration), but instead only occasionally inserts citations selected to support its negative dialectical presuppositions, these most frequently being taken from the *Grundrisse* and earlier drafts and editions of *Capital* in which the influence of Hegel's logic remains most pronounced.[56]

Here too, we can say that Arthur's procedure confirms Macherey's critique of interpretation, in its tendency to conceal the complex, overdetermined work and its constitutional dissonance behind the gleaming image of the vision of totality it artfully constructs: primarily directed toward 'an external end' (the articulation of his own original understanding of the negative dialectical sys-

---

55 See above, p. 26.
56 As for example Arthur's reliance upon Marx's formulation in the *Grundrisse* of the contradiction of money as value 'for itself' as opposed to the immediate relation of specific commodities as 'values "in themselves" to each other', from which Arthur draws the imaginary conclusion that 'money cannot realise the concept of value because of the contradiction that in striving to be value for itself it must be alienated but cannot be' (2002, p. 31). Bidet argues in this vein that Arthur's interpretation and its reliance on the Hegelian concepts of totality and system 'leans chiefly on the *Grundrisse*' (Bidet 2005, p. 124). I will argue below against this widespread assumption that Arthur shares, i.e., that Marx presents the concept of the commodity as constitutively contradictory. On the intensive relation between *Grundrisse* and Hegel's *Logic*, see Uchida 2016 [1988]; the classic reference is Roman Rosdolsky's *The Making of Marx's Capital* (1992 [1968]): 'The Rough Draft [i.e., the *Grundrisse*] must be designated as a massive reference to Hegel, in particular to his *Logic* – irrespective of how radically and materialistically Hegel was inverted! The publication of the *Grundrisse* means that academic critics of Marx will no longer be able to write without first having studied his method and its relation to Hegel' (Rosdolsky 1992 [1968], p. 323).

tematic dialectic of capital) rather than an explication of the necessary and complex dynamics of the text itself,[57] Arthur's interpretive effort amounts to 'a mythical task that endows [the work] with a unity and totality into which it vanishes'.[58] This process of reduction and revelation culminates in Arthur's schematic and reductive chart of correspondences between Hegel's *Logic* and *Capital*.[59]

5   The Problem with Totality

Capital is not a totality, whether considered materially or logically. This general conclusion follows simply as a logical consequence of the nature of all axiomatic logical systems.[60] Any logical system requires an axiomatic foundation to establish the basic principles allowing for its demonstrations, and the largely informal logical system of *Capital* is no different. I argue throughout this book that the first sentence of *Capital* provides such an axiomatic starting point to Marx's argument – that capitalism is the social form characterized by the generalization of commodity production and exchange, with the commodity as its basic unit – and that many of Marx's propositions follow apodictically from this initial axiom – that in the capitalist social form, all commodities require a value form; that generalized exchange requires a general equivalent form; that labour power is the only commodity capable of creating surplus value; that the value and price of a commodity tend to diverge, etc.

Now, any axiomatic system can be said to be *complete* – a logical totality – if it can derive whether any proposition formulated within its language is true or false, and it can be said to be *consistent* as a totality if its derived proposi-

---

[57] 'The literary work is not ... a quest for its own vanishing point. The linear simplicity that gives it boldness and freshness is actually only its most superficial aspect; we must also be able to distinguish its real and fundamental complexity. And in this complexity we must recognise the signs of a necessity .... In all literary works can be found the tokens of this internal rupture, this decentring, the evidence of its subordinate dependence on precise conditions of possibility. Thus the work is never – or only apparently – a coherent and unified whole' (Macherey 2006, pp. 44, 46, translation modified).

[58] Macherey 2006, p. 27. In such an interpretation, 'the work is only the expression of this meaning, which is also to say, the shell that encases it, which must be broken to reveal [this meaning]. The interpreter accomplishes this liberating violence: he dismantles the work to refashion it in the image of its meaning, to make it denote directly that of which it was the indirect expression .... Translation and reduction: to reduce the apparent diversity of the work to its unitary signification' (Macherey 2006, p. 85, translation modified).

[59] Arthur 2002, pp. 108–9.

[60] Thanks to Burhannudin Baki for helping me to think through this logical question.

tions do not result in logical contradictions. While I argue that this is the case for the great majority of Marx's propositions and demonstrations, Macherey, Balibar, Antonio Negri, Jacques Bidet, Riccardo Bellofiore and others have all shown that there exist multiple points of logical rupture and discontinuity in *Capital*: in other words, that the logic of *Capital* is incomplete because its own consistency or inconsistency cannot be derived from its initial axioms.[61] Without needing to rehearse their various readings, I will simply argue below that it is Arthur himself who undermines his own assumption for the logical totality of *Capital*, insofar as he can only present this ideological image of a complete functional system by excluding from consideration the anomalous, disjunctive, disruptive power of living labour.

Following his private critique of Althusser's use of the concept of totality in the first edition of *Reading Capital*,[62] Pierre Macherey would develop a more sustained critique of the concept in *Theory of Literary Production* and his writings on Spinoza.[63] Macherey's critique is extensive, if not systematically argued: totality, he argues, can and should only refer to the fabrication of imaginary, inadequately determinate sets (such as Arthur's undemonstrated position), and necessarily remains a tendential, incomplete construction of a thought object. In Macherey's understanding, the explication of a text must seek instead to construct an analysis of the necessity that governs its overdetermined, dissonant complexity:

> Rather than sufficiency and ideal consistency, a determinate insufficiency and incompleteness actually shapes the work. The work is necessarily incomplete in itself: not extrinsically, in a fashion that could be completed to 'realise' the work. This incompleteness, indicated by the confrontation of distinct meanings, is the true reason for its articulation. The thin line of the discourse is the temporary appearance behind which we recognise

---

61 See RC, Ch. 3; Balibar 1991, Bellofiore 2009, Bidet 2009, and Negri 1985.
62 See Montag 2013, Ch. 5.
63 As discussed in the previous chapter, while Macherey does not discuss *Capital* in *Theory of Literary Production*, he does explicitly apply its general critique to the case of *Capital* in his 1967 intervention at the Cérisy 'Centennaire du *Capital*': 'The enterprise of a total or "totalising" reading is ideological in its essence .... A scientific text can only be taken up on the condition of being continued: a closed, repetitive reading is itself an ideological reading .... The object of *Capital* is an object constructed theoretically, and this is precisely why *Capital* is not a formal system. If we were to read it as a closed system, this would constitute an interpretive reading, a repetition and reprisal of a completed system' (2006, pp. 57, 61, 92).

the determinate complexity of a text: on the condition that this complexity is not that of a 'totality', illusory and mediate.[64]

Constitutionally finite and incomplete, the work is never a terminate totality or unified whole. This position, one that Macherey articulates so resolutely, nonetheless itself remains underdetermined: what, we may ask, does the concept of totality in fact indicate, and why does Macherey, following Spinoza, so vigorously assert its epistemological inadequacy?

Derived from the Greek *To holon* [τὸ ὅλον], the Latin *totalis* indicates a *complete* and *integral* whole.[65] Conceptually, the notion of totality thus implies that which has nothing essential to its nature outside itself: it is the thing entirely self-sufficient and in-itself [*in se est*]. This as opposed to all finite singular things [*res in suo genere finita* (EID2)], which, as finite, necessarily depend causally upon other things for their determination, and, via the infinity of these reciprocal determinations, are in fact, Macherey observes, *overdetermined* by other things within their genre or attribute: a body (in the sense of any extensive material thing) will always be limited and essentially determined by other bodies, just as any finite thought [*cogitatio*] will necessarily be limited and determined by other thoughts.[66]

The conclusion Macherey draws from Spinoza's incipient definitions constitutes a rejection of the notion of totality as applied to any finite thing: Spinoza's 'logic of the finite [indicates that] a finite thing, whatever it may be, can never be thought absolutely for itself, but only relatively by the intermediary of its relation to another thing'.[67] The implication of this initial position is thus that to speak of any finite, determinate thing as *a* totality (such as the capitalist mode of production and/or the logical system of the book *Capital* for Arthur) is to have recourse to a merely *imaginary* figure based on our sense impressions of that object as a discrete and self-sufficient thing, as opposed to adequately grasping its necessarily infinite determinations by other things. Consequently, this imaginary figure (say, Arthur's abstract hypostatisation of *the* capitalist mode of production) is then imagined to produce effects upon the various moments of the system. Marx, in *Capital*, proceeds in precisely the opposite fashion, from the logical demonstration of the essential nature of a thing (such as the commodity) to its necessary effects, without the imputation of what Lukács called 'the standpoint of totality'.

---

64   Macherey 2006, pp. 88–9, translation modified.
65   Cassin 2014, p. 1234.
66   Macherey 1998, pp. 35, 36.
67   Macherey 1998, pp. 72–3.

Indeed, Macherey indicates in his commentary that the topic of Book I of *Ethics* is precisely not some finite, determinate thing, but 'an object that is infinite, and even infinitely infinite: the set [*ensemble*] of reality considered *in its totality and as a totality*, according to the principles that found its unity [and] develop a rational thought on the subject of *all* [*au sujet de tout*] by treating this whole according to its nature as *whole* [*sa nature de tout*]'.[68] It would thus seem that Macherey expressly limits the notion of totality or whole [τὸ ὅλον] to Spinoza's substance, not as the hypostatisation of a thing, but as the starting point for the adequate knowledge of nature.

I would argue, moreover, that Macherey's initial use of the terms *totality* and *whole* in reference to Spinozist substance that I have just cited is itself merely imagistic, in the sense that the indefinite article ('*a* totality') tends to hypostatise into a determinate thing, what Macherey goes on to steadfastly and repeatedly argue is precisely not *a* thing, determinate and countable (as one monist substance): 'to think the real *in totality* according to the synthetic procedure or geometric order that proceeds from the cause to its effects, and not the reverse' requires a conception of substance not as *a* thing but as Being, understood as the presupposition that 'conditions the set of its [determinate] affections'.[69] To think of substance as *a* thing is 'to transfer onto [the concept of

---

68   Macherey 1998, p. 65, my emphasis. Note how Macherey's phrasing in the French original seeks to avoid any definite or indefinite articles that would reify substance and to speak instead 'au sujet de tout', a formulation difficult to render in English.

69   Macherey's critique of the substantivisation of Spinozist substance implicitly pursues Althusser's initial polemical and underdeveloped rejection of Plekhanovist, monist understandings of dialectical materialism (discussed in Chapter 1). After Plekhanov himself, the determinant figure in this regard is the Spinozist Marxism of Plekhanov's disciple Abram Deborin, editor of *Pod Znamenem Marxsizma* (Under the Banner of Marxism). Tasked by Lenin and Trotsky from 1922 with developing the theoretical foundations of Bolshevism, Deborin's contributions to the journal were crucial in particular for orienting the extensive Soviet reception of Spinoza (Oitinnen 2022, pp. 4–5). In this regard, it is notable, for example, that in a 1927 article in which he discusses Spinoza's 'remarkably dialectical formulation of the problem of finite and infinite', Deborin speaks repeatedly of '*the whole* of nature' and 'nature as *a whole*' (cited in Oikinnen 2022, pp. 7–8, emphasis added). (Of course, the Russian original, like all Slavic languages other than Macedonian, would not use articles to identify the nominal referents of phrases, as in English or French). On the debates in Soviet philosophy more generally, as well as its reception of Spinoza more particularly, see Yakhot 2012 [1981]. Landon Frim and Harrison Fluss articulate a richly argued contemporary version of Marxist substance monism, for example via a critique of Deleuze's reading of Spinoza in 'Substance Abuse: Spinoza contra Deleuze' (2018). Fluss and Frim more generally reaffirm the Plekhanovist-Deborin tendency to hypostatise Spinozist substance as countable thing, for example in their theoreticist-materialist intervention 'Reason is Red', where they write that 'Marxism ... demands monism, the idea that the entire universe is *an intelligible Whole*' (2022).

substance] characteristics that belong only to its affections .... Substance, insofar as it exists necessarily [i.e., as *causa sui*], thus by virtue of its proper [*seule*] nature, does not exist in the manner of a finite thing, and thus in the mode of an individual existence, as a singular entity finding its place next to others within a series that can be enumerated'. Substance, in other words, is not *one* or *a* substance or totality; 'it is not "an" existence, in the sense of a particular existence that would depend upon causes exterior to its nature, but existence itself thought as absolute ... the fact of existing understood in itself, thus independent of reference to any particular existence whatsoever'.[70]

To think of Spinozist substance as a determinate thing or totality is to grasp this most difficult concept inadequately, through the imagination.[71] 'To attentively think the nature of substance', Macherey observes,

> is a new manner of thinking existence, in itself and no longer in number [*non plus en nombre*], and thus without bringing to bear consideration of exterior causes .... The nature of substance is such that it is subtracted from the grasp of the imagination, which can only denature it in replacing it in a network of exterior determinations in which it figures as an existing thing next to or above others [as a transcendent instance or subject of monism, Althusser would have said], which amounts to denying its absolute relation to itself that excludes all relation to anything other than itself.[72]

---

[70] Macherey 1998, p. 86. Let me reiterate that despite our unyielding disagreement on this point, the generous and probing comments of Landon Frim and Harrison Fluss while drafting this chapter, not to mention their informed and original understanding of the relation between Spinoza, Hegel, and Marx, have been essential in pushing me to better articulate my own position.

[71] Macherey emphasises that the process of enumeration in general is fundamentally linked to the imagination: Spinoza indicates in this way 'the privileged relation that the imagination bears, not only with the consideration of singular existences, but with the very fact of enumerating them, and thus as well with that of counting in general, a preoccupation from which the rational analysis of substance ... is completely removed in principle' (1998, p. 86).

[72] Macherey 1998, p. 87. Macherey continues to develop this point a few pages further in his commentary on the second Scolium to EIP8: 'Substance can only be unique, not in the sense of a nature that would be realised in only a single copy [*exemplaire*], and thus more than zero and less than two, but of a thing of which all possible forms of realisation enter into the nature that defines it .... In the expression "a single substance of the same nature", [the indefinite article] "a" is not to be taken in the sense of the number "one" as an element of quantification' (Macherey 1998, p. 90).

To think Spinoza's idea of substance, then, is to refuse to speak of 'a' substance at all, but instead, Macherey continues, of 'subsisting [*le subsister*], or existing [*l'exister*] considered as such'.[73]

If the concept of totality or the whole as hypostatised thing is thus necessarily inadequate and imaginary, both in the case of substance (because to speak of substance as a thing is to reify it as an existing thing) as well as of any determinate object of thought (since the process of adequate construction of an object of thought is infinite), how does Spinoza, in Macherey's reading, allow for the adequate understanding of any existing thing or 'whole' (such as the capitalist social form)?

In his letters of 10 and 14 May 1965 to Althusser on the problem of totality in *Reading Capital*, Macherey somewhat cryptically suggests that Spinoza's 1665 letter XXXII to Oldenberg contains the theoretical resources to overcome Althusser's ungrounded references to 'the structured whole' in the first edition of *Reading Capital*: 'It seems to me', Macherey writes, 'that when you speak of a set [*ensemble*] or of a whole, you thereby add a concept that is absolutely unnecessary to the demonstration, and which may later become an obstacle (the idea of the real whole in opposition to that of the spiritual whole is not very clear: the idea of the whole is really the spiritualist conception of structure) .... Each time I have encountered the phrase "structured whole" in what you have written, I was struck by the problems that it raises'.[74] Macherey's point is that reference to totality or a whole, whether expressive totality, the explicit object of Althusser's critique in *Reading Capital*, or structured whole (as Althusser suggests positively) is 'absolutely unnecessary to the demonstration'. In what sense is this the case, following the Spinozist logic Macherey refers to?

Let us look at Spinoza's letter XXXII more carefully than Macherey does in his suggestion to Althusser. There, in answer to Oldenberg's inquiry into

---

73   Macherey 1998, p. 90n1. It is interesting to note how Macherey's critique of the hypostatisation of substance has distant, far cruder echoes, in the 1920s debate between the mechanistic Spinozism of Liubov Akselrod, with its emphasis on substance as *causa sui*, and Deborin's Plekhanovist position that 'substance is matter' (Yakhot 2012, Chapter 6.4). Despite basing her critique of Spinoza on a racist antisemitism that deterministically reduces Spinoza's thought to its putative 'Jewish origins', Akselrod argues: 'What an absurdity to assert that Spinoza's substance is matter. To recognise it as matter means to design a very strange entity: substance is matter, one of its attributes is matter, and another attribute is thinking' (Akselrod, cited in Yakhot 2012, Ch. 6.4). To indicate the base nature of this impassioned debate (to say nothing of Akselrod's antisemitism), one need only observe that for Spinoza it is not 'matter' that is an attribute, as Akselrod claims, but extension, which is an entirely different concept.

74   Cited in Montag 2013, p. 75.

'the grounds of our belief that each part of Nature accords with the whole', Spinoza begins by pointing out that 'the actual manner of this coherence and the agreement of each part with the whole ... is beyond my knowledge. To know this it would be necessary to know the whole of Nature and all its parts'. Instead, Spinoza argues to his correspondent that our knowledge of any putative whole, and not only being qua being, remains inadequate and imaginary in the absence of its systematic, adequate demonstration, whether through common notions or intuitive knowledge. Rather than developing a systematic and comprehensive demonstration of this point as he does in the *Ethics*, however, Spinoza fabricates for his correspondent a striking, hauntingly graphic and even fantastic image, his famous parable of the worm in the blood. The point of Spinoza's allegory is that the decision as to whether an object (such as the blood in which Spinoza's imaginary worm swims) constitutes a whole or a part is necessarily subjective.[75] It is possible to understand any determinate thing as either part or whole, depending on how this knowledge is constructed, whether things are understood to 'adapt themselves to one another so that they are in closest possible agreement', such that each is a part of a whole, or, alternatively, 'are different from one another', such that each is understood to constitute a whole. As objects of knowledge, the parts of the blood (what we today identify as white and red blood cells, plasma, etc.), in Spinoza's example, can readily be understood either as whole or part: from the perspective of their 'agreement [they] form all together one fluid', but were we to consider each in its singular

---

75   To be sure, in this letter Spinoza does explicitly speak of 'the whole of Nature' and of 'the universe as a whole', which seems to imply for his reader a conviction that *there is* an objective totality of Nature, though our finite minds cannot know its infinitely infinite determinations. This, however, stands in marked contrast to his definitions of substance and God (Nature) in the *Ethics*, which make no reference of any kind to a whole or totality. In my view, Spinoza's epistolary recourse to this image of the 'whole of Nature' marks a rhetorical compromise intended to engage his reader's inadequate understanding of Spinoza's position, analogous to Marx's parable of the linen and coat that speak to one another in 'the language of commodities' in *Capital*. Rather than speaking more adequately of substance without reference to totality or the whole, as *causa sui* and the *in se* as he does in *Ethics*, Spinoza here instead adopts the relatively unclear and imaginary language of his interlocutor ('I presume that you are asking for the grounds of our belief that each part of Nature accords with the whole'), a rhetorical device he regularly adopts in the Scolia of *Ethics* (Macherey is at pains to indicate many of these passages in his *Introduction*, for example in his lengthy commentary on the Appendix to Book I). Spinoza regularly does so, Macherey insists, through an ethical commitment to meet his interlocutor halfway, as it were, and to communicate more effectively with a reader who, from habit, necessarily understands something entirely different by familiar terms such as God, Nature, substance, or whole than what Spinoza means by them.

difference from the others (white vs. red cells, etc.), 'to that extent we regard them each as a whole, not a part'.

To call a thing either a whole or a part is thus for Spinoza merely relative and subjective, fundamentally dependent upon how an object of knowledge is constructed, more or less adequately, as a figure of the understanding. As Macherey summarises in *Hegel or Spinoza*, 'For Spinoza, the notion of totality ... does not represent the positive existence of a being ... but [depends] on the point of view of the understanding that cuts it up in the infinite chain of singular things, by considering it as a whole'. This position, moreover, indicates Spinoza's fundamental antagonism with Hegelian logic, as the absolute distinction between substance and subject, insofar as the former, by definition for Spinoza absolute and thus indeterminate, can never be figured as a determinate whole.[76]

That said, Spinoza is not propounding the relativism of all judgements. He clearly indicates to Oldenberg an entirely different path to adequate knowledge of any singular thing: beginning from a true idea, it is possible adequately to understand the essential nature of that thing, and then, constructively, to proceed from one adequately constructed idea to another. This synthetic logic proceeds to construct the 'coherence [*cohaerentiam*] of parts' via a cumulative understanding by which 'the laws or nature of another part adapts itself to the laws or nature of another part', absent all teleology.[77] While we cannot know in totality either the infinite determinations of any singular thing (such as the capitalist social form) nor the infinitely infinite determinations of the whole of Nature, the mind can nonetheless proceed constructively, from an adequate knowledge of one true idea, to the (logical) successor with which it additively forms a part of a larger body.[78]

---

76   Macherey 2011, p. 184.
77   Cavaillès modulates this Spinozist position as a philosophy of the mathematical science of the infinite: 'The body of a theory is a certain operatory homogeneity – as described by the axiomatic presentation – but when the theory is carried to the infinite, the iteration and the complications provide results and an intelligible system of contents that are ungovernable, and an internal necessity obliges itself by way of an enlargement, which moreover is unforeseeable'. Cavaillès 2021, p. 81.
78   Arthur himself seems to admit to imagining totality and the constitutive negative dialectic of *Capital* precisely because – as Spinoza argues to Oldenberg – of the (Hegelian) perspective he chooses, ie., as what Lukács called the 'point of view of totality': 'There is a contradiction in the commodity *only* if it is claimed that it is imbued with a universal, namely value, as a result of its participation in a whole network of capitalist commodity production' (Arthur 2002, p. 70). Precisely so: if one examines the concept of the commodity in itself, as Marx does in the first pages of *Capital*, then, as a *whole*, the concept possesses two parts or attributes: its use and exchange-values. If, as subsequently in Marx's presentation, the commodity is instead examined within the general system of exchange,

Instead of Arthur's claim for a negative dialectical knowledge based on the contradiction between any determinate concept such as money or value and the (merely presupposed, imaginary) totality of the capitalist social form in all its infinite determinations, Marx's argument in *Capital*, in this view, should be understood to proceed constructively, from the adequate knowledge of one concept (the general form of appearance of any society 'in which the capitalist mode of production predominates', the commodity form, the substance of value, etc.) to the next with which it is most closely linked (the passage from use-value to exchange-value, for example). This is precisely to indicate what Macherey only suggests to Althusser: the reference to totality is not simply 'absolutely unnecessary to the demonstration', but utterly misleading, in the sense that the concept of totality inherently refers to 'the *complete* set of elements of a whole' (Lalande), a terminally and wholly complete object rather than an inherently infinite construct.[79] Neither *Capital* the book nor the capitalist mode of production, the object of knowledge Marx constructs, is subject to the completion of totality, but only the more or less adequate construction of each of its logical steps and their infinitely complex ramifications and network of correspondences, the sum of which do not make up a whole.

A case in point is Marx's concept of total surplus value: 'Equal amounts of capital, no matter how they are composed, receive equal shares (aliquot parts) of the *totality* of surplus-value produced by the total social capital'.[80] Marx's analysis here explicitly takes as its object not the investigation of specific individual commodities, as did classical economics, but the total mass of commodities, initially in the first sentence of *Capital* impressionistically described as an undifferentiated, 'immense heap' (*ungeheure Warensammlung*), and subsequently and with increasing theoretical concretion, as identical subdivisions or 'aliquot parts' that constitute the general substance of capital.[81]

---

then it appears as a single component *part* of that system, precisely as Spinoza argues in his parable of the worm in the blood stream.

79 'Totalité', in Lalande 2010, p. 1137, emphasis added.
80 Marx 1981, p. 274, emphasis added.
81 'In capitalist production, each capital is assumed to be a unit, and aliquot part of the total capital'. Marx, quoted in Moseley 2017, p. 46. Marx's fractional perspective has confused many readers, since Marx repeatedly frames the rhetoric of his argument in terms of individual examples (coats, linen, tailoring and weaving, and the like), above all in the first chapters of Volume I. Moseley emphasises the purely theoretical nature of Marx's analysis, observing that 'It is not always clear that Marx's theory in Volume I is about the total capital and the total surplus value produced in the economy as a whole, because the theory is usually illustrated in terms of an individual capital and even a single, solitary worker .... However, the individual capitals in Marx's examples represent the total social capital of the capitalist class as a whole. Individual capitals are not analysed as separate and distinct

As Fred Moseley has shown, Marx meticulously constructs this concept across the three volumes of *Capital*, such that it serves, in Volume III, as the crucial theoretical object that allows Marx to distinguish between profit and surplus value. The concept has no empirical or even quantitative basis or nature, there exists no Fort Knox of total surplus value, but remains from the first page of *Capital* to the last a purely theoretical object of increasing theoretical complexity. For all the rigor and adequacy of Marx's construction, 'the total mass of surplus-value' remains in *Capital* an inherently incomplete concept, as Moseley's 400-page analysis amply demonstrates. In the place of Arthur's impressionistic gesture to capital as a logical totality, a concept such as total surplus-value, which Marx rigorously, if necessarily incompletely, develops, serves to lucidly distinguish Marx's theoretical analysis from the inherent contradictions of mainstream economics' individualist, summative process. From this we might even conclude that Marx's reference to the 'totality' of surplus-value that I cited above is a terminological lapsus, a usage limited to a single instance in the uncorrected 1864 manuscript that Engels reworked into Volume III; instead, Marx in every other case refers to the '*total* mass of surplus-value', arguably tending to avoid the implication of surplus-value as a complete and closed conceptual set.

Arthur, like Lukács before him, plays the role of the worm in Spinoza's blood: reassuringly swathed in the balm of absolute knowledge (whether that of the logic of *Capital* or the theodicy of the proletarian revolution), the point of view of expressive totality bestows the aura of absolute truth via its mere assertion. In *The New Dialectic*, as it had for Lukács, the subjective hypostatisation of the actually existing concept of capitalism as negative dialectical totality offers a reassuring image, the function of imputed totality magically bestowing on every partial, expressive determination of the whole its necessary and sufficient reason. Affectively, the transcendent monism of totality, whether logical or revolutionary theodicy, serves in this view to repress the *anxiety* of the knowing subject before its constitutive not-knowing, to repress the necessary incompletion of any object of knowledge. It was not for nothing that Lacan initially founded the singularity of any analysis on this Spinozist epistemology: it is Spinoza who most forcefully refuses the imaginary, regressive figure of totality as guarantee. The *Ethics*, principle among its many virtues, instead

---

real capitals, but rather as representatives and 'aliquot parts' of the total social capital' (2017, pp. 45–6). In this sense, one could say of Marx's examples of specific commodities such as coats and linen what he says of his historical example of English capitalism, i.e., that coats and linen, like 'England [are] used as the main illustration of the theoretical developments [he] makes' (Marx 1976, p. 90).

initiates a treatment, offering the subject the means to sustain the anxiety of not-knowing via the progressive amendment of the intellect, in the certainty that the finite human mind is capable of more adequate understanding than such imaginary chimera, even to realise a *scientia intuitiva* – not of totality – but of the absolute.[82]

6 The Systematic Dissonance of *Capital*

Materially, it is quite obvious that Marx's book *Capital* is a radically incomplete project. Even Volume I of *Capital* – the publication of which Marx oversaw through its second, revised German edition and first French translation (1872–75) – remains a work-in-progress; Marx made notes for a further complete revision of it in 1881 (which he never carried out). What we know today as Volume I is a bricolage Engels made of the second German edition of 1872 and the French edition of 1872–75. While the bulk of the first draft of Volume I from 1863 is lost, the first German edition of 1867 as well as Marx's notes for the 1872 edition and his intended further 1881 revision contain many important formulations and developments of his demonstration (in particular, a radically different presentation of the key first chapter on the value-form), aspects absent from Engels's posthumous 'definitive edition'. Volume III, assembled by Engels after Marx's death, is based upon a single manuscript from 1864–65; it is thus not only theoretically immature compared to Marx's subsequent work on Volumes I and II, but in fact terminates abruptly with Marx's comment 'etc.', a mere five paragraphs into its twenty-fifth chapter dedicated to what presumably would have been one of the essential results of Marx's analysis, the concept of 'Classes'.[83]

In fact, attention to the totality of Marx's drafts, notebooks, and letters from 1857 to 1881, gradually becoming available in the definitive MEGA² edition of Marx and Engels's works, leads Michael Heinrich to draw the distinctly Althusserian conclusion that 'in a strict sense, a three-volume work "Capital" written by Marx does not really exist. ... There is no clear difference between drafts and the final work – we have only differently developed drafts of a shifting, unfinished and incomplete project'.[84]

---

82 'Sensing what the subject can tolerate, in terms of anxiety, is something that puts you to the test at every moment. ... As regards anxiety, there isn't any safety net. ... It's upon the cutting edge of anxiety that we have to hold fast'. Lacan 2014, pp. 5, 9, 15, translation modified. See McNulty 2009, pp. 1–39.
83 See Moseley 2016.
84 Heinrich 2009, p. 96.

Given this genetic complexity, it is patently obvious that Marx's intellectual project of a critique of political economy that we know as *Capital* does not constitute a totality in any sense of the word, and that the presumption of totality by proponents of Systematic Dialectics such as Arthur and Reuten is a mere article of faith. Their unquestioned certainty underwrites a distinctly theological reading of *Capital*. This imaginary totality, that of the theoretical object Marx constructed, as well as its materialist basis in the putative totality of actually-existing capitalism, constitutes for this Hegelian school of thought the transcendent instance that bestows meaning on each moment of the (imaginary) whole:

> Only on completion of the presentation, [Reuten writes, citing Hegel,] will we know that 'the truth of the differentiated is its being in unity'. ... Once the presentation is complete – and thus when the initial unifying concept [of the commodity] is shown to be inherent in the object-totality, in its full concreteness (γ) – will we have come full circle, confirming the truth of the abstract starting point.[85]

This providential day of theoretical plenitude is one that will never arrive, as Reuten himself knows as well as Althusser or Heinrich: *Capital* Volume I as we know it, Reuten observes parenthetically, 'requires further concrete grounding of the moments presented in this sequence (*Capital* Volumes II and III, as well as the books which Marx had planned but did not even begin to draft)'.[86] The Hegelian theoretical commitments of this school of Marxology thus lead them – despite their intensive knowledge of the extreme genetic complexity of Marx's *Capital* project that makes of it an unequivocally 'unfinished and incomplete project' (Heinrich) – to adhere to this Lukácsian-Hegelian theoretical imperative, and to bestow upon *Capital* the aura of a transcendent, emanant totality. Their analytic pursuit recommences a perpetually-in-process inquest into the theoretical promised land that is Marx's alleged Hegelian palimpsest, as they fervently continue to invoke 'the lonely hour of the last instance [that] never comes'.[87]

Similarly, it should be obvious on even the most cursory reading that Marx deploys a multiplicity of demonstrative modalities across the pages of *Capital*, from Marx's recurrent recourse to classical *modus ponens*, if-then propo-

---

85 Reuten 2014, p. 253.
86 Reuten 2014, p. 254.
87 Althusser 2005, p. 153.

sitions,[88] to imaginary phantasmagorias[89] and other quite original modes of demonstration Macherey, Althusser, and Balibar identify as the 'exhaustion' of concepts (Macherey), the non-dialectical, discrete 'positioning' (*position*) of concepts (Althusser), and the methods Balibar calls 'comparison' and 'results'.[90] While Chris Arthur does not literally claim that Marx's demonstration in *Capital*, unlike that of Hegel's *Logic*, proceeds *solely* via a dialectic of constitutive, negative contradiction and sublation, his unrelenting and unquestioned focus on this mode of demonstration certainly implies such a belief.

Arthur's exclusively Hegelian understanding of *Capital* as a substantive, expressive totality – the presentation of which is driven by the contradictory relation of any of its moments with that totality – grounds his presentation of its logic univocally, to the exclusion of any other mode of presentation:

> The [logic of *Capital*] depends upon the presupposition that there is a whole from which a violent abstraction has [initially] been made so as to constitute a simple beginning ...; and thus there arises a contradiction between the character of the element in isolation and its meaning as part of the whole. The treatment of this moment as inherently in contradiction with itself, on account of this, is given if it is assumed throughout the dialectical development that the whole remains immanent or implicit

---

88   A great many of Marx's principal propositions in *Capital* are articulated in variations of this form, for example: 'It follows from this that ...'; 'If then we disregard the use-value of commodities, only one property remains, that of being products of labour'; 'If we leave aside the determinate quality of productive activity, and therefore the useful character of the labour, what remains is its quality of being an expenditure of human labour-power'; 'since the magnitude of the value of a commodity represents nothing but the quantity of labour embodied in it, it follows that all commodities, when taken in certain proportions, must be equal in value'; '[Commodities'] objective character as values is therefore purely social. From this it follows self-evidently that [value] can only appear in the social relation between commodity and commodity' (Marx 1976, pp. 127, 128, 134, 136, 139).

89   'If commodities could speak, they would say this: our use-value may interest men, but it does not belong to us as objects' (Marx 1976, p. 143).

90   Balibar proposes the latter two categories in one of his rare analyses of Marx's method of demonstration in *Capital*, 'Un texte de methodologie'. This brief analysis appeared only in the first edition of *Lire le Capital*, in the form of an 'Annex' following his well-known chapter. One senses that Balibar cut this short, five-page text from subsequent editions because it would require much greater development actually to demonstrate what it only briefly proposes: that the distinction between the concepts of 'production en général' and 'production générale' in Marx's 1857 Introduction depends upon two distinct and 'parallel' forms of abstraction, and furthermore that this distinction proves that Marx's method unfolds 'toute entière dans la connaissance', (Balibar 2012, p. 657) rather than in the form of a traditional empiricist theory of knowledge. See Balibar 2012, pp. 655–61.

in it. This provides the basis for the transitions in the development of the categorial ordering. There is an impulse to provide a solution to a contradiction – a 'push' one might say – and there is the need to overcome the deficiency of the category with respect to its fulfilment in the whole.[91]

In this fashion, with no more than sporadic, selective textual references, Arthur bases his claim for the negative dialectical logic of *Capital* upon the priority of its status as an expressive totality: it is only because *Capital* is presupposed to form a substantive totality that each of its moments, in its incompletion, can be argued to enter into negative contradiction with that supposed-totality, logically propelling its sublation from one moment to the next.

On my reading of *New Dialectic*, Chris Arthur variously presents three distinct arguments for the consistency of Marx's logic of the capitalist social form as a totality, none of which is either systematic (to adopt Arthur's own term) or even directly relevant to showing that 'Capital [the book and its logic? The concept? The social form?] is closed in form'.[92] The first of these 'arguments' points to the totalising nature of capital, its tendency subsume all things within its logic, and to commodify all things and social relations: 'If value depends for its reality on the full development of capitalist production, then the concepts of Marx's first chapter can only have an abstract character, and the argument itself as it advances develops the meanings of these concepts, through grounding them adequately in the comprehended whole'.[93] Arthur's statement seems to confuse its categories, its first clause on the reality of value apparently indicating the real, material subsumption via commodification of means and relations of capitalist production, the second, confusingly addressing 'the concepts of Marx's first chapter'.

Were we to assume, for argument, that Arthur rigorously remains at the level of Marx's logic, and instead means 'the [concept] of value' and '[Marx's concept of] the full development of capitalist production', this obscure claim (even granted all this the reader must still guess at Arthur's exact meaning) has been more adequately and systematically explicated by Fred Moseley. In *Money and Totality*, Moseley comprehensively shows that throughout the expanse of Marx's economic manuscripts he presumes that 'the means of production in capitalist production are commodities, which have been purchased at the

---

91   Arthur 2002, p. 67.
92   Arthur 2009, p. 172.
93   Arthur 2002, p. 26.

beginning of the circuit of money capital, and which therefore enter the valorisation process with already existing specific prices'.[94]

Even so, while Arthur's claim may be true that 'only at the end of the reconstruction of the totality is its truth unfolded', this is true not because this so-called 'end' – a point Arthur never concretely indicates within Marx's exposition, nor could he, since it does not in fact exist within the incomplete and unfinished three volumes we know as *Capital* – would realise the putative negative dialectical totality of *Capital*'s logic of exposition, but only, as Moseley shows, because Marx, like Spinoza in the *Ethics*' Scholia, chose to simplify for his readers this aspect of his initial presentation in the second edition of 1872, such that this 'totality' represents no more than a mere reductive, summary position.

In contrast to Arthur's ungrounded claim, Marx explicitly emphasises this situated, subjective, provisional nature of the concept of the circularity of the reproduction of capital as a whole when, in the final paragraph of chapter 23 he indicates that 'The capitalist process of production, ... seen [*betrachtet*] as a total, connected process, i.e. a process of reproduction, produces not only commodities, not only surplus-value, but it also produces and reproduces the capital-relation itself'.[95] Coming at the end of Volume I, this position is no

---

94 Moseley 2017, p. 141. 'Capital', Moseley summarises, 'exists first in the form of money advanced in the sphere of circulation, then in the form of means of production and labour power in the form of means of production and labour power in the sphere of production, then in the form of commodities produced at the end of the production process, and then finally back again in the form of money recovered, including more money than was originally advanced at the beginning of this real historical process' (2017, p. 11, emphasis in original). See also Marx 1976, p. 709. Moseley further shows that in volume 1 of *Capital*, Marx simplified for readers, at Engels's repeated urging, his initial, comprehensive formulation of the circuit of capital as a wholly monetary process in which both the constant and variable means of production are initially purchased as actual commodities already possessing a price form. This has resulted, in Moseley's view, in the 'common interpretation of Volume I that it is only about labour times, not money or prices, and that Marx's theory deals with money and prices only in Volume III' (Moseley 2017, p. 9). Through a comprehensive reading of Marx's various drafts and manuscripts, Moseley shows that the 'interpretation of these passages [in traditional Marxism] ignores and is contradicted by all the textual evidence ... – that the circuit of money capital is the analytical framework of Marx's theory, and the circuit of money capital begins with an independently existing quantity of money capital (M) ... which is "thrown into circulation" in order to make more money; ... the inputs to capitalist production and the valorisation process are commodities with already existing prices' (2017, pp. 185–6, emphasis in original). On the wholly monetary nature of the circuit of capital, see also Murray 2017, p. 135; and Bellofiore 2018.

95 Marx 1976, p. 724, emphasis added.

doubt infinitely more developed and concrete than the initial, minimal true idea with which Marx began *Capital* (i.e., that the capitalist mode of production *appears* [*erschient*] as a general accumulation of commodities); for all that, it is still a partial, incomplete position, a viewpoint obviously possessing none of the further conceptual determinations to be introduced in Volumes II and III.[96]

The fact that the circuit of money capital constitutes a constant in the capitalist social form, in other words, hardly makes of Marx's logic or the system itself a totality: the concept of this feedback loop is only one among the throng of dissonant concepts Marx develops, existing alongside quite heterogeneous, but nonetheless crucial concepts such as class struggle, the theory of ground rent, cost price, and a hundred others composing the logical body Marx constructs, step by step, concept by concept, as the finite, dissonant thing without totality that is *Capital*.

Related to but distinct from this first claim for the logic of *Capital* as totality is Arthur's similarly obscure implication that because capital requires not just the valorisation of *value* (as in the previous argument), but its unceasing *accumulation*, Marx's logic thus 'treat[s] a given whole', this because 'it is characteristic [of *Capital* like the works of Hegel] that it demonstrates how [this given whole] *reproduces* itself .... The movement winds back upon itself to form a *circuit* of reproduction of these moments by each other'.[97] Certainly, Marx shows the necessity of this circularity of reproduction and accompanying linear accumulation; nonetheless, my response is identical: Arthur's claim is true and just as wholly irrelevant to the status of capital (whether the book or the social form) as totality, as it is only one among innumerable dissonant concepts in Marx's logical construct.

Finally, the most developed but just as problematic argument Arthur puts forward for capital as totality is, paradoxically, its partial nature. Building on the previous points regarding the generality of value and subsumption, Arthur

---

96 Here too, among the members of the Systematic Dialectic school of reading *Capital*, it is Bellofiore who has the position closest to the one I am arguing here, stressing as he does that *Capital* is composed of 'fragments of a systematic reasoning' such that he refuses the 'attempts [of Arthur and Reuten in particular] to 'rewrite' Marx in Hegelian fashion' and insists instead (while rightly indicating various moments where Marx deploys aspects of Hegelian logic) that 'we are forced to remain in a fragmentary reading of Marx'. It is likewise surely no coincidence, given this orientation, that Bellofiore is perhaps the only member of this school actually to refer to Althusser and *Lire le Capital* both explicitly and affirmatively. Bellofiore 2018, pp. 359–60, 357.

97 Arthur 2002, p. 64.

argues that 'It is inherent to the concept of capital that it must reproduce and accumulate, and in this it seeks to overcome all obstacles and to make the material reality it engages with conform as perfectly as possible to its requirements'. But this it cannot do, 'its ideal world of frictionless circulation and growth' is inevitably dependent upon recalcitrant externalities, namely, living labour and its resistance to subsumption and the objective social demands of the valorisation process.[98]

Arthur makes this interesting and subtle point, one that in fact subverts the general argument of his book, in the context of a wider claim for the comprehensive logical, as opposed to historical, argument of *Capital*. He asserts for example that the discussion of the historical struggle over the length of the working day in chapter ten of Volume I 'is strictly illustrative and does not advance the [logical] argument'.[99] While literally correct, I think Arthur's position fails to indicate the *necessity* that governs Marx's inclusion of this material at this point in his analysis. When Marx writes that between the buyer and seller of the commodity labour power there exists 'an antinomy, of right against right, both equally bearing the seal of the law of exchange', he clearly indicates a point in his analysis that cannot be decided theoretically, one which, having as always first explicated the theoretical parameters of this struggle (between necessary and surplus labour), *requires* reference to this historical conflict.[100]

Note, however, how Arthur has *externalised* the category of class struggle from his governing framework of the 'ideal world of [capital's] frictionless circulation and growth': first as merely 'illustrative' historical data,[101] then as a 'material reality'[102] that impinges on this ideal logical form (totality). While the

---

98 Arthur 2002, p. 76.
99 Arthur 2002, p. 75.
100 Marx 1976, p. 342. As Michael Heinrich observes, 'Theorising capitalism in its "ideal average" ... constitutes a precondition [for Marx] for analysing the history of developed, fully-formed capital .... The "theoretical development" of the categories, however, does not just constitute a general background for analysing concrete struggles. The categorical presentation itself leads to points where nothing further can be developed conceptually, and we must turn to the contested historical process instead. Chapter 10 of the first volume, which deals with the working day, demonstrates this in an exemplary way. We cannot determine the limits of the working day based on the "laws of commodity production". Instead, it is the "violence" (*Gewalt*) of class struggle and the state that decides these limits, which are repeatedly brought into question. Hence, there are historical depictions in *Capital* that are not just "illustrations" and go beyond telling how capitalist relations emerged. Nevertheless, the location and meaning of these passages are by no means arbitrary but rather are based strictly on the theoretical development of the categories' (Heinrich 2021, p. 398).
101 Arthur 2002, p. 75.
102 Arthur 2002, p. 76.

data Marx cites may well be merely 'illustrative', is it not the case that the presentation of this data nonetheless depends not just upon 'material reality', but precisely upon a *concept* of class struggle, a concept obviously vital and necessarily internal to Marx's entire critique of political economy, for the data Marx presents to make sense in his argument?

When Arthur writes that 'The logical form of capital is by no means absolute but totally insufficient to maintain itself and it requires a transition *to the domain of reality;*' that 'while capital has the form of self-realisation it still lacks control *over its bearers*'; or that 'the logic of the development can issue only in tendencies, which in truth depend on *material premises*',[103] he unwittingly reveals the nature of the imaginary logical totality he constantly presumes:[104] in contrast to the object of Arthur's analysis, a purely imaginary logical form purged of class struggle, Marx's (critical) logic of the capitalist social form *integrally* and *essentially* positions the dissonant concepts of class struggle and the recalcitrance of living labour as necessary *logical* components of his logical system.[105]

In contrast to Marx's critique, in which concepts such as class struggle and the working day form integral, dissonant moments, the ideal system Arthur presents as 'frictionless' totality, from which these dissonances have been externalised, is none other than the ideological apology for capitalism that is *classical political economy* itself (and neoliberalism more generally), precisely the imaginary totality from which class struggle has been magically erased by an 'invisible hand'. If capital is indeed a totality, it is so only in the imagination of its apologists and benefactors. As Arthur himself is obviously not to be counted among these, one is left to conclude, with Spinoza, that the powerful impression of the univocal Hegelian philosophy of totality has blinded the Marxist analysis of *The New Dialectic* to the discordant, polyphonous logics of Marx's theoretical critique.

---

103 Arthur 2002, pp. 104, 106.
104 Arthur similarly claims in 'Contradiction and Abstraction' that 'capital, as the totalising Subject, is at home with itself only in the world of *forms*. At that level, it may well be conceded that it is grounded on itself, and achieves closure when producing commodities on the basis of *ex nihilo* bank credit. [But] the *human* and *natural* basis of the economic metabolism remains .... Capital is a closed totality only in form; *in reality*, capital cannot posit its presuppositions where its material conditions of existence are concerned' (Arthur 2009, p. 175, emphasis added).
105 And Marx does so precisely, one might add, in order to critique the *theoretical* incapacity of classical political economy to theorise the substance and nature of surplus value (*Hic Rhodus, hic salta!*).

7 Negation and Contradiction

In the sixth chapter of *New Dialectic*, Arthur explicates in detail the negative dialectical logic of chapter 32 of *Capital* Volume I, 'The Historical Tendency of Capitalist Accumulation'. While the previous chapters of *New Dialectic* only punctually cited and analysed Marx's text to support Arthur's interpretive reconstruction of the logic of capital, here, Marx's sole reference to the Hegelian concept of the 'negation of the negation' in the whole of *Capital* serves Arthur as the occasion actually to cite and closely analyse the logic of this moment in Marx's demonstration. Beginning with an extensive, two-page citation (to 'remind ourselves of Marx's text'), Arthur goes on to construct a detailed, original interpretation of the logic of this passage.

Though the arch-Hegelian figure of the 'negation of the negation' amply vindicates Arthur's decision to analyse this long passage in detail, in other respects the section is an odd choice for a study of 'systematic dialectic'. For not only have this chapter's summary, teleological claims, as Arthur himself notes, long been an object of ridicule from Dühring on, but their very formulation is precisely the opposite of the painstaking, systematic dialectic (of whatever type) to be found in the initial chapters of *Capital*. In the place of the apodictic logic of a rigorous demonstration that moves precisely, step by step, sentence by sentence, to demonstrate the essential nature of the commodity and its forms, of surplus value, of capital, etc., in this concluding chapter of volume one, Marx famously makes sweeping, unfounded claims for the inevitable, unitary movement of history: 'At a certain stage of development [the precapitalist mode of production] brings into the world the material means of its own destruction .... Its annihilation ... forms the pre-history of capital'. With the further development of social productive forces, Marx continues, 'the monopoly of capital becomes a fetter upon the mode of production which has flourished alongside it .... The knell of capitalist private property sounds. The expropriators are expropriated'.[106]

Stuck at the very end of Marx's thousand-page volume, its penultimate chapter retains the grandiose, undemonstrated logic of an inevitable, automatic collapse of capitalism characteristic of the *Grundrisse*'s famous 'Fragment on machines', claims buttressed not by rigorous demonstration but instead by the unrevised, teleological Hegelianism of Marx's *Grundrisse* notebooks that is precisely the object of Arthur's fascination: 'Capitalist production begets, with the inexorability of a natural process, its own negation. This is the negation of

---

106 Cited in Arthur 2002, p. 112.

the negation'.[107] Whether Marx's grandiose claims do justice to the intricacy of Hegel's logical demonstrations is doubtful; at the very least, though, their articulation through the Hegelian category of negation constitutes a further instance of my argument in this chapter: that Marx's process of exposition in *Capital* follows not one single logical model (Hegelian or otherwise), but deploys a multitude of demonstrative logics.

Despite Arthur's close attention to the letter and movement of Marx's text in this passage, its grandiose, telegraphic nature forces him to revert to the process of interpretation (as opposed to textual explication) that guided the previous chapters of *New Dialectic*. Arthur's intention, then, is to show that Marx's deployment of the logic of the negation of negation in this chapter 'is more than just metaphor or parody', but instead that its high degree of abstraction in fact constitutes 'the *form* of the transition [from one mode of production to another] at the most general level, however highly mediated and contingent is the real process'.[108]

Arthur thus proceeds interpretively to reconstruct the logic of the 'two negations' Marx indicates in the passage: from pre-capitalist to capitalist social forms, and from the latter to the point at which, in Marx's words, 'The knell of capitalist private property sounds. The expropriators are expropriated'. This analysis is predicated on the founding distinction of *New Dialectic*, i.e., between a traditional historical reading of *Capital* as describing the passage from simple exchange to the capitalist mode of production, in favour of a 'structural problematic requiring an account of the "genesis" [of the capitalist social form] in logical terms'.[109] Given the resolutely historical terms in which Marx presents his claims in this chapter (in this, it is of a piece with the entire concluding historical section eight of *Capital* on so-called primitive accumulation), Arthur's point seems to be that even here, in what is argumentatively the weakest chapter of the entire book, *Capital* remains a resolutely, unflaggingly *logical* work (as opposed to a historical study of capitalism, its antecedents, and successors).

---

107   Cited in Arthur 2002, p. 113. Marx's pre-1860 reliance on the Hegelian figures of estrangement, objectification, and alienation, absent from the first seven chapters of *Capital*, remains predominant in this penultimate one: 'Before he enters the process [of capitalist production], his own labour has already been estranged from him, appropriated by the capitalist, and incorporated with capital, it now, in the course of the process, constantly objectifies itself so that it becomes a product alien to him' (Marx 1976, p. 716). Arthur rightly notes how this language is 'reminiscent of a parallel passage in [Marx's] *1844 Mss*' (2002, p. 133n18).
108   Arthur 2002, p. 114.
109   Arthur 2002, p. 116.

Arthur's focus is on the source of the original capital to initiate the capitalist production process (this being the topic of section eight of *Capital* more generally). Here, Marx castigates the ideological faith that the capitalist gets these funds from his own hard labour. This, Marx observes ironically, is 'the unanimous answer of the spokesmen of political economy. And in fact', Marx adds slyly, 'their assumption *appears* to be the only one consonant with the laws of commodity production'.[110] The point of Marx's irony, as any reader of *Capital* will know, is that this appearance is not just an ideological justification on the part of the capitalists themselves, but possesses its own necessity, given the *theoretical inadequacy* of the analysis of the question prior to Marx.

Arthur's claim then is that Marx's ensuing rectification of this ideological – though necessary – misapprehension adheres to a negative dialectical logic of 'the transformation of the laws of exchange, appropriation, and property, into their opposites'.[111] And indeed, Marx's language in this passage, which Arthur cites extensively, seems to indicate the automatic transformation characteristic of dialectical sublation:

> It is quite evident ... that the laws of appropriation ... *become changed* into their direct opposite *through their own internal and inexorable dialectic* .... The property laws of commodity production *must undergo an inversion* so that they become laws of capitalist appropriation.[112]

This passage incontrovertibly constitutes, as Arthur rightly maintains, an instance of Hegelian negative dialectic that Marx continued to deploy at certain moments in *Capital*, a movement of sublation that Marx presents as a passive process of transformation that occurs automatically, as more adequate categories sublate previous inadequate, ideological ones in the progression of his argument.

This passage should be compared, however, with the strictly analogous preceding passage from chapter five to six and seven, the very crux of Marx's critique of classical political economy. There, he shows that the 'contradictions in the general formula of capital', i.e., the inability of the classical economists to account for the source of surplus value given the inadequate conceptual terms in which they posed the problem, requires not an automatic sublation of those concepts based on their inner contradictions, one that would retain them in their transformation, but, as Jacques Bidet and Riccardo Bellofiore have

---

110 Arthur 2002, p. 119, emphasis added.
111 Arthur 2002, p. 119.
112 Marx 1976, pp. 729, 734, cited in Arthur 2002, p. 119.

both argued, a logical break or leap to another theoretical terrain, one in which Marx's original concept of labour power – crucially absent from the conceptual framework of classical political economy – can be analysed in its use by its purchaser, the capitalist, to reveal the source of surplus value as the difference between necessary and surplus labour.[113]

While the object in question differs, Marx's basic demonstrative procedure is identical in these two passages: he first shows the necessity governing inadequate, ideological forms of appearance of a phenomenon (respectively, the origin of a capital fund and the source of surplus value), and then offers its more adequate analysis in his own theoretical terms. Despite this superficial similarity, the terms of Marx's demonstration are radically different, fully constituting two singular modes of logical demonstration in the pages of *Capital*. In both cases, the transformation in question is a transformation in the adequacy of our understanding of the logic governing the capitalist social form; in both cases, Marx contrasts an initial, inadequate and ideological form of appearance of a phenomenon, with the greater adequacy our understanding can attain thanks to the original concepts he has constructed.

For Arthur, the conclusion to be drawn from chapter 24 is merely that even in this most superficially 'historical' analysis, 'Marx speaks "virtually" [i.e., logically] rather than historically, [which] refutes any interpretation of *Capital* that equates the systematic presentation of the existing totality with historical stages, as if the first chapter explicated some prior regime of simple commodity production'.[114] While Arthur's defence of the entirely logical status of *Capital* is in my view correct, the more interesting question, I think, is one that precisely subverts the claims to logical totality ('the systematic presentation of the existing totality') that accompany this assertion. A comparison between this passage and the transition from chapter five to six and seven incontrovertibly shows that the unrevised negative dialectical form of presentation in chapter 32 constitutes an epistemological impediment, obscuring Marx's lucid, apodictic argument behind the foggy automatism and passivity of a putative 'internal and inexorable [negative] dialectic'.

In its place, Marx's famous invocation to his readers to solve the riddle that had confounded the greatest minds of classical political economy, '*Hic Rhodus, hic saltus!*' invokes not the imaginary automatism of a Hegelian dialectic but the real power of the intellect to emend its comprehension of an object through the difficult labour of Marx's concepts. In comparison with the con-

---

113   See Bidet 2006, pp. 161–3; Bellofiore 2018, p. 365.
114   Arthur 2002, p. 121.

ceptual gymnastics Arthur must perform to reveal the logical kernel of Marx's eschatological historicist claims in chapter 24, the blatant superiority of Marx's process of exposition in chapters five, six, and seven lies in the very simplicity of his presentation of a series of powerfully creative critical concepts: when two commodities are exchanged at their value without cheating, the source of profit cannot be readily discerned; for labour power to be sold as a commodity requires that the labourer own their own person as a free subject, not a slave; upon its sale, the commodity labour power is entirely at the disposition of its owner who has purchased it, the capitalist, who may continue to use it beyond what is necessary for the sustenance and reproduction of the labourer, in order to produce surplus value.

As such, Marx's presentation in part two of the first volume of *Capital* discards his earlier reliance on the logical automatisms of a negative dialectic in the *Grundrisse* and other preparatory manuscripts, directly to invoke the fulsome powers of the human intellect more adequately to understand the object of its analysis ('*Hic Rhodus, hic saltus!*'), an invocation analogous to Spinoza's subjective presentation of the initial definitions of the *Ethics*. In those opening statements, Spinoza defines each of his founding concepts (*causa sui*, substance, God, etc.) in resolutely subjective terms, via the concerted repetition of the qualification *intelligo* [I understand]: 'By substance I understand that which is in itself and is conceived through itself' ['Per substantiam intelligo id, quod in se est, et per se concipitur'].[115]

Macherey's illuminating commentary on this crucial dimension of Spinoza's presentation is worth citing in whole for its resonance with Marx's method in part two of *Capital*:

> It is important to note that the first statements that confront the reader of the *Ethics* make an appeal to his capacity to 'understand' (*intelligere*), that is to say, to his 'intellect' (*intellectus*), through which he is called to know things in themselves, as they are really [*réellement*] and not only as they could be in the abstract. In this manner, [Spinoza's] philosophical discourse installs itself immediately in the movement [*mouvance*] of the third genre of knowledge. It is furthermore notable that Spinoza, in these inaugural definitions, conjugates the verb *intelligere* in the first-person indicative present ['I understand'], which necessarily associates the formulation of the idea in question in each of these definitions with an activity of effective thought [*pensée effective*], fully engaged in its affir-

---

115   EID3.

mation .... It is evident that in constructing in this way the first definitions of the *Ethics*, Spinoza sought to confer on their expression, and at the same time to the entire sequence of discourse that will be elaborated from them, a personal character, something unusual [*décalé*] compared to the impersonal form typical of abstract scientific discourse. The reader thus implicitly receives the following message, which amounts to a provocation [*défi*]: here is what I myself understand, here is how things irrecusably present themselves to my mind, on the model of eternal truths; it is up to you to see whether this thought experiment [*expérience*] imposes itself on you with the same necessity, or whether you find it possible to understand things otherwise .... Spinoza practices philosophical thought as a free spirit [*esprit libre*] who elaborates the conditions of a communication with other free spirits.[116]

Like that of Spinoza, Marx's audacious challenge 'Hic Rhodus, hic saltus!' is an encomium to the infinite powers of the human intellect progressively to emend its capacity for understanding. While Marx's early subjection to the fascination of Hegel's negative dialectic remains determinant in certain marginal moments of *Capital* even in its second revision, such as its thirty-second chapter, nowhere is this progressive emendation more evident than in the revisions Marx operates upon his extraordinary and unparalleled analysis of the concept of the commodity, as he reworked an initial presentation based upon its putative contradiction-based determinations of reflection [*Reflexionsbestimmungen*], to formulate instead a novel ramified, additive synthetic dialectic for the 1872 and 1875 editions of *Capital*.

8   Constituting the Commodity

To argue as Arthur does that Marx deploys a Hegelian totality-based logic of negation in a marginal, historicist *recoin* of *Capital* such as its thirty-second chapter is in some ways to offer too easy a target for the post-Althusserian reading of *Capital* I am developing here. Far more consequential would be to show this negative dialectic at work in the crucial initial chapters of *Capital*, along with its supersession in the course of Marx's revisions by an alternative mode of apodictic demonstration. 'Beginnings', Marx observed in the Preface to the First

---

116   Macherey 1998, pp. 29–30.

Edition of *Capital*, 'are always difficult in all sciences'.[117] This is undoubtedly true not only for the readers of *Capital* whom Marx cautions in this passage, but for the author himself, who struggled mightily to find the proper mode of demonstration for this crucial initial moment in his argument, and constructed no less than four published versions of his analysis of the value-form (two in the 1867 edition, and two others in the second, 1872 German edition and the 1875 French translation he carefully rewrote), along with an entire manuscript from January 1872 in which he points to the shortcomings of his initial (1867) presentation, in order to revise and emend his analysis in what would become the 1872 edition.[118]

In fact, as Arash Abazari has shown, Marx's analysis of the commodity form in the first chapter of the first (1867) edition of *Capital* 'is the *only* place in Marx's entire oeuvre where he systematically deploys and develops the concept of dialectical contradiction'.[119] Abazari argues that Marx's initial analysis of the commodity form deploys the Hegelian logic of constitutive negation [*Reflexionsbestimmungen*], comparing Marx's analysis with Hegel's discussion in the *Logic* of the 'thing' [das Ding].[120] Abazari argues that in the *Logic*, Hegel distinguishes two forms of the contradictory nature of the thing.[121] In the initial logic or doctrine of being, Hegel analyses how the thing constitutes its identity as a positive entity through its negative, contrastive exclusion from other things: salt gains its self-same identity through its negative distinction (differ-

---

117   Marx 1976, p. 89.
118   On the latter, see Heinrich 2021, pp. 375–80.
119   Abazari 2019, p. 182, emphasis in original. Abazari's article reprises that of W.A. Suchting's 'Marx, Hegel, and Contradiction' (1985, p. 409), though without the former clearly indicating his proximity to Suchting's analysis, whom he does not cite in his bibliography.
120   This is one point at which Abazari goes beyond Suchting's earlier piece, which based its presentation of Hegel's logic of contradiction on Chapter 6 of the *Encyclopedia* rather than, as with Abazari, the analysis of the *Ding* in the *Science of Logic*. This difference in approach allows Abazari, in my view, to bring out much more sharply than Suchting the homologous logics of contradiction and *Reflexionsbestimmung* in Hegel and the 1867 edition of *Capital*. In the following paragraphs I follow Abazari's suggestive comparison of the Hegelian logic of *Reflexionsbestimmungen* and Marx's 1867 analysis of the commodity, rejecting Abazari's argument only in its further, undemonstrated claim that 'although Marx omits [explicit reference to dialectical contradiction] in later editions of *Capital*, [this Hegelian logic], I believe, remains central to his analysis even in the later editions' Abazari 182. In *Wissenschaft vom Wert* Heinrich criticises Helmut Brentel's systematic argument for the predominance of a Hegelian logic of determinations of reflection in *Capital* in Brentel's *Widerspruch und Entwicklung bei Marx und Hegel* (Heinrich 2022 [1999], p. 168; 2023, p. 264).
121   Abarazi 2019, p. 183.

ence) from pepper and all other spices, or, in the case of *Capital*, we could say that capitalism gains its identity through its difference from feudalism and all other modes of production.

In such contrastive negation, Abazari observes, 'there is no contradiction *in* something. Something excludes other somethings, and, as it were, remains a harmonious ensemble of qualities and quantities'.[122] While this form of external contradiction is determinant in the first book of Hegel's *Logic*, only occasionally and in passing does Marx define the capitalist mode of production in this exclusive manner, through its distinction from feudalism, slavery, or communism; instead, he develops his critique through the analysis of the categories proper and internal to the capitalist social form itself (the commodity, surplus value, competition, etc.).[123]

In the second Book of the *Science of Logic*, the 'doctrine of essence', however, Hegel shows the object to gain its essential determination not through its contrastive exclusion from other things, but instead through the sublation of such external reflection as the inner, constitutive contradiction that he names the 'determination of reflection' [*Reflexionsbestimmung*].[124] By this he indicates the inner, contradictory determination of the thing by dyadic categories such as cause and effect or essence and appearance, categories that are in internal relation to the thing they define.[125] The key point for Hegel is that such inner

---

122   Abarazi 2019, p. 185, emphasis added.
123   Marx repeatedly invokes feudalism, but only in passing, as a contrastive example or aside in his systematic demonstration, i.e.: 'The medieval peasant produced a corn-rent for the feudal lord and a corn-tithe for the priest; but neither the corn-rent nor the corn-tithe became commodities simply by being produced for others' (1976, p. 130).
124   'Determining reflection is in general the unity of positing and external reflection .... The positing is now united with external reflection; in this unity, the latter is absolute presupposing, that is, the repelling of reflection from itself or the positing of determinateness as its own. As posited, therefore, positedness is negation; but as presupposed, it is reflected into itself. And in this way positedness is a determination of reflection .... The determination of reflection is on the contrary positedness as negation – negation which has negatedness for its ground, is therefore not unequal to itself within itself, and hence essential rather than transient determinateness .... The determination of reflection ... has taken its otherness back into itself. It is positedness – negation which has however deflected the reference to another into itself, and negation which, equal to itself, is the unity of itself and its other, and only through this is an essentiality' (Hegel 2010b, pp. 352–3).
125   Abazari focuses his analysis on the Hegelian dyad of form and matter, which becomes problematic when he argues for their direct homology with Marx's concepts use-value ('matter') and exchange-value ('form'). Problematic because while the use-value of a commodity may bear a physical form or shape, many commodities are immaterial (the use-value of services for example); on the other hand, exchange-value, as the form of appearance of value, has material attributes (the number printed on a bill or coin, for example).

determinations, unlike those of the doctrine of being, stand in negative contradiction to each other:

> The self-subsisting determination of reflection [*Reflexionsbestimmung*] excludes the other in the same respect as it contains it and is self-subsisting for precisely this reason, in its self-subsistence the determination excludes its own self-subsistence from itself. For this self-subsistence consists in that it contains the determination which is other than it in itself and does not refer to anything external for just this reason; but no less immediately in that it is itself and excludes from itself the determination that negates it. And so it is *contradiction* [*Widerspruch*].[126]

This is to argue that the object is not merely a positive entity, its being consisting of a synthetic addition of its various qualities (as shown in Hegel's doctrine of Being), but constitutes instead, from the perspective of its essence, a negative or contradictory totality: 'The thing as this totality is contradiction [*Das Ding als diese Totalität ist der Widerspruch*], … the form in which the matter is determined … and at the same time consisting of sorts of matter that … are at once both self-standing and negated'.[127]

The question in the case of the commodity is thus whether use-value and exchange-value, what Marx calls the two 'factors' [*Faktoren*] of the commodity, simultaneously contain and exclude one another to constitute a contradiction in Hegel's sense, or, instead, stand in positive 'opposition' [*Gegensatz*] to one another without contradiction. Note carefully Hegel's contention: '[Self-subsistence] contains the determination which is other than it in itself …; but no less immediately … excludes from itself the determination that negates it'. Each determination of reflection, in other words, contains its opposite within itself, which I will argue does not obtain in Marx's analysis of the commodity. There, in contrast, I will seek to show that the determinations or what Marx calls the 'factors' of the commodity such as use- and exchange-value merely stand in positive 'opposition' to one another without mutual reflection, precisely as Marx will state in the revised versions of this analysis.

Here, I can only agree with Roberto Fineschi, who writes that 'I do not think that we have to look for analogies or homologies between Marx's theory of capital and Hegel's logic; this alleged 'Hegelian approach' has paradoxically resulted in a very non-dialectical attitude in many scholars. In fact, Marx himself criticised any external application of categories to a given content' (Fineschi 2014, p. 140).

126 Hegel 2010b, p. 374, emphasis in original.
127 Hegel 2010a, p. 196, translation modified.

In Hegel's recuperation of the concept of contradiction, the object – in its essential, constitutive nature rather than its mere external being – is 'the absolute contradiction [*der absolute Widerspruch*]' of form and matter.[128] While this position famously constitutes the originality of Hegel's reconstruction of logic as a negative, contradiction-based dialectic,[129] it is far from clear that Marx adopts and, above all, holds to this same logic of the determinations of reflection in his analysis of the concept of the commodity.

9 From Dialectical Contradiction to Additive Synthesis

What Abazari does show convincingly is that in the analysis of the concept of the commodity in the first edition of *Capital*, Marx systematically adopts this Hegelian logic of constitutive negation [*Reflexionsbestimmung*], the commodity, that is to say, as it has commonly been understood in traditional Marxism 'as the contradictory unity of use-value and exchange-value'.[130] It is not merely the case that Marx initially adopts the Hegelian vocabulary of externalisation, contradiction [*Widerspruch*], the determinations of reflection [*Reflexionsbestimmung*], and essence and appearance in the first chapter of the 1867 edition.[131] Abazari argues more generally that in Marx's analysis of the value-form:

---

128 Hegel 2010a, p. 268.
129 'Contradiction [is] the negative in its essential determination, the principle of all self-movement .... Only when driven to the extreme of contradiction are the many of that manifold quickened and alive to each other: they hold the negativity in them which is the inner pulse of self-movement and life' (Hegel 2010b, pp. 382, 384).
130 Abazari 2019, p. 188.
131 Examples of this Hegelian vocabulary from the 1867 edition that are absent from the 1872 edition include: 'Since it is, as value, of the same essence [*Wesens*] as the coat, the natural form of the coat thus becomes the form of appearance of its own value'; '[The coat's] status as an Equivalent is (so to speak) only a reflection-determination [*Reflexionsbestimmung*] of the linen'; 'The commodity is the immediate unity of use-value and exchange-value, i.e., of two opposites [*zweier Entgegengesetzten*]. It is therefore an immediate contradiction [*unmittelbarer Widerspruch*]. This contradiction [*Widerspruch*] must enter upon a development just as soon as it is no longer considered as previously in an analytic manner (at one point from the viewpoint of use-value and at another from the viewpoint of exchange-value) but is really related to other commodities as a totality [*ein Ganzes*]'; (Dragstedt's translation of first chapter of the first German edition of *Capital*, entitled 'The Commodity', pp. 13, 16, 29–30, translation modified, available at https://www.marxists.org/archive/marx/works/1867-c1/commodity.htm. For the original German text, see MEGA II5 [1867]). Heinrich points out that in the 1872 edition, Marx never uses the term essence [*Wesen*] before page 458 of the Penguin translation (Heinrich 2021, p. 58). I will make a similar point about the systematic absence of the term *Widerspruch* (contradiction) from the first chapter of *Capital*, and its replacement by the term 'opposition' [*Gegensatz*], without

> The simple form of value, for Marx, is constituted by a contradiction; since, first, the exchange-value of A is contained in the use-value of B, and yet, since the two commodities are necessarily two distinct things, the exchange-value of A is excluded by the use-value of B. The relation is contradictory, since it is composed of two moments that contain, and yet exclude, each other.[132]

This, then, is the familiar claim for the 'contradictory' nature of use- and exchange-value in the commodity, but does it hold up when measured against the actual terminology and argument to be found in Marx's demonstration in the 1872 edition of *Capital*?

It is important to distinguish this first chapter of the 1867 edition that founds Abazari's claim, the argument of which, Marx warns his reader, will 'present the greatest difficulty', from what Marx calls the 'supplementary, more didactic exposition of the form of value' that he added as an appendix to that same first edition, at the request of Engels and Kugelmann.[133] The latter material then formed the basis of Marx's 1872 revision of this chapter. In that 1867 appendix – Marx tells the reader in his Postface to the second edition – the process of exposition '[was] completely revised'. While the 1867 appendix thus already begins the tendential elimination of this Hegelian vocabulary, a process that will culminate in the 1872 and 1875 editions, a systematic comparison of the five versions of this chapter shows that this tendency is both uneven and incomplete, such that none of Marx's varied analyses of the value form can be considered as definitive.[134]

The revision manuscript that Marx drafted in December 1871-January 1872,[135] for example, develops the social, communal nature of value-objectivity to a degree unparalleled in any of the three published versions of his analysis,[136] while the 1875 French translation by Joseph Roy, which Marx personally and extensively revised, inserts, for example, a negative dialectical passage absent from both the 1867 and 1872 German editions: 'Les contradictions que renferme la forme équivalente exige maintenant un examen plus appro-

---

hesitating to draw Althusserian conclusions from this absence, conclusions that Heinrich steers clear of in his commitment to reading *Capital* literally and without interpretation.

132   Abazari 2019, pp. 190–1.
133   Marx 1976, pp. 89, 94.
134   Heinrich 2021, pp. 363, 370.
135   'Ergänzungen und Veränderungen zum ersten Band des Kapitals (Additions and Changes to the First Volume of Capital)'.
136   Heinrich 2021, p. 375.

fondie'.[137] Similarly, the 1872 edition, while abandoning the vocabulary and logic of contradiction [*Widerspruch*] in its body text, nonetheless inserts a note observing that 'determinations of reflection [*Reflexionsbestimmungen*] of this kind [i.e., in the analysis of the value form] are altogether very curious'.[138]

Given this complexity and unevenness between Marx's various presentations of the value form, it is notable that Marx already distinguishes in 1867 between his materialist derivation of the form of value as 'an external material in which labour objectifies [*vergegenständlichen*] itself ... as determinate labour [*bestimmten Arbeit*]', and Hegelian idealism, in which, he observes ironically, 'it is only the 'concept' [*Begriff*] in Hegel's sense that manages to objectify itself without external material'.[139] Marx's 1867 critique of Hegelian idealism is thus precociously analogous to that which Badiou will develop of Frege in *Being and Event*: thought cannot imperiously determine being, but must remain subject to a materialist determination.[140]

Heinrich observes, however, that this position nonetheless remains a mere negative critique; it will only be with the further revision in the 1872 version of this chapter that Marx would develop the *conceptual* means to distinguish the 'chimerical' objectivity of the commodity form from the tangible value form. According to Heinrich's reading,

> both in chapter 1 of the first edition and in [Marx's 1872] revision manuscript, Marx seems unsure about how exactly to present the relation between the 'purely chimerical' objectivity of value and its tangible form of existence in the shape of another commodity. It's clear that this relation is not to be grasped in the manner of Hegel's philosophy. In fact, Marx first found an adequate solution [only] in *Capital*'s second edition. There, he distinguishes between two levels of investigation: (1) The examination of the *exchange relation* between two commodities [as ...] value-objectivity, which cannot be grasped in the case of the individual commodity; (2)

---

137   MEGA II7 1989, p. 38.
138   Marx 1976, p. 149.
139   Dragstedt's translation of *Capital*, [Chapter 1]: 'The Commodity' (p. 13), https://www.marxists.org/archive/marx/works/1867-c1/commodity.htm.
140   Here is Heinrich: 'In the second edition of *Capital*, Marx put the rational kernel of this conceptual form of expression into words: "Our analysis has shown that the form of value, that is, the expression of the value of a commodity, arises from the nature of commodity-value" (Marx 1976: 152). That is, the value-form does not arise from the concept of value, but rather from that which the concept of value expresses scientifically, namely the "nature of commodity-value"' (Heinrich 2021, p. 374). On Badiou's critique, see below, Chapter 4.

The examination of the *value-relation* between two commodities, which already assumes the result of the analysis of the exchange relation in level (1).[141]

Here we have one of the clearest examples of the furtive and uneven tendency of development across the multiple versions of Marx's exposition of the value form, from an initial rejection of Hegelian idealist, negative dialectic that still lacks the means replace this with a positive demonstration, to Marx's further development by 1872 of what Heinrich and Fred Moseley agree is an additive synthetic method of presentation without negation, one that clearly distinguishes between and synthetically proceeds from an analysis of what Heinrich identifies as the 'exchange relation' to that of the 'value relation', and Moseley, from the substance and magnitude of value in the first two sections of chapter 1, to its necessary form of appearance in the third.[142]

Abazari, in contrast, finds Marx's 1872 insertion of the footnote 22 referring to the 'Determinations of reflection [*Reflexionsbestimmungen*]' in the value-form to be certain proof of a continued reliance on Hegelian logic. In comparison with the body of the text, from which the concept of contradiction is strictly absent, I believe, in contrast, that the insertion of this new footnote in 1872 is rather an example of Marx falling back on an old and familiar category to inadequately indicate a new, post-Hegelian process he is in the process of inventing, an original form of additive, synthetic dialectic.

This would then be another example of what Althusser identified as the symptomatic tendency of a novel theory in its deployment to run ahead of subjective recognition of its novelty:

---

141 Heinrich 2021, p. 380. Heinrich's contention that the first chapter of *Capital* is divided between analyses of the exchange relation and the value relation has not gone unchallenged, in particular by Fred Moseley (2023). I will discuss the dispute between Heinrich and Moseley over the nature of value in *Capital* below.

142 Here is Moseley: 'The overall logical structure of Marx's analysis of the commodity in Chapter 1 is in terms of the concepts of the substance of value, the magnitude of value, and the form of appearance of value. The substance and magnitude of value are derived in Sections 1 and 2, and then the form of appearance of value is derived in Section 3, with the predetermined substance and magnitude of value presupposed' (Moseley 2023, p. 236). The distinction I make throughout this chapter between Marx's *analytic* method of research in preparatory notebooks such as the *Grundrisse* and the *synthetic* method of *Darstellung* characteristic of *Capital* is also held by the systematic dialectical school of Marxist epistemology, including Heinrich's vehement critic Fred Moseley, and is explicitly developed for example in Reuten 2014, p. 251. Though I agree with Reuten, Arthur and Tony Smith on the relevance of this analytic/synthetic distinction, as noted above, I reject the positions of this school regarding the concepts of capital as a totality and the putatively contradiction-based process of Marx's exposition.

This is what Marx tells us. And there is no *apparent* reason not to take him at his word .... [And yet,] at certain moments, in certain symptomatic points, this silence [i.e., the absence of a proper name for a novel concept or procedure Marx has invented] emerges as such in the discourse and forces it against its will to produce real theoretical lapses, in brief blank flashes, invisible in the light of the proof: words [such as *Reflexionsbestimmungen*] that hang in mid-air *although they seem to be inserted into the necessity of the thought*, judgements which close irreversibly with a false obviousness the space of which seemed to be opening before reason .... Marx has not thought what he is doing to the letter.[143]

It would be incongruous to condemn Marx's failure to find the time to name and theorise the novel process of exposition he develops in *Capital*, as Althusser observes more generally, for 'no one can be convicted for not saying everything at once. But his too hurried readers can be attacked for not having *heard this silence*'.[144] Althusser's more general claim holds as well for this putative obviousness of the constitutive contradiction between use- and exchange-value, i.e., that it indicates precisely such a 'point at which the theoretical incompleteness of Marx's judgement of himself has produced the most serious misunderstandings'.[145] To determine whether in fact *Capital* continues to rely on the Hegelian logic of determinate reflection requires actually to follow Marx's demonstration line by line in the first chapter of *Capital*, asking furthermore whether the elimination of the category of *contradiction* and its replacement by that of *opposition* indicates a fundamental change in the nature of Marx's demonstration.

10   Toward an Additive Demonstration, Without Contradiction

While the word *Widerspruch* (contradiction) does not appear at all in Chapter 1 of the 1872 edition, Marx comes to prioritise in its place the concept of *Gegensatz* (opposition) to indicate the precise nature of the relation of use- and exchange-value in the concept of the commodity. The word *Gegensatz* (which is only used 4 times in the 1867 version of Chapter 1) appears some twenty-five times in Chapter 1 (1872), as Marx's term of preference to indicate the relation of use-value and value: i.e., 'The simple form of value of a commodity is the

---

143   RC, pp. 231, 237, emphases added.
144   RC, p. 235, emphasis in original.
145   RC, p. 238.

simple form of appearance of the opposition [*Gegensatz*] between use-value and value which is contained within the commodity'.[146]

Gegensatz, synonymous with the German *Opposition*, does indeed indicate something quite different from Hegelian contradiction and determinations of reflection: the relation of extreme difference, diversity, or contrast between two things, in other words, an intensive positive distinction without contradiction.[147] While this etymological distinction seems merely suggestive, it in fact clearly and succinctly indicates for Marx a profound and longstanding theoretical distinction, between Hegelian logical negation and Marx's own development of a positive, materialist mode of demonstration, a distinction that originates in his intensive engagement with Hegelian and Aristotelean logic in the period 1839–1842.

Briefly put, in the period 1839–1841, Marx initially studied Hegelian and Aristotelean logic not only to prepare his highly original deployment of Hegelian logic in his dissertation, but intending as well, as Charles Barbour has shown, to compose a never-completed Hegelian rebuttal to the leading proponent of Aristotelean logic of the time, Adolf Trendelenburg. Trendelenburg was famous in philosophical circles for his 1833 critical edition of Aristotle's *De Anima*, and this likely motivated Marx's decision to initiate a competing translation of *De Anima*, as well as his explicit critiques of Trendelenburg in the dissertation.

It was, however, Trendelenburg's highly influential 1840 critique of Hegelian logic, *Logische Untersuchungen*, that was the primary focus of Marx's theoretical ire in March 1841, when he hatched a plan with Bruno Bauer to compose a Hegelian rebuttal to Trendelenburg in the journal the two projected, to be enti-

---

146 In the 1872 edition, Marx first uses the word *Widerspruch* only toward the end of chapter 3.1, 'The Measure of Values': 'The price-form … may also harbour a qualitative contradiction [*qualitativen Widerspruch*]' (1976, p. 197). Marx refers once to the mere illusory appearance [*scheint*] that exchange-value is 'something accidental' as a pseudo 'contradiction in adjecto', but translates the Latin as 'Widersinn' rather than the more Hegelian synonym *Widerspruch* [1976, p. 126] (1976, p. 153).

147 In *The Science of Value*, Michael Heinrich casually equates the two terms in passing: 'Das Mangelhafte an einer Kategorie wird von Marx oft als "Gegensatz" oder "Widerspruch" ihrer verschiedenen Bestimmungen bezeichnet' ('What is deficient in a category is often defined by Marx as the "opposition" or "contradiction" between its different determinations') (Heinrich2022, p. 174; 2023, p. 270, my translation). In *Hegel or Spinoza*, Macherey, in contrast, observes that 'The contradiction (*Widerspruch*) distinguishes itself from the opposition (*Gegensatz*) in that it is not a fixed relation between distinct and antagonistic terms but the irresistible movement that discovers in each of these elements the truth of the other and thus produces them as moments of a unique process in which they appear as inseparable' (2011, p. 121).

tled *Annals of Atheism*.[148] While Marx's initial intent in 1839–1841 was to defend Hegelian logic against Trendelenburg, on at least one count, the latter's learned exposition of Aristotelean logic and critique of Hegelian dialectics seems to have hit home, and to have provided for this brilliant and learned young reader of Aristotle a signal theoretical distinction between Hegelian idealist and scientific materialist methods of logical demonstration.

In *Logische Untersuchungen*, Trendelenburg vehemently criticizes Hegel for confusing quite basic Aristotelean logical principles, primary among which in Trendelenburg's judgment is Hegel's failure to grasp the fundamental distinction Aristotle makes between what Trendelenburg calls 'logical negation' and 'real opposition [*Gegensatz*].'[149] If Marx had not already gleaned this theoretical distinction from his reading of Aristotle, it would have been impossible to overlook its primacy in Trendelenburg's critique. It is, moreover, this distinction between Hegelian 'logical negation' and Aristotelean, materialist 'real opposition' that, I wish to argue, becomes a fundamental theoretical distinction for Marx, from his 1843 'Critique of Hegel's Philosophy of Right' through his revisions to *Capital* three decades later.

When Marx first came to critique Hegelian logic in the 1843 "Critique of Hegel's Philosophy of Right," he reproached Hegel throughout for his logical idealism, for his derivation, that is to say, of the empirical existence of the orders of the state – sovereign, executive, legislative, and the Estates – from their logical Idea. This process inevitably leads, Marx argues, to an uncritical defence of the status quo:

> Hegel's purpose is to narrate the life-history of abstract substance, of the Idea, and in such a history human activity etc. necessarily appears as the activity and product of something other than itself; he therefore represents the essence of man as an imaginary detail instead of allowing it to function in terms of its real human existence. This leads him to ... the inevitable result that an empirical existent [*eine empirische Existenz*] is uncritically enthroned as the real truth of the Idea. For Hegel's task is not

---

148 Barbour 2023, 18.
149 Here is Barbour: 'In pure logic or [what Trendelenburg calls Hegelian] "logical negation," it is possible to claim that the one term is determined by its difference from another, or through purely logical negation. Being, for example, has meaning insofar as it is not nothing, and nothing insofar as it is not being. But the same is not true in nature or [what Trendelenburg calls] "real opposition." For in nature there are no negative terms, only positive facts. The natural existence of a cat, for example, is not to be found in the idea "not dog," but in an empirical description of a cat.' Barbour 2023, 22.

to discover the truth of empirical existence but to discover the empirical existence of the truth.[150]

Marx instead calls for an opposing materialist-scientific method, one that would arrive at "the truth of empirical existence" through the critical analysis of real, actually-existing entities (in this case, the orders of the state).

Marx's primary critique of Hegel in this early text, however, is Hegel's representation of the orders of the state as existing in a negative dialectical relation to one another, such that they derive their identity and legitimacy through their mutual, negative dialectical relations to one another, the contradictions of each order resolving those of the others. This, Marx argues, is to treat actual differences between real, actually-existing entities, what Marx calls "real extremes," as mere logical differences that harmoniously sublate one another's contradictions.[151]

It is precisely here that Marx deploys Trendelenburg's distinction between "logical negation" and "real opposition," distinguishing the materialist method he calls for – as the analysis of real "opposition" or "extremes" – from the logical idealism of Hegel's negative dialectic of *Reflexionsbestimmungen*:

> It is remarkable that Hegel could have reduced this absurd process of mediation to its abstract, logical and hence ultimate undistorted form, while at the same time enthroning it as the speculative mystery of logic [*spekulatives Mysterium der Logik*], as the scheme of reason, the rational mode of deduction par excellence. Real extremes cannot be mediated precisely because they are real extremes. Nor do they require mediation, for *their natures are wholly opposed* [*sie sind entgegengesezten Wesens*].[152]

It is precisely this theoretical distinction, first developed in the "Critique of Hegel's Philosophy of Right," that will govern Marx's variable recourse throughout his drafting and revisions to *Capital* to these two modes of theoretical demonstration: the logical idealism of Hegelian negative dialectical "contradiction" [*Widerspruch*] versus the materialist analysis of the real order of existence that takes each thing in its real "opposition" [*Gegensatz*] to others.

In light of Marx's reading of Trendelenburg and his argument in the "Critique of Hegel's Philosophy of Right," my claim is straightforward: when decades

---

150   Marx, 1974, 98; MEGA² I.2, 40, translation modified.
151   Barbour 2023, 26.
152   Marx, 1974, 155; MEGA² I.2, 97, emphasis added.

later Marx came to draft and subsequently revise the various sections of *Capital*, it would be this nominal distinction between "contradiction" and "opposition" that would serve to clearly indicate to an informed reader the distinction between two theoretical procedures of analysis and demonstration. It is a theoretical doublet that allowed Marx succinctly to realise in his various revisions, in part, the task he had given himself in the *Grundrisse*: the systematic elimination of the impression that the various categories of his analysis are derived from the Idea of the capitalist social form, rather than scientifically constructed from his analysis of a real thing, a society typified by the accumulation and exchange of commodities.[153]

If now we return to reading *Capital* to the letter, we do in fact find that what Marx demonstrates in his analysis of the commodity is an "opposition" rather than a Hegelian "contradiction" between use- and exchange-value.[154] Indeed, Marx begins his demonstration by introducing each dimension of the commodity positively, as what he calls 'factors' [*Faktoren*] or attributes. There is no derivation of use-value or exchange-value in the opening paragraphs of *Capital*; instead, they are simply additively posed or 'positioned', as Althusser will say, one after another: 'The commodity is, first of all, an external object, a thing which through its qualities satisfies human needs of whatever kind ... The usefulness of a thing makes it a use-value'. And then, in his fifth paragraph, with neither transition nor derivation of any kind, Marx immediately poses the second factor of the commodity: 'Exchange-value appears first of all as the quantitative relation, the proportion, in which use-values of one kind exchange for use-values of another kind'.[155]

If we abstract from Marx's intervening analysis of the characteristics of these two factors or attributes of the commodity (satisfying a human need, having both quality and quantity, etc.), we are left with two positive, underived propositions:

A. The commodity has the attribute ('factor') use-value.
B. The commodity has the attribute ('factor') exchange-value.[156]

---

153   "It will be necessary later," Marx noted to himself in the *Grundrisse*, "to correct the idealist manner of the presentation, which makes it seem as if it were merely a matter of conceptual determinations and of the dialectic of these concepts" Marx, 1973, 151.
154   Here I only summarize relevant moments in Marx's exposition of the commodity form in *Capital*, chapter One (1872), referring readers to Michael Heinrich's more detailed exposition of this chapter's logic in *How to Read Marx's Capital*.
155   Marx 1976, pp. 125–6.
156   To call these factors 'attributes' of the commodity implies that, analogously to the infinite attributes of substance that Spinoza identifies, use-value and exchange-value are 'that

In the relation between Marx's initial proposition that the 'individual commodity' constitutes the 'elementary form' [*Elementarform*] of the capitalist mode of production and the additive introduction of these two attributes in the four succeeding paragraphs,[157] there is no trace of any deduction or inference whatsoever, to say nothing of a putative negative dialectical sublation such as is to be found in the first lines of Hegel's *Science of Logic* (Being|Nothing→Becoming).[158] At the same time, this additive positioning of concepts is no a priori formalist or abstract axiomatic exercise, but comprises a properly materialist critique, thanks to the necessary determination of this starting point – the true idea that we as subjects of capitalism always already possess of its nature (as general commodification).[159] Marx has determined precisely these as the attributes of the commodity, thanks to his painstaking research or 'enquiry' [*Forschungsweise*] prior to the elaboration of his reproduction [*Darstellungsweise*] of the capitalist real in the attribute of thought.[160]

---

which the intellect perceives of' the 'substance' of the capitalist mode of production – i.e., what Marx has just called its '*Elementarform*', the commodity – 'as constituting its [the commodity's] essence' at its greatest level of abstraction (EID4).

157   Marx 1976, pp. 125–6.
158   This absence of a contradiction-based logic in *Capital* is one of the principal themes of Althusser's 'Avant-propos du livre de G. Duménil' (written in February 1977), along with his subsequent (unpublished) seminar of March 1978, the 'Cours sur le mode d'exposition chez Marx' (IMEC 20 ALT 28.5): 'In what respect could use-value ... be said to contradict the value it "carries"? Mystery' ('Avant-propos', p. 253). 'The relation between use-value and exchange-value is not a relation of contradiction (as the result of a scission) ... the scission of an abstraction of value into use-value and exchange-value .... Marx insists on the difference in function of use-value [which] can in no sense be thought of as contradictory to exchange-value' IMEC 20ALT 28.5, pp. 16–17. Althusser's assertion remains little more than that, however, this claim in both these texts cryptically referring to Marx's passing observation that use-values are the 'bearers' [Träger] of value ('In the form of society to be considered here [use-values] are also the material bearers [Träger] of ... exchange-value') (Marx 1976, p. 126).
159   What Macherey says of Spinoza's starting point in *Ethics* holds identically for Marx's beginning to *Capital*: 'If the exposition of the Spinozist doctrine begins with definitions, axioms, and postulates, if it begins with substance rather than God, this does not at all indicate that these primitive notions constitute a source of truth from which all that follows could be simply deduced, following a rigid and predetermined course in the form of an explication. Substance, attributes, and modes, as they appear in these liminary principals, are precisely the equivalent of the rough, unpolished stone that the first smiths needed to "begin" their work: these are still abstract notions, simple words, natural ideas that will only truly take on meaning from the moment they function in demonstrations' (Macherey 2011, p. 76).
160   Marx 1976, p. 102. In the *Avant-propos to G. Duménil*, Althusser offers a qualified agreement with Duménil's assertion (equivalent to that which Arthur makes in *New Dialectic*) that ' "Political economy is not an axiomatic". Certainly', Althusser observes, this is the case

What I am calling Marx's additive synthetic method is essentially a development, on my part, of Althusser's abstract assertion that Marx's exposition proceeds via the 'positioning' [*la position*] of one concept after a preceding one has been adequately analysed. 'Marx's thought', he writes in the *Avant-propos au livre de G. Duménil*, 'proceeds by the *positioning* [*la position*] of concepts, inaugurating the exploration (analysis) of the theoretical space opened and closed by this positioning, followed by the positioning of a new concept, thus enlarging the theoretical field, and so forth, to the point of constituting theoretical fields of extreme complexity'.[161] This thesis of the additive positioning of concepts, Althusser observes, 'excludes all appearance of an auto-production of the concept (and *a fortiori* of the real by the concept) in Hegelian fashion, [versus] the intervention at a given moment of the exposition of the key concepts around which is organised the constitution and exploration of the theoretical field in its multiple combinations'.[162]

It's notable in particular how by this late moment in Althusser's reflection, his analysis of *la position* proceeds in purely additive fashion, from Marx's initial research [*Forschungsweise*] to its demonstration, and within the latter, from one concept to the next, never referring to a putative totality or whole (as does Arthur or as Althusser himself had in the first edition of *Reading Capital*) that would govern and guarantee the truth of this exposition (as opposed to the crudely suppressed paragraphs in the second edition of *Reading Capital* that were the object of Macherey's 1966 critique). This additive procedure that

---

'in the sense of an ideological axiomatic: Marx neither positions [*pose*] nor adds [*ajoute*] a given concept [merely] to "explore" what would follow from it, as a pure hypothesis, or to produce consequent effects. He doesn't indulge in arbitrary variations, nor in the "apprehension" of a given phenomenal totality as a mere indulgence [*par plaisir*]. His exposition is patently guided, behind the scenes, by the great realities discovered by the silent "method of research" [*Forschungsweise*]' (Althusser 1998, p. 259). Althusser writes in the 1978 'Cours sur le mode d'exposition', in terms that similarly emphasise the materialist determination of Marx's method, that 'this method is not without resemblance [*analogie*] with an axiomatic method, with the understanding that the positioning of concepts ... plays the role of the conceptual introduction of real [materialist] determinations that must be introduced in abstract form in order simultaneously to think the discontinuity of the field within a previously constituted theoretical continuity' IMEC 20ALT 28.5, pp. 18–19.

161   Althusser 1998, p. 257.
162   Althusser 1998, p. 258. In the 'Cours sur le mode d'exposition' Althusser observes in a similar vein that the additive procedure of the positioning of concepts 'is the condition of the discontinuity of the theoretical field [of *Capital*] .... [While] Hegel proceeds by the auto-production of concepts, Marx proceeds by the positioning of a concept, [such that] the positioning of each concept opens and closes a new theoretical field' (IMEC 20ALT 28.5, p. 17).

Althusser describes, I would add, thus coheres perfectly with Spinoza's critique of totality in his 1665 letter to Oldenburg, despite its telegraphic nature in this late moment of Althusser's thought.

While the variegated analysis of exchange-value and that of the even more complex value relation characteristic of these two attributes will occupy Marx in the rest of chapter one, his three-paragraph analysis of the concept of use-value in the first two pages of *Capital* starkly illustrates Macherey and Althusser's claim that Marx's demonstration proceeds sequentially, via the 'exhaustive' (Macherey) analysis of each concept; a given concept's essential nature having been thoroughly analysed at the corresponding level of abstraction, all without logical contradiction, Marx can then presuppose that analysis as a given, and move to the next level of abstraction as what Althusser calls an additive *positioning*.

Now, if this were all there were to Marx's process of exposition, the case for the tendential suppression of *Aufhebung* in *Capital* would be closed; indeed, Macherey has it easy on this score by only considering the first five pages of Chapter 1 in his brief contribution to *Reading Capital*. That said, Marx's process of exposition throughout *Capital*, if we look beyond Althusser's elliptical assertions and Macherey's brief analysis, is indeed impelled not by contradictory reflections of determinations [*Reflexionsbestimmungen*], but instead due to what Marx variously calls the 'insufficiency' [*Unzulägliche*], 'defects' [*Mängel*] or 'peculiarities' [*Eigentümlichkeit*] of a concept, terms that indicate its various *inadequacies* at that level of abstraction.

Indeed, the real and telling complexities can be said to begin in the third section of the first chapter, precisely the section, that is, that Abazari, and, indeed, Marx himself in footnote 22, identify as the locus of various *Reflexionsbestimmungen*. It is in this section 1.3 that Marx examines not use-value, exchange-value, and what Heinrich identifies as the basic *exchange relation* of commodities in abstraction from their value form, but – at this subsequent degree of concretion – the *value relation*, the complex interrelation of use- and exchange-value in the analysis of the value form, which necessarily culminates in the general equivalent and money form.[163]

Close attention to Marx's analysis of the value form in this section unequivocally shows that he additively builds upon his analysis of the exchange relation in the preceding two sections, without those demonstrations being superseded or invalidated. In the initial moment of his demonstration (sections 1.1–1.2), Marx first analysed the exchange relation between two commodities, from

---

163 See Heinrich 2021, pp. 92–143.

which he concluded that they must share a 'common element', value, the substance of which he shows to be abstract labour. In section 1.3, he then proceeds to the analysis of the *form* of value, as the section title clearly indicates: 'The Value-form, or Exchange-Value'. In this logical progression from sections 1.1 and 1.2 to section 1.3 – the latter arguably one of the most crucial demonstrations of *Capital* – there is not a trace of negative dialectical, contradiction-based Hegelian logic determining the development of these categories.

Instead, Marx deploys an original process of logical demonstration that I am calling additive synthesis. The demonstration is additive, in the sense that Marx's analysis of the value relation presupposes his prior adequate and complete demonstration of the exchange relation, the analysis of the value relation constituting a subsequent degree of concretion relative to the initial high level of abstraction of section one.[164] This additive mode of positive dialectic in Part One of *Capital* confirms Jacques Bidet's abstract assertion, in his review of Arthur's *New Dialectic*, that there is no Hegelian, contradiction-based 'fluidity' of Marx's concepts in the movement from one part or section to another (as Arthur asserts):

> It is not the concept that changes [from one section to another]; rather, there is a change of concept, through conceptual determinations .... The 'theory of value' [in Part One of *Capital*] is in no way transformed by the theory of surplus-value [in Part Two], which, on the contrary, expressly presupposes it, unchanged, in the pure and perfect form that Marx has given it in his exposition in Part One.[165]

---

164 Marx initially abstracts from the category of the *form* of value, in addition to the many other variables held at bay in his incipient analysis of the commodity, such as prices, money, other commodities, commodity owners and buyers, capital, etc. In this, I follow Heinrich's conclusion: 'If we speak of the "value-relation" between two commodities, then value is already presupposed as a result of the exchange relation .... What is new here is that Marx has introduced the concept of form and undertakes a detailed analysis of the value-form' (Heinrich 2021, pp. 98, 99). In this section of my argument, I am building on Heinrich's comprehensive but theoretically agnostic presentation, to argue that Marx deploys a novel process of demonstration that I am calling the additive synthetic. Hegel, in *The Science of Logic*, indicated precisely the methodological procedure Marx would adopt in *Capital*: '[One must begin a scientific exposition] with the subject matter in the form of a universal .... The *prius* must be ... something simple, something abstracted from the concrete, because in this form alone has the subject-matter the form of the self-related universal .... It is easier for the mind to grasp the abstract simple thought determination than the concrete subject matter, which is a manifold connection of such thought determinations and their relationships' (cited in Musto 2020, p. 16).
165 Bidet 2005, p. 133. Though unattributed, Bidet's argument clearly develops the late Althusser's concept of *la position*, described above.

In the first chapter of *Capital* that I discuss here, Marx implements a purely additive synthetic method, in which the process of logical synthesis operates in a fashion analogous to that which Macherey identifies in his commentary on Spinoza's method. Basing his comments on Spinoza's Preface to the *Principles of the Philosophy of Descartes*, the only site at which Spinoza reflected on method, Macherey observes that for Spinoza, '*synthesis* [as opposed to Cartesian *analysis*] is the method of formal exposition that allows for the presentation of truths [that have been previously discovered and analysed in the research process] in a demonstrative form that proceeds from the known to the known .... Synthesis proceeds from the knowledge of causes to that of their effects, in conformity with the real order of things'.[166] For both Spinoza and Marx, such additive demonstration, as a science of causes without superfluous reference to a putative totality or whole, constitutes the adequate modality of a materialist demonstration, the synthetic reproduction of the real order of things in the attribute of thought.

This synthetic mode of demonstration [Macherey continues],

> mentally reproduces ... the order in which things effectively are and produce one another [*sont et se font*] .... Synthesis concomitantly expresses the productivity of the real [as] a form of discourse, the organisation of which, which is to say its necessary progression, adheres to that of the causal process, and reproduces the order of the real as it is in itself, leading to understanding as if from the interior of things, as they are and as they develop [*telles qu'elles sont et telles qu'elles se font*], following the rational movement that leads from causes to effects, rather than the inverse.[167]

Synthetic demonstration, in this view, constitutes a rigorous form of materialist demonstration, an organisation of discourse whose object is to make visible what Macherey calls 'the syntax of the real' in its effective constitution and 'intrinsic intelligibility'.[168] Spurning all constraint and guarantees, all formal obligation and teleology, this mode of demonstration, one that I am arguing is shared by Marx and Spinoza as a science of causes, invites the reader to follow the logic of the real, step by necessary step, as a materialist 'restitution of the texture of the real in the form of the order of ideas'.[169] Marx suggests nothing less by his otherwise strange self-quotation from the 1859 *Introduction*, that

---

166 Macherey 1998, p. 17.
167 Macherey 1998, p. 18.
168 Macherey 1998, p. 19.
169 Macherey 1998, p. 20.

he inserts in the first sentence of *Capital*, as if to say: 'This, reader, is what I have come to understand as the effective constitution of the real order of things and relations of value in the capitalist social form: follow my reasoning carefully, and judge for yourself if this is the case'.[170]

Let's look at Marx's analysis of the value relation more carefully. In Marx's initial analysis of the exchange relation in sections 1.1–1.2, he determined that the value of commodities – a 'residue' obtained by abstracting entirely from their characteristics as use-values – *has no material form at that level of abstraction*, and thus cannot *exist* as a sensuous singular thing, but instead constitutes a mere 'spectral objectivity'.[171] This first stage of analysis showed that the substance of the commodity's value is abstract labour, but did so in abstraction from its phenomenal manifestation in any determinate form whatsoever.

The substance of this value, abstract labour, will only obtain objective, material form, and thus actual existence, as opposed to this mere spectral objectivity, when Marx's logical demonstration investigates the concrete social relation of one commodity to another, and it is to the nature of this relation that Marx turns in section 1.3.[172] At stake in this section, the development of which will culminate in Marx's unprecedented demonstration of the logical (as opposed to historical) genesis and necessity of the money form, is a problem that had previously remained at best a riddle, and at worst entirely invisible, in the history of political economy: while it is obvious to anyone that money allows for the exchange of commodities, this does not at all explain how it is that money possesses this strange power, and why it must necessarily be so in any society governed by commodity relations: only Marx's logical genesis of the money form can answer this question.[173]

My point here is simply to show that each logical step in Marx's demonstration fully preserves the findings that precede it, and, as opposed to any alleged negative dialectical *Aufhebung*, proceeds instead through a positive, additive logic of *implication*. Marx begins this analysis in section 1.3a by con-

---

170 'I welcome every opinion based on scientific criticism', Marx writes in the Preface to the first edition. 'As to the prejudices of so-called public opinion, to which I have never made concessions, now, as ever, my maxim is that of the great Florentine: "Segui il tuo corso, e lascia dir le genti"' (1976, p. 93).

171 Marx 1976, p. 128. This point will prove crucial when I come to discuss Moseley's critique of Heinrich in the next section.

172 'Commodities possess an objective character as values only in so far as they are all expressions of an identical social substance, human labour, [such] that their objective character as values is therefore purely social' (Marx 1976, p. 138).

173 Heinrich 2021, p. 97. See also Bellofiore's analysis of this spectral aspect of Marx's demonstration, Bellofiore 2018, pp. 360–1.

structing the value relation in its most abstract form, one that is 'simple' (it investigates only two commodities), 'isolated' (bearing no relationship to commodities other than these two he has chosen), and 'accidental' (because any two commodities could be chosen as examples of this abstract relation).[174] This simple isolated and accidental form of the value relation, he next specifies, possesses two 'poles' [*Pole*] that coexist and allow for this relation, mutually determining and barring one another, all without contradiction, precisely as the poles of a compass coexist in their opposing, non-contradictory difference to define North and South.

Marx first recalls the results of his prior analysis of the exchange relation, which involved the exchange of two commodities of equal value such that both commodities identically and symmetrically shared a 'common element' (value).[175] In marked contrast, when Marx now turns to the analysis of the form of expression of value, that value relationship is by no means symmetrical. Instead, the first commodity (linen) is said by Marx to *actively* expresses its value in the second commodity (coat), while the second commodity remains *passive*, serving as the material expression of something else, the value of the first. Marx names these two forms the 'relative' and the 'equivalent' form of value. Like the two attributes of the commodity that Marx introduced in the first pages of *Capital*, Marx here observes that these two forms of value bear two non-contradictory aspects or attributes: they are 1. mutually dependent, each requiring the existence of the other, as well as being 2. mutually exclusive, such that a given commodity can only play the role of one of these two forms at a time.[176]

Having presented these attributes, in section 1.3.2, Marx next proceeds to analyse the first of these two forms of value, the relative. Though Marx's initial analysis of the exchange relation has shown that the value of any and all commodities can be reduced to an identical unit (abstract labour), in now analysing the *form* that this value must take, he proceeds to investigate the particularities of these differential roles (relative and equivalent forms of value), explicitly calling attention to the difference between these two levels of his analysis:

> If we say that, as values, commodities are simply congealed quantities of human labour [i.e., the principal finding of his initial analysis of the exchange relation], our analysis reduces them, it is true, to the level of an abstraction, value, but does not give them a *form of value* distinct from

---

174 Heinrich 2021, p. 97.
175 Marx 1976, p. 139.
176 Heinrich 2021, p. 99.

their natural forms. It is otherwise in the value relation of one commodity to another. The first commodity's value character emerges here through its own relation to the second commodity.[177]

While it is the case that as values, at the level of the *exchange* relation, commodities are what Marx describes as 'congealed' abstract human labour, *this common unit, since it possesses not an 'atom of matter'*,[178] *cannot be apprehended in the sensuous, actually existing form of a singular, isolated commodity*.[179]

Now, however, additively building upon this prior determination of an initial 'value-abstraction', Marx proceeds to show that when considered at the higher level of logical concretion of the *value* relation, the value of the commodity that plays the relative role in this relation (linen) does in fact acquire the material expression of its value in and through the equivalent form possessed by the second, actually existing commodity (coat), a material form necessarily different from its own (the value of linen cannot be expressed in linen).[180] From this demonstration, Marx draws a simple, minimal inference: that 'the value of the commodity linen is therefore expressed by the physical body of the commodity coat, the value of one by the use-value of the other'.[181] This then leads him to offer a summary statement of this stage of his analysis:

> Commodity A, then, in entering into a relation with commodity B as an object of value, as a materialisation of human labour, makes the use-value B into the material through which its own value is expressed.[182]

This completed, in the next step of his analysis, in section 1.3.2.ii, Marx introduces the quantitative aspect of this value relation from which he had abstracted to this point ('The quantitative determinacy of the relative form of value'). As a material expression or actually existing embodiment of value, in

---

177 Marx 1976, p. 141 f., emphasis added.
178 Marx 1976, p. 138.
179 Once again, this point will prove crucial to rebut Moseley's critique of Heinrich.
180 'Human labour-power in its fluid state, or human labour, creates value, but is not itself value. It becomes value in its coagulated state, in objective form …. The value of the linen as a congealed mass of human labour can [thus] be expressed only as an "objectivity" [*Gegenständlichkeit*], a thing which is materially different from the linen itself and yet common to the linen and all other commodities' (Marx 1976, p. 142, cited at Heinrich 2021, p. 104).
181 Marx 1976, p. 143.
182 Marx 1976, p. 144, cited at Heinrich 2021, p. 106.

contrast to the nonexistent 'spectral' nature of value when considered in the exchange relation, this value form must furthermore be 'quantitatively determined' as a determinate 'magnitude'.[183] This being the case, Marx proceeds to consider the four logically possible variations of the relative value of the two commodities in question in this basic form of the value relation: either the value of one or the other changes, while the second remains constant, or both change in identical proportions, or both change in different proportions.[184]

Having enumerated these cases, Marx next turns to examine the nature of the equivalent form of value in a passage that clearly indicates the additive, non-contradictory nature of his demonstration:

> The commodity linen brings to view its own *existence* as a value through the fact that the coat can be equated with the linen although it has not assumed a form of value distinct from its own physical form. The coat is directly exchangeable with the linen; in this way the linen in fact expresses its own *existence as a value*. The equivalent form of a commodity, accordingly, is the form in which it is directly exchangeable with other commodities.[185]

While the first sentence summarises Marx's analysis of the value form to this point, the second and third add to this a new proposition: the actually existing, material form of the linen expresses the coat's direct 'exchangeability' with it, such that the equivalent form 'is the form in which it is directly exchangeable with other commodities', which is to say, that it requires no mediation (of another commodity) for the exchange process to occur.[186]

Marx next indicates three 'peculiarities' [*Eigentümlichkeiten*] (none of which constitute 'contradictions') of the equivalent form, in which he stresses the necessity that governs this form, such that the appearance of the value of the linen in the form of the coat requires and can only occur within this value-relation:

> The natural form of the commodity becomes its value-form. But, note well, this substitution only occurs in the case of a commodity B (coat, or maize, or iron, etc.) when some other commodity A (linen etc.) enters into a value-relation with it, and then only within the limits of this relation.

---

183   Marx 1976, p. 144.
184   Marx 1976, pp. 145–6.
185   Marx 1976, p. 147, emphasis added.
186   Heinrich 2021, p. 109.

Since a commodity cannot be related to itself as equivalent, and therefore cannot make its own physical shape into the expression of its own value, it must be related to another commodity as equivalent, and therefore must make the physical shape of another commodity into its own value-form.[187]

Here again we find Marx stressing the systematic necessity that governs the value relation between two commodities: since no commodity can express its value in its own material form, it *must* relate to another, materially distinct commodity as its equivalent, the actually existing material form of its value. The linen (in Marx's example) must take the physical form of the equivalent commodity (coat) as the form of its value, since the value of linen cannot be expressed in linen. This, Marx shows, is the real, necessary, and positive form of the value relation, involving no contradiction whatsoever between use- and exchange-value, but only a peculiarity that he insightfully notes, one that allows for the value relation materially to exist.

Next, following his famous excursus on Aristotle's socially determined incapacity to grasp the nature of the value relation,[188] Marx summarises his qualitative and quantitative analysis of the simple form of the value relation, to which he adds the important terminological clarification that the two factors or attributes of the commodity introduced at the beginning of chapter one should, strictly speaking, have been identified as use-value and 'value' (rather than exchange-value), since exchange-value is merely the 'form of manifestation' of value, not something a given commodity possesses in and of itself. Instead, Marx specifies, 'the commodity never has this form when looked at in isolation, but only when it is in a value-relation or an exchange relation with a second commodity of a different kind'.[189] As Heinrich specifies, 'A commodity "is" something double: use-value and an object of value. But it is not exchange-value; it has exchange-value, when another commodity expresses its value'.[190] While it may seem that Marx is splitting hairs, the point is important in the context of my argument (and I will argue it applies analogously in Moseley's dispute with Heinrich), since it clearly indicates a key conceptual and logical difference from the 1867 edition, where Marx did not yet clearly distinguish between value and exchange-value.

---

187 Marx 1976, p. 148.
188 Marx 1976, pp. 151–2.
189 Marx 1976, p. 152.
190 Heinrich 2021, p. 119.

Even more crucial is the next step in Marx's argument, and in fact the interpretation of this passage condenses and radicalises my entire argument for Marx's additive, positive dialectical method. Here is Marx's observation, which I cite in full:

> The *internal opposition* [*innere Gegensatz*] between use-value and value, hidden within the commodity, is therefore represented on the surface by an *external opposition* [*äusseren Gegensatz*], i.e. by *a relation* between two commodities such that the one commodity, whose own value is supposed to be expressed, counts directly only as a use-value, whereas the other commodity, in which that value is to be expressed, counts directly only as exchange-value. Hence the simple form of value of a commodity is the simple form of appearance of the opposition [*Gegensatzes*] between use-value and value which is contained within the commodity.[191]

Here, perhaps more than anywhere else in the first chapter of *Capital*, we would expect to find a statement of the 'contradictory' nature of use-value and exchange-value. Instead, Marx does not simply refuse outright the Hegelian terminology of contradiction [*Widerspruch*]; what's more, he clearly and otherwise defines the nature of this relation – both within the single commodity possessing its two attributes of use-value and value when initially analysed at the level of the exchange relation, and now, at the level of the value relation – as an *opposition* [*Gegensatz*].

As I have throughout this book, let me pause to invoke the lucidly contrasting definitions André Lalande offers for these two concepts:
- 'Contradiction' [D. *Widerspruch*]: the relation existing between the affirmation and the negation of a *same element* of knowledge, in particular, between two terms, one of which is the negation of the other, such as *A and not-A*.
- 'Opposition' [D. *Gegensatz, Opposition*]: the relation of *two contrary* objects placed facing one another in contrast or distinction.[192]

---

191   Marx 1976, p. 153, emphasis added. 'Der in der Ware eingehüllte innere Gegensatz von Gebrauchswert und Wert wird also dargestellt durch einen äußeren Gegensatz, d.h. durch das Verhältnis zweier Waren, worin die eine Ware, deren Wert ausgedrückt werden soll, unmittelbar nur als Gebrauchswert, die andre Ware hingegen, worin Wert ausgedrückt wird, unmittelbar nur als Tauschwert gilt. Die einfache Wertform einer Ware ist also die einfache Erscheinungsform des in ihr enthaltenen Gegensatzes von Gebrauchswert und Wert'. MEGA II 6, *Karl Marx, Das Kapital: Kritik Der Politishen Ökonomie. Erster Band, Hamburg 1872*. Berlin: Dietz Verlag, 1987, p. 93.
192   Lalande 2010, pp. 183, 717, emphasis added. I have added the specification 'in contrast or distinction' to Lalande's from the OED definition of opposition.

The crucial difference between Hegelian contradiction and the 'opposition' of use-value and exchange-value in Marx's analysis is that while the former indicates the simultaneous affirmation and negation of 'a same element' or object (A and not-A), opposition indicates the contrast or distinction between two *different* objects.

As a point of contrast, take for example Hegel's famous beginning to the *Science of Logic*. Hegel here unequivocally indicates a relation of contradiction, as 'A and not-A', as opposed to Marx's indication by the concept of 'opposition' a relation of contrast, a determination without any implication whatsoever that use-value and exchange-value are in any sense the same thing. In other words, for Hegel, a thing ('Being, pure being – without further determination'), through the necessity governing its essential nature as this phrase defines it ('without determination'), reveals its selfsame identity to be, 'in fact nothing, pure nothingness', i.e., all at once one and the same thing, both A and not-A, both being and nothingness, in what constitutes a real contradiction in the full sense of the word.[193]

In marked contrast to Hegel's analysis of Being, Nothing, and Becoming, at no point does Marx ever state or imply that use-value and exchange-value are in any sense *the same thing* (A and not-A). Instead, he goes to painstaking logical detail to precisely formulate the nature of the differential relation of these two always distinct concepts, and in the case of both the exchange and value relations, and he defines this relation as an *opposition*. He introduces this concept in the passage I have cited above to indicate at once the dependent and necessary nature of these two distinct attributes of the commodity form, as well as the important distinction that in the more abstract exchange relation, the differential opposition of use-value and exchange-value is internal to ('hidden within', Marx says) any given, individual commodity, while in the value relation between the relative and equivalent forms of the commodity, the differential opposition finds its 'representation' on the surface (as the forms of appearance of the value relation), as an 'external opposition'.

This differential opposition of use-value and exchange-value, Marx has shown, is neither contradictory nor contingent. Instead, in each logical form, it

---

193   Hegel 2010b, p. 59. Compare Hegel's argument with that of Spinoza in proposition 3 of *Ethics* III, as Macherey reads the latter: 'There is nothing in the essence of a thing, following from its definition, which can cause it not to be [*qui puisse faire qu'elle ne soit pas*], or that its reality encompass [*soit marquée*] any negativity whatsoever [and thus Spinoza writes:] "the definition of any thing whatsoever affirms the essence of that thing itself, but does not negate it; that is to say, it posits the essence of the thing but does not suppress it" (*definition cujuscunque rei ipsius rei essentiam affirmat sed non negat; sive rei essentiam point, sed non tollit*)'. Macherey 1997 p. 382.

is emphatically and logically necessary, he shows, for this very distinction (as A and B rather than A and not-A) to exist such that commodity and commodity relations may themselves *exist* (and Marx has begun *Capital* by defining societies in which the capitalist mode of production predominates, his object of investigation, as the general *existence* (appearance) of commodities and commodified relations).

In fact, these two contrasting starting points of Hegel's *Logic* and Marx's *Capital* could not be more radically opposed, though each thinker at the same time fully comprehends and calls attention to the difficulty and crucial nature of the beginning of any scientific analysis.[194] For the one, a word, a notion, Being, conceived and defined as a maximum of abstraction, as 'without content'. For the other, a (maximally abstract but positive) definition of capitalism as the general accumulation of commodities, one that is quite the opposite of nothing (it is an '*ungeheure Waarensammlung*'); instead, having come to this definition and starting point by necessity through his materialist enquiry, Marx's beginning indicates something very concrete, full of positive implications that remain to be concretised.

The negative dialectical dice are loaded if one picks a notion with no determinate content to start with: then of course this 'thing' without content will of necessity immediately reveal itself as a contradiction, as the negation of itself, as nothing, as A and not-A.[195] On the one hand, a logic that begins with a logical contradiction and develops this into an entire science of negative dialectical logic, on the other, a critique of a real social form, one that begins in materialist fashion in media res, with an abstract definition of this determinate mode of production to initiate an increasingly concrete analysis via the logic of ramified additive synthesis and implication.

To prepare the necessary logical passage to the expanded and then general equivalent forms of value, Marx simply indicates that the simple form of the value relation he has analysed to this point in section 1.3 possesses an 'insuffi-

---

194 Here is Hegel: 'That which constitutes the beginning, the beginning itself, is to be taken as something unanalysable, taken in its simple, unfilled immediacy; and therefore as being, as complete emptiness .... Let those who are still dissatisfied with this beginning take upon themselves the challenge of beginning in some other way and yet avoiding such defects' (2010b, p. 53); while Marx famously warns his readers that 'Beginnings are always difficult in all sciences' (1976, p. 89).

195 Compare with Caligaris and Starosta, who write, 'In so far as [Hegel's] systematic dialectic begins with the simplest *thought-form* (*that is, with a purely ideal or formal abstraction*), his subsequent derivation of categories is bound to follow the immanent necessity of 'pure thought' as such, which does not express the inner movement of the simpler determinations of "real material being"' (Caligaris and Starosta 2014, p. 96, emphasis in original).

ciency' [*Blick*] (as opposed to a *Widerspruch*) relative to the general equivalent and price-form.[196] This is to say that while Marx's analysis of the simple form is fully coherent and non-contradictory, that simple form is nonetheless logically deficient or inadequate, in the sense that the forms of value (relative and equivalent) inhering between only two commodities cannot account for the *general* exchange and accumulation of commodities, the defining feature of capitalism for Marx at its most general and abstract level. Simply because linen expresses its value in the form of actually existing coats, it cannot therefore be directly exchanged, in this form of relation, for any other commodity than coats.

In other words, the simple value relation of two commodities cannot express the relation of any given commodity to all other commodities, which, Marx logically assumes from his point of departure, is nonetheless essential in a social form determined by general commodification. Capitalism is not defined by the exchange of two or even a small set of commodities, but by the general commodification and exchange of all things of value, and thus the demonstration of the form of value must proceed adequately to account for the level of generality of exchange this specific social form requires.

Marx's analysis of the value form therefore progresses sequentially to investigate the 'expanded' and 'general' forms, indicating along the way both the necessity of each as well as various 'defects' [*Mängeln*] of the former, here again proceeding additively to indicate the (logical) development of the (non-contradictory) *Gegensatze* that positively, if inadequately, constitute each 'pole' of the value form: from the symmetrical, and thus 'unfixed' simple form to its subsequent fixation in one commodity set aside as the general equivalent form.[197] I leave to the reader to follow the development of this additive logic in

---

196   Marx 1976, p. 154. Heinrich at this point underscores the purely logical nature of this demonstration in terms that again evoke Althusser's concept of *la position*: 'The transition from the simple form of value to the expanded form is not a historical transition, which we are merely describing; rather, it is a transition to a new level of analysis, which we are carrying out. It's a conceptual development – a development of our conceptual constructions – that aims to dissect what is always mixed up and interconnected in capitalist reality, so that we can understand it' (Heinrich 2021, p. 124).

197   While Marx continues to speak only of 'Gegensatze' ('In demselben Grad aber, worin sich die Wertform überhaupt entwickelt, entwickelt sich auch der Gegensatz zwischen ihren beiden Polen, der relativen Wertform und Äquivalentform'), Fowkes inconsistently, if suggestively, at this point translates the term as 'antagonism' (1976, p. 160). For the original German of the 1872 edition, see MEGA II/6, *Karl Marx, Das Kapital: Kritik Der Politischen Ökonomie. Erster Band, Hamburg 1872*. Berlin: Dietz Verlag, 1987, p. 99. The wording of this passage is identical as well in the 1890 edition; cf. MEGA II 10, *Karl Marx, Das Kapital: Kritik Der Politischen Ökonomie. Erster Band, Hamburg 1890*. Berlin: Dietz Verlag, 1991, p. 67.

the remainder of chapter 1, to turn now to the dispute between Heinrich and Moseley over the substance of value in *Capital*.

11   When Does Socially Necessary Labour Exist?

In the previous section I have based my own anti-Hegelian argument upon Heinrich's distinction between the exchange and value relations in the first chapter of *Capital*.[198] Heinrich's reading has not gone uncriticised, however: Robert Kurz, Barbara Lietz and Winfried Schwarz, and Fred Moseley have all disputed Heinrich's contention (as they read him) that value is only created through the exchange of commodities, or, to cite Heinrich himself, that 'Abstract human labour, as the substance of commodities' value, does not emerge on the basis of the individual commodity but is based on the exchange relation between commodities'.[199] Heinrich's critics argue instead that Marx clearly and repeatedly indicates that, as Moseley puts the matter, 'each commodity is assumed [by Marx] to possess a common property, the "substance" of value (objectified abstract human labour) in definite quantities ... determined in production, independently of exchange'.[200] Moseley's value realism, as I would call it, thus stands opposed to Heinrich's relational understanding of the substance of value: 'Commodities', Heinrich summarises, 'have value-objectivity only in the social relation of one commodity to another'.[201] In turning to this debate over the substance of value, I wish to argue against Heinrich's critics, that Marx's analysis of the substance of value is not uniform and unchanging, but instead undergoes an important process of auto-critique. This critique – while revising Marx's initial Hegelian position that an existing but imperceptible essence or substance of value must appear through its dialectical sublation as exchange-value – remains obscure, since Marx only clearly articulated it in long-unpublished revision notes for the second edition of *Capital*.

---

198   Heinrich, as noted above, follows Althusser in rejecting the theoretical commonplace that Marx's dialectic is a materialist revision of Hegel's *Logic*, but, to my knowledge, does so only in passing, as opposed to the more sustained attention I seek to give the question in these pages.

199   Heinrich 2021, p. 66. Note already that in this passage (which Moseley cites on page 117 of *Marx's Theory of Value*), Heinrich does not say that value is 'created' by exchange (as Moseley repeatedly reads him), but only that it 'emerges' in this process.

200   Moseley 2023, p. 50. Here I will primarily address Moseley's critique, which develops in more systematic, book-length form a position on Heinrich essentially identical to that of Kurz and Lietz and Schwarz. See also Kurz 2016 and Lietz and Schwarz 2023.

201   Heinrich 2021, p. 95.

In my view this dispute between Heinrich and Moseley has resulted in a persistent *dialogue des sourds* in large part due to the failure by Moseley in particular to clearly formulate the terms of their disagreement, relying instead on a hodgepodge of vague, unexamined terms either imputed to or taken directly from Marx. The commodity is repeatedly claimed by Moseley to 'possess', 'contain', or 'have' value, a value which is said to 'emerge', 'congeal', 'exist', 'be', or 'become' as a result of the production process. All of these varied expressions can in my view be reduced to a single, theoretically clear (though false) claim on Moseley's part: that value *exists* already in the production process of any single commodity, that, as Moseley writes, 'the value of the coat ... does *exist* by itself', or as Lietz and Schwarz write, 'value *exists* as a form-determination ... in production, where it arises'.[202]

We should cut this Gordian knot simply by holding here as well to Marx's Spinozist distinction between a nonexistent thought-construct [*Gedankenkonkretum*] and actually existing singular things. My interest in addressing this question is not merely to break through this protracted dispute on the origin of value between Heinrich and his opponents; my principal claim is that Marx eventually articulated this clear distinction between the nonexistent abstraction of a thought-construct such as value and that of actually existing, sensuous things such as singular commodities and their price forms, but only in the little-known 1872 *Ergänzungen Und Veränderungen* preparatory manuscript and in a single, but crucial sentence added only to the 1875 French translation. It was only in these obscure passages that he managed fully to escape the Hegelian hermeneutics of revelation still prevalent in the discussion of the substance of value in the 1867 and 1872 editions of *Capital*.

These earlier texts do in fact suffer from a conceptualisation of the substance of value as a hermeneutic, in which a latent, formless yet putatively existent essence, simultaneously claimed to be 'congealed' in the commodity yet 'spectral', is said to acquire its sensuous form in a moment of sublation. While Marx overcame this mystical Hegelian logic of incarnation by 1875, it nonetheless continues to haunt Moseley's otherwise sober analysis into the present. I will first recall the purely theoretical status of abstraction in *Capital*, before discussing the implication of this on the debate over the substance of value.

That *Capital* is an abstract theoretical construction of the capitalist social form, and not a historical study of capitalism (as Kautsky argued in *Karl Marx: Oekonomische Lehren*) is a point on which Heinrich and Moseley (as well as Althusser and Chris Arthur) all agree. As Heinrich points out,

---

202   Moseley 2023, p. 155, emphasis added; Lietz and Schwarz 2023, p. 26, emphasis added.

such a conception [as Kautsky's] baldly contradicts Marx's claims in the Preface to the first volume. There, he emphasises that the work deals with 'theoretical developments', and that the text makes reference to conditions in England only as an 'illustration' of such developments.[203]

Not only is *Capital* a 'theoretical' study in its entirety; Marx famously identifies for his reader in the Preface to the First Edition the fundamental tool he deploys for this analysis of the capitalist social form: abstraction. 'In the analysis of economic forms neither microscopes nor chemical reagents are of assistance. The power of abstraction must replace both'.[204] Abstraction, as Lalande comments, 'isolates by thought that which cannot be isolated in representation'.[205] The point is simple, but far-reaching and, indeed, eminently Althusserian: abstraction is fundamentally opposed to the *representation* of an empirical object. Instead, abstraction indicates the *sui generis* construction of a non-existent thought object, what Marx called in the 1857 Introduction a *Gedankenkonkretum*.

Marx was no doubt familiar with Hegel's anti-empiricist appraisal of abstraction in the *Encyclopedia*: 'Ordinary consciousness deals with sensory representations which crisscross and get entangled. In the act of abstraction, however, the mind is concentrated on a single point and, by this means, the habit is acquired of preoccupying oneself with the interiority [of things]'. He emphatically rejected, however, Hegel's ensuing condescending judgement of Aristotelean ἀφαίρεσις [abstraction] as no more than training wheels for the mind till it learns to practice true, i.e. negative dialectical, thought: 'To occupy oneself with this kind of formal logic is no doubt useful. It clears the head, as they say. One learns to concentrate'.[206]

Instead, Marx explicitly deployed 'the power of abstraction' as the fundamental tool for his entire critique of political economy, such that Heinrich can devote an entire Appendix of his *How to Read Capital* to the multiple 'Levels of Abstraction and the Course of Argument in the First Seven Chapters of Capital'.[207] What's more, this understanding of abstraction as the construction of nonexistent *Gedankenkonkretumen* constitutes, since the very beginning of his research in 1857 when Marx first articulated this basic epistemological position, a further confirmation of Althusser's assertion that Marx rejects Hegel's

---

203 Heinrich 2021, p. 397.
204 Marx 1976, p. 90.
205 Lalande 2010, p. 8.
206 Hegel 2010a, p. 54, bracketed insertion in original.
207 Heinrich 2021, p. 391.

model of abstraction as the representational extraction of a kernel of truth from an object (Hegel's 'preoccupying oneself with the interiority of things'), to instead undertake the fabrication of nonexistent concepts.[208] Heinrich repeatedly emphasises this very Althusserian point in his reading of *Capital*, the subtlety of which is quite surprisingly absent in Moseley's rebuttal: 'The object of inquiry, the 'commodity', is not simply drawn from experience. Instead, it is constructed, by means of abstraction'.[209]

While throughout this book I have repeatedly emphasised this Spinozist-Althusserian distinction between the object of thought and real, actually existing things, the point I wish to make here in appraising Moseley and Heinrich's debate over the substance of value is simply that the concept of *existence* should be taken in its rigorous definition as 'the fact of being *independently* of knowledge, [as] actually presented in [sensuous] perception',[210] in other words, as the distinction between nonexistent thought objects and actually existing singular things in sensuous extension. If this is the case, one must conclude that as concepts, *none* of the original *Gedankenkonkretumen* that Marx constructs in *Capital*, concepts such as use-value, exchange-value, and value, relative and absolute surplus value, and the like, *actually exists*.[211]

---

208 RC, p. 36. This distinction between Hegel's empiricist understanding of abstraction and Marx's Spinozist usage reproduces to some degree the founding distinction in Aristotle between two models of abstraction, respectively, 'abstractive induction' ('epagôgê [ἐπαγωγή]'), the additive grouping of similar elements under a single concept, versus the 'stripping' ('aphaireisthai [ἀφαιρεῖσθαι]') [of] the image or representation of a thing of its individualising characteristics (essentially material). Alain de Libera, 'Abstraction', in Cassin 2014, p. 1.

209 Heinrich 2021, p. 53. I say the absence of awareness of this distinction is surprising in Moseley's argument because the entire, elaborate argument of his finely constructed previous book *Money and Totality* is based upon the distinction between actually existing capitals and the purely theoretical construction of aliquot subdivisions of a total mass of surplus value. See Moseley, 2017, 45–46; Nesbitt 2022, 224 n. 68.

210 Lalande 2010, p. 318. On the extremely complex history of the related concepts of the Latin *existentia*, the French and English 'existence,' and the German pseudo-synonyms *Existenz* and *Dasein*, see David, 2014. Bolzano argues that the fundamental, universal characteristic of all *Vorstellungen an sich* – his preeminent logical concept, analogous to Spinoza's *res singulares non existentes* (EIIP9) – is that '*Vorstellungen an sich haben kein Dasein*' (Bolzano 1978, 75). I discuss Bolzano's logic in the next chapter.

211 Of course, the general theoretical point regarding 'existence' that I am making here at the high level of abstraction of the first chapter of *Capital I* (the site of Moseley and Heinrich's debate) in no way exhausts the complexity of the relation between living labor and the commodity labor power at greater levels of concretion, for example as what Riccardo Bellofiore calls 'the ambiguity built into the notion of abstract labor itself [:] abstract labor, on the one hand, is the *immediately private labor* which is *becoming* social in circulation; on the other hand, it is the private labor which *has become socialized* on the commod-

At the same time, *some* of those nonexistent concepts are *also* sensuously manifest as singular existing things. The nonexistent concept of concrete labour, for example, also exists as the actual physical activity, the physiological labour, involved in producing any singular commodity, a real coat or yard of linen. Similarly, the nonexistent concept of exchange-value also exists in sensuous form, for example as the singular price of any given commodity (as a price on a tag), i.e., as the material form of appearance of the value of that actually existing commodity.

The form of value as exchange-value thus constitutes at once a nonexistent abstraction in thought (a concept), as well as indicating actually existing *real abstractions* to be found in the material world of commodity exchange.[212] It is precisely this distinction, between the non-existent thought abstraction, Marx's *Gedankenkonkretum*, and the actually existing real abstractions of the manifest, material price-forms of value, that is entirely missing from Moseley and Heinrich's debate.

Now, Moseley and Heinrich, astute, seasoned readers of *Capital* that they are, both agree that Marx derives the concept of the substance of value (abstract human labour) as an *abstraction* from the sensuous, tangible qualities of any singular, actually existing instance of concrete labour, in other words, as a concept that Marx constructs in his analysis.[213] Marx summarises this point quite clearly in the *Ergänzungen*:

> The magnitude of value represents a specific quantity of labour, but this quantity is not the coincidental quantity of labour that A or B expend in the production of a commodity. It is socially determined, the labour socially necessary for the production of a thing. ... Equality in the full

---

ity market. ... The origin of the trouble goes back to the fact that Marx mostly deduces abstract labor from exchange "as such," but he also sometimes defines it as the labor which is opposed to capital' (Bellofiore, 2023, 6). In my view, however, the point Bellofiore makes is a merely apparent contradiction, as I will argue below.

212 Adorno gives a succinct definition of real abstraction in *Introduction to Sociology*, confusingly conflating at the same time, however, two different forms of real abstraction, the real act of exchange and the material monetary form of value: In 'exchange in terms of average social labour time the specific forms of the objects to be exchanged are necessarily disregarded instead, they are reduced to a universal unit. The abstraction, therefore, lies not in the thought of the sociologist, but in society itself' (2002, p. 32). On the concept of real abstraction, see Sohn-Rethel 2021; Toscano 2008; and Jappe 2013.

213 'I agree [with Heinrich] that Marx is not looking for the common property of commodities in the production process of a single commodity'. Moseley 2023, p. 108. Marx's 'focus', Heinrich writes, 'is therefore upon a reduction (and abstraction) that only scientific analysis can make visible' (2021, p. 64).

sense between different kinds of labour can be arrived at only if we *abstract* from their real inequality, if we *reduce* them to the characteristic they have in common, that of being the expenditure of human labour-power, of human labour in the abstract.[214]

Yet while being fully aware of this point, Moseley nonetheless repeatedly reaffirms the real *existence* of the substance of value in any single, isolated commodity: 'The value of the coat cannot be grasped by itself, but *it does exist by itself*, [as] the values of all commodities (including the linen) *exist by themselves*'.[215] If we take *existence* in the strict sense, however, to mean any real, sensuous thing, sensible to us via what Spinoza calls the attribute of extension, then it is clear that Marx's *abstraction* constructs a *nonexistent* concept: lacking a form of appearance or value-form, there is no actually existing 'human labour in the abstract' or 'identical human labour-power'; these phrases indicate instead a *conceptual construct* without sensuous reality. In the attribute of sensuous extension, there are only singular acts of concrete labour.[216]

The next step in Marx's argument that both Heinrich and Moseley retrace is to construct, in terms that follow directly from this initial abstraction, the concept of the *quantity* of the substance of value in any commodity as such. One of Marx's great advances over the classical labour theory of value is to have understood that this quantity cannot consist in the actual concrete time it took to make any single existing commodity. Marx makes the point simply and memorably in *Capital*:

> It might seem that if the value of a commodity is determined by the quantity of labour expended to produce it, it would be the more valuable the more unskilful and lazy the worker who produced it, because he would need more time to complete the article. However, the labour that forms the substance of value is equal human labour, the expenditure of identical human labour-power.[217]

This 'equal human labour' is an *abstraction* from actually existing concrete acts of labour, and as such, it cannot *exist* in space and time without a form of

---

214   Marx, cited in Moseley 2023, p. 183, emphasis added.
215   Moseley 2023, p. 155.
216   Riccardo Bellofiore similarly points out that 'in a fully monetary exchange society like capitalism, the real abstraction of labor is only completed ex-post in the final circulation of commodities' (Bellofiore, 2023, 6).
217   Marx 1976, p. 128.

appearance, which Marx will only introduce as a further degree of concretisation in the third section of chapter one.[218] While Moseley indeed 'agree[s] with Heinrich that value is "shown" or "revealed" only in exchange', he immediately adds the mistaken proviso that 'the revelation of value in exchange presupposes an *already existing value* ... created in production and revealed in exchange'.[219]

In repeatedly taking this position against Heinrich throughout *Marx's Theory of Value*, Moseley is arguably misled by taking Marx too literally, citing Marx's published formulations without sufficiently taking into account Marx's own auto-critique in the *Ergänzungen*. Unfortunately, Marx only clearly formulates this obvious point – that concepts as abstractions do not exist in the strict sense of the word – in the *Ergänzungen*, such that numerous descriptions of the quantity of the substance of value read as if Marx were referring to the actual labour time that went into the production of any single commodity. In other words, reading Marx to the letter, Moseley is arguably misled by a problematic lack of clarity already present in Marx's analysis, prior to his self-criticism in the *Ergänzungen*, as when Marx writes for example that 'The value of *a commodity* ... varies directly as the quantity, and inversely as the productivity, of the labour which finds its realisation *within the commodity*. ... A given quantity of *any commodity* contains a definite quantity of human labour'.[220]

Moseley then reproduces in turn this same ambiguity inherent in the 1867 and 1872 editions of *Capital*: 'Note that the magnitude of value is a distinct quantity of objectified labour contained in *each commodity* and thus is an intrinsic property of *each commodity*'.[221] Moseley places particular emphasis on Marx's definition of the magnitude of value of any commodity as, in Moseley's

---

218   Here is Moseley: 'The labour that produces commodities is private independent labour, and private commodity producers come into contact with each [other] only through the exchange of their products, and, therefore, the labour expended to produce their commodities can only "appear" or manifest itself as the exchange-value of the commodities they produce. The exchange-value of commodities is the form of appearance of the social character of the labour expended to produce the commodities' (2023, p. 178).
219   Moseley 2023, p. 180.
220   Marx 1976, pp. 131, 144, cited in Moseley 2023, pp. 122, 160.
221   Moseley 2023, p. 40, emphasis added. Other examples include: '[Marx's phrase] "quantitatively comparable magnitude" presupposes that *each individual commodity* contains a given quantity of objectified human labour (the magnitude of value)'; 'Sections 1 and 2 of Chapter 1 presuppose that *individual commodities* contain definite quantities of objectified human labour-time, as determined in production' (Moseley 2023, pp. 68, 70 emphases added).

words, 'the quantity of objectified labour-time contained in *the commodity*, measured in hours, days, etc.'.[222] Despite Moseley's recurrent denials that he considers the substance of value to pre-exist in any single commodity in isolation,[223] he repeatedly takes Marx's initial ambiguity literally.

Rather than stating clearly and simply that the scientific object he has constructed – abstract human labour – is, as its name indicates, an abstract concept without spatio-temporal existence, Marx presents his finding in a vivid and unforgettable image, one that seems to confuse even Heinrich. Without a value form, Marx argues, the concept of the substance of value – abstract human labour measured as socially necessary labour time – takes on a disembodied existence, an oxymoron that Heinrich struggles to puzzle through:

> Marx describes what remains of the products of labour *after abstracting* from their use-value, the 'residue', as a 'phantom-like' [or 'spectral', *gespenstige Gegenständlichkeit*] objectivity. ... This objectivity can no longer be grasped by the senses. If we associate it with weight, color, form, or any other quality, we always come back to use-value – but we've just abstracted from use-value! Thus, the objectivity is present but is as intangible as a ghost; hence it is a 'spectral objectivity'.[224]

Now, the one advantage of Marx's image is to clearly indicate what it means to believe in the existence of an object without sensuous qualities, as Moseley apparently does: it is to believe in phantoms and spectres. Marx's initial formulation in the 1867 and 1872 editions of *Capital* of an 'objectivity' that can, as Heinrich writes, 'no longer be grasped by the senses', is needlessly confusing. And in fact, this does confuse Moseley, who, despite his repeated denials that he is not speaking of a single commodity in isolation, constantly reiterates that any commodity 'possesses' a quantity of the substance of value, as if this were the case for any actually existing commodity in isolation from all

---

222 Moseley 2023, p. 39. Here is Marx: 'How then is the magnitude of value to be measured? By means of the "*value-forming substance*", the *labour*, contained in the article. The quantity is measured by its *duration*, and the labour-time itself is measured on the particular scale of hours, days, etc.' (Marx 1976, p. 129, emphasis in original, cited in Moseley 2023, p. 39).
223 'My interpretation does not consider a single commodity by itself. Rather (as I have emphasised), my interpretation is about a single commodity as a representative of all commodities (the "elementary form" or the "cell-form") and the properties that all commodities (i.e. each and every commodity) have in common' (Moseley 2023, pp. 118–19).
224 Heinrich 2021, p. 64, emphasis added.

others.²²⁵ This leads Moseley confusingly to claim, for example, that 'the *unobservable* equal human labour that *exists* in production *appears* for the first time in exchange'.²²⁶

Moseley's critique of Heinrich suffers from a failure clearly to distinguish the nonexistence of Marx's conceptual abstractions from actually existing phenomena such as real, singular commodities, the concrete labour that produced them, and the actually existing price form of their value.²²⁷ To be sure, a certain quantity of value actually exists in the production process of any singular commodity, for example as the commodified inputs the capitalist purchases for the production process, whether in the form of constant (machinery and raw materials) or variable capital (labor power).²²⁸ These actually existing values, however, are merely transmitted as such to the commodity in the production process; at issue in this debate as I read it is instead whether a *newly produced surplus* value obtained via the exploitation of labor power already comes to exist in the production process. Extrapolating on Heinrich's reading to Marx's discussion of the working day and unpaid work hours in chapter 10 of *Capital*, we should say that what exists in the production process on this score are only unpaid hours of real, concrete labor expended to produce any given commodity; for these to exist as surplus value requires, Heinrich rightly argues, that they take a value form and go on to achieve their social validation through commodity exchange.

---

225 'Heinrich's explanation confuses *expressing* value with *possessing* value. The coat *expresses* the value of the linen only in relation to the linen, but the coat *possesses* value on its own, independent of its relation to the linen, as a result of the homogeneous human labour-power expended to produce the coat' (Moseley 2023, p. 155, emphasis in original).

226 Moseley 2023, p. 186, emphasis added. Numerous passages in Heinrich's *How to Read Capital* also suffer from a terminological vagueness regarding the existence or non-existence of the substance of value prior to appearance in a value-form: 'Commodities *have* value-objectivity only in the social relation of one commodity to another – which is why it first *comes to light* here. Prior to and outside of this relation, they are mere use-values: they are *on the way to becoming* commodities, but far from *being* commodities'. Heinrich, cited in Moseley 2023, p. 151, emphasis added.

227 Given this terminological vagueness, Moseley can even (correctly) formulate Heinrich's position in the terms I here insist on, only immediately to reject this position: 'Heinrich's interpretation is that abstract human labour does not *exist* in production, but instead abstract human labour comes to *exist* only in exchange' (Moseley 2023, p. 130, emphasis added).

228 Marx presumes in his analysis a fully developed capitalist social form, such that, Moseley writes in *Money and Totality*, "The means of production in capitalist production are commodities, which have been purchased at the beginning of the circuit of money capital, and which therefore enter the valorisation process with already existing specific prices." Moseley, 2017, 141.

Heinrich, while more consistently asserting that value only comes to 'emerge' or exist in the exchange relation,[229] nonetheless does not formulate this distinction between nonexistent abstractions and actually existing singular things as a theoretical position. Instead, focusing on Marx's image of the 'phantom-like' nature of the substance of value, he seeks to puzzle through this conundrum by asserting that already in the first two sections of chapter 1, Marx implicitly analyses the commodity in an 'exchange relation'. 'Only based on the exchange relation' Heinrich argues, 'can Marx say that there is an abstraction from the use-value of the commodity, and then go on to draw further conclusions'.[230]

Moseley argues at length that Heinrich autonomously imputes the concept of the 'exchange relation' to the first two sections of chapter one in order to make sense of the intangibility of abstract human labour, when Marx in these initial sections only speaks of the concept of the commodity as such in isolation.[231]

> Heinrich presents no textual evidence in this appendix [where he defines his concept of exchange relation] to support his interpretation of exchange relation in Chapter 1, except the one sentence from Marx's 'Marginal Notes on Wagner', which mentions only the commodity and does not mention an act of exchange at all. ... Heinrich's very unusual interpretation of 'exchange relation' as an abstraction from two acts of exchange between commodities and money on the market is just asserted by [him] with no explicit textual evidence.[232]

---

229   'Abstract human labour, as the substance of commodities' value, does not emerge on the basis of the individual commodity but is based on the exchange relation between commodities' (cited in Moseley 2023, p. 117).
230   Heinrich 2021, p. 59.
231   Here is one example among countless similarly fastidious statements by Moseley, each of which repeats the same point: 'Marx's first sentence does not say anything about an "exchange relation" of two commodities. Instead, Marx's sentence says "our analysis reduces them", and "them" clearly refers to "commodities", and thus "our analysis" means our analysis of commodities and the value of commodities, not our analysis of the "exchange relations" of commodities' (Moseley 2023, p. 154).
232   Moseley 2023, pp. 98, 99. 'The term "exchange relation"', Moseley continues, 'occurs only 11 times in Chapter 1: 5 times in Section 1, 0 times in Section 2, 5 times in Section 3 and 1 time in Section 4. None of these passages defines "exchange relation" as an abstraction from presupposed acts of exchange between two commodities and money on the market' (Moseley 2023, p. 99).

What Moseley convincingly shows, in my view, is that Heinrich needlessly introduces a conceptual conflation absent from Marx's presentation: it is only in section 1.3.2 on 'The Relative Form of Value' that Marx will analyse the relation between two commodities as what Heinrich calls their 'value relation', in which 'the coat [in Marx's example] counts as the form of existence of value' of the linen.[233] Prior to this, Marx analyses the concept of the commodity in abstraction from its relation to other commodities.s

What Moseley does not and cannot show, however, is how Marx's 'phantom-like' concept of abstract human labour can *exist* without a form of appearance. This instead is a mere faith-based assertion in his otherwise scrupulous argument. Moseley arrives at this untenable position because of his uniformly Hegelian reading of Marx's argument, assuming without discussion that an abstract concept can exist prior to its incarnation in a material form.[234] 'Essence', Hegel famously asserted without proof, 'must appear', a position to which Moseley subscribes without reserve.[235]

To be sure, Moseley adopts this position underwritten by Marx's own phrases in the first two editions of *Capital*, such as the following particularly unclear assertion:

> In the production of linen, a particular quantum of human labour *exists* in having been expended. The linen's value is the merely objective reflection of the labour so expended, but it is not reflected in the body of the linen. It *reveals* itself (i.e., acquires a sensual expression) by its value-relationship to the coat.[236]

Marx's language implies that he is speaking of the private, concrete 'quantum of human labour' expended in making an actually existing length of linen, but we know this cannot be the case (or else the existing length of linen's value would automatically be greater the longer it had taken to produce it), and that instead Marx must be speaking of an abstraction, abstract human labour. His language nonetheless clearly reveals the theoretical result of this muddle: a mystical logic of *revelation*, in which the unseen but 'existing' spirit (phantom,

---

233 Marx 1976, p. 140.
234 'Even though Marx did not follow Hegel's idealist conceptual speculation, Marx's theory of the value-form is a materialist version of Hegel's logic of essence and appearance' (Moseley 2023, p. 31).
235 Hegel's famous assertion appears as the subheading that begins 'Section II: Appearance' of Book II of the Greater Logic. Hegel 2010b, p. 418.
236 Marx 1976, p. 20, emphasis added.

spectre) becomes incarnate, sublated in a material object (not bread or wine, in this case, but *coat*).

It is precisely the accomplishment of Marx's exercise in self-clarification in the *Ergänzungen* notebook to have worked through this point of mystified theoretical confusion, to have abandoned his previous Hegelian hermeneutic of revelation and incarnation, but without, unfortunately, having sufficiently rewritten his manuscript to reflect this theoretical development:

> The coat and the linen as values, each for itself, were reduced [in the first section of chapter 1] to objectifications of human labour as such. *But this reduction forgot that neither is in and of itself value-objectivity [Werthgegenständlichkeit]*; they are this only in so far as this objectivity is held in common [*gemeinsam*] by them. Outside of their relationship with each other – the relationship in which they count as equal – neither coat nor linen possess value-objectivity or objectivity as congelations of human labour per se. *They only possess this social objectivity as a social relationship* (in a social relationship).[237]

Marx only managed to insert a single but crucial sentence into the 1875 French edition that reflects this auto-critique, while letting stand without clarification sentences such as that cited above ('In the production of linen, a particular quantum of human labour *exists* in having been expended'), sentences that continue to confuse astute readers such as Moseley into the present.

That new sentence – the meaning of which in the *Ergänzungen* Heinrich and Moseley disagree on (neither Moseley nor Heinrich discuss the actual published French rendition) – marks a crucial amendment to Marx's argument, but one that Marx fails explicitly to flag as a general position in his text, even in its more expansive French articulation:

> L'égalité de travaux qui diffèrent *toto cœlo* les uns des autres ne peut consister que dans une abstraction de leur inégalité réelle, que dans la réduction à leur caractère commun de dépense de force humaine, de travail humain en général, et c'est l'échange seul qui opère cette réduction en

---

237 Cited in Moseley 2023, p. 212, emphasis added. Moseley interprets Marx's 'as congelations of human labour' to imply that this congelation actually exists already in the individual commodity, when the sentence says just the opposite: that they only 'possess' this in social relationship with other commodities, not individually in isolation from the social network of exchange.

mettant en présence les uns des autres sur un pied d'égalité les produits des travaux les plus divers.

The equality of labours that differ entirely one from another can only consist in *an abstraction* from their real inequality, only in the reduction of their common character as an expenditure of human force, of human labour in general, and it is exchange alone that operates this reduction, by placing the most diverse products of labour in the presence of one another as equals [in value].[238]

While Heinrich correctly reads Marx's 'opère' [*vollzieht sich*, 'carried out' in the German *Ergänzungen*] to mean that 'the abstraction of equal human labour only *exists* in exchange', Moseley instead perversely seeks to force the phrase 'to be consistent with [Marx's] earlier paragraphs' (i.e., precisely the text Marx seeks to correct here) paragraphs that putatively state that, in Moseley's words, 'equal human labour exists in production'.[239]

In fact, however, Marx's clarification is not yet clear enough: when Marx writes in the French edition that 'The equality of labours that differ entirely one from another can only consist in *an abstraction* from their real inequality', he should have added the obvious implication of this, i.e., that this 'abstraction from their real inequality' results in, precisely and self-evidently, *an abstraction*, the nonexistent concept of abstract human labour. To clarify the theoretical obscurity that confounds Moseley, and given that his difficult, highly abstract presentation in Chapter 1 relies upon singular examples (coats, linen) to help the reader grasp his argument, Marx should have inserted in his text an analogous clarification to his extremely important note on the difference between value and exchange-value, which he only came to present clearly in the 1872 edition: 'Once we know this, our manner of speaking does no harm; it serves, rather, as an abbreviation'.[240] Once we know that the abstraction of

---

238   MEGA II/7: 55 (my translation). In the original German in the *Ergänzungen*, Marx writes more briefly that 'The reduction of various concrete private acts of labour to this abstraction of equal human labour is only carried out [or accomplished, *vollzieht sich*] through exchange, which actually equates products of different acts of labour with each other' ('Die Reduction der verschiednen konkreten Privatarbeiten auf dieses Abstractum gleicher menschlicher Arbeit vollzieht sich nur durch den Austausch, welcher Producte verschiedner Arbeiten thatsächlich einander gleichsetzt'). MEGA II/6: 41.

239   Moseley 2023, p. 185, emphasis added.

240   Having been inserted already in the 1872 German edition, this crucial moment of self-clarification therefore found its way into all subsequent editions and translations, and is thus common knowledge to any attentive reader of *Capital* the world over: 'When, at the

equal human labour only *exists* as a real abstraction in the exchange relation via its value-form, and is until then a nonexistent concept, our manner of speaking – for example that 'In the production of linen, a particular quantum of human labour *exists* in having been expended' – does no harm.

12 The Raw Materials of Marx's Additive Synthetic Method

As he repeatedly rewrote the first chapters of *Capital* – from the simplified Appendix of the 1867 edition, to the second, 1872 edition and its accompanying preparatory notebooks, to his corrections of Roy's 1875 French translation – in the explicit intention to clarify and improve the process of exposition in those initial chapters, Marx in fact gradually abandoned the negative dialectic of totality that predominates in his initial scientific works. While from the 1841 dissertation through the *Grundrisse*, and as late as the 1867 edition of *Capital*, this negative dialectical mode of exposition still plays an important role, I have argued that in the process of rewriting, Marx developed an additive synthetic process of exposition, in which the Hegelian logic of totality, contradiction and determinations of reflection [*Reflexionsbestimmung*] play no further role.

There is no evidence that Marx consciously undertook this process as the invention of a novel materialist dialectical *method*; instead, he continued to pay homage to the centrality of Hegel's logic in his own formation, most famously in the Postface to the 1872 edition where he celebrates 'that mighty thinker' in the face of the 'ill-humoured, arrogant and mediocre epigones who ... take pleasure in treating Hegel in the same way as the good Moses Mendelssohn treated Spinoza ..., namely, as a "dead dog"'.[241] This transformation in Marx's process of exposition instead involved a practical development, in the form of the reconceptualisation, clarification, and rewriting of these crucial initial chapters, most visibly for example in Marx's preparatory notebook for the 1872 edition entitled *Ergänzungen und Veränderungen zum ersten Band des Kapitals*

---

beginning of this chapter, we said in the customary manner that a commodity is both a use-value and an exchange-value, this was, strictly speaking, wrong. A commodity is a use-value or object of utility, and a "value". [... Its] form of manifestation is exchange-value, and the commodity never has this form when looked at in isolation, but only when it is in a value-relation or an exchange relation with a second commodity of a different kind. Once we know this, our manner of speaking does no harm; it serves, rather, as an abbreviation' (Marx 1976, p. 152).

241   Marx 1976, p. 103. Michael Heinrich points out that Marx's parallel explicitly and admiringly posits Spinoza on equal terms with Hegel in Marx's judgement, a point to which I will return below. Heinrich 2019, p. 331.

(Additions and Changes to the First Volume of Capital).[242] Since Marx made no systematic statement or reflection on this process, it must be reconstructed immanently from Marx's text, as I have tried to do here.

What's more, for all his customary polemical conviction, Marx's two well-known statements on his relation to Hegelian dialectic in the 1872 Postface are quite ambiguous. On the one hand, he famously asserts that due to 'the mystification [*Mystifikation*] which the dialectic suffers in Hegel's hands ... it must be inverted [*umstülpen*], in order to discover the rational kernel within the mystical shell', a process of mere inversion that, Althusser famously argued, were it true, would have left intact the principal Hegelian logical categories (negation, contradiction, *Aufhebung*, etc.).[243]

Instead, in *Reading Capital*, Althusser merely asserts what I have here tried to demonstrate: that Marx's claim fails to do justice to the real transformations manifest in the process of exposition concretely deployed in the second and all subsequent editions of *Capital*, as what Althusser rightly calls 'the apodictic character of the order of [Marx's] theoretical discourse'.[244] At the same time, a few lines before that famous statement, Marx does in fact seem to go much further in that very direction, asserting unequivocally (though without presenting any evidence that would indicate more precisely his meaning) that 'My dialectical method is, in its foundations [*Grundlage*], not only different from the Hegelian, but exactly opposite [*direktes Gegenteil*] to it'.[245]

If by 1872, in the practical process of revision, Marx had transformed his mode of exposition in the opening chapters of *Capital* into what I have termed a method of additive synthesis,[246] without ever committing to paper the systematic analysis of his understanding of method that he never found time to write, he seems to have done so spontaneously, amply drawing on the resources of his own genius to construct an original process of materialist critique. That

---

242 *Ergänzungen und Veränderungen zum ersten Band des Kapitals* [1871–72], in MEGA 11/6, *Karl Marx, Das Kapital: Kritik Der Politischen Ökonomie. Erster Band, Hamburg 1872*. Berlin: Dietz Verlag, 1987, pp. 29–32. See Heinrich's commentary on this text (2021, pp. 375–6).
243 See Althusser 2005, 'On the Young Marx'.
244 RC, p. 50.
245 Marx 1976, p. 102.
246 The analogy with musical sound synthesis is no mere homonymic: the temporal articulation of timbral singularity through the *additive* composition of sine waves to construct complex harmonic overtone sequences might be said to adhere to Marx's fundamental (logical) imperative: always to proceed from the most abstract (whether a minimal definition of the capitalist social form or a single pure sine wave) to encompass the fullest degree of concretion, whether that is the composite body of *Capital* or the most complex timbre frames of an NED Synclavier's synthesis engine.

said, here I wish to indicate a number of theoretical resources in Marx's theoretical toolkit that necessarily played decisive roles in this process.

The first of these has long been overlooked in Marx studies. In Heinrich's judgement, however, Marx's thorough training in law and legal argumentation was decisive for his intellectual formation:

> Marx's knowledge of law left behind clear traces in his work. Directly legal arguments are found in a few of his articles for the *Rheinische Zeitung*, [and] his *Critique of Hegel's Philosophy of Right* from 1843 and some passages in *Capital* also demonstrate Marx's legal knowledge. And last but not least, in February of 1849 in Cologne, Marx successfully pleaded before the court twice when the *Neue Rheinische Zeitung* was charged with insulting a magistrate and in a further trial for inciting rebellion.[247]

This is relevant in the present context because this training gave Marx what Heinrich describes as 'a reasonably solid (theoretical) training in law', one that in addition to his study of logic with Georg Andreas Gabler, for which he unsurprisingly received a mark of 'extremely diligent', would necessarily have grounded him in the subcategory of positive logic that is legal argumentation.[248]

Etienne Balibar argues even more strongly that though 'there remains a remarkable blindness in the detailed commentaries on Marx's *Capital* to the issue of juridical forms and the function of law in Marx's analysis', in fact, 'juridical form is key to the understanding of Marx's reasoning'.[249] Balibar shows that the category of legal subject as property owner is crucial to the entire demonstrative arc of *Capital*, from the initial analysis of exchange in chapter Two, to that of the wage form, and finally that of the accumulation of capital in chapter 24, such that there exists 'a homology of the juridical form with the value form', in the sense that without the category of legal person the process of valorisation cannot proceed.[250]

---

247   Heinrich 2019, p. 310.
248   Heinrich 2019, p. 299. Marx also took a course on Hegel's *Logic* with Gabler in the summer semester of 1838 (Heinrich 2019, p. 300). While the exact content of Marx's studies in legal argumentation is unknown, legal reasoning at its most abstract follows a syllogistic form, in the sense that a general legal rule or law (major premise) is argued, in relation to a specific claim or case (minor premise), to apply conclusively (conclusion). See Huhn 2022.
249   Balibar 2023, pp. 75–6.
250   Balibar 2023, p. 88.

Second, Günther Schmidt has argued that given Marx's extensive knowledge of the works of Aristotle – including the *Physics, Metaphysics*, and *On Generation and Corruption*, to the point of having translated in 1841 sections of *On the Soul* – he in fact originally intended to write his doctoral dissertation as a comparison of Epicurus not with Democritus, but with Aristotle himself.[251] While there is no direct evidence that Marx studied Aristotle's *Prior* and *Posterior Analytics*, the works in which Aristotle literally invented logic as a domain of scientific, philosophical reflection, there is every reason to suppose that given his training in logic, Marx was familiar with these canonical works as well. In any case, Aristotle's positive logic pervades at every moment the philosophical works that Marx knew intimately, such as the *Physics* and *Metaphysics*. Marx's respect for Aristotle is, moreover, a constant of his intellectual universe, to the point that in *Capital* he will unequivocally name the inventor of the Peripatetic School, 'the great investigator who was the first to analyse the value-form, like so many other forms of thought, society and nature, ... the greatest thinker of Antiquity'.[252]

Finally – and here the question of influence is both significantly more obscure but equally crucial to the argument of this book as a whole – there is the problem of Spinoza and Marx.[253] Compared to his extensive engagement with thinkers such as Epicurus, Aristotle, Feuerbach, or Hegel, Marx has little to say about Spinoza, all of it rather superficial and in passing (though always positive and admirative). In its generality, Marx's one theoretically substantive citation of the author of the *Ethics*, in a footnote to *Capital*, ('These gentlemen [the vulgar economists] would do well to ponder occasionally over Spinoza's *"Determinatio est nagatio"* ') most likely relays Hegel's misrepresentation of Spinoza rather than a substantive engagement with Spinoza himself, repeating Hegel's erroneous word order rather than the original ('*determina-*

---

251   Heinrich 2019, pp. 412–15. Charles Barbour has shown that this extensive familiarity with Aristotle arose in part from Marx's intensive engagement with post-Aristotelean logic more generally in the period 1839–1842. Marx did so, Barbour shows, not just in preparation for writing his dissertation, but with the intention of writing a never-completed response to the foremost scholar of Aristotelean logic of the time, Adolf Trendelenburg, and his highly influential 1840 critique of Hegelian logic, *Logische Untersuchungen* (Barbour, "The Logic Question"). See above, pp. 158–60.
252   Marx 1976, pp. 151, 532.
253   For systematic enquiries into Marx's relation to Spinoza, none of which, however, even raises the possibility that Marx's familiarity with Spinoza may have impacted the epistemology and method of exposition of his critique of political economy, see Maximilien Rubel's classic article 'Marx à la rencontre de Spinoza' (1977); Matheron 1977; and more recently, Matysik 2023, Chapter 3, 'When Marx Met Spinoza', pp. 97–134; Bianchi 2018; Tosel 2008; Fischbach 2005; Lordon 2010.

tio est negatio' rather than Spinoza's '*determinatio negatio est*').[254] For Marx in this footnote, the phrase '*Determinatio est negatio*' is taken to refer in general to 'Hegelian "contradiction", which [Marx continues] is the source of all dialectics', something quite different than its limited application in Spinoza's letter to Jelles.[255]

It would seem that Marx's other principal reference to Spinoza ('In opposition [*Gegensatz*] to Spinoza, [vulgar economics] believes that "ignorance is a sufficient reason" [*die Unwissenheit ein hinreichender Grund ist*]') is, if anything, even less promising in its vagueness.[256] I wish in conclusion, however, to pause to consider this phrase that does not seem to have merited the attention of previous commentators on Marx's relation to Spinoza. It is my conviction that taken in context, and given the importance Marx seems to attribute to it judging from the phrase's repetition from his 1841 dissertation through the 1872 edition of *Capital*, this seemingly cliched, even throwaway catchphrase in fact indicates, as a sort of signpost or marker, precisely the additive synthetic epistemological process that brings Marx's revisions to *Capital* in proximity to Spinoza's apodictic, positive logic.

13   On Ignorance and Common Notions

In the existing literature on Spinoza's possible influence on Marx, the focus has remained unrelentingly limited to questions of the critique of religion and mir-

---

254 Marx 1976, p. 744. Spinoza's letter of 2 June 1674 to Jelles, in which the phrase appears, is not among those transcribed in Marx's 1841 notebook on Spinoza, similarly indicating that Marx based his knowledge of the proposition on Hegel's misreading of Spinoza (MEGA² VI.1, Berlin, 1977). In contrast, Marx, unlike Hegel, actually cites Spinoza correctly in the identical citation in *Grundrisse* (1973, p. 90). Macherey argues that Hegel's addition of the single word '*omnis*' in his analyses of Spinoza symptomatically transforms a specific, situated comment on Spinoza's part into a general proposition on Being as such. See Macherey 2011, Chapter 4, '*Omnis determinatio est negatio*'. Marx also substantively engages with Spinoza in *The Holy Family* (1844), but merely to indicate him as a thinker 'representative of a rationalist and abstract metaphysical system' (Bianchi 2018, p. 49; see also Tosel 2008, p. 141). Marx's characterisation of Spinozist thought in his pre-1845 texts repeats aspects of the Hegelian misreading that Macherey has critiqued, for example in the claim that 'Spinoza's substance ... is metaphysically disguised *nature separated* from man' (cited in Bianchi 2018, p. 50). Bianchi, however, proposes that in arguing against Hegel's Spinoza, Marx was in fact targeting Hegelian idealism itself (2018, p. 51).

255 Macherey 2011, p. 162. For Spinoza the determinate figure, the topic of this interjection, serves to constitute any totality as limited to a subjective point of view, as an actually existing singularity rather than a nonexistent thing or even substance itself.

256 Marx 1976, p. 422.

acles, freedom of speech, and the autonomy of the political. Bernardo Bianchi remains squarely within this field of interpretation, noting only that 'After 1844, Marx drifts away from Spinoza as well as ... the problems relating to the autonomy of the political'.[257] No commentator to my knowledge has reflected on the epistemological implications of the statement that 'ignorance is no argument', though there is unanimous consensus that the source of this phrase in the first volume of *Capital* is the Appendix to *Ethics* 1P36.[258]

On at least three occasions spanning his intellectual production, from the 1841 dissertation to the final revisions of *Capital*, Marx cites Spinoza's phrase that 'ignorance is no argument'.[259] In *The German Ideology*, Marx briefly cites the phrase to indicate Max Stirner's ignorance of real human suffering, but in the case of Marx's 1841 dissertation, *On the Difference between Democritean and Epicurean Physics*, Rubel suggests a far more consequential, epistemological dimension, one that I will argue is carried over, amplified, and clarified when Marx repeats it in *Capital*. While Marx's lost Appendix to the Dissertation, judging by the Notes that have survived, addressed potentially Spinozist themes related to the TTP such as 'On Individual Immortality', 'The Theology of Epicurus' and 'The Relationship of Man to God', in the second chapter, Marx writes that 'Spinoza says that ignorance is no argument' in order

---

257   Bianchi 2018, p. 54.
258   As for example Fowkes, who adds a translator's note at this point to the Penguin edition, that states: 'Spinoza, in the Appendix to Part I of his *Ethics*, rejects the teleological argument for the existence of God, stating that ignorance of other causes is not a sufficient reason for the view that God created Nature with some particular end in view' (Marx 1976, p. 1121). Bianchi points out, however, that 'the same argument may also be based on Chapter VI from the *Theological-Political Treatise*' in which Spinoza analyses miracles (2018, p. 39). The latter, moreover, is the chapter from TTP that Marx placed at the head of his selection of excerpts and personally copied in his own hand, as opposed to later sections of these notebooks that were the work of a copyist (Rubel 1977, p. 15). Furthermore, while there is a similar consensus that Marx was familiar with Spinoza's *Ethics*, little attention has been paid to Marx's citation of one of Spinoza's most original epistemological positions: in his article "Comments on the Latest Prussian Censorship" from January 1842, Marx notes that "Truth is as little modest as light .... *Verum index sui et falsi*." Cited at Bianchi 2018, 44. Bianchi comments, "Both the light metaphor and Spinoza's sentence expressed as an aphorism – *verum index sui et falsi* – refer to E11P43: 'Indeed, just as light defines itself and darkness, so truth sets the standard for itself and falsehood'" (44).
259   There is no literal equivalent to this phrase in Spinoza's writings; perhaps the closest is to be found in E1VP17S: 'My purpose ... is not to conclude that ignorance is preferable to knowledge, or that there is no difference between a fool and a wise man in the matter of controlling the emotions. I say this because it is necessary to know both the power of our nature and its lack of power, so that we can determine what reason can and cannot do in controlling the emotions'.

to reject the platitudes of commentators who 'attributed no qualities to the atoms' based merely on their inability to 'reconcile the qualities of the atom with its concept', in other words, based merely on the inadequacy of their own thought.[260]

Rubel's commentary on this reference to Spinoza is suggestive, if hesitant. He argues that this seemingly offhand reference to Spinoza in fact indexifies the dissertation's fundamentally Spinozist epistemology:

> One is tempted to speak of a Spinozist reading of Epicurus on Marx's part; at both the level of atomist physics as well as its ethics, the [dissertation's] concepts of reason, the sensible [*sensibilité*], consciousness and superstition all contribute to the conception of a 'materialism' that is not without connection to the rationalism defined by Spinoza in relation to the 'second genre of knowledge'.[261]

Marx's dissertation in its surviving form is divided between the theoretical anti-empiricism of its first part, a position coherent with both Spinoza and Hegel,[262] and the purely Hegelian negative dialectic of its second section.[263] In the former, Marx articulates the fundamental distinction between Democritus' empiricism and the purely conceptual orientation of Epicurus. Setting off across the Mediterranean world in an endless search for knowledge, Democritus, Marx observes, 'is driven into *empirical* observation [*empirische Beobachtung*]. Dissatisfied with philosophy, he throws himself into the arms of empirical knowledge [*empirischen Wissen*]'. Democritus 'applies himself to empirical natural science [*empirische Naturwissenschaft*] and to positive knowledge, and represents the unrest of observation, experimenting, ubiquitous learning [*überall lernenden*], ranging over the wide, wide world'. Marx's Epicurus, in contrast, 'scorns the empirical [*verachtet die Empirie*]; embodied in him are the

---

260 Marx 1975a, p. 119.
261 Rubel 1977, p. 11.
262 In the *Encyclopedia*, Hegel writes for example that 'perception is the form in which matters are supposed to be comprehended [*begriffen*], and this is the deficiency of empiricism …. In perception, one possesses something concrete in multiple ways whose determinations one is supposed to take apart like peeling away the layers of an onion. This process of splitting them up [*Zergliederung*] is therefore intended to dissolve the determinations that have grown together, breaking them up [*zerlegen*] without adding anything but the subjective activity of breaking them up. Analysis is, however, the progression from the immediacy of perception to thought' (Hegel 2010a, p. 80).
263 See Levine 2009; McIvor 2008; Labelle 2020.

serenity of thought satisfied in itself, the self-sufficiency that draws its knowledge *ex principio interno*'.[264]

Epicurus' position amounts to the refusal of all supernatural or miraculous explanations of causality, all teleologies of divine intent, and asserts instead the adequacy of a physics-based, 'atomistic' account of nature. 'The atom is perceived only through reason', Marx flatly observes.[265] There are no sensations of atoms from which to construct their concept; instead, Epicurus' philosophical project seeks to articulate the rational order of nature, beginning from the purely theoretical, anti-empiricist concept of the atom and the void, to culminate in a materialist cosmology. Marx's Epicurus squarely locates the production of knowledge within scientific reflection – as opposed to the extraction of truth from empirical observation so characteristic of Democritus – as the positive construction of an adequate intellection of the real. This position, despite its rudimentary development in the dissertation, nonetheless indicates a purely Spinozist materialist position, in which the real order of nature finds conceptual articulation in the attribute of thought; Marx's reading of the *TTP* and *Ethics* in preparation for the dissertation in all certainty contributed to the articulation of this epistemological position.

The Spinozist theoretical anti-empiricism of Marx's first chapter stands in marked contrast, however, to the negative dialectical logic of its succeeding sections, the latter deploying a none-too-subtle application of Hegel's logic of *Reflexionsbestimmung* to the Epicurean theory of the atom. If Democritus' assertion of the necessarily, eternally linear fall of atoms through the void describes for Marx a realm of pure necessity, Epicurus' introduction of the concept of their *clinamen* or swerve, in Marx's reading, introduces negation not as the mere external definition of the atom as not-void, but internally, as the negative unity of its becoming-other, its swerve the theoretical basis of self-consciousness and the freedom of human action:

---

264 Marx 1975a, pp. 99, 107, translation modified. The original German can be found in MEGA II, *Karl Marx Werke, Artikel Literarische Versuche bis März 1843*. Berlin: Dietz Verlag, 1975, pp. 27, 30.

265 Marx 1975a, p. 134. '*Das Atom, ihr Fundament, nur durch die Vernunft geschaut wird*' (MEGA II, p. 49). In the First Notebook on Epicurean Philosophy, Marx observes in more Hegelian terms that 'the motion of the atoms is in principle absolute, that is, all empirical conditions in it are sublated [*alle empirischen Bedingungen sind in ihr aufgehoben*] .... What is lasting and great in Epicurus is that he gives no preference to conditions over notions, and tries just as little to save them. For Epicurus the task of philosophy is to prove that the world and thought are thinkable and possible' (Marx 1975a, pp. 186, 189, translation modified). For the German original, see MEGA IV1, *Karl Marx Friedrich Engels Exzerpte und Notizen bis 1824*. Berlin: Dietz Verlag, 1976, p. 19.

The mode of being which [the atom] has to negate [*negiren*] is the straight line. The immediate negation [*unmittelbare Negation*] of this motion is another motion, which ... is the declination from the straight line .... Epicurus objectifies the contradiction [*Widerspruch*] in the concept of the atom between essence and existence .... In Epicurus *atomistics* with all its contradictions [*Widersprüchen*] has been carried through and completed as the natural science of self-consciousness [*Selbstbewusstseins*].[266]

Here, the Hegelian logic of the determinations of reflection that would remain a constant in Marx's thought through the first edition of *Capital* already offers the young Marx the theoretical means to develop an original reinterpretation of Epicurus' materialism. The contrast with Marx's return to Spinoza in chapter 11 of *Capital*, as we shall see in a moment, could not be greater.

That said, Rubel's hesitant, passing mention of the importance for the young Marx of Spinoza's 'second genre of knowledge', that of common notions [*notiones communes*], puts us on the trail of the true and penetrating significance of Spinoza for Marx's process of exposition, the final piece in the puzzle of what I am calling in this book *Capital*'s Spinozist epistemology. For while in the dissertation this Spinozism remains superficial, if determinant in Marx's argument, by the time of its reappearance in *Capital*, the reference to Spinoza, in the context of Marx's argument in chapter 11, precisely and exactingly indicates what Rubel could only vaguely infer from the 1841 dissertation and its accompanying notebooks: a full-fledged theoretical reconstruction and deployment on Marx's part of what Spinoza called general or common notions, notions that Marx names the 'law of motion' of the capitalist social form. In other words, taken in the context in which it appears in the eleventh chapter of *Capital* ('The Rate and Mass of Surplus-Value'), in saying that 'ignorance is not a sufficient reason' Marx is not merely pointing to the 'ignorance' of the classical political economists he criticises, but does so in the context of his contrasting *positive* elaboration of an adequate mode of knowledge: specifically, the concept of the 'law' of the rate and mass of surplus value that it is the remit of chapter 11 to formulate.

---

266   Marx 1975a, pp. 112, 125, 146. MEGA I/1, pp. 36, 44, 58.

14 Marx's Spinozist Theory of Knowledge

'Ignorance is not a sufficient reason'. For reasons he never explains, it is this unassuming insight of Spinoza's, gleaned from his readings and notes in 1841, that permanently stuck in Marx's mind. When Marx repeats this reference to Spinoza three decades later, in chapter 11 of *Capital* Volume I, he tellingly does so in the immediate context of a critique of the illusions and misapprehensions of the classical economists regarding the nature of surplus value.[267] Immediately following his eminently clear and concise statement of the general 'law' (*Gesetz*) governing the 'Rate and Mass of Surplus-Value' (henceforth 'LRMSV') in the first three pages of the chapter, Marx notes that 'This law clearly contradicts all experience based on immediate appearances'.[268] This is necessarily the case, he argues, because, as 'everyone knows', the amount of profit made from a commodity by 'a cotton spinner' or 'a baker' does not vary according to the relative amounts of variable and constant capital either has invested to produce their cotton or bread, but only according to the general cost of 'inputs' (in mainstream economic jargon) relative to their market price.[269]

While Marx can assume that 'everyone knows' this is the case from their lived experience of commodity production and exchange, this ready familiarity nonetheless directly contradicts the law Marx has just before stated; at this point in his exposition, however, he has not yet explained the real and necessary distinction between surplus value and profit, and Marx will continue to hold their difference in abstraction and to assume instead that the two coincide until many hundreds of pages later, when he will explicate the dynamics and laws governing competition in Volume III via concepts such as cost price and average rate of profit.[270]

Here, Marx simply indicates that the authors of 'classical economics' are just as subject to this empiricist illusion as 'everyone', and necessarily so: in the absence of an adequate theory of value and its necessary concepts such as Marx has developed to this point in his exposition in chapter 11, classical economics can only 'hold instinctively to this law, although it has never for-

---

[267] To my knowledge, while many have repeated the assumption that Marx's citation refers to the Appendix of Spinoza's *Ethics* Book I, no one, surprisingly, seems to have reflected on the context in which he inserts this reference in *Capital*.

[268] Marx 1976, p. 421.

[269] As the US Bureau of Labor Statistics puts the matter with naïve simplicity, 'Inputs are any resources used to create goods and services. Examples of inputs include labour (workers' time), fuel, materials, buildings, and equipment' ('What Are Inputs?', at https://www.bls.gov/k12/productivity-101/content/what-is-productivity/what-are-inputs.htm).

[270] See Nesbitt 2022, pp. 138–52.

mulated it, because it is a necessary consequence of the law of value'.[271] In other words, the only difference between 'everyone' and classical economics is that while the former simply observes and follows what is empirically the case, the latter experiences this same fact as a theoretical contradiction that it cannot solve: having posited labour as the source of value, but lacking concepts such as labour power and socially necessary labour time, classical economics embroiled itself in insoluble contradictions trying to explain, for example, how it can then be the case that a commodity is not 'more valuable the more unskilful and lazy the worker who produced it, because he would need more time to complete the article'.[272]

Lacking adequate theoretical concepts, 'vulgar economics' can only make 'violent [as opposed to scientifically adequate] abstractions'; condemned to its empiricist illusions, it 'must rely ... on mere semblance as opposed to the law which regulates and determines the phenomena'.[273] One could hardly imagine a more perfectly Spinozist critique of the necessarily illusory and inadequate nature of empirical, sensuous experience, and it is indeed precisely at this point that Marx then inserts his reference to Spinoza.

The obvious conclusion is not merely that chapter 11 of *Capital* is explicitly constructed as a perfectly Spinozist critique of the *necessity* governing the illusions of empiricist, ideological forms of knowledge such as those of 'vulgar economics', but furthermore, that Marx offers in contrast an equally perfect demonstration in the immediately preceding paragraphs of what should necessarily take its place to constitute a properly scientific, adequate analysis of a concept such as the rate and mass of surplus value: 'the law that regulates and determines the phenomena', or, in Spinozist terms, its *common notion*.

Marx thus begins his analysis of this law, in the first paragraph of chapter 11, by reminding his reader that 'In this chapter, as hitherto, the value of labour-power ... is assumed to be a given, constant magnitude'.[274] Superficially, this reminder simply prompts the reader to recall the abstract concept (the value of labour power) that allowed Marx, in chapter 7, to distinguish between necessary and surplus labour, and thus to indicate the source of surplus value in the production process. More importantly, however, this proviso also squarely replaces Marx's forthcoming analysis of the LRMSV in the purely theoretical domain of thought; the law of the rate and mass of

---

271   Marx 1976, p. 421.
272   Marx 1976, p. 129.
273   Marx 1976, p. 421.
274   Marx 1976, p. 417.

surplus value is, in other words, not an empirical, sensuous thing, but unambiguously a *Gedankenkonkretum*.

I say *replaces* because Marx must here forcibly return his reader to the high level of abstraction of the first nine chapters of *Capital* following the extensive empirical *illustration* of these concepts in chapter 10 ('The Working Day'); equally, however, this initial prompt must be kept in mind in what follows, because it clearly indicates that the initial presentation of this law stands in utter distinction from the empiricism of both 'everyone' and the classical economists he will then excoriate midway through the chapter in the passage discussed above.

This point should not be forgotten when Marx immediately, in the second paragraph, launches into a discussion of 'the worker' and 'the capitalist', offering as well specific numerical quantities of work time ('6 hours a day') and its monetary expression as a specific value ('3 shillings') to calculate a 'specific mass of surplus-value'.[275] How are 'the worker' and 'the capitalist' different, a casual reader might ask, from the 'baker' or 'cotton spinner' whose empiricist point of view he will condemn just after presenting this law? In fact, it will shortly become clear – when Marx directly scales his analysis from a single labour process to the 'total capital of a society' ('for example ... the social working day of ten million hours') – that they inhabit utterly distinct theoretical realms: the baker and spinner actually existing, singular examples of productive labourers with their distinct points of view and lived experiences of the production and exchange processes, the 'worker' and 'capitalist' mere theoretical, abstract markers or stand-ins, imagistic ciphers of an abstract thought construct that Marx will call 'aliquot parts' of a whole that can be directly scaled up or down at will.[276] Marx thus proceeds, in his third paragraph, to scale his

---

275 Ibid.
276 Marx 1976, p. 422. Patrick Murray writes that 'Marx replaces the failed classical theory of value, which explains individual prices in terms of individual values and individual profits in terms of individual surplus values, with a labour theory of value that holds at the aggregate level (the level of total capital) and explains subordinate phenomena on that basis .... Marx revolutionises the classical labour theory of value by making the aliquot or representative commodity the object of inquiry' (Murray 2017, pp. 22, 23). This fractional orientation can easily confuse the reader of *Capital*, however, since Marx repeatedly frames the rhetoric of his argument in terms of individual examples (of coats, linen, tailoring and weaving, or here in chapter 11, bakers and cotton spinners). As discussed above, Fred Moseley observes in this sense that 'It is not always clear that Marx's theory in Volume I is about the total capital and the total surplus value produced in the economy as a whole, because the theory is usually illustrated in terms of an individual capital and even a single, solitary worker .... However, the individual capitals in Marx's examples represent the total social capital of the capitalist class as a whole. Individual capitals are not

analysis from aliquot, representative figures of the individual worker and capitalist, to address 'the total value of all the labour-powers the capitalist employs simultaneously'.[277]

Marx next examines factors governing the variation on this simple formula for the production of surplus value: when variable capital invested diminishes or increases, and when the corresponding rate of surplus value increases or diminishes, the total mass of surplus value produced will directly vary according to these given proportions.[278] These variations, Marx insists, nonetheless remain governed by absolute 'limits, which cannot be overcome', in the form of both limits to the working day (24 hours) and to reductions in the number of workers employed (to the theoretical and potentially real limit of zero).[279]

All of this combines, in Marx's various simple, algebraic examples, to indicate the 'self-evident' nature of the LRMSV: 'With a given rate of surplus-value, and a given value of labour-power, therefore, the masses of surplus-value produced vary directly as the amounts of the variable capitals advanced'.[280] Though Marx's exposition in volume I to this point has focused on the relative division of capital into its constant and variable forms, 'the law just laid down is not affected by this'. This is the case since it is only the element of variable capital, by definition and whatever its relative quantity to constant capital employed in production, that effects 'the valorisation process performed by the labour-powers which set the means of production in motion'.[281]

This final observation thus allows Marx to summarise in natural language the LRMSV in its simplest form: 'The masses of value and of surplus-value produced by different capitals – the value of labour-power being given and its degree of exploitation being equal – vary directly as the amounts of the variable components of these capitals, i.e. the parts which have been turned into

---

analysed as separate and distinct real [empirical] capitals, but rather as representatives and "aliquot parts" of the total social capital' (Moseley 2017, pp. 45–46). In contrast to the examples of chapter one, here in chapter 11 Marx will make explicit this fractional scope of his analysis through the explicit distinction between bakers and cotton spinners on the one hand, and what he calls 'the social working day' as a whole, the overarching frame of reference for the LRMSV.

277   Marx 1976, p. 417.
278   Marx 1976, p. 419.
279   On the latter point in relation to capitalist slavery, see Nesbitt 2022, pp. 145–50.
280   Marx 1976, p. 420.
281   Marx 1976, p. 421.

living labour-power'.[282] Having done so, Marx turns to his critique of both the common sense of 'everyone' as well as the necessary contradictions governing the 'vulgar economists' discussed above.

Now, the epistemological point I wish to make about Marx's algebraically simple LRMSV is that on at least eight counts, Marx's law constitutes a perfect example of what Spinoza called a common notion, i.e., general concepts or formulae that are, in contrast to imaginary ideas, Spinoza insists, always and in all cases *necessarily adequate*. It is quite extraordinary, I think, that both Spinoza, in propositions 37, 38, and 39 of *Ethics* II, and Marx in *Capital* chapter 11:

1. Reject empirical knowledge as radically and necessarily inadequate;
2. Propose in its place an abstract science of nonexistent things (*res singulares non existentes*) without sensuous determination;[283]
3. Emphasise the absolute scalability of this knowledge between aliquot part and whole;
4. Understand this form of knowledge as relational and proportional as opposed to the observation-based study of actually existing singular things;
5. Articulate this form of knowledge as a process of *formalisation* that models reality through the power of abstraction ...
6. To produce a necessarily and universally adequate mode of knowledge ...
7. The nature of which follows a necessary genesis that gradually transitions from the inadequacy of imaginary, empirical knowledge to the adequacy of the general, in order to ...
8. Constitute the paradigm of a political epistemology as *epistemological commons*

In his analysis of Spinoza's exposition of the concept of 'notions common to all humans' [*notiones omnibus hominibus communes*], Macherey initially emphasises the same distinction Marx makes, described above, between the inadequacy of empirical observations and a general notion: while the former are produced 'by the chance encounters of bodies, [common notions] differ fundamentally from those produced by the mechanisms of perception and imagination, under conditions subject to infinite variations, which prevents their meaning, always elaborated in a determinate context, in the here and now, to be extended beyond the moment of their appearance'.[284] In contrast, Macherey

---

282   Ibid.
283   On Macherey's explication of Spinoza's crucial and difficult distinction between nonexistent things (idealities) and actually existing singular things (*res singulares actu existentes*) in EIIP8,9, see above, pp. 53–4
284   Macherey 1997, p. 274.

argues that such notions common to all humans by their very nature escape from 'the instability inherent in opinions' insofar as they possess a fixed and determinant form that allows for their deployment 'by all in common'.[285]

What then is the nature of such common notions? For Spinoza, the crucial distinction between the inadequate, imaginary ideas we necessarily form from sense impressions, and common notions, is that the latter are ideas not about any given, actually existing singular thing (such as coats and linen or bakers and cotton spinners, among Marx's examples), but about certain qualities common to all things in general. In the wake of Galileo, who died in 1642, Spinoza's privileged example in these propositions is that of physical bodies as such, universally existing in space and following the general laws that govern their relations. If it is the case that 'all bodies agree in certain things'[286] – i.e., that aside from their particular existences, they possess common characteristics, which is to say their extension – then they therefore have in common that 'they are determinations of extension, and are universally and identically subject to the same laws of movement and rest'.[287]

For Spinoza, this common nature is what allows for the development of a general science of bodies, one that is founded on purely mathematical principles. The essential characteristic of this scientific understanding of the physical, material world, Macherey observes, is that it does not 'take into consideration the existence of any specific body in particular, and is thus *completely abstract*'.[288] This immediately recalls Marx's famous defence of the powers of abstraction for the analysis and critique of political economy: 'In the analysis of economic forms neither microscopes nor chemical reagents are of assistance. The power of abstraction must replace both'.[289] Like Marx's scientific critique of political economy ('The ultimate aim of this work [i.e., *Capital*, is] to reveal the economic law of motion of modern society'), Spinoza's 'science', as Macherey reads him, 'determines figures of regularity that, despite the perpetual variations impressed on [actually existing, singular] bodies due to the fact that they exist *en acte*, constitute the manifestation of a permanence regarding which laws can be formulated independently of the existence of any particular body'.[290]

Spinoza further specifies a characteristic of common notions, one that applies not only to physical bodies in extension, but to all actually existing

---

285 Macherey 1997, p. 275.
286 EIIP13L2.
287 Macherey 1997, p. 278.
288 Ibid., emphasis added.
289 Marx 1976, p. 90.
290 Macherey 1997, p. 281.

singular things as such: these common characteristics apply equally and absolutely to the part and whole [*quod aeque in parte ac in toto est*], and are, Macherey stresses, completely independent of any distinction between part and whole, precisely in terms of the *scalability* that Marx stresses in the example of the LRMSV: when considering aliquot, representative parts of a whole such as the total mass of surplus value rather than actually existing labourers such as bakers and cotton spinners and their lived experience, the law governing the rate and mass of surplus value holds absolutely.

This is necessarily the case, since a common notion such as Marx's LRMSV represents not actually existing singular things, but *relations* and *proportions*, the nature of which, Macherey notes, 'remains identical in every dimension [*ordres de grandeur*], as long as the rule that defines these relations is sustained'. As such, a common notion informs by this equivalence all 'composed and composing' things, which, in their entirety and universally, constitute relational systems as singular structures of causality that through formalisation come to *nonexist*, and do so independently of the particular conditions of existence of singular existing things (such as, for Marx, the particular characteristics of baking bread or spinning cotton).[291]

Now, the astute reader will have noted that in my initial presentation of chapter 11 of *Capital*, I skipped over what is perhaps the most striking confirmation of my argument that the LRMSV is a Spinozist common notion: Marx's graphic formula summarising the law itself in schematic form:[292]

$$S = \begin{cases} \frac{s}{v} \times V \\ P \times \frac{a'}{a} \times n \end{cases}$$

I did so because Marx's introduction of this formula – though it adds no further information to his presentation of the LRMSV – not only synthesises in schematic form this common notion, but, what is more, its specific history across the various editions of *Capital* can stand as a final confirmation of my proposition that Marx tendentially supresses his initial reliance on the Hegelian logic of determinations of reflection and contradiction for a properly Spinozist additive synthetic method.

---

291 Marx 1976, p. 279.
292 Marx annotates this formula as follows: 'Let the mass of the surplus value be S, the surplus-value supplied by the individual worker in the average day s, the variable capital advanced daily in the purchase of one individual labour-power v, the sum total of the variable capital V, the value of an average labour-power P, its degree of exploitation [= a'/a or: surplus labour divided by necessary labour,] and the number of workers employed, n' (1976, p. 418).

In fact, this schematic reduction and formalisation of the LRMSV, along with the paragraphs directly preceding and following it, is absent from both the 1867 and 1872 editions of *Capital*.²⁹³ Retained by Engels in the 1890 'definitive' edition of *Capital*, Marx in fact only inserted this formula, along with a number of abbreviations and clarifications, in his revisions to Roy's 1875 French translation. In the third paragraph, for example, he added a second sentence that more clearly states, at a high degree of abstraction, the additive and scalable nature of variable capital: 'Sa valeur [that of the variable capital employed] égale la valeur moyenne d'une force de travail multipliée par le nombre de ces forces individuelles ; la grandeur du capital variable est donc proportionnelle au nombre des ouvriers employés'.²⁹⁴ Immediately following the formula, Marx further emphasises the purely abstract nature of the values it represents: 'We assume throughout, not only that the value of an average labour-power is constant, but that the workers employed by a capitalist are *reduced to average workers*'.²⁹⁵ The overall tendency of Marx's final, 1875 revisions to the first paragraphs of this chapter are clear: simplifying its presentation, while above all emphasising the scalability of his propositions as well as their purely abstract character.

Now, I find it quite extraordinary that in his proof to EIIP37, Spinoza characterises the abstract, general nature of the properties common to all things (i.e.,

---

293 *Schematisation* in this sense refers not to the Kantian empiricist application of a category to sense perception, but instead to the systematic replacement of referential terms in a proposition by variables (n), while *formalisation* refers more generally to the establishment of the logical form of a proposition. See Lapointe 2008, p. 29.

294 MEGA II7 [1875], *Le Capital, Paris, 1872–1875*, Dietz Verlag, 1989, p. 257. The English in the Penguin translation reads: 'Its value is therefore equal to the average value of one labour-power multiplied by the number of labour powers employed' (Marx 1976, p. 417). Marx also cut out the succeeding sentence from the end of the third paragraph in the 1867 and 1872 editions, presumably because it made much the same point more verbosely: 'Der Werth des vorgeschossenen variablen Kapitals ist also gleich dem Durchschnittswerth einer Arbeitskraft multiplicirt mit der Anzahl der verwandten Arbeitskräfte. Bei gegebnem Werth der Arbeitskraft wechselt also Werthumfang oder Größe des variablen Kapitals mit der Masse der angeeigneten Arbeitskräfte oder der Anzahl der gleichzeitig beschäftigten Arbeiter' (MEGA² II5 [1867], p. 242; MEGA² II6 [1872], p. 303).

295 Marx 1976, p. 418, emphasis added. 'Es wird fortwährend unterstellt, nicht nur dass der Werth einer Durchschnitts-Arbeitskraft konstant ist, sondern dass die von einem Kapitalisten angewandten Arbeiter auf Durchschnitts-Arbeiter reducirt sind' (MEGA² II10 [1890], p. 274). In fact, this sentence, a footnote in the French, replaces in the 1890 addition within the body text an inconsequential one unique to the French, in which Marx had written: 'Or, un produit ne change pas de grandeur numérique, quand celle de ses facteurs change simultanément et en raison inverse' (MEGA² II7 [1875], *Le Capital*, 258). An online scan of the original French 1875 edition can be consulted at https://gallica.bnf.fr/ark:/12148/bpt6k1232830/f1n351.pdf.

their common notions) by an abstract variable, 'B', precisely as does Marx in the formula he inserts between the fourth and fifth paragraphs of Chapter 11.[296] Common notions apprehend not actually existing singular things but *relations*, in effect constructing an atemporal formal model of the real. The ethical and political result of this process of abstraction, Macherey observes, is to multiply the powers of the intellect adequately to grasp the essential, relational nature of all things:

> It is as though the intellect ... surpassed itself, escaping from the limitations of its particular situation as the idea of a particular thing as a body in action, which is how it ordinarily perceives all other things. Instead, [through the development of common notions] it is led to form ideas that are not themselves ideas of particular things, but [nonexistent] ideas, the object of which is the relations among things.[297]

In fact, Spinoza argues, common notions, though they do not grasp the essential nature of singular things (this he reserves to the third, 'intuitive' form of knowledge), are nonetheless necessarily and universally adequate, and as such constitute an instance of the political epistemology with which this book as a whole is concerned.

'Those things that are common to all things and are equally in the part as in the whole can be conceived only adequately'.[298] Aside from the laws governing the movement and rest of physical bodies, Spinoza also refers to axioms as common notions, in the sense that they hold for 'all things that are' [*omnia que sunt*].[299] When the apparatus of thought moves in this fashion away from the empirical consideration of various actually existing things, to construct instead ideas whose object is the purely abstract relations between things, Macherey observes,

> It moves to a new mode of operation [*régime de fonctionnement*], one that makes it see the things it apprehends in a completely new fashion: no longer via contingent encounters tied to the existence in act of bodies, but

---

296 'Conceive, if possible, that it does constitute the essence of one particular thing, B. Therefore, it can neither be nor be conceived without B (Def. 2, II). But this is contrary to our hypothesis. Therefore, it does not pertain to B's essence, nor does it constitute the essence of any other particular thing' (EIIP37Pr).
297 Macherey 1997, pp. 286–7.
298 EIIP38.
299 EIP8.

from a completely disincarnated point of view .... Relating to no specific thing in particular, such an idea, by its nature, can indicate or consider no other thing than that of which it is the idea: it can only be a clear and distinct idea, the transparency of which cannot be corrupted by opacity. It is, therefore, an idea 'that is for us absolute or adequate and perfect' [*quae in nobis est absoluta sive adequate et perfecta*].[300]

Common notions are absolute and complete ideas, precisely in the sense that schematisation (via the introduction of variables, A or B, to replace all reference to actually existing singular things) affords the passage from our inadequate ideas about the actually existing, empirical things we *perceive* (like Marx's bakers and cotton spinners) to our *conception* of universally and eternally valid relations (such as Marx's LRMSV).

This political epistemology of common notions is grounded in what Macherey terms 'a dynamic of rational knowledge', via the perfecting and emendation of the capacity to grasp the real by means of ideas, in which the intellect is led 'from the activity of [sensuous] perception, in which it is at its most passive, to that of conception, in which it is the most active ... passing from the particular to the general through a progressive process of abstraction'.[301]

The common notion as such thus possesses an inherent ethical and political dimension: ideas that express properties common to all things are as such necessarily 'common to all humans', Macherey comments, 'which is to say that they compose a *common knowledge* that can be universally shared'. This common knowledge, accessible to all humans and necessarily identically conceived by all who follow this democratic path, thus constitutes 'the condition for a mental community among all people .... In so far as people form common notions that are necessarily adequate, they are actually united, and constitute as such a single intellect and a single body'.[302] Macherey insists above all on the real actuality of this intellectual commons of theoretical practice: 'In the intellect of man, whoever he or she may be, there always exist common notions [such as, I suggested above, a minimal idea of the nature of capitalism such as Marx expresses in the first sentence of *Capital*] through which can be established the forms of their union with other people, which is to say, with the maximum possible others, and tendentially, with all'.[303]

---

300 Macherey 1997, pp. 282, 287.
301 Macherey 1997, pp. 289, 290.
302 Macherey 1997, p. 290.
303 Macherey 1997, p. 291.

If this political dimension of theoretical practice holds for a universal understanding of the law of gravity or logical axioms, in Spinoza's examples, how much more then is this true of Marx's critique of political economy in *Capital*, in which the reader is swept up by Marx's bracing rhetorical devices and compelling argument, to develop for herself a dynamic of increasingly adequate knowledge of the nature of capitalism, to grasp its essential nature in the fullest complexity of its systematic dynamic, to pierce the ideological untruth of its mere forms of appearance, and to join Marx in the construction, at the highest pitch of an active knowledge, of nothing less than a universal theoretical commons, a communism of the active intellect, as the necessary and adequate prolegomenon to the real 'death of capital' with which this book began.

CHAPTER 4

Toward an Axiomatic Analysis of the Commodity in Badiou and Marx

The publication of *Reading Capital* in 1965 initiated a theoretical intervention that would both culminate in and be extinguished by the events of May '68. In this and the following chapter, I wish to argue that the thought of Alain Badiou, beyond the historical and epistemological break that was 1968, though never explicitly engaging Marx's magnum opus, provides crucial theoretical resources that carry forward the apodictic, anti-empiricist and anti-historicist reading of *Capital* initiated by Althusser that I have analysed to this point. In this sense, I wish to pursue Althusser's original assertion that in *Capital*, Marx 'really did invent a new form of order for axiomatic analysis, ... a new order in the theoretical, a new form of apodicticity or scientificity'.[1] Badiou does so not by considering *Capital* directly, but by theorising 1) the general imperative of an *axiomatic* orientation of thought and 2) reconceptualising logic as the science of the appearance of things in a given world. These imperatives, fundamental to Badiou's entire philosophical project, can be brought to bear on the reading of *Capital* itself, to further specify and develop Marx's tendency, discussed above, to develop an additive synthetic demonstration of the structure of the capitalist social form. In other words, Badiou's elaboration of a logical materialism (in his early texts 'Mark and Lack' and *Concept of Model*) and an ontological materialism (in *Being and Event* and related texts such as *Number and Numbers*) constitutes a direct development of the Althusserian critique of empiricism and idealism, one that further specifies the tendency of Marx's revisions to *Capital* toward formalisation and schematisation as a materialist critique determined by the axiomatic starting point Marx chooses for his argument.

That said, Badiou's relation to *Capital* is nonetheless an uncanny mixture of manifest disinterest to the point of disavowal and censorship (is it not odd for such a committed philosopher of Marxist communism never to have discussed *Capital* at some point in over two hundred monographs?), and the corresponding recurrent, unacknowledged reinscription of the order of Marx's critique within the abstract terms Badiou's universal logic. This insistent reinscription constitutes an objective process of displacement [*Verschiebung*] within the

---

1 RC, p. 52. See above, note 55.

greater topography of theory, passing from a latent order (the critique of political economy) to a manifest one (Badiou's reconstruction of abstract logic).[2]

The insistent recurrence of this process gives the objective and obscure impression (uncanny on the part of a Marxist) that the structure of the capitalist social form can, for Badiou, only be addressed indirectly; in short, that the various discursive iterations of Badiou's logics (not at the level of a spurious psychology but through the analysis of real discursive objects) rewrite Marx's *Capital*, but with its charge censored and diminished via its displaced reinscription within the more abstract terms of post-Cantorean logic.

In these two concluding chapters, I will argue that if 1968 marks the end of the Althusserian initiative to construct a Marxian, anti-humanist 'philosophy of the concept' (to redeploy Jean Cavaillès's famous imperative), the Althusserian theoreticist position ended by '68 nonetheless takes on its purest form as Badiou's logical materialism of the mark (in 'Mark and Lack' and *Concept of Model*), lectures whose oral presentation was itself short-circuited by the event of May itself. The appearance of *Being and Event* two decades later in 1988, in turn, dismisses the materiality of the logical mark to sound the call for an *axiomatic* reorientation of philosophy as an ontological materialism of generic multiplicity, against both empiricism and logicist idealism, including that of the early Badiou himself.

While this tendency, I will argue in the following chapter, will culminate in *Logics of Worlds*, it is already decipherable in Badiou's 1967 contribution to *Cahiers pour l'Analyse*, 'Mark and Lack: On Zero'. Here, as if in a logician's dream of *Capital*, is that essay's dense opening paragraph:

> Epistemology breaks away from ideological recapture [*reprise*], in which every science comes to mime its own reflection, insofar as it excludes that recapture's institutional operator, the notion of Truth, and proceeds instead according to the concept of a mechanism of production, whose effects, by contrast, one seeks to explain through the theory of its structure.[3]

Here we find Badiou already moving in silent parallel with Marx: not with the political Marx of the *Communist Manifesto*, but with the theorist of the scientific critique of capitalism.

---

2   Laplanche and Pontalis define 'Displacement' as 'The fact that an idea's emphasis, interest or intensity is liable to be detached from it and to pass on to other ideas, which were originally of little intensity but which are related to the first idea by a chain of associations' (2018, p. 121).

3   Badiou 2012, p. 159.

Badiou's 1967 statement should be read, I am suggesting, as the objective, formal reduction of the methodological programme Marx sketches out in the '1857 Introduction' to the *Grundrisse*.[4] In his 1857 text, Marx set himself the project, in what would become *Capital*, of breaking away from the recapture of political economy as the mere articulation of the ideology of bourgeois capitalism, a theoretical recapture typical of classical economics, the consummate example of which is Adam Smith. For Smith, the theoretical articulation of a true image of capitalism was an empiricism based on the mere *representation* of the concrete. This entailed an analytic process that sought to articulate abstract conceptual generalisations drawn from the phenomenological manifestations of capitalism, an abstraction based on the observed regularities of its universal features. The classic example of this procedure is Smith's famous assertion of a universal and transhistorical 'human propensity to barter and truck'.

In contrast, Marx rejects both Hegelian Idealism and the methodology of classical political economy alike, as various modes of *representation* of the concrete. In their place, to deploy Badiou's more abstract phrasing in 'Mark and Lack', Marx refuses the logic of conceptual *representation* for a novel 'concept of a mechanism of production, whose effects, by contrast, one seeks to explain through the theory of its structure'.[5] This, in a formulation analogous to Althusser's reading of the same passage, albeit at a far higher degree of abstraction, is what Marx terms in the 1857 Introduction the 'reproduction' of a 'thought-concrete [*Gedankenkonkretum*]'.[6] Only here, in the manifest content of Badiou's 1967 formulation (to pursue this Marxian chain of associations I am imposing on Badiou's abstraction), 'Truth', as in Adam Smith's 'propensity to truck and barter', or the image of the magic hand, constitutes the operator of ideological illusion, and is to be replaced by Marx's categorial logic, a logic that Badiou, in essence furthering Marx's tendency toward the abstraction of nonexistent idealities described in the previous chapter, pursues what Badiou calls the systematic production of formal marks.

Badiou's fundamental assertion in his formalist essays of 1967–68 is that 'The concept of identity holds only for marks. Logic never has recourse to any self-identical *thing*, even when thing is understood in the sense of the object of scientific discourse'.[7] One way to read this statement is as a formalisation of the Spinozist distinction between actually existing and nonexistent things: the abstract schematisation process of logic does not indicate actually exist-

---

4   Marx 1973, pp. 109–21. See also Iñigo Carrera 2013; Nesbitt 2019.
5   Badiou 2012, p. 159.
6   Marx 1973, p. 101. See RC, p. 41.
7   Badiou 2012, p. 165.

ing singular things, but purely atemporal relations.[8] In this view, one could say that Adam Smith certainly produced a scientific, natural language discourse on political economy, but Marx's critique reveals that Smith's analysis is an ideological representation of the mere forms of appearance of capitalism in their superficial regularity (as the 'tendency to truck and barter').[9] In other words, the putatively self-same concepts of classical political economy are revealed in Marx's critique as fetishised forms of appearance of the true objects that only conceptual critique can produce: the substance of value, abstract labour power and the general social form of relation that he names the 'value-form', and the like. 'Nothing here warrants the title of *"object"*', observes Badiou. 'Here the thing is null: no inscription can objectify it. Within this space, one finds nothing but reversible *functions* from system to system, from mark to mark-nothing but the mechanical dependencies of mechanisms'.[10] Badiou's ultra-formalism thus radicalises in the mathematically grounded abstraction of nonexistent idealities, I am arguing, Althusser's initial reading of Marx's 1857 Introduction in *Reading Capital*, where Althusser famously asserted the fundamentally conceptual nature of Marx's project, stressing Marx's materialist rejection of empiricism and the destruction of all merely humanist Marxism.[11] This reinscription of Althusser's critique then becomes even more pressing in Badiou's 1968 lectures, *The Concept of Model*.

---

8   See above, pp. 53–4.
9   Hegel had already formulated in the *Logic*'s 'Doctrine of Concept' an analogous critique of empiricism as the mere abstract reflection of appearances: 'Since the predicates immediately drawn from the appearances still belong to empirical psychology, so far as metaphysical consideration goes, all that is in truth left are the entirely inadequate determinations of reflection'. Hegel then continues – and here one should simply replace the more general 'metaphysics of the *soul*' that Hegel criticises in this passage for Adam Smith's more specific search for a *metaphysics of man's economic nature* that is the object of Marx's critique – with the point that such empiricism is 'intent on determining the *abstract essence* of the soul; it went about this starting from observation, and then converting the latter's empirical generalisations, and the determination of purely *external* reflection attaching to the singularity of the actual, into the form of the *determinations of essence*' (Hegel 2021b, pp. 689, 690). It is no coincidence, then, that this chapter of the *Logic* ('The idea of cognition') appears to be precisely the section of the *Logic* that most decisively influenced Marx's formulation of the 1857 'Introduction' (Meaney 2015, p. 45).
10 Badiou 2012, p. 165.
11 RC, pp. 40–2.

1 1968: Logical Materialism

The Concept of Model consists of two brief lectures, along with a 2007 Preface by Badiou written for its reedition.[12] These two lectures proceed in three moments: the first five sections rearticulate Althusser's critique of Lévi-Strauss's combinatory structuralism, rejected as an empiricist idealism, to which Badiou then appends a similar critique of logical formalism, followed in conclusion by Badiou's presentation of his own materialist concept of logical structure.

Although the text itself is a punctual intervention, one that addresses the singular epistemological problem that Badiou calls the concept of 'model', it nonetheless allows us, when read in the broader historical perspective Badiou suggests in his 2007 introduction to the reprint of these lectures, to figure a broader, three-part typology of this period. Its first moment stretches from the initiation of the Althusserian philosophy of the concept, from the publication of *For Marx* and *Reading Capital* in 1965 to May '68, including as well the journal, *Cahier pour l'Analyse* that emerged out of the Althusserian project to specifically develop this conceptual orientation and the articulation of a philosophy of the concept and the formalisation of conceptual categories.[13] This is followed by a second period marked by the retreat from theory into political militancy (the 'Red Years', 1968–89). This is above all the moment of an *in*-formal politics, a *politique de l'informel*, a period in which Foucault and Deleuze famously invoked, against all universalism, a withdrawal into local, situated politics – a politics of local situations, problems, and interventions, refusing the overarching attempts to rearticulate the structural determinants of a given social configuration or order that arguably determine both Marx's critique of capitalism and the dynamic of twentieth-century Marxism itself.[14]

This period of retreat into local politics is followed, according to Badiou's chronology, by a third period: at the level of politics, universalism returns as tragic farce with the triumph of neoliberalism as a putative global destiny, while at the level of conceptual thought, Badiou bestows on this period (that extends into the present) a vital determination characterised by the axiomatic orientation initiated by *Being and Event*.[15]

---

12 Badiou 2007 [1968].
13 See Hallward and Peden 2012.
14 Foucault and Deleuze 1977, pp. 205–17.
15 Althusser 2005; Badiou 2013 [1988].

Badiou begins *The Concept of Model* by reiterating term for term Althusser's critique of Lévi-Strauss.[16] He first defines empiricism as the (ideological) scientific discourse that articulates the distinction between empirical reality and theoretical form as a relation of representation, 'the formal representation of a given [empirical] object'. Within this ideological figure, Lévi-Strauss's structural anthropology is then said (in section 3) to constitute a specific form of this ideology, one in which

> The pair empiricism/formalism takes the form of an opposition between the neutral observation of facts and the active production of a model. In other words, science is thought [by Lévi-Strauss] as the confrontation [*vis-à-vis*] between a real object, which one examines (ethnography), and an artificial object destined to reproduce and imitate the real object (ethnology) via the law of its effects.[17]

Lévi-Strauss implements precisely the empiricist procedure Althusser had condemned in the abstract in *Reading Capital*, extracting, in other words, the essential kernel from the observed object, to fashion it into a faithful representation of the real.[18]

The principal fault of Lévi-Strauss's empiricist combinatory, for Badiou as it was for Althusser, is the incomprehensible, aleatory nature of any observable case or situation, the impossibility of determining, from mere observation of the case at hand, the necessity that has determined this phenomenon. Instead, the truth of scientific empiricism amounts to no more than the mere measure of the 'fit' between fact and model:

> If the model represents the truth of scientific work [for Lévi-Strauss], this truth is never anything more than that of the best model. This is to restore the dominance of empiricism: theoretical activity cannot choose between necessarily multiple models, since its activity is precisely the fabrication of such models. It is then the 'fact' that decides, designating the best model as the best approximation of itself.[19]

The model, in this empiricist procedure, is no more than the constructed object that best accounts for, in the sense of representing, the observed facts. 'To the

---

16 See above, pp. 72–4.
17 Badiou 2007, 19.
18 RC, p. 37.
19 Badiou 2007, 23.

question, what is the criterion of this "accounting for"', the empiricist observer has no other response than the circular reasoning of Lévi-Strauss, i.e., 'the one that accounts for all the facts'.[20]

To this critique of Lévi-Strauss, which takes up the first half of Badiou's lecture without adding anything substantial to Althusser's previous critique, Badiou appends, in his fifth section, a similar critique of logical positivism. In Badiou's presentation, the scientific doctrine of logical positivism is not at all gratuitous, but similarly depends upon a strict correlation between a formal system and its empirical objects. A formal system, as a system of necessary deductions, constitutes the accurate expression or representation of its objects, as 'the correspondence between the statements of the formal system and the domain of scientific objects under consideration'. The formal system adheres to a syntactic regime of constraint at the level of its chain of deductions, without, however, deriving the materialist necessity that would determine the necessity of any specific axiomatic orientation.

When Badiou then turns to his own 'construction of the concept of model' in the final sections of his talk, it is conspicuous that this rigorous demonstration of 'logical materialism', as he will appropriately name this orientation in his 2007 Preface, no more attends to its axiomatic starting point then do the empiricisms of Lévi-Strauss and logical positivism he has just rejected. Badiou's 2007 auto-critique is spot-on:

> What is striking [in the talks comprising *Concept of Model*] is that of the two general determinations of the paradigmatic function of mathematics (the axiomatic decision and the logical constraint of its consequences), it is the second that receives attention. [In these lectures] the recourse to the normative script of formal logic is the principal focus, in so far as it imposes, through the materiality of marks and symbols, a mechanism of inscription opposed to all empiricist and idealist interpretations.[21]

Badiou's definition of his earlier position as a logical materialism is revealing: rather than a (Spinozist) science of causes in which the axiomatic starting point (for example *causa sui* for Spinoza or Marx's initial true idea of capitalism as general commodification) determines the materialist basis of a critique, here it is instead the mere materiality of the logical mark that produces a material*ism*, in which matter again stands as the emanant source, not of being qua

---

20   Lévi-Strauss, cited in Badiou 2007, 25.
21   Badiou 2007, 25.

being as in ontological, monist materialisms, but merely as a materialist guarantee of what Badiou terms the 'mechanism of inscription'.

Indeed, Badiou's exposition of the 'construction of the concept of model' consists of little more than a virtuosic manipulation of basic set theory materials. Despite his recognition that 'the choice of axioms makes all the difference in a demonstration', he simply begins immediately with the problem of syntax, admitting that his only concern is 'to convey the articulation of the construction of the concept [of a model]'.[22] The only difference from the rigor of logical positivism is that Badiou has detached the model he constructs from any and all reference to empirical objects to which it would correspond; neither determined at the front end by the sensuous given, nor idealistically via the rigor of proof which would determine being, Badiou's 1968 concept of model amounts to little more than a free-floating formal system that finds its adequacy in the mere 'material sequence of the proof'.[23] The closing invocation of Dialectical Materialism is in this sense telling, clearly indicating this as an ultra-formalist version of traditional matter-based material*ism*, the destiny of which, Badiou claims, would be to find 'its efficacious integration within proletarian ideology'.[24]

In retrospect, Badiou coherently qualifies his subsequent rejection of this 'logical materialism' ('my materialism of the sixties is a logical materialism') via the decisive turn in his thought formulated by the publication of *Being and Event* in 1988, as the initiation of a quite different problematic, one that he names in turn an 'ontological materialism':

> I moved from a positive reading of mathematics [in *The Concept of Model*] as the site of regulated inscriptions to one according to which the mathematics of the multiple is the thought of being qua being. In brief, I passed from a structural materialism that privileged the letter (the mark), to an ontological materialism that privileges the evidence of being-there [*l'évidence du 'il y a'*] in the form of pure multiplicity.[25]

At the same time, I would add that this ontological materialism nonetheless fails to constitute a science of causes in the sense of the materialist critique of Spinoza or Marx, as Badiou himself seems to sense: 'the fact that logical struc-

---

22   Badiou 2007, 30.
23   Badiou 2007, 31.
24   Badiou 2007, 40.
25   Badiou 2007, 19.

tures are valid for any model only signifies their real vacuity, the fact that they make possible thinking the transcendental form of different possible localisations' in what he will eventually call a 'world' (in *Logiques des mondes*).

While the virtue of this later position, as we shall see in more detail in the following chapter, is that it limits logic, against all empiricist and idealist tendencies, to the rigorous description or science of the appearance of things in a world, I will nonetheless argue that it remains, as Badiou himself calls it, a mere material*ism*, one that, in the absence of a materialist axiomatic starting point, holds true only at the level of ontology as generic multiplicity; it is, in other words, a mere *generic materialism* that in its utter abstraction ignores the singular structural logic of any specific world, such as the logic of our world, the capitalist social form. Before developing this critique of Badiou's generic materialism as a logic of worlds in the next chapter, I wish to first take stock of the real force of Badiou's post-1988 ontological materialism, since it constitutes a powerful critique of logical idealism such as that of Frege (the object of Badiou's explicit critique) and, implicitly, that of Hegelian Absolute Idealism more generally.

2   Bolzano and the Formalisation of Axiomatic Thought

Badiou's turn after 1988 to an axiomatic orientation constitutes a structural materialism of the letter or the sign. This is a materialism in which ontology is strictly subordinate to logic in a philosophy of the concept, a tendency that in fact originates with the Czech logician, Bernard Bolzano, and only subsequently develops from Bolzano through Frege, through Cavaillès, Desanti, and the Badiou.[26] Although Badiou engages explicitly with the latter figures, it is Bolzano who initiates and articulates the turn from Hegelian negative dialectical thought toward an axiomatic philosophy in the decades prior to his death in 1848, and given his relative invisibility in post-Althusserian thought, it is important to indicate his key role for thinkers such as Cavaillès and Badiou.

Badiou never mentions the pioneering, long-overlooked Czech-German logician Bernard Bolzano in the three volumes of *Being and Event*. In fact, his name only appears in passing on two occasions in Badiou's oeuvre: once in *Number and Numbers*, in a list of the modern founders of *the thought of number*, and once, in a passing reference to Bolzano's pioneering formalisation of the concept of the infinite in *Paradoxes of the Infinite*, in Badiou's 1994–95 seminar on

---

26   See Lapointe 2011.

Lacan.[27] Badiou has, moreover, admitted that his knowledge of Bolzano's work is in fact limited and largely second-hand.[28]

Badiou's neglect of Bolzano's thought is hardly surprising, since the great Czech-German philosopher's pioneering and foundational work, in set theory, in the critique of post-Kantian Idealism and intuitionism, in the semantic formalisation of mathematics and logic, in the formal nature of axiomatisation, his precocious articulation of a realist, mathematics-based platonism a century before Albert Lautman's 'transplatonism', and in many other fields, remained little acknowledged and even less studied until quite recently.[29] As late as 1993, Jacques Bouveresse could still decry this 'historical injustice' done to 'the most gifted and original adversary of German Idealism'.[30]

Decades before Frege, Husserl, Cantor, Tarski, and Gödel, Bolzano founded or made possible many of the crucial discoveries of modern analytic philosophy and set theory, innovations for which the former would become famous. Following the prohibition of his publications and his early retirement to the Czech countryside, Bolzano's discoveries remained overlooked after his death in 1848, and thus the breakthroughs of his major, posthumous works *Paradoxes of the Infinite* and *Theory of Science* were only belatedly recognised by Cantor and famously celebrated by Husserl in the *Philosophical Investigations*.[31]

Bolzano's vast and still underexplored body of work announces Badiou's thought in a series of crucial dimensions, of which I will briefly indicate three:[32]

1) Bolzano's thought remains the most original and decisive critique of post-Kantian Idealism in the first half of the nineteenth century. While Badiou can-

---

27   'Les noms de cette première modernité [de la pensée du nombre] ne sont pas Proust et Joyce, ce sont Bolzano, Frege, Cantor, Dedekind, Peano'. Badiou 1990, p. 24. 'Après que l'infini eut reçu dans la mathématique un statut clair, grâce à Bolzano, Weierstrass et Cantor, il cesse de jouer un rôle dans l'argumentation philosophique'. Badiou 2013b, pp. 256–7. In English: Badiou 2008. Badiou 2018. See also Bolzano 1950 [1851].
28   Personal communication, New York, 18 October 2017.
29   Badiou 2013a, p. 12.
30   Bouveresse, 'Préface', in Laz 1993, p. iv.
31   'Bernhard Bolzano's *Wissenschaftslehre*, published in 1837, a work which, in its treatment of the logical 'theory of elements', far surpasses everything that world-literature has to offer in the way of a systematic sketch of logic'. Husserl 2001 [1900], p. 68. See Bolzano 2014; 2011. On Bolzano's life, see the biographical information in Rusnock and Šebestík 2019. Bolzano publicly articulated as radical a critique of Viennese militarism as was perhaps possible in his Austro-Hungarian milieu, and it was this in particular that led to the banning of his publications and his forced early retirement from Charles University.
32   I develop other points at which Bolzano announces Badiou's thought, for example on the concept of the infinite, in Nesbitt 2021.

not be said to reject Hegelian dialectical modes of thought entirely, and in fact has returned repeatedly to interrogate its modalities, it is arguably Bolzano who initiates a tendency in European philosophy to supplement and complete philosophical investigations with apodictic demonstrations formulated in the precise, emphatically un-Hegelian mathematical terms of set-based theory. This mode of demonstration culminates in Badiou's mathematical apparatus deployed throughout the three volumes of *Being and Event*.

While Bolzano's *Theory of Science* reiterates and refines the terms of Bolzano's initial critique of post-Kantian Idealism, Jacques Laz has shown that Bolzano's 1810 *Beiträge zu einer begründeteren Darstellung der Mathematik* [*Contributions to an Exposition of Mathematics on a Firmer Basis*], written when Bolzano was only twenty-nine, already sets forth the principal propositions of his thought.[33] Key among these is his systematic critique of Kantian philosophy, attacked at its root via what Bolzano shows to be the contradictory nature of Kant's claims for an *a priori intuition* that would ground the entire project of the *Critique of Pure Reason*.[34] While the extraordinary brevity of the Appendix to Bolzano's *Contributions* ('The Kantian Doctrine of the Construction of Concepts by Intuitions') articulates its powerful critique in a mere eleven dense and methodically parsed paragraphs,[35] elsewhere Bolzano decries more generally the 'love of imagistic language', lack of expressive precision, and reliance upon 'analogies, paradoxes, and tautologies' dominant in the Schellingian and Hegelian thought of the age.[36]

Bolzano unequivocally condemns what he views as a catastrophic tendency of philosophy, 'the essence of [which] consists in ... playing with images and passing off the slightest superficial analogy between two objects as an identity'.[37] The core of this limitation, Bolzano concludes, is that 'the thinkers of our age do not feel themselves in the least subject to ... the *rules of logic*, notably to the obligation always to state precisely and clearly *of what* one is speaking, in what *sense* one takes this or that word, and then to indicate from what *reasons* one affirms this or that thing'.[38] Bolzano's critique proved decisively productive for his invention of what Jean Cavaillès would famously call a 'philosophy of the concept'.[39] Badiou can be said in turn to have taken from Cavaillès' critique a

---

33   Bolzano 2010.
34   Kant 1998.
35   See Bolzano 2010.
36   Cited in Laz 1993, p. 33.
37   Cited in Laz 1993, pp. 32–3.
38   Cited in Laz 1993, p. 32.
39   Cavaillès 2008. Note that beginning with his critique of Fregean logicism in 'Meditation 3'

positive notion of ontology in its intrinsic relation to science and to mathematics in particular as the adequate language of being as being.[40]

2) Bolzano, decisively influenced on this count by Leibniz, is arguably the first modern philosopher to clearly define mathematics as the adequate language of ontology in the form of a *mathesis universalis* based upon predicate logic derived from Aristotle's *Posterior Analytic*.[41] Bolzano argues in the *Contributions* that philosophy is the science addressed to the question 'what things are necessarily *real*', while mathematics, in contrast, addresses the question 'What properties must things *necessarily* possess to be *possible*?'[42] While philosophy attempts to prove the reality of particular objects *a priori* and unconditionally, mathematics, in Bolzano's formulation, constitutes the *a priori* science of the set of universal laws to which all possible objects are subject.[43]

Scientific method in general is for Bolzano coterminous with the logical rigor of mathematical method.[44] While for Bolzano philosophy seeks to deduce the real existence of things (analogous to Badiou's project to define an asubjective phenomenal logic in *Logics of Worlds*), mathematics applies its analysis, Bolzano argues, to the *possible* existence of all objects as governed by general laws. Bolzano can in this sense be said to announce Badiou's demonstration of the laws governing the *phenomenal* appearance of things in *Logics of Worlds* (to be discussed in the next chapter): mathematics, Bolzano affirmed, develops a general theory of forms, which he defined as 'a science that treats of the general laws (forms) to which things must conform in their existence'.[45] While for Bolzano this constitutes an ontological affirmation, Badiou will reject categorial logic as identical with being as such, to argue instead that while mathe-

---

of *Being and Event*, Badiou decisively rejects the notion of logic as a purely syntactic operation: 'Logic is not a formalisation, a syntax, a linguistic apparatus. It is a mathematised description of possible mathematical universes, under the generic concept of Topos'. Cited in Hallward 2003, p. 109. I will return to this point below, in reference to Bolzano's innovative formalisation of axiomatic method. While Cavaillès celebrates, in *On Logic*, Bolzano's rigorous attention to the necessary modalities of adequate, apodictic demonstration, he nonetheless criticises the ahistorical nature of these conditions, to offer instead a historically developmental concept of adequate demonstration. Hourya Benis Sinaceur has argued that Cavaillès' critique of Bolzano indicates a subterranean Hegelianism latent in Cavaillès' thought. Sinaceur 2013, pp. 114–16.

40 Thanks to David Rabouin for clarifying this point.
41 On Leibniz's influence on Bolzano, see Laz 1993, pp. 33–5; and on Bolzano's reconfiguration and critique of Aristotelean logic, see Laz 1993, pp. 27–30.
42 Cited in Laz 1993, p. 29.
43 Cited in Laz 1993, p. 45.
44 Laz 1993, pp. 46–8.
45 Cited in Rusnock and Šebestík 2019, p. 417.

matics constitutes the adequate language of what is *dicible* (sayable) of being, a categorial logic offers the means to conceptualise an asubjective *phenomenology of worlds*.

3) Finally, Bolzano crucially announces the axiomatic position Badiou will develop in *Being and Event*: 'Axiomatisation', Badiou writes there, 'is not an artifice of exposition, but an intrinsic necessity. Being-multiple, if entrusted to natural language and to intuition alone, produces an undivided pseudo-presentation of consistency and inconsistency. ... Axiomatisation is required such that the multiple, left to the implicitness of its counting rule, be delivered without concept, that is, without implying the being-of-the-one'.[46] While, as David Rabouin points out, Badiou's notion of axiomatisation draws upon Hilbert and Bourbaki, one might note that Bolzano already presents in the second section of the *Contributions* the first explicit model of axiomatisation, decisively rejecting Kantian intuitionism.[47]

There, Bolzano does not proceed via a demonstration of the nature of the axiom, which would return precisely to the very logicism axiomatisation seeks to overcome (and for which Badiou takes Frege to task in both *Being and Event* and *Number and Numbers*). The axiom, Bolzano argues in terms that decisively announce those of Badiou, is derived neither through an intuition, nor even as a minimally and generally acceptable common notion, which would rely on a psychological recognition and agreement, but is instead, he argues, indemonstrable, and objectively so. Bolzano argues that it is precisely and minimally the indemonstrability of an axiom, rather than its essential nature, that can in fact be proven. This minimal proof is merely the verification that allows axioms to found the subsequent propositions subject to apodictic demonstration. 'Neither deduction, nor demonstration of the truth of a proposition', Jacques Laz writes, 'the [Bolzanean] *Deductio* of an axiom is the exposition of its status as principle [*statut de principe*] in an objective sequence of connections between propositions. It is the operation by which are revealed the propositions that are the principles for other propositions'.[48] Objective without being a logical demonstration of the truth of an axiom, the *Deductio* founds the effective *conditions* of demonstration, deducing only that a given proposition possesses an axiomatic character, in the sense that it cannot be analytically reduced into subsidiary components.[49]

---

46 Badiou 2005, p. 43, translation modified.
47 David Rabouin, personal communication.
48 Laz 1993, p. 55.
49 Laz 1993, pp. 52–6.

Bolzano can thus be said to announce not only central features of Badiou's thought, but more generally the structuralist analysis of what Marx called 'social form' that is the topic of this book as a whole; structuralist analysis, that is to say, in the quite specific sense in which Louis Althusser and Pierre Macherey developed it in *Reading Capital*. Here, Bolzano's concerted critiques of intuitionism, psychologism, and empiricism, and above all his concept of propositions in themselves can be said to second and further develop the Spinozist critiques that Althusser, Rancière, Macherey, and Balibar deployed in their readings of Marx's *Capital*.

If Althusser and Macherey in particular looked back three hundred years prior to Spinoza in order to develop their critiques of Hegel and Hegelian Marxism, it is surely no less plausible to suggest that Bolzano, who developed the single most rigorous critique of Kantian and Hegelian Idealism prior to 1848, might offer compelling theoretical arguments to further develop this anti-Hegelian line of thought. Bolzano argued for an objective semantics governing not subjective, hermeneutic knowledge of objects, but their objective properties and relations. He inaugurates, this is to say, the affirmation that Badiou will formalise in 1988 as the governing imperative of *Being and Event*: that mathematics 'writes that which, of being itself, is expressible [*dicible*]'.[50] This, Bolzano argues, implies the independence of these concepts apart from conscious representation. Their meaning, he argues, is rigorously objective and independent from acts of judgement. In fact, I would willingly push this argument even further, to suggest that Bolzano can rightly be said to formulate crucial theoretical resources in the path leading to the Lacanian theory of the symbolic and real, above all perhaps via his realist, semantic critique of the Kantian thing in itself. As Badiou writes of Lacan's notion of the real,

> Lacan is not a critic. To be sure, the real differs from reality, which attaches its regime to knowing. But Lacan immediately says: I don't mean to say the real is unknowable. I'm not a Kantian. ... Although the real, as distinct from reality, is exempted from the knowable, which is the essence of reality, *the real nevertheless does not end up being the absolute unknowable but is instead exposed to being demonstrated*.[51]

Bolzano's asubjective order of propositions and representations – in a precise and limited sense analogous to what Lacan will call the symbolic order (in what

---

50   Badiou 2005, p. 5, translation modified.
51   Badiou 2013b, p. 151.

Badiou calls Lacan's 'hyperstructural axiomatic' phase of the 1950s) – is eminently knowable through acts of formalisation and judgement, in contrast to Bolzano's anti-Kantian notion of the thing in itself as much as the Lacanian real.[52] While this objective order presents things as they are in what Bolzano calls the matter [*Stoff*] of a semantic, symbolic order, it is for Bolzano (unlike Kant) the real, as Lacan famously stated, that constitutes the *impasse* of formalisation.[53] Or as Laz writes, for Bolzano, 'we will never be able to grasp the objects of our representation, but only their [objective] meaning through which we represent them'.[54]

To suggest a Bolzanian reading of Badiou along the lines that I am suggesting here is surely no more implausible than was Macherey's reading of Hegel.[55] It is to articulate a transversal relation; unlike that which Macherey articulates, however, in Badiou's case, there is no obscure disavowal on his part of a hidden proximity to Bolzano's historically prior thought, but rather a complex field of relations and implications that remains to be developed and articulated, an investigation that Badiou himself might be the first to welcome.

3   Ontological Materialism in Its Limits

That said, the explicit referent for Badiou's critique of idealist ultra-formalism is not Bolzano, but Frege, a thinker with whom he engages repeatedly across his work – in 'Mark and Lack', in *Being and Event*, and again in *Number and Numbers*. Already the object of Badiou's critique in 'Mark and Lack', the inventor of formal logic will become, in both the Meditation Three of *Being and Event* and the second chapter of *Number and Numbers*, the object of a critique of formalist idealism that will motivate and justify Badiou's essential turn from his initial logicism of 1967–68 to an axiomatic of Being as the pure presentation of inconsistent multiplicity prior to all logic.

The key moment in the development of Alain Badiou's thought, the crucial turn is undoubtedly this conceptual decision to reorient ontology around an axiomatic, anti-logicist, anti-Fregean position. This takes form in Badiou's axiomatic displacement and debasement of logical formalism, the destitution of the entitlement of Logic to legislate over Being classically sought after by Frege and David Hilbert. Badiou instead relegates logic to an unimpeach-

---

52   Badiou 2013b, p. 237.
53   Badiou 2005, p. 5.
54   Laz 1993, pp. 121–2.
55   Macherey 2011 [1979].

ably secondary status in strict subordination to an ontological materialism, the inaugural presentation of Being as inconsistent multiple without a One.

What we observe is a movement between Badiou's initial logical materialism, a culmination of this long tradition, an anti-phenomenological tradition in thought from Bolzano, Cavaillès, and Althusser to Badiou – and an axiomatic formalism, in which the process of formalisation in Badiou's works, such as *Being and Event* and *Logics of Worlds*, is retained, but to become strictly subordinate to ontology and philosophy. Mathematics, that is to say, reduced to the status of a subordinate, proper, and adequate mode in which to speak of being, longer assures the being there of being itself, as with Frege.

We find this Bolzanean, axiomatic turn or reorientation of Badiou's thought at work, drawn and measured against the demonstrative force of Frege's logicism, in the key founding 'Meditation Three' of *Being and Event*. If 'Meditation One' sets forth the absolute necessity of inconsistent multiplicity, it does so in the philosophical rhetoric of natural language. 'Meditation Three', in contrast, indexifies the necessity of inconsistent multiplicity not only to Bertrand Russell's paradox, a merely negative presentation of the limits of natural language, but to the actual demonstration of these limits via Gödel's proofs of completeness and incompleteness.

This is the moment in which Badiou affirms the contingent, axiomatic orientation of his thought as a refusal of all first principles, even those of logic as they were first systematised by Frege in his 1879 *Begriffsschrift*. There Frege sought to construct a comprehensive language for formal logic:

> It is necessary [Badiou writes,] to abandon all hope of explicitly defining the notion of set. ... Axiomatisation is required such that the multiple, left to the impliciteness of its counting rule, be delivered *without concept* .... [Contrary to Frege,] language cannot induce existence, solely a split within existence .... The power of language does not go so far as to institute the 'there is' of the 'there is'. It confines itself to positing that there are some distinctions within the 'there is'.[56]

Frege's effort to secure the concept of set 'guaranteed by a well-constructed language'[57] such that the 'control of language (of writing) [would amount to] control of the multiple'[58] founders on the shores of Russell's paradox, and this limit to a totalising symbolic formulation is then formalised in Gödel's proof

---

56 Badiou 2005, pp. 43, 47.
57 Badiou 2005, p. 39.
58 Ibid.

of, first, the completeness of first-order logic as the predicate calculus – the proof, in other words, that 'every consistent formal system has a model' – along with Gödel's proof of the existence of arithmetically true but unprovable statements, the effective *separation* of the criteria for semantic truth from those of provability.[59] Gödel demonstrates that 'there are provably unprovable, but nevertheless true, propositions in *any* formal system that contains elementary arithmetic, assuming the system to be consistent'.[60]

Badiou draws the ontological implication of incompleteness as the destitution of monism with remarkable force: Since given not just Russell's paradox, but above all incompleteness, 'it is necessary to abandon all hope of explicitly defining the notion of set, ... axiomatisation is required such that the multiple, left to the implicitness of its counting rule, be delivered *without concept*, that is, *without implying the being-of-the-one*'.[61] Even more strongly, we read in the concluding lines of 'Meditation Three' this summation of the ineluctable ontological conclusion to be drawn from incompleteness: 'The power of language does not go so far as to institute the "there is" of the "there is". It confines itself to posing that there are some distinctions within the "there is"'.[62]

For what, after all, is Zermelo's axiom of separation if not the restrictive warrant of the symbolic to operate critically upon a necessarily prior given in its merely provisional totality, counted-as-one? Under the aegis of Separation, it is the case, Badiou tells us, that 'a property only determines a multiple under the supposition that there is already a presented multiple'.[63] There is always already a presented multiple in Badiou's ontological materialism, a generic multiplicity prior to any counted-as-one. If this is the case, the ontological necessity of Zermelo's axiom, required to save the operations of first-order logic from the proof of incompleteness, logically necessitates the initiation of any critique from the prior givenness of a world, as opposed to the idealist engendering of existence from the loins of logic.

The axiom of separation certifies the absolute necessity that apodictic critique begin not from the absolute of an esoteric logical demonstration of a logical structure as a closed, complete system, but, instead, as an ontological materialism, from the most universal and immediate, a multiplicity as the givenness, the *il y a*, of a generic plurality (for example, of commodities as an

---

59 See Goldstein 2013, pp. 186, 160.
60 Goldstein 2013, p. 168.
61 Badiou 2005, p. 43.
62 Badiou 2005, p. 47.
63 Badiou 2005, p. 45.

immense, undifferentiated heap, the underived axiom of an *'ungeheure Warensammlung'*). The axiom of separation, we could say, tells us that in our world, in the capitalist mode of production, in this world in which everything under the sun has its price, the world of commodities names a pure, perhaps *the* paradigmatic instance of a consistent multiple, in which each is counted, everything has its price, but *counts* in subtraction from any and all specific determination of singular form, any of the specific determinate use-values of various commodities in their differentiated multiplicity. Use-value, though necessary, is always secondary; from atom bombs to zaffre, the valorisation of value is the universal logic of our world.

The axiom of separation can be said to formalise the critical procedure itself as strict necessity. For the very meaning of critique – from the Greek *kritikē*, *krinein*, becoming after 1838 the French neologism *criticité*, to designate after Kant the examination of the rational foundations of knowledge – indicates precisely the operation of discerning, sorting, dividing, in a word, *separating*, that very procedure the axiom of separation formalises as absolute necessity. Here is Badiou: 'Language cannot induce existence, solely a split [*scission*] within existence'.[64] The logical requirement of an axiom of separation formalises the critical operation itself as absolute necessity. As Badiou writes in *Number and Numbers*, 'We can only move to an existence that is somehow carved out of a pre-given existence. We can "separate" in a given domain those objects within it that validate the property exposed by the concept'.[65]

Critique in these terms is precisely the operation Marx deployed as the systematic destruction of the fetishistic illusion of totality, of the illusion that there are, in other words, natural beings we call commodities, in the pure inviolability of their self-same identity. There are only inconsistent multiples prior to the localised, provisional presentation of any One. 'The existence-multiple anticipates what language retroactively separates out from it as implied existence-multiple'.[66] In sum, the priority of being as inconsistent multiplicity, confirmed and supported by its axiomatic separation from the demonstrative critique that is the power of language, assures for Badiou the priority of an ontological materialism against all Hegelian and Fregean Idealisms alike.

A turn occurs, following the 1988 publication of Badiou's first major ontological work, *Being and Event*: from that point on, Badiou recognises the impera-

---

64 Badiou 2005, p. 47.
65 Badiou 2008, p. 20.
66 Badiou 2005, p. 47.

tive to retain a process of formalisation and reflection at a conceptual level, a 'certain' structuralism, a certain variant of structuralism as an axiomatic formalism. Nonetheless, this new form of thought is not a formal combinatory of fixed, unchanging structural essences as in the structuralism of Lévi-Strauss, but rather an axiomatic one, one in which politics and the critique of capitalism more specifically takes any given orientation as a decision, as a process of decision, one that allies with that orientation a formal process of reflection.

This is to say, literally and specifically: with 1989 and the coming neoliberal 'triumph' or generalisation of capitalism as a global sequence, it suddenly becomes imperative for Badiou to carry forward political thought axiomatically, and to invent a critique and politics adequate to the vast and encompassing generalisation of capitalism after 1989 as the tendential totalisation of global society. What we see is precisely the necessity of revisiting, and carrying forward into the post-'89 period, both a contingent axiomatic orientation toward the critique of capital, based not on an *a priori* moralism, or pre-given norms or normativity, but one that refers instead to the capacity to orient oneself in relation to universal categories – justice as equality, for example. The enormous difficulty of comprehending the rapidity with which capitalism dominates and transforms our experience (particularly since the turn of the century) is so overwhelming, that it becomes very difficult, if not impossible, to conceive of a politics that would truly be not just local politics, but also veritably anti-capitalist, given our existing and lingering categories of political critique from the twentieth century; to understand what that might mean implies, of course, understanding the forms, limits, structures of capitalism itself.

It is precisely in revisiting the conceptual categories that Marx developed in his critique of political economy in the three volumes of *Capital*, that we can recover the basic elements that still today define the structure of structures that is capitalism, a social form that is, nonetheless, a contingent structure: a structure of structures in which we see contemporary mutations of the orientation, the domination, and the subordination of those various categories in ways that require us to step back to invoke a conceptual moment and process of reflection in order to grasp precisely what it means to live in a period that I would call 'posthuman capitalism', in which there unfolds a general devalorisation of the capacity of labour power to create surplus value, the very substance of capital. To grasp that process, and then to put forward and to think politics in the contemporary conjuncture is precisely to require what I am calling an axiomatic formalism. This would constitute an effect or derivation from a general philosophical project, an ontological project that following Badiou sutures the axiomatic to the process of formalisation and conceptual reflection, to provide resources to begin such a re-foundation, reconceptualisation, and reorientation: the initiation of a critique adequate to our contemporary conjuncture of posthuman capitalism.

4   The Displacement of *Capital*

As such, among the most striking features of *Being and Event* and *Number and Numbers* is their reiteration and further development of the association noted above in 'Mark and Lack' and *Concept of Model*, as the pressing refiguration of Marx's critique. Here too, these later texts schematise the logical reduction and restatement of Marx's initial derivation of the concept of exchange-value and the commodity in Chapter One of *Capital*, Vol. 1. Here is Badiou on Frege: 'To say that two concepts are equinumerate is to say that they have the "same quantity", that their extensions are the same size, abstracting from any consideration as to what the objects *are* that fall under those concepts'.[67]

And here, beside that formal statement of equinumeracy, is a passage from Marx's famous presentation of exchange-value in the first chapter of Volume I of *Capital*:

> Let us take two commodities, such as a coat and 10 yards of linen, and let the value of the first be twice the value of the second, so that, if 10 yards of linen = W, the coat = 2W. ... *Just as, in viewing the coat and the linen as values, we abstract from their different use-values, so, in the case of the labour represented by those values, do we disregard the difference between its useful forms, tailoring and weaving* [etc ....][68]

The essence of Badiou's critique is that while Frege's idealism claims to conjure the self-same object – zero, that is – through the pure powers of logic, for

---

67   Badiou 2008, p. 17.
68   Marx 1976, p. 132, emphasis added. The formal resemblance of these two texts grows even greater if we then consider Badiou's schematic reduction of Frege's idealist derivation of number in *Number and Numbers*: 'Concept→ Truth→ Objects that fall under the concept (that satisfy the statement attributing the concept to the object) → Extension of the concept (all truth-cases of the concept) → Equinumeracy of two concepts (via biunivocal correspondence of their extensions) → Concepts that fall under the concept of equinumeracy to a given concept C (that satisfy the statement 'is equinumerate to C') → The extension of equinumeracy-to-C (the set of concepts from the preceding stage) → The number that belongs to concept C (number is thus the name for the extension of equinumeracy-to-C)'. Badiou 2008, p. 18.

Marx and Badiou both, the thought-object can only be the production of an entirely secondary operation. Marx calls this process in the 1857 Introduction the *reproduction* of the concrete as materialist thought-concrete, while Badiou names this secondary derivation, more generally, the operation of the count-as-one.[69]

5   A Materialist Axiomatic

In what sense then can we say that Marx's beginning to *Capital* ('The wealth of societies in which the capitalist mode of production prevails appears as an "an immense collection of commodities"') constitutes a *materialist axiomatic*? It is axiomatic, to begin with, in the minimal sense Lalande gives the term, as 'a premise considered evident, and taken as true without demonstration by all those who understand its meaning'.[70] Marx chooses as his starting point just such a 'premise considered as evident'; he proposes a minimal, true idea, that all its subjects, he wagers, already possess of the nature of capitalism: that it appears as the general commodification of things.

Throughout this book, however, I have argued that the first sentence of *Capital* furthermore functions in a stronger, logically determinant sense, firstly that of an axiom as Lalande further defines the concept as 'every proposition, in a hypothetico-deductive system ... that is not deduced from another, but which is posed by a *decisionary* [*décisoire*] act of thought, at the beginning of a deduction'.[71] This emphasis on the decisionistic aspect is precisely the sense in which Badiou qualifies axioms, 'which must', he argues, 'be affirmed, taken into account [*assumés*], explicit, and which, as such, introduce into every rational

---

69   One could, I think, follow through nearly every step of this presentation to translate and formalise Marx's discursive analysis of exchange-value into Badiou's more logically adequate form, in which each logical step of derivation is indicated, beginning with the famous initial postulation of the concept of commodities as given, as pre-existent materialist fact in the first sentence of *Capital*: 'The wealth of societies in which the capitalist mode of production prevails appears as "an immense collection of commodities"' (Marx 1976, p. 125). From this follows the proposition that there are, in fact, commodities that fall under that concept; this is followed by the extension of the concept of the commodity to name the set of all commodities; to assert in turn the equinumeracy of all such concepts in their consistent multiplicity, as differing quantities of use-values that relate to one another as equivalent exchange-values (1 coat = 2 yards of linen); next the set of concepts that is the consistent multiplicity of use-values that fall under the concept of equinumeracy, etc.
70   Lalande 2010, p. 105.
71   Lalande 2010, p. 105, emphasis added.

system an element of decision'.[72] Marx explicitly addresses the contingency of the starting point of his critique, for example in the *Grundrisse*, when he rejects the seemingly obvious option to begin the critique of political economy from the fact of ground rent.[73]

Yet this leaves in suspension a third aspect of the axiomatic starting point, the axiom as what Lalande calls 'a general rule of logical thought', which is to say, the manner in which the choice of this axiom prescribes and determines the nature of the exposition that follows from it. I have repeatedly emphasised, in the previous chapters, the way in which the starting point of *Capital* determines the course of the demonstration that follows from it: for example the necessity, in a society of general, as opposed to occasional, exchange, that that exchange be mediated by a general equivalent (monetary) form of value.[74]

While Marx's demonstration of the 'simple' form of value is logically coherent and non-contradictory in the case of two commodities (coats and linen in Marx's example), it is nonetheless 'insufficient' or inadequate to account for a society characterised by the general exchange of all things of value as commodities, as Marx has defined the capitalist social form in the first sentence of *Capital*, and it is this axiomatic insufficiency (rather than some internal contradiction) that compels his exposition in the first chapter of *Capital* to move from the simple to the general form of value.[75] Marx's axiomatic demonstration shows that *if* capitalism is a social form of general commodification, *then* it necessarily and by absolute implication requires a general, monetary form of value for that exchange.

Badiou's ontological materialism, in its refusal critically to investigate the parameters of an actual, given world (such as that of capitalism), suffers from

---

72   Badiou 2007, p. 40. Similarly, Macherey emphasises how Spinoza's definitions in their axiomatic contingency forgo 'all attempts at rhetorical persuasion, since these truths proposed for examination are to take or leave as such, addressed to [the reader's] completely free mind, free to pursue – or not – the path they open', (1998, p. 30).

73   'Nothing seems more natural than to begin with ground rent, with landed property, since this is bound up with the earth, the source of all production and of all being, and with the first form of production of all more or less settled societies – agriculture. But nothing would be more erroneous .... Capital is the all-dominating economic power of bourgeois society. It must form the starting-point as well as the finishing-point, and must be dealt with before landed property. After both have been examined in particular, their interrelation must be examined' (Marx 1973, pp. 106, 107).

74   Analogously, Macherey emphasises the determination Spinoza's initial starting point, the definition of *causa sui*, governs the entirety of his ensuing exposition: 'the concept [of *causa sui*] sustains from beginning to end Spinoza's entire philosophy, which one could present in a general manner as an effort to explain all things by their causes' (1998, p. 31).

75   Marx 1976, p. 154. See the previous chapter on this point.

a materialist deficit. While its axiomatic orientation determines the necessity governing its ensuing demonstration, the choice of a given starting point remains indeterminate, even arbitrary. It is, in other words, a mere *generic* materialism, applicable to any world whatsoever. In contrast, Marx's apodictic exposition in *Capital* derives its starting point from the capitalist real itself: 'I do not start out from "concepts"', Marx writes in his 'Notes on Adolph Wagner', 'hence I do not start out from "the concept of value", and do not have "to divide" these in any way. What I start out from is the simplest social form in which the labour-product is presented in contemporary society, and this is the "commodity". I analyse it, and right from the beginning, in the form in which it appears'.[76]

Marx's painstaking analytical enquiry into the nature of the capitalist social form extended from the 1850s to the end of his life, to constitute the materialist determination not only of his additive synthetic exposition, but of the axiomatic starting point that initiates and determines that demonstration.[77] This materialist determination is evident, for example, in Marx's crucial finding in the final paragraph of *Grundrisse*, when, nearly 900 pages into his analysis, Marx at last determines the proper starting point for his exposition. Not, for example, ground rent, a beginning point he explicitly rejects already in his 1857 Introduction (as noted above), but 'Value', the analysis of which, he adds in a note to himself immediately following this section title, should necessarily constitute his materialist starting point: it is the 'section to be brought forward' to the beginning of what will become *Capital*.[78]

In contrast to Badiou's generic materialism, Marx's science of causes in *Capital* begins from the materialist position he develops not from empirical reflection on the lived experience of capitalism, but from his critical analysis of the contradictions and insufficiencies of classical political economy and French socialism. Despite this comparative insufficiency of Badiou's ontological materialism, it is nonetheless possible and even fruitful, I wish to argue, to continue to read Badiou's abstract logic as the objective displacement (*Verschiebung*, in the Freudian terminology) of *Capital*, as a body of work that in its incessant commitment and faithfulness to the Marxian political project of communism, objectively reinscribes Marx's critique of political economy within terms that raise to a point of extreme abstraction and schematisation that same initial tendency to formalisation identifiable (as I argued in the previous chapter) in Marx's own revision process of his manuscript.

---

76   Marx 1996, p. 241.
77   Musto 2020. On Marx's materialist enquiry as a guarantee against Hegelian idealism, see Heinrich 2022, p. 170.
78   Marx 1973, p. 881.

CHAPTER 5

Capital, Logic of the World

Alain Badiou's oeuvre sits uneasily astride a bewildering paradox. Badiou repeatedly asserts that the single most imposing impediment to our subjective access to truths, to our finite, yet substantial and materialist participation in the infinite, is the tyrannical domination of global social relations and subjectivity by the economic rationality of capitalism. In *Number and Numbers*, he writes: 'Number governs the economy; and there, without a doubt, we find … the "determination in the last instance" of its supremacy'.[1] Similarly, in one of his most recent books, *Happiness*, he tells us that the good and real life, '*la vraie vie absente*' as Rimbaud writes in *Une saison en enfer*, is systematically reduced in the world of global capitalism to the specious freedom of consumerist choice: 'Freedom is coded or precoded in the infinite shimmer of commodity production and in what monetary abstraction institutes on that basis'.[2] In the face of this overdetermined and seemingly universal untruth, the name Badiou has steadfastly maintained to indicate the political dimension of the true life, is, of course, the 'Idea of Communism'.

And yet, for all that, one could assert with little exaggeration that Badiou's engagement with Marx's critique of political economy is a veritable empty set. Badiou's repeated, sustained, admiring and attentive engagement with this great thinker is, in other words, addressed almost univocally to the *political* Marx, the Marx of the *Communist Manifesto* and *The Civil War in France*. But if capitalism constitutes the dominant logic of our untrue world, and not merely a passing epiphenomenon, how can a reader hope to formalise the logic of the true life, life subtracted from the reign of commodity fetishism, without a systematic, formal construction of the categories and logic of the world of capitalism?

Like Adorno's superficial comments in *Negative Dialectics* on capitalism as universal fungibility, Badiou's explicit pronouncements on capitalism are not false, but remain manifestly inadequate to the real complexity of their object, betraying only the vaguest sense of the complexity of the logic governing the valorisation of value, the many laws of the tendencies determining production, circulation, exchange, and accumulation that Marx painstakingly develops. We

---

1 Badiou 2008, p. 3.
2 Badiou 2019, p. 43.

know as much as Badiou tells us about the logic of capitalism from even the first sentence of *Capital* volume one: that the form of appearance of social relations in which the capitalist form of production predominates is that of universal commodification and exchange.³

This disinterest is of course odd coming from Badiou, who devotes meticulous care precisely to the formalisation of his primary objects of inquiry in systematic, philosophical and mathematical-logical terms. But while this is the case, for example in *Logics of Worlds*, it is nonetheless striking that the worlds in question there, along with the events that break free from them remain either entirely generic, worlds as such, events as such, or else constitute decidedly minor, even 'baroque' subsets of what Marx called the general social forms (*gesellschaftliche Formen*) that govern social existence in any specific historical domain and period:

> a country landscape in autumn, Paul Dukas's opera *Ariadne and Bluebeard*, a mass demonstration at Place de la République, Hubert Robert's painting *The Bathing Pool*, the history of Quebec, the structure of a galaxy ... Rousseau's novel *The New Heloise* ... Sartre's theatre, Julien Gracq's novel *The Opposing Shore* and the architectural form of Brasilia [or] a poem of Valéry.⁴

To take two other examples of events named in *Logics of Worlds*, it is certainly the case that Toussaint Louverture and Schoenberg name world-historical events in the political and musical domains respectively. But in both these cases, there is no substantial demonstration of the structures either from which these events break free nor the worlds into which they subsequently open. Only the briefest presentation of the Haitian Revolution, and nothing of the essence of slavery and capitalism in the Caribbean, arguably the logics governing these two worlds, before and after Toussaint Louverture. Similarly, in Badiou's 'Scholium' to Book I of *Logics*, one finds no substantial demonstration of the logic of traditional western harmony and the various points and sites where Schoenberg ruptures this logic to implement two entirely novel operational procedures, free atonalism and dodecaphonic composition.

Now, no one can know or say everything, and it may be fine to leave the details to others, given the suggestive nature of Badiou's propositions. But my point is rather that while *Logics of Worlds* casts its remit explicitly as the apodic-

---

3 Marx 1976, p. 125.
4 Badiou 2009, p. 96.

tic exposition of the 'logic of appearance' (*la logique de l'apparaître*) governing any world (and thus the plural of its title), none of the examples in *Logics of Worlds* in fact addresses the general logic and laws governing the forms of appearance of any specific object in *capitalism*. Perhaps Badiou simply is not interested in developing in his own terms the structural categories and logic of capital that Marx initiated. Indeed, Badiou often appears more interested in the novelty of events than the mundane regularity of the dominant logic of the world: 'Philosophy is asked to be capable of welcoming or thinking the event itself, not so much the structure of the world, the principle of its laws or the principle of its closure, but how the event, surprise, requisition, and precariousness can be thinkable in a still-rational configuration'.[5]

I wish to argue in this final chapter that Badiou has, in the three monumental volumes of *Being and Event*, in fact produced the materials for precisely such a logic, but in the form of an arsenal of concepts that remain to be precisely measured against Marx's critical and formal reproduction of capitalism, confronted with what Marx called his *Gedankenkonkretum*, a materialist, scientific 'thought-concrete', the systematic exposition of which consumes the three volumes of *Capital*. In what follows, I will proceed in two moments, the first critical, the second comparative. While Badiou's disinterest in the logic of capitalism and Marx's *Capital* specifically constitutes a silence that traverses his entire oeuvre, this absence takes on a strongly symptomatic, spectral presence in the 1994–95 seminar recently translated to English as *Lacan: Anti-philosophy 3*.[6]

Secondly, while the previous chapter indicated certain general aspects in which Badiou's ontology reproduces the fundamental gestures of Marx's materialist critique, here I wish to push this claim further and more strongly: while it is true that *Logics of Worlds* never discusses the logic of appearance that governs all *capitalist* things (i.e., commodities), we should nonetheless read *Logics* in a quite specific sense as the (objective, likely unintentional) abstract displacement (*Verschiebung*) and formalisation of Marx's *Capital*. In this view, *Capital* should quite simply be read as the systematic demonstration of the logic of what Marx calls the *capitalist social form*, which is to say in Badiou's jargon, as the logic of the appearance of things in the *capitalist world*.

This will then entail two subsidiary claims: 1) that the notion of a materialist logic bears the same meaning for Marx and Badiou, and 2) that the domain Badiou calls a 'world' encompasses what Marx calls *social form*. In a sense,

---

5 Badiou 2019a, p. 63.
6 Badiou 2018a.

then, this means nothing more, though nothing less, than subjecting *Logics of Worlds* to a Marxian torsion: what Badiou has neglected, Marx has in fact already accomplished (with his own specific formal, conceptual, and discursive means): the systematic, synthetic demonstration of the necessary forms of appearance of commodities in the capitalist social form.

1   Badiou's Lacan, Badiou's (Marx)

While Badiou fully grasps the essential nature of formal demonstration for Lacan, his 1994–95 seminars circle around, and yet nonetheless betray a symptomatic repression or blindness regarding Marx's critique of political economy. In these lectures, Badiou explicitly names Marx alongside Lacan as occupying a very particular status in the pantheon of anti-philosophy, insofar as both Marx and Lacan mount a critique of philosophy and truth in the name of *science*, rather than Nietzsche's poetic utterances or Wittgenstein's language games. Despite this crucial insight, Badiou nonetheless remains symptomatically deaf in these lectures, as elsewhere, to Marx's scientific discourse – to *Capital*, that is to say.

This repression results in a highly problematic *suturing* in Badiou's discourse, a suturing of the ideological imaginary to a politics of the real. In suppressing any consideration of scientific discourse – whether of Marx's *Capital* or even Lacan's systematic demonstration in the 1950s of the structure of the unconscious, a demonstration that Badiou suggestively names a 'hyperstructural axiomatic'[7] – Badiou enacts a short-circuiting of analytical critique. The result of this suture as theoretical short-circuit is that politics in Badiou's *Lacan* seminar lacks any consequential formalisation of the categorial structure of capitalism understood as social form, as the *value-forms of abstract labour*, that is to say. In its absence, politics can take the form not of a true act, but only and ever the mere acting-out of ideological fantasy.

This becomes eminently clear in what is for me the key passage in the entire seminar. Here is Badiou's citation from Lacan's *Radiophonie*:

> What Marxism has shown by its actual revolution: that there's no progress to be expected from truth, nor any well-being, but only the shift from imaginary impotence to the impossible, which proves to be the real by

---

7   Badiou 2018a, p. 203.

being grounded only in logic: in other words, where I claim the unconscious is located, but not so as to say that the logic of this shift shouldn't hasten the act.[8]

Badiou's commentary of this passage is revealing, both in what it says and does not say:

> In short, in Lacan's view, Marx showed that, instead of philosophical fantasies about the good state or the good society, it was the logic of Capital that had to be identified at the point of the real. Marx's actual revolution is a liquidation of philosophy. *Should we say that Marx substituted a science or knowledge for the philosophical imaginary? No, says Lacan, because we must maintain that the 'logic of this shift' must 'hasten the act'.*[9]

The first point to note in Lacan's original statement is his indication of Marx's refusal of 'truth' and 'well-being'. This formulation reiterates Lacan's post-May '68 rejection of traditional, Leninist Marxism, as both a moralism of the proletariat as the universal class, and Bolshevism as a mere programmatic redistributionism of wealth. It is Lacan's rejection of the Leninist misreading of Marx's critique, the reduction of the critique of political economy to an ideological moralism of the working class in the form of a politicised redistribution of the wealth of production, in short, Left Ricardianism.[10] Leninist Left Ricardianism ignores Marx's systematic demonstration of the laws of the tendencies of capitalism as a structure and social form, while the mere superficial forms of appearance of modes of market exchange become the target of political redistributionism.

---

8   Jacques Lacan, 'Radiophonie', cited in Badiou 2018a, p. 155. Note the tortuous, ambivalent grammar and tense structure of Lacan's original phrasing: 'Ce que le marxisme a démontré par sa révolution effective: qu'il n'y a nul progrès à attendre de la vérité ni de bien-être, mais seulement le virage de l'impuissance imaginaire à l'impossible qui s'avère d'être le réel à ne se fonder qu'en logique: soit là où j'avertis que l'inconscient siège, mais pas pour dire que la logique de ce virage n'ait pas à se hâter de l'acte' (Lacan, cited in Badiou 2013b, p. 155).
9   Badiou 2018a, p. 132, my emphasis.
10 This programme is encapsulated by the famous Leninist slogan 'Communism is Soviet power plus the electrification of the whole country', the redistribution, that is to say, of the wealth of production under the directives of the dictatorship of the proletariat, while leaving untouched, and even expanding as a general productivist imperative, the general social form that to this day demands the endless valorisation of value.

It is clear from his many disparaging comments on the proletariat and proletarian politics after May '68, a number of which Badiou cites in the course of the seminar, that Lacan discounted all mythification of the proletariat as ideological, as what he calls here the 'impotent imaginary'. Virtually no attention, including Badiou's presentation, however, has been devoted to a number of brief but incisive comments Lacan makes on the formal logical structure of Marx's analysis in *Capital* in the seminars from the 1950s, precisely the period when Lacan was elaborating his own systematic formalisation of the symbolic structure of the unconscious. That said, Badiou rightly reads Lacan as here, in the wake of May '68, affirming in place of all utopian 'philosophical reveries on the good state and good society' the systematic analysis of the structure of capitalism. The point though is that this work, both Lacan reading *Capital* and Lacan articulating his own structural demonstration of the nature of the unconscious, had occurred long before, in the 1950s seminars, a period of his thought Badiou studiously ignores in these seminars.

In this passage, Badiou reads in Lacan's assertion a rejection of philosophy ('no clamor of being or nothingness'), revealingly identifying Marx as an anti-philosopher of the same stripe as Lacan himself. In this vein, in order to analyse Lacan's assertion that philosophy merely plugs the hole of politics, Badiou had reminded his listeners of Marx's famous taking leave of philosophy in the eleventh thesis on Feuerbach: 'Philosophers have only interpreted the world; the point is to change it'. While this disparagement of philosophy and truth casts both Lacan and Marx as anti-philosophers, they are, as Badiou points out regarding Lacan, different from all others in that for both, the rejection of philosophies of truth is enacted in the name of the rigour of scientific, apodictic demonstration; for Lacan, the demonstration of the structure of the unconscious, for Marx, the demonstration of the structure of capitalism.[11]

---

11   In articulating his critique of Freudian Ego-psychology, Lacan had striven to give a materialist turn to the notion of the symbolic, one that draws it into more direct proximity to Marx's Spinozist, materialist dialectic. In his 1954 Seminar II, Lacan displaced the process of signification from the intentionality of a subject, to argue instead that the figures of machine language (cybernetics) offered a perfect illustration of the function of the Symbolic. Lacan there reduces meaning (*le sens*) to the logical assemblage and concatenation of signs, the purely formal relation of logical marks, such that Lacan can assert that 'the symbolic world is the world of the machine' (Lacan 1991, p. 47). The symbolic, as Lacan formulated it at this point, is understood to constitute an asubjective system of codes that are supported, in Lacan's example, by the materiality of computing (rather than the intentionality of an ego). In this view, the Lacanian symbolic would constitute the asubjective system of meaning into which we are thrown, to be interpellated as subjects of Capital.

Badiou cites Lacan in a further development of what I would call Lacan's scientific anti-philosophy: 'Thus the real differs from reality. This is not to say that it's unknowable, but that there's no question of knowing about it, only of demonstrating it'.[12] Here, and although his name is never mentioned in the whole of Badiou's seminar, we are resolutely on the terrain of Spinoza. Not the Nietzschean misreading of Spinoza as an invocation of the mere affect of beatitude as a joyful wisdom or Gay Science, but the precise categories of adequate knowledge that Spinoza terms the general and the intuitive (the imaginary remaining a necessary, but wholly inadequate form of knowledge, as we first learn in the famous Appendix to Book I and more fully in Book II of the *Ethics*). If Lacan is an anti-philosopher, Spinoza nonetheless remained the crucial formative philosophical reference for Lacan, prior to Hegel and Kojève, most explicitly in the 1932 dissertation, where the entire presentation is framed by citations and analyses of key propositions from the *Ethics*.[13] No less is Spinoza the crucial reference, as I have argued throughout this book, to grasp Marx's epistemology of the substantial unity of the real and the synthetic production of analytic thought, as Althusser and Macherey famously argued in their analysis of the 1857 Introduction in *Reading Capital*.

It was Spinoza whose demonstrations already put Hegelian negative dialectics in its proper place: things (such as the unconscious or capital) adequately grasped in their singular essences, know no contradiction or negation. Here is Badiou:

> The real is the remainder of the disjunction between the knowable and the unknowable. Here we take the measure of the anti-dialectical dimension of every anti-philosophy: the point of access to the real cannot be reached negatively. As compared with knowable reality, no negation procedure provides any access to the real.[14]

Contradiction adequately understood is a figure of experience, of the forms of appearance of things. While this has been well-understood of the unconscious since Freud's *Traumdeutung*, in Marx's case, I have argued (in Chapter 3 above) that we witness across the development of his critique in the wake of the dialectical Hegelianism of the *Grundrisse* a series of theoretical revolutions

---

12   Lacan, 'Radiophonie', cited in Badiou 2018a, p. 151. 'Ainsi le réel se distingue de la réalité. Ce, pas pour dire qu'il soit inconnaissable, mais qu'il n'y a pas question de s'y connaître, mais de le démontrer' (Lacan, cited in Badiou 2013b, p. 178).
13   Roudinesco 1997, pp. 52–4.
14   Badiou 2018a, p. 152.

in the notes and manuscripts of the 1860s and 70s: there, what Jacques Bidet has called various Hegelian theoretical impediments (the identity and nonidentity of production and consumption, for example, or the merely apparent contradiction between the exchange of equivalents and the realisation of surplus value) are removed and in their place Marx develops, or tends increasingly to develop in his unfinished masterpiece, the full relational complexity of the laws of the tendencies and counter-tendencies as they determine the increase in the organic composition of capital: not the mere falsity, but the absolute necessity governing the phenomenal, fetishistic forms of appearance of capital (profit, rent, finance, for example).

Adequate knowledge, knowledge of both the general laws governing the unconscious as well as the essence of any singular case, governs Lacan's understanding of analysis. While in the *Écrits* and seminars Lacan develops a systematic exposition of the structure of the unconscious, it is no accident that we are left, as Badiou laments toward the end of his seminar, without a theory of the act. For the analytic act occurs on the register of Spinoza's third, intuitive mode of knowledge, as the knowledge of the singular essence of any given case. We cannot know what to do in the case of a given, real analysis, no matter how adequate our knowledge of the laws governing the structure of the unconscious may be. We can only approach the real of a given subject via an adequate understanding of the singular essence of that case, a process that indeed requires, along with the scientific mastery of general laws, an improvisational genius attendant to Spinoza's third genre of knowledge.[15]

Badiou's commentary is revealing: 'Although the real, as distinct from reality, is exempted from the knowable, which is the essence of reality, the real nevertheless does not end up being the absolute unknowable but is instead exposed to being demonstrated'.[16] 'Demonstration' is arguably the key epistemological concept in the French tradition from Cavaillès and Koyré to Althusser and Badiou himself. Beyond the knowable and the unknowable, lies not the will

---

15   In the third section of 'L'Unique tradition matérialiste', Althusser – in the course of a broad reflection on the centrality of Spinoza to his thinking – turns to Spinoza's invention of an adequate materialist ('nominalist') knowledge, a knowledge Althusser argues encompasses Spinoza's discovery of 'generic constants or invariants ... which arise in the existence of singular "cases"'. Such constants are to be distinguished from the universal generality of 'laws', (which would fall under Spinoza's second genre of knowledge); equally, it is their genericity as constants of any singular case that allows for what Althusser revealingly calls in clinical terms their 'treatment', as distinct from any empirical or experimental verification. See Althusser 1997, pp. 3–20.

16   Badiou 2018a, p. 151.

to power, or language games, but the adequate, asubjective, apodictic demonstration of the essential necessity governing an object of knowledge such as the unconscious.

All this is, I think, a fully adequate reading of these two typically enigmatic Lacanian pronouncements that Badiou cites. The problem, however, arises in Badiou's final gesture: 'Should we say', Badiou concludes, 'that Marx substituted a science or knowledge for the philosophical imaginary? No, says Lacan, because we must maintain that the "logic of this shift" must "hasten the act".[17] Where in the original text Lacan loads his typically baroque pronouncement with ambiguous negatives and subjunctive conditionals ('Be there where I announce that the unconscious reigns, but not to say that the logic of this turn may not hasten to the act') Badiou declares an unambiguous imperative to proceed directly to the political act itself. This '*devoir*' ('we *must* [*on doit*] maintain that the logic of this shift *must* [*doit*] hasten the act'), this obligation Badiou imposes on Lacan's ambiguity betrays a problematic disinterest – in fact an extraordinary indifference given the systematic, logicist nature of Badiou's philosophy – in scientific knowledge of the object. It is at this point that Badiou's interpretation becomes not merely problematic, but wholly symptomatic, symptomatic of a general oblivion and lack of engagement not only with Lacan's scientific discourse on the structure of the unconscious from the 1950s, but above all with Marx's *Capital* specifically.

Surprisingly, it is Badiou himself who unintentionally makes precisely this point – presented here as a symptom of traditional Marxism's lack of engagement with Marx's categorial demonstration – when he summarises Lacan's critique of the political Marx in the following terms: 'Politics is glued to meaning, and, insofar as it's glued to meaning, it makes an imaginary, or if you will, religious, hole in the real of Capital'.[18]

In the absence of any substantial engagement with Marx's scientific demonstration on Badiou's part and the rush to pronounce the imperative of the political act, Marx remains a mere (hysterical) political activist, and revolutionary desire remains 'stuck' to mere ideological meaning, overdetermined by the empty, even 'religious' hope of moving beyond capitalism to something called communism.

> Strictly speaking, there is no discourse of politics. And it's because there isn't any that, in fact, politics always makes a hole in the discourses. And

---

17   Badiou 2018a, p. 132.
18   Badiou 2018a, p. 110.

more precisely in what, in these discourses, is based on imaginary consistency, or, in other words, is based on semblance.[19]

The complexity of social form, of capitalism as the social logic of compulsory valorisation, is reduced to mere imaginary ideological semblance, both in traditional Marxism (as Lacan and Badiou both note), as well as in Badiou's own suturing of politics to the Idea of Communism.

In the face of the immense theoretical complexity and simultaneous abstraction of Badiou's logic of worlds and events, how is one to know where the weak points and sites lie in the capitalist system, what constitutes its weakest links and limits? How to organise and articulate political militancy without an adequate understanding of the social form that is its object? The result of such reflexive politics invites the very conclusion Lacan never tired of bestowing on the pseudo-events of May '68 as the mere acting out of imaginary desires sutured immediately to the inflammatory act and the messianic hope that the system would magically crumble: 'Sous les pavés, la plage'.

This brings us directly and imperatively to the limits of any formalisation of the world of capital, to the very problem Badiou terms the *'recherche du réel perdu'*, the search for the capitalist real. There is, in other words, a capitalist Real, in the strong, Lacanian sense of the term. In *À la recherche du réel perdu*, Badiou draws on Lacan to argue that the capitalist 'real' is no mere empirical, ready-at-hand substance or experience of the everyday; instead, the capitalist real consists of the very impasse or impossible limit of capital understood as a process of formalisation.[20] I would argue, though, that a more appropriate proper name for this real is not equality, as Badiou suggests. Equality is certainly a necessary subcategory of the capitalist real – for example in capitalism's dependence upon abstract labour as the substance of value. The essential conclusion of *Reading Capital* still holds: we do not yet truly live as more than the subjects (*Träger*) of what Marx named the 'automatic subject': subjects of the general social structure of compulsion that he formalised as the system of *Capital*. To live, then, beyond mere fleeting intimations of life in evental moments such as 1789 and 1804, the Paris Commune and May '68, requires the deployment of a politics adequate to the demands of such events as a general possibility, the transformation of the transcendental categories of social structuration and subjectivity themselves, toward the construction of a post-

---

19   Badiou 2018a, p. 118, translation modified.
20   Badiou 2015.

capitalist transnationalism, one that surpasses the mortal crisis of valorisation that is the actuality of posthuman capitalism and its real and attendant threat of anthropocenic catastrophe.

Badiou eloquently describes such an orientation as our finite participation in the infinity of Number, real and true life, that is, beyond the tyranny of mere numericality:

> To think Number ... restores us, either through mathematics, which is the history of eternity, or through some faithful and restrained scrutiny of *what is happening*, to a supernumerary hazard from which a truth originates, always heterogeneous to Capital and therefore to the slavery of the numerical. It is a question, at once, of delivering Number from the tyranny of numbers, and of releasing some truths from it. ... It proceeds, effectively and theoretically, to the downfall of numbers, which are the law of the order of our situation.[21]

2   'Qu'en est-il de la logique?': Reading *Logics of Worlds* After *Capital*

Let me restate in the most deliberate terms the paradox that determines the limits of Badiou's philosophical and political critique: On the one hand, Badiou clearly and repeatedly states the obvious, that the overarching and predominant form of contemporary global social relations is, quite simply, capitalism. Most recently, for example, Badiou has repeated this in the form of an axiomatic truism: 'Allow me to begin ... from a perfectly banal conviction: the dominant socio-economic structure, which is today in place at a global scale, is capitalism. Everyone, or nearly so, agrees'.[22] Who could disagree? On the other hand, while I have argued above that the corresponding absence of any concrete *analysis* of the capitalist social form on Badiou's part occasionally, as in the Lacan seminars, reaches symptomatic proportions, the one moment where one would most expect such an engagement with 'the dominant socio-economic structure' that governs the contemporary world is precisely in Badiou's second magnum opus, *Logics of Worlds*. Instead, in the vast complexity of its 638 pages comprising seven books and dozens of chapters,

---

21   Badiou 2008, p. 214.
22   Badiou, 'Comment vivre et penser en un temps d'absolu désorientation?', talk given at La Commune Aubervilliers, 4 October 2021. Transcription available at http://www.entretemps.asso.fr/Badiou/21-22.html?fbclid=IwAR1oOVauXtOuGfACRHIjSXrDLmBzDgRf87rpEQxokTe__gzC-5PakoiHack, accessed 21 November 2021. My translation.

alongside the analyses of worlds from painting to poetry, mathematics to music, love and revolutions past and present, the word *capitalism* appears exactly once, in a banal and utterly indeterminate aside, when Badiou early on castigates the *nouveaux philosophes* of the 1970s for their ideological role in the unleashing of 'an unbridled capitalism'.[23]

Stated as such, this stunning absence from a book proposing to analyse with abundant examples the logic governing the forms of appearance of things in any world would amount to no more than a final *pièce de conviction* in an absurd and illegitimate condemnation of the author of some 200 books for not having talked about a topic of particular interest to this reader; were it not that *Logics of Worlds*, without ever explicitly mentioning capitalism, in fact provides the means precisely and adequately to understand the philosophical status of Marx's critique of the political economy of capitalism as a *materialist logic*. It is as if *Logics of Worlds* objectively takes up the long-forgotten conclusion of Althusser's 1947 thesis 'On Content in Thought of G.W.F. Hegel'. There, Althusser called for a reading of *Capital* as transcendental analytic of the capitalist social form, a reading that it would be left to Badiou to take up six decades later: 'The *transcendental* which conditions the a priori activity (theoretical or practical) of man', Althusser writes in his conclusion, 'has, now, conquered its nature: it is the concrete historical totality. ... In the fundamental structure of the human totality, Marx gives us the table of human categories that govern our time. *Capital* is our transcendental analytic'.[24]

Here again, Badiou seems to *displace* Althusser's explicit, 1947 invocation of Marx's *Capital* as transcendental analytic into a theoretically generic domain of representation, as if *Logics of Worlds* conducted its dreamwork upon the conclusion of Althusser's 'On Content in Thought of G.W.F. Hegel'. To reread *Capital* after *Logics of Worlds*, to analyse the latter as the abstraction of the former, is to read Marx's three volumes as a *logic* of capital, to account for its status as an utterly contemporary presentation of a materialist logic of the dominant structure of the world.

In this vein, Badiou recasts and precisely delimits logic, after Aristotle, Kant, and Hegel, after the linguistic turn of analytic philosophy, as what he calls the 'science of the forms of appearance' (*la science de l'apparaître*) of objects in any world. In the case of capitalism, following Marx, this will mean quite simply to grasp the precise ontological status of the critique of political economy, understood as the science of the necessary forms of appearance of value in the capitalist social form, as, in other words, Marx's *monetary labour theory of value*.

---

23   Badiou 2009, p. 55.
24   Althusser 2014, p. 169.

'*Qu'en est-il de la logique?*', 'What then of logic?' Badiou asks in his theoretical prolegomenon to *Logics of Worlds*, the 1998 *Court traité d'ontologie transitoire*.[25] To answer this question will require that Badiou reconceive the ontological status of logic – this is the project of the *Short Treatise* – which will then allow him to deploy this new, *categorial* logic of the forms of appearance of things in any given world in *Logics of Worlds*. Badiou is forced to turn to the problematic status of logic in the wake of *Being and Event* because, he argues, that book left unaddressed a crucial aspect of any ontology: the being-there, existence, and forms of appearance of beings that manifest themselves in any determinate situation:

> My goal [in *Logics of Worlds*] is to define what existence is ... and to introduce the fundamental philosophical difference between being [the subject of *Being and Event*] and existence ... *Logics of Worlds* is the logic of existence. It establishes the possibility of the logic of existence; that is, the possibility of different forms of singularity, of different forms of relationship between a multiplicity and a world in which this multiplicity is localised.[26]

To 'establish the possibility of the logic of existence', Badiou first steps back in the *Short Treatise* to condense the problem of logic in the form of an axiomatic decision between 'Plato or Aristotle'.[27] Either logic remains integrally linked to the Idea of mathematical truths, as it does for Plato, he argues, or, in the case of Aristotle, 'thought is the [mere] construction of an adequate descriptive framework', the weaving together, in the form of demonstrations that construct a 'purely ideal' set of admissible consecutions, an aesthetic 'art of calculation'.[28] In Badiou's reading, Aristotle's logic remains ontologically determined ('For Aristotle, ontology prescribes logic') in a manner analogous to that of Frege, whom (as discussed in the previous chapter) Badiou had criticised in the crucial Meditation 3 of *Being and Event*.

Badiou's initial presentation would seem to relegate Aristotelean logic to the dustbin of the history of philosophy, but in fact, surprisingly (and crucially in the case of Marx, for whom Aristotle, not Plato, stands as 'the greatest thinker of Antiquity'[29]), this refoundation of logic as a categorial science of appear-

---

25   Translated as Badiou 2006, p. 153, translation modified.
26   Badiou 2019, pp. 103, 105.
27   Badiou 2006, p. 105.
28   Badiou 2006, p. 102, translation modified.
29   Marx 1976, p. 532.

ances will ultimately refashion Aristotle for a contemporary logic of worlds. To do so, Badiou must address the immediate object of his critique, the linguistic turn of logic since Bolzano and Frege. Badiou formulates this critique as a second contrast, one that forces an axiomatic philosophical orientation: logic will either be understood as the syntax of a linguistic semantics or, as Badiou will propose, as a *categorial* logic, in which among plural 'universes' (a term he will subsequently replace with 'worlds' in *Logics*) each necessarily bears its own singular logic as an immanent, 'internal dimension'.[30]

Key to this categorial reconceptualisation of logic is the notion of the plurality of worlds and their attendant logics (as the title *Logics of Worlds* will forcefully proclaim). Given that, as Russell's Paradox first determined, there exists no set of all sets, no totality of worlds (what Badiou will call in *Logics* the 'universe' of worlds), there can correspondingly exist no single logic that would govern the existence of all beings. Instead, logics in their plurality must be conceived of as necessarily *local*:

> It is an essential property of the existent qua existent [*de l'étant en tant qu'étant*] that there can exist no totality of beings, in so far as they are thought uniquely from their beingness (*étantité*). A crucial consequence of this property is that every ontological investigation is irremediably *local*. In fact, there can exist no demonstration or intuition bearing upon Being as the totality of beings, or even as the general site in which beings are disposed.[31]

This plurality of logics that Badiou will formalise in *Logics of Worlds* is not only a necessary characteristic of any adequate materialist logic since Cantor, but, I would add, indicates the relevance of a *categorial* logic to Marx's *critique* of political economy. Any world and its attendant logic of the existence of beings must, Badiou argues, necessarily be local and contingent; there exists, Marx argues analogously, no overarching ontology or anthropology of production, labour, or commodities and their value as such, understood transhistorically; each of these and other categories of political economy always necessarily exist within a historically and conceptually distinct 'social form' (*gesellschaftlich Form*) (feudalism, capitalism, communism, etc.).[32]

---

30   Badiou 2006, p. 113.
31   Badiou 2006, p. 161, translation modified.
32   This is among the key points Moishe Postone first developed in his influential critique of traditional, Left Ricardian Marxism, to substitute instead a reading of Marx as what he calls a 'categorial' critique: 'I use "categorial" to refer to Marx's attempt to grasp the forms

The principal consequence of Badiou's categorial reformulation of logic as a plurality of situated logics is therefore that to the description of any given world there correlates a specific structure of logic: 'The descriptive characterisation of a thinkable ontological state induces certain logical properties, which are themselves presented in the space of Being, or the universe, that thought describes'.[33] This categorial reformulation allows Badiou to escape the formalist dead-end of the linguistic turn of modern logic[34] and to construct a novel 'contemporary theory of logic'. When logic is no longer understood as a normative syntax, but instead as an 'immanent characteristic' of possible worlds, it escapes its reduction to the status of a formal science of adequate discourse, to regain instead the ontological dimension it had born from Aristotle to Hegel, but now relegated to its limited and proper domain, as the science of possible worlds according to the 'cohesion' or necessary forms of appearance therein.

The final consequence of this reformulation is thus that the remit of logic becomes necessarily limited to the ontological domain of existence, with logic understood specifically as the science of the necessary *forms of appearance* of any existing object in a given world.[35] Since a necessary aspect of Being is that it must take on forms of appearance,[36] and since in this view 'the essence of appearance is relation', categorial logic can thus demonstrate how any given

---

of modern social life by means of the categories of his mature critique. ... A categorial reinterpretation, therefore, must focus on Marx's distinction between value and material wealth; it must show that value is not essentially a market category in his analysis, and that the "law of value" is not simply one of general economic equilibrium'. Postone 1993, pp. 17, 123.

33 Badiou 2006, p. 113, translation modified.
34 'For a long time I had believed this superseding of Platonism involved a destitution of formal logic as the royal path by which we have access to rational languages. Accordingly, and so deeply French in this respect, I rallied to the suspicion that, in the minds of Poincaré and Brunschvicg, was cast upon what they called "logistics"'. Badiou 2006, pp. 159–60.
35 Badiou defines appearance as follows: 'what links a being to the constraint of a local or situated exposure of its manifold-being we will call the "appearing" of this being [*l'apparaître de cet étant*]'. Badiou 2006, p. 162, translation modified.
36 Badiou restates this Hegelian point categorically and without demonstration, but, against both Kant and Hegel, in the form of an asubjective phenomenology: 'It is the being of the existent to appear [*Il est de l'être de l'étant d'apparaître*], insofar as the totality of Being does not exist. ... Appearing in no way depends on space or time, or more generally on any transcendental field whatsoever. It does not depend on a subject whose constitution would be presupposed. The manifold of beings [*L'étant-multiple*] does not appear for a subject. Instead, it is rather the essence of a being to appear as soon as, unlocalizable within the whole, it must assert the value of its being-multiple [*fasse valoir son être-multiple*] from the point of view of a non-whole'. Ibid., translation modified.

world can both be pure, inconsistent multiplicity (as *Being and Event* had described), as well as intrinsically determined as the existence of beings and their attendant and necessary forms of appearance. This affirmation of the strict equivalence of logic and appearance then becomes a shibboleth in *Logics of Worlds* ('"Logic" and "appearance" are one and the same thing') such that for Badiou the compass of any given logic, as it governs the existence of things in any singular world as such (rather than a particular world or social form such as capitalism), remains strictly limited to the laws that determine the 'cohesion of appearing'.[37]

3   Logics of (Capitalist) Worlds

Following his refoundation of contemporary logic as the science of appearing ('science de l'apparaître') in the *Short Treatise*, *Logics of Worlds* sets itself the consequent task of grasping 'the requirements of a contemporary materialism' in the form of a systematic 'materialist logic'.[38] To do so, Badiou sets forth in the crucial second book of *Logics* what he calls a 'Greater Logic' (*Grande logique*), which he defines as 'a materialist theory of the coherence of what appears'.[39] This Greater Logic takes the form of an exposition and demonstration of the concepts required for the apprehension of the existence, or 'being-there' (*être-là*) (Badiou uses the terms interchangeably) of any multiplicity whatsoever. If *Being and Event* had articulated Badiou's understanding of ontology as such, *Logics* turns to the subordinate problem of the 'worldly' existence of any being, apprehended not as pure multiplicity, but according to the laws governing its appearance or 'localisation' in the form of a general theory of objects and relations:

> The mathematical theory of the pure multiple doubtless exhausts the question of the being of a being, except for the fact that its appearing – logically localised by its relations to other beings – is not ontologically

---

37   Badiou 2009, pp. 100–1. 'We are speaking here of any appearing whatsoever in any world whatsoever. In other words, our operational phenomenology identifies the condition of possibility for the worldliness of a world, or the logic of the localisation for the being-there of any being whatever'. Badiou 2009, p. 102.

38   Badiou 2009, p. 95.

39   Badiou 2009, p. 94. This 'Greater Logic' Badiou distinguishes from 'ordinary logic, [i.e.] the formal calculation of propositions and predicates' which he considers a mere subset of Greater Logic as such. Badiou 2009, p. 173.

deducible. We therefore need a special logical machinery to account for the intra-worldly cohesion of appearing.[40]

It is thus the task of *Logics*' Greater Logic to set forth this 'logical machinery' in the form of a novel series of concepts or 'logical operators', the functions that provide any world with its singular coherent forms of appearance, the most important of which for this task is what Badiou names, after Kant, the 'transcendental'.[41]

Reasserting in the wake of Russell's paradox the inexistence of totality as a necessary and governing condition of any contemporary materialist logic, *Logics* analyses both worlds and their attendant logics in their plurality.[42] One of the few significant differences between the refoundation of logic in the *Short Treatise* and its systematic exposition in *Logics* is a terminological one. Where the *Short Treatise* spoke ambiguously of multiple 'universes', in *Logics* Badiou reserves this term to indicate not a world but only the inexistence of the Whole figured as an empty set or void (*le vide*).[43] In its place, he substitutes the more precise term of 'world', and crucially indicates by this not a material, extensive space to be filled with beings, but instead only the governing *logic* of that world.[44] This is to formalise the concept of world in the order of thought, to grasp the real structuration that allows for the manifestation of objects as they appear in sensuous lived experience.

---

40 Badiou 2009, pp. 121–2.
41 In explicit contrast to the Kantian transcendental subject, Badiou's materialist logic is radically pre-subjective, and necessarily so, since Badiou's conception of the subject – which Book I of *Logics* further articulates in the wake of the formal simplicity of the concept in *Being and Event* – appears in subtraction from the governing logic of any world as the bearer, faithful or otherwise, of an Event: 'The transcendental that is at stake in this book is altogether anterior to every subjective constitution, for it is an immanent given of any situation whatever. ... It is what imposes upon every situated multiplicity the constraint of a logic, which is also the law of its appearing, or the rule in accordance with which the 'there' of being-there allows the multiple to come forth as essentially bound'. Badiou 2009, p. 101.
42 Russell's 1902 Paradox, Badiou summarises, 'means that it is not true that to a well-defined concept there necessarily corresponds the set of the objects which fall under this concept. This acts as a (real) obstacle to the sovereignty of language: to a well-defined predicate, which consists within language, there may only correspond a real inconsistency (a deficit of multiple-being)'. Badiou 2009, p. 153.
43 'We will call universe the (empty) concept of a being of the Whole'. Badiou 2009, p. 102.
44 'A world is not an empty place – akin to Newton's space – which multiple beings would come to inhabit. For a world is nothing but a logic of being-there, and it is identified with the singularity of this logic'. Ibid.

It is the concept of the transcendental that then enables Badiou to pass, logically, from the inconsistency of any set in its abstract, 'neutral' multiplicity, to account for the existential consistency of any object in a given world. Badiou develops this process in four steps, steps that correspond, in the abstract, to Marx's initial and familiar demonstration of the basic categories of the commodity form in the first three chapters of *Capital*: use-value, exchange-value, value as such and its substance (abstract labour), along with the necessary form of appearance of any commodity, the price-form. These steps, given their high degree of abstraction in *Logics of Worlds*, can be rapidly summarised.

Badiou's demonstration sets off from the ontological standpoint of *Being and Event*, and its description of the abstract multiplicity of the elements of any set in its bare neutrality.[45] To this corresponds Marx's concept of the commodity's use-value: every commodity possesses, and must possess if it is to be sold, its singular identity. The set of all commodities in the capitalist social form consists of an infinite variety of things, each of which – at this general level of abstraction of use-values as such – exists in its singularity, unique unto itself, in its abstract nature as use-value devoid of any systematic relation to other commodities, each existing in sheer externality to all others within this set. 'The commodity is, first of all', Marx writes, 'an external object, a thing which through its qualities satisfies human needs of whatever kind'.[46] The set of commodities taken solely as use-values refers each use-value to its singular possession of any given quality whatsoever, the only requirement being the most abstract one, that a commodity in fact have some use-value of whatever kind (lest it be unsellable, and thus, in the capitalist social form, worthless). Were we to reproduce capitalism analytically in this fashion as a structured totality of the Symbolic, a Badiouian rearticulation of the opening sentence of *Capital* might thus read: 'The wealth of a society subject to the logic of the world of capitalism appears as a consistent multiplicity of commodities'. To posit being as the abstract multiplicity of the objects in any world entails for *Logics of Worlds* no more than a passing reference to *Being and Event* ('A multiple is only identical to itself, and it is a law of being-qua-being').[47] Marx similarly spends a mere three paragraphs analysing the use-value of commodities.

---

45 To initiate his Greater Logic, Badiou explicitly invokes this starting point: 'Previously, I identified [in *Being and Event*] situations (worlds) with their strict multiple-neutrality. I now [in *Logics of Worlds*] also envisage them as the site of the being-there of beings'. Badiou 2009, p. 99.
46 Marx 1976, p. 125.
47 Badiou 2009, p. 155.

Exchange-value, in turn, is the crucial category that in Marx's demonstration initially explains how commodities can enter into relation with one another: the commodity form *requires* that materially distinct commodities, commodities *differing* in their nature as use-values, possess *identical* exchange-values (in their relative amounts) in order to be exchangeable one for the other. Crucially, and even in Marx's initial, abstract examples of simple exchange logically prior to the price form ('a quarter of wheat for example, is exchanged for x boot-polish, y silk or z gold'), each exchange requires a definite, numerical quantity through which it relates to all others.[48] While it is only with the price form that this quantity will *appear and thus exist* as identical – if in the barter example 'x boot-polish, y silk or z gold', the variables x, y, and z all constitute different amounts, the dollar value of two exchangeable commodities must be identical – the key point to note here is simply the necessity of this numerical count.

Badiou analogously characterises a necessary quantification as the degree of difference between any two things that appear in a world. 'The logic of appearing', he writes, 'necessarily regulates degrees of difference, of a being with respect to itself and of the same with respect to others. These degrees bear witness to the marking of a multiple-being by its coming-into-situation in a world'.[49] Badiou argues that every object that exists in a world bears a certain degree of strength of its appearance in relation to all other existing things in that world. It is this relational logic of a world that 'regulates' the local manifestation of an object, 'affecting a being with a variable degree of identity (and consequently of difference) to the other beings of the same world'.[50] While Badiou argues that this logic of the transcendental holds for any world whatsoever, his examples often remain obscure (what do we learn from an analysis of the relative strengths of appearance of the objects – leaves, a wall, a shadow – in a painting?), in the case of capitalism, it is luminously clear that every commodity, to be exchangeable, must bear a numerary exchange-value

---

48   Heinrich analyses in detail the various levels of abstraction in Marx's presentation across the initial chapters of *Capital*, pointing out for example that in Chapter One (which I am discussing here), 'Marx is analysing a capitalistically produced commodity, which is normally exchanged for money, but he is doing so initially not only in abstraction from capital but also in abstraction from money [as well as from the human subjects that exchange commodities]. For that reason, Marx does not yet mention prices. The relation between the money price that we are familiar with in everyday life and exchange-value still has to be explained. ... The object of inquiry, the "commodity", is not simply drawn from experience. Instead, it is constructed, by means of abstraction'. Heinrich 2021, p. 53.
49   Badiou 2009, p. 118.
50   Badiou 2009, p. 119.

that precisely determines its 'strength of appearance' in the world of commodities and their exchange, in other words, its numerical price or exchange-value. 'There must exist values of identity which indicate, for a given world, to what extent a multiple-being is identical to itself or to some other being of the same world'.[51]

Marx asked for the first time why under capitalism labour must appear as what he called its 'value-form' (*Wertform*), manifest as the price of labour power (wage), and, furthermore, demonstrated how the formal equality of commodity exchange is nonetheless able to create surplus value. Money, in the form of exchange-value (manifest as the price form), in this view, is no mere convention, but the key relational intermediary that governs and regulates social interaction under capitalism, crucially enabling the socialisation of all private labour. Marx for the first time distinguished transhistorical, material-physiological processes of commodity production (concrete labour) from their specific social forms in a commodity-based society (as abstract labour, the 'substance' of value). In this fashion, he demonstrated why in a society governed by commodity exchange, labour must take the historically distinct form of a monetary exchange-value that Marx termed labour power. To count as a value in the capitalist social form, a concrete object or service must necessarily, by definition, have an exchange-value, a value that can and must be manifested in the form of a price. A commodity without a price is simply not a commodity, regardless of whether we treasure or despise it.

The price form of a commodity, Marx crucially shows in the first three sections of *Capital*, is no mere nominal contrivance or clever invention to facilitate exchange, but is essential and absolutely necessary to the nature of the commodity.[52] Since the capitalist social form is axiomatically defined, in Marx's view, by the predominance of commodities and commodity relations, a thing without an exchange-value simply cannot appear as a thing of value within that social form.[53] There is nothing mystical in Marx's mundane observation: that

---

51 Badiou 2009, p. 102.
52 See Murray 2017, p. 273. 'For classical labour theory', Murray writes, 'labour of whatever social sort was the source of value, and money was an afterthought, a "ceremonial form", as Ricardo called it; the answer to a merely technical problem'. Murray 2017, p. 278. Marx vehemently rejected and critiqued such monetary nominalism of Proudhon and his followers such as Darrimon in the first section of the *Grundrisse*.
53 'All other commodities relate to [the general equivalent] as their expression of value. It's only this act of "relating" within the world of commodities that makes a certain commodity into the general equivalent, thus endowing it with the ability to buy everything. Importantly, this "relating" is not at all accidental or arbitrary; it is necessary, for only by relating to a general equivalent can commodities relate to each other as values'. Heinrich 2021, p. 143.

commodities require a price form is simply another of the necessary consequences of Marx's initial premise in the first sentence of *Capital*.[54] A thing on the store-shelf without a price, for example, simply cannot be exchanged for money, it remains a tangible thing, perhaps even a privately useful thing, but, under capitalist social relations, it cannot take the *social* form of an exchangeable *commodity*.

Marx is not content to describe the dual nature of the commodity as use- and exchange-value; he asks, furthermore, what is it that a numerical exchange-value actually measures? What, in other words, constitutes the *substance of value* of a commodity? Marx's famous answer, *abstract labour*,[55] indicates a further point of congruence of Badiou's abstract logic of worlds with Marx's systematic demonstration of the singular logic of the capitalist social form, as what Badiou calls the scale (*échelle*) of evaluation of the strength of appearance of any object. An object's indexification to a transcendental, what Badiou calls its 'function of appearance', must, he argues, offer a numerical measure of something. What, in other words, does the degree of a transcendental measure? Badiou's answer is perfectly agnostic, given the abstract level of his analysis, and yet its relevance to Marx's analysis of the substance of value in the capitalist social form is uncanny:

> But what are the values of the function of appearing? What measures the degree of identity between two appearances of multiplicities? Here too there is no general or totalising answer. The scale of evaluation of appearing, and thus the logic of a world, depends on the singularity of that world itself. What we can say is that in every world such a scale exists, and it is this scale that we call the transcendental.[56]

---

54 'The busiest streets of London', Marx observed matter of factly in the 1859 'Contribution to the Critique of Political Economy', 'are crowded with shops whose show cases display all the riches of the world, Indian shawls, American revolvers, Chinese porcelain, Parisian corsets, furs from Russia and spices from the tropics, but all of these worldly things bear odious, white paper labels with Arabic numerals and then laconic symbols £ s. d. This is how commodities are presented in circulation'. Cited in Murray 2017, p. 471. See Heinrich 2021, pp. 92–143 for an extraordinarily meticulous, word-by-word analysis of Marx's demonstration of the logical and materialist necessity governing Marx's monetary labour theory of value.

55 'How, then, is the magnitude of this value to be measured? By means of the quantity of the "value-forming substance", the labour, contained in the article … The labour that forms the substance of value is equal human labour, the expenditure of identical human labour-power'. Marx 1976, p. 129.

56 Badiou 2009, p. 156.

Translating Badiou's jargon to Marx's analysis, we can say that the quantitative degree of strength of an object, what Marx calls a commodity's exchange-value, is the monetary form of appearance of the substance of value of that commodity, what Badiou terms the scale of values inhering in any world. In capitalism, this scale is simply the price or exchange-value of any commodity.

Capitalist society, Marx argues, is that specific historical epoch in which every thing and relation that counts as a value must bear a monetary price. 'In this form', Marx concludes, 'when they are all counted as comparable with the [general equivalent, money], all commodities appear not only as qualitatively equal, as values in general, but also as *values of quantitatively comparable magnitude*'. Any commodity, under the general, monetary form of value, can thus *relate* to any other through its *equation* with the universal equivalent: x (quantity) of (any given commodity) a = \$1. This, the general capitalist form of appearance of value, is quite simply the price form: in Marx's example, '20 yards of linen = 2 £'.[57]

Here we should note that Badiou furthermore argues, again analogously to Marx, that the existence of the things composing any world forms a *relational system*; no single thing (such as a commodity) can exist on its own. Rather, the logic of the necessary forms of appearance of things in a world necessitates a relational order: 'What is measured or evaluated by the transcendental organisation of a world is in fact the degree of intensity of the difference of appearance of two beings in this world, and not an intensity of appearance considered [ontologically] "in itself"'.[58] Badiou's transcendental logic of appearance of any world demands that each thing that appears in that world do so in relation to all other things; the intensity of appearance of one thing must be relational, 'measured by the intensity of appearance of one of them'.[59] This 'conjunction', Badiou states, is 'carried' by one of the two things in relation. The parallelism with Marx's analysis is here as well uncanny: in Marx's derivation of the necessity of the price form of appearance of any commodity in the capitalist social form, he famously begins by defining exchange-value as a necessarily relational determination.

While Badiou's abstract point can be briefly stated as such, Marx's more complex analysis of the relational nature of the commodity can be summarised in four crucial steps of his argument. In the famous opening sentence of *Capital*, Marx chooses to begin his demonstration with an axiomatic declaration of the nature of the capitalist social form: 'The wealth of societies in which

---

57 Marx 1976, pp. 159, 163, emphasis added.
58 Badiou 2009, p. 123.
59 Badiou 2009, p. 126.

the capitalist mode of production prevails appears as an 'immense collection of commodities'; the individual commodity appears as its elementary form. Our investigation therefore begins with the analysis of the commodity'.[60] Marx thus asks his reader to accept axiomatically, initially and without prior logical derivation, that in capitalism – the immediate form of appearance of which is the massive accumulation of commodities – the predominant form of *existence* as well as the *relations among existing things* are those laws that govern the exchange of commodities. This is to say that the capitalist social form is, minimally but essentially, distinguished from other social forms by the predominance of both commodities and commodified social relations. His analysis, his initial statement informs the reader, will take as its object this specific social form, and furthermore will investigate not specific individual commodities, as did classical economics, but the total mass of commodities, an undifferentiated, 'immense heap' (*ungeheure Warensammlung*), in relation to which Marx will analyse individual commodities as identical subdivisions or 'aliquot parts'.[61] Marx initiates in this manner not a semantics of capital nor a representation of the structure of capitalism, but instead undertakes a logical demonstration of the essential nature of the real (commodified) social forms of relation in capitalism, to *construct*, under the aspect of thought (rather than sensuous material extension), as the logic of this world or social form, actual capitalist social relations.[62]

One could imagine other axiomatic definitions of capitalism. Marx chooses an initial, readily acceptable proposition (that capitalism appears as the accumulation and generalisation of commodities and commodified relations) and from it, the many implications he will demonstrate in his critique follow necessarily. More specifically, if the reader accepts that the predominant form of appearance of capitalism is the accumulation of commodities, this already implies, as Marx will demonstrate, that only commodified things bearing a monetary price form can appear as values under the capitalist social form. Non-

---

60   Marx 1976, p. 125.
61   See Fred Moseley's penetrating analysis of this point in *Money and Totality* (2017).
62   As Marx affirms in his 'Notes on Adolph Wagner': 'I do not start out from "concepts", hence I do not start out from "the concept of value". ... What I start out from is the simplest *social form* in which the labour-product is presented in contemporary society, and this is the "commodity". I analyse it, and right from the beginning, *in the form in which it appears*. Here I find that it is, on the one hand, in its natural form, a useful thing, alias a "use-value", on the other hand, it is a bearer of exchange-value, and from this viewpoint, it is itself "exchange-value". Further analysis of the latter shows me that exchange-value is only a "form of appearance", the autonomous mode of presentation of the value contained in the commodity'. Marx 1996, pp. 241–2, emphasis added.

commodified things and relations certainly continue to exist (though tend to be monetarised whenever possible), but they do not and cannot *count* as commodified values when the capitalist social form predominates: they can have no value in capitalism since they have no value-form and thus cannot be objects of commodity exchange.

If, as Marx proposes, the substance of value is social (as abstract labour in general, rather than any specific concrete form of labour), this must mean that value 'can only appear [as exchange-value] in the social relation between commodity and commodity'. Marx argues that it is only when two (or more) commodities actually confront each other in the exchange process that they take on the social form specific to capitalism, a commonplace value-form of which 'everyone knows [:] the money-form'.[63] To do so, he demonstrates that the value of labour must be expressed not simply as an isolated exchange-value, but must take the specific form of appearance of the universal equivalent, money. To do so, Marx systematically develops his analysis of the social nature of commodity relations:

1) One commodity (sugar, cotton, indigo) taken in isolation cannot have an exchange-value expressed by itself, since this would be to 'exchange' one thing for the same. The exchange-value of a commodity can only be expressed *relatively*, in a relative form, in some other, second commodity.[64]

2) This 'relative form' of the expression of value, which Marx analyses in great detail,[65] simply describes how one commodity can come to have its value expressed in another commodity. There must, by this reasoning, exist a minimal relation between (at least) two commodities for the substance of value (abstract labour) to find expression (as an exchange-value). Only then does the commodity take a form (in its equivalent) that is distinct from its material, natural form as a use-value, a dual form that Marx has already shown any thing must possess to count as an exchangeable commodity. The social nature of this binary relation lies not merely in the comparison of these two things (as exchange-values). The social aspect of the commodity form finds its first (logical) mode of expression in this simple relative form of relation insofar as the substance of that value (which Marx

---

63 Marx 1976, p. 139.
64 'I cannot', Marx observes, 'express the value of linen in linen', for this would simply express a concrete quantity of this item 'as an object of utility'. Marx 1976, p. 140.
65 Marx 1976, pp. 139–54.

has argued is abstract, rather than any specific concrete labour), what exchange-value is actually measuring or expressing, is given real concrete form in the social act of equating these materially distinct concrete practices when two use-values (linen, coats) are equated (X coats = Y yards of linen).

3) This simple relative form of value, however, is 'insufficient', Marx notes, and 'must undergo a series of metamorphoses before it can ripen into the price-form', the form of appearance adequate to the capitalist social form. A society in which only two commodities are exchanged simply is 'insufficient' to determine the capitalist social form as Marx has axiomatically defined it from the first sentence of *Capital*. In what Marx calls the 'expanded relative form of value', a commodity expresses its value not just in a single opposing commodity, but in each and every other commodity; there thus arises an infinite sequence of relative values. The social relation of any given commodity now becomes all-encompassing, and all commodities stand 'in a relation ... with the whole world of commodities [as] an endless sequence'.[66]

4) Commodities consequently must find their adequate form of expression in one single commodity, a general equivalent that is socially specified to stand apart and to serve as the measure or expression of value (traditionally, gold). It is finally in this general form of value that commodities achieve their full social form of expression, insofar as only this universal equivalent 'permit[s] them to *appear* to each other as exchange-values'.[67] This general, social form of relation to all other commodities is therefore *necessary* given the axiomatic assumption that the capitalist social form is characterised by the general predominance of commodities and commodification.

Badiou's abstract summary of the relational nature of any system of the transcendental valuations governing the strength of appearance of the objects in a world constitutes, therefore, a precise reformulation of Marx's analysis of the systematic logic governing the forms of appearance of commodities in the capitalist social form. 'The transcendental values', Badiou concludes,

66 Marx 1976, p. 155.
67 Marx 1976, p. 158.

do not directly measure intensities of appearance 'in themselves', but rather differences (or identities). When we speak of the value of appearance of a being, we are really designating a sort of synthetic summary of the values of transcendental identity between this being, in this world, and all the other beings appearing in the same world.[68]

The logic of the forms of appearance of existence in any world, Badiou argues, can be succinctly summarised at this high level of abstraction with only three basic operations: 1) the determination of a minimum value for any thing to appear in that world (in capitalism, that a commodity bear a numerical price); 2) that there exist the possibility of conjoining the degrees of value of any two objects (in capitalism, the determination of what Marx calls a *relative* exchange-value between two commodities); and 3) the possibility of a 'global synthesis' of these values among a specific number of multiples (in capitalism, the necessity of the monetary price form to allow for the universal exchangeability of any and all commodities one for another). The degree of congruence between Badiou's abstract analysis of the logics of worlds and Marx's analysis of the necessity governing the forms of appearance of commodities in the capitalist social form is uncanny, all the more so as judging at least by his writings, Badiou seems never to have closely studied Marx's synthetic demonstration of this logic in the third chapter of *Capital*.

4   Reading *Capital* as the Logic of a World

This book has argued that Marx's demonstration of the nature of value in the capitalist social form, of its forms of appearance (above all as money), and of the essence of surplus value, are not derived from obscure metaphysical elucubrations (as Marx's academic and empiricist critics have often asserted), nor from the theoretical reversals of a negative-dialectical (Hegelian) logic.[69] Marx's theory is at heart a materialist logic of the real process of the circuit of capital as it passes, without logical negation, through its various forms. Marx was not improvising when he methodically, revision after revision, constructed the various drafts of *Capital* from 1861 to 1883, but instead sought the most adequate (logical) form of demonstration to present the conceptual order of the capitalist social form. Though he certainly continued to develop and fine

---

68   Badiou 2009, p. 127.
69   On the putative Hegelian, negative-dialectical structure of *Capital*, see for example Arthur 2002 and Moseley and Smith 2014.

tune the diverse categories of his analysis till his last days, he had already conducted his fundamental 'inquiry' into the structure of the capitalist social form to arrive at his central notion of the monetary labour theory of value in the final pages of the *Grundrisse* notebooks.[70] Among the greatest accomplishments of *Capital*, in this view, is to have constructed for readers the real, dynamic logic of the capitalist social form, the immanent logic of a social form, to reveal, as Marx proudly proclaims in his first Preface from 1867, 'the natural laws of capitalist production, ... these tendencies winning their way through and working themselves out with iron necessity'.[71]

If capitalism appears as the general accumulation of commodities, and *if* its predominant form of social relations is that of the exchange of commodities, *then*, Marx argues, a series of necessary consequences immediately follow. What Marx will argue, in the limpid terms of a synthetic logical demonstration, is that given this predominance, abstract labour, the substance of value, *must* take a monetary form of appearance. To do so, he takes his reader step by step to discover the essential nature of the commodity form. From the dual nature of the commodity as both use- and exchange-value to the substance of value (abstract labour) as the determination of what exchange-value measures in the capitalist social form, Marx's demonstration of the logic governing the commodity form culminates in his demonstration of the necessity of its monetary form of appearance. If a thing does not possess this dual form, if, specifically, it does not possess an exchange-value, Marx tells us, it cannot appear as, and thus is not, a commodity. Marx categorically and unambiguously affirms this often-overlooked point: 'Money as a measure of value is the necessary form of appearance of the measure of value which is immanent in commodities, namely labour-time'.[72]

As does Badiou in his general theory of the logics of worlds, Marx repeatedly emphasises the criterion of *appearance* in his analysis, not just critically, but positively. This is to say that the object of his critique of the commodity, the substance of its value, and its various value-forms is not only to reveal the illusory, ideological nature of social relations under the capitalist social form. Marx undertakes in his analysis not just a negative critique of commodity fetishism, but also a positive construction of the commodity in the form of a thought-object, to demonstrate the logical necessity of its monetary form of appearance. In arguing that in commodity relations, value must take a monetary form of appearance, Marx is constructing not an adequate syntax of capital, but a

---

70 On Marx's monetary labour theory of value, see Bellofiore 2018, p. 256.
71 Marx 1976, p. 91.
72 Marx 1976, pp. 138.

materialist logic of the immanent necessity governing the existence of what counts as a thing and possesses value in the capitalist social form (a commodity). *Capital* is not a well-ordered linguistic apparatus of semantic analysis that would *infer* or prove the necessary existence of the capitalist social form and its attendant value-forms; instead, given the *a priori existence* of this social form, *Capital* simply reconstructs, in the attribute of thought (as opposed to extension), as the logic of this world, a real object. Marx proceeds in materialist fashion from the unproven, axiomatic and reasonable presupposition that accumulated commodities and generally commodified social relations do in fact exist and prevail, and furthermore define the capitalist social form per se, to then reproduce in thought the real structure of this social form via the demonstration of the necessary consequences of this predominance.

The expression of the value of any commodity in the form of the universal equivalent (money) fully abstracts not only from the material use-value of that commodity, but universally, from the material specificity of all commodities, finally to 'express what is common to all commodities': abstract labour. The general form of value thus fully expresses the (commodified) social relations of the capitalist social form, in the form of the quantitative abstractions of exchange-values. 'By this [general] form', Marx writes, 'commodities are, for the first time, really brought into relation with each other as values, or permitted *to appear to each other as exchange-values*'.[73] Here again, Marx underscores in his logic of capital the 'positive nature' of a form of *appearance* that allows for a general social relation – between the commodities people exchange – at the same time that it fetishistically obscures the substance of those exchange-values, abstract labour.

Since Marx's analysis is not an economic theory, but a *critique* of economic theory, what the demonstration of the necessity of the quantitative, monetary form of appearance of value reveals are not specific numerical values (the object of econometric analyses, from profit rates to unemployment figures), but rather the nature and substance of the various categories that constitute the forms of appearance of the capitalist social form.[74] The categorial logic of *Capital*, in other words, is not a philosophy of 'substance' in the sense of

---

73 Marx 1976, p. 158, emphasis added.
74 As Paul Mattick writes, 'Marx's model of the capitalist economy does not yield quantitative results that could be compared with economic data; it is capable neither of accounting for the actual price of goods on the market nor of predicting (or even accounting for) such phenomena as the rates of profit obtaining at one time or another. [Rather,] the phenomena (price representations of labour time) with which it is concerned ... serve social functions involving the concealment of real relationships rather than their direct manifestation'. Mattick 2019, p. 33.

the econometric, analytic manipulation of collections of objects or sets (commodities, profits, employment data, GDP, etc.); rather, from the moment Marx defines the substance of value as abstract labour, derivable only as a socially validated relation, *Capital* unfolds as a *category* theory of the capitalist social form.[75] Among Marx's unprecedented accomplishments, in his logic of the forms of appearance of value in capitalism, is to have systematically demonstrated the absolute necessity that value take a monetary form of appearance in commodity society.

The consequence of Badiou's reformulation of the domain and remit of logic as a categorial science of the necessary forms of appearance and existence of the beings in any given world is that without ever considering Marx's *Capital* or even the capitalist social form in general, Badiou has quite surprisingly produced a theoretical formalisation of the object of Marx's critique of political economy, one that constructs the adequate notion of a materialist logic of capitalism. It is not that *Logics of Worlds* accounts in the abstract, point by point, for the enormous complexity of *Capital* (though *Logics* contains many extraordinary formulations that begin to do just that, only a few of which I have indicated here), but, rather, that Badiou's materialist logic for the first time adequately accounts for the ontological status of Marx's critique. For while Marx famously takes leave of philosophy in the eleventh thesis on Feuerbach ('Philosophers have only interpreted the world, in various ways; the point is to change it'), the various ongoing attempts to map the movement of concepts in *Capital* back onto Hegel's *Logic* cannot account for the theoretical and, indeed ontological specificity of this critique, but instead, implicitly or explicitly, tend to reinscribe Marx's critique of a singular social form as a monist and transhistorical (Hegelian) ontology. Instead, following Badiou, it is clear that despite its incompletion, *Capital* constitutes nothing less than the historically and theoretically delimited, adequate, and systematic demonstration of the necessary forms of appearance of value in (and only in) the capitalist social form. In other words, *Capital* should and indeed must be read and understood as the science of the logic governing our world, the capitalist social form.

---

75 See Badiou's comments on this distinction – in response to Jacques Desanti's critique of the latent 'substantialism' of *Being and Event* – where he presents *Logics of Worlds* as a category theory of *relations between existing things*, in Badiou 2019b, pp. 97–105.

CONCLUSION

Theory and Practice Today

When Althusser articulated the concept of theoretical practice (*la pratique théorique*) in his introduction to *Reading Capital*, he intended the concept not as a conflation of the traditional pairing of theory and practice, nor by any means as an elimination of other forms of revolutionary practice, but just the opposite, as an enlargement of the concept of practice to include that of theoretical production, bypassing the subject-object doublet of traditional theories of knowledge.[1] He did so, moreover, by deploying the central Spinozist epistemological tenet, *verum index sui et falsi* to make the famous claim that underlies the argument of this book:

> The criterion of the 'truth' of the knowledges produced by Marx's theoretical practice is provided by his theoretical practice itself, i.e., by the adequacy of demonstration [*valeur demonstrative*]. Marx's theoretical practice is the criterion of the 'truth' of the knowledges that Marx produced.[2]

Against empiricism, Althusser categorically asserted in this manner the autonomy of adequate demonstration, against traditional theories of knowledge as the correspondence of thought with its empirical referent.

Equally Spinozist is Althusser's categorical assertion that Marx constructs *Capital* not from observation of the empirical real, but from the critique of pre-existing ideas – of classical political economy, French socialism, and even the English *Factory Reports* – such that Marx's analysis takes place entirely within the attribute of thought, or, as Etienne Balibar puts it in his Methodological Annex to the first edition of *Lire le Capital*, 'an analysis that remains entirely within thought [*intérieure à la connaissance*]':[3]

> Knowledge working on its 'object' [writes Althusser] does not work on the real object but on the peculiar raw material, that constitutes ... its 'object' (of knowledge), and which, even in the most rudimentary forms of knowledge, is distinct from the real object.[4]

---

1 RC, pp. 41–4, 61–2.
2 RC, pp. 61, 62 [LC, pp. 65, 66], translation modified.
3 Balibar, 'Un texte de methodologie', in LC, p. 659, my translation.
4 RC, p. 43; LC, p. 43.

Holding to Spinoza's rigorous distinction between the attributes of thought and extension, Althusser's position constitutes a coherent rejection of both traditional theories of knowledge as the correspondence of a concept with its empirical object, as well as of Hegelian sublation of the real of Nature within the Idea. One would think these are terms so transparently Spinozist, that for any reader with even a passing knowledge of his thought, Althusser's subsequent, repentant admission ('We were Spinozist') should have been wholly superfluous.[5] Instead, criticism of Althusser has tended to focus on his critique of the idealist subject,[6] largely ignoring his original epistemological theory.

In this book, in contrast, I have sought to remain faithful to Althusser's equally Spinozist rejection of universals, manifest in the position that there is no 'practice' in general, standing in diametrical opposition to an idealist notion of 'theory'. There are only singular modes of practice; among which, alongside the revolutionary, political, economic, musical, postcolonial, and a thousand others, is to be counted *theoretical practice*:

> There is no practice in general, but only distinct practices that are not related in any Manichaean way with a theory which is opposed to them in every respect. For there is not on one side theory, a pure intellectual vision without body or materiality – and on the other side a completely material practice which 'gets its hands dirty'. This dichotomy is merely an ideological myth in which a 'theory of knowledge' reflects many 'interests' other than those of reason.[7]

In these pages, I have tried to further develop in this fashion the singular modality of theoretical practice that is Marx's critique of political economy, following its transformations across the drafts, editions, and notes to *Capital* from 1857–75, reading the history of these mutations through the thought of Althusser, Macherey, Balibar, and Badiou.

That this conception of plural, singular practices maintains into the present a certain validity is perhaps confirmed by the counter-example of Badiou's essential *division* of theory and practice, strikingly manifest for example in

---

5 Althusser 1972, p. 29.
6 'This definite system of conditions of theoretical practice is what assigns any given thinking subject (individual) its place and function in the production of knowledges. ... This determinate reality is what defines the roles and functions of the "thought" of particular individuals, who can only "think" the "problems" already actually or potentially posed; hence it is also what sets to work their "thought power", in the way that the structure of an economic mode of production sets to work the labour-power of its immediate producers' (RC, p. 42; LC, pp. 41–2).
7 RC, p. 59, translation modified; LC, p. 64.

his 2023 *Mémoires d'outre politique*. Here we find a conspicuous distinction between the extreme abstraction of Badiou's ontological system, on the one hand, and a surprising poverty of 'communist' practice. Badiou describes at length in his memoir the history and activity of the political party he cofounded with Sylvain Lazarus and Natasha Michel, the *groupe pour la foundation de l'union des communists français (marxiste-léniniste)* (UCFml) in the period 1970–85. In this rich and varied history of Badiou's transformation in the wake of May '68, from local member of the Parti Socialiste in Reims to Maoist militant founder of the UCFml, Badiou recounts memorable moments in the latter's history.

Among the varied anecdotes composing Badiou's memoir, what stands out to this reader is the glaring disparity, not so much with the pure abstraction of Badiou's ontology, though this is striking as well, but between the grandiose rhetoric of Badiou's 'Idea of communism' and the targeted (not to say limited), local nature of the militant interventions of the UCFml.

In *The Communist Hypothesis*, we read in this vein that:

> An Idea is the subjective operation whereby a specific real truth is imaginarily projected into the symbolic movement of a History, we can say that an Idea presents the truth as if it were a fact. ... In order to anticipate, at least ideologically, or intellectually, the creation of new possibilities, we must have an Idea. ... By combining intellectual constructs, which are always global and universal, with experiments of fragments of truths, which are local and singular, yet universally transmittable, we can give new life to the communist hypothesis, or rather to the Idea of communism.[8]

The Idea of communism, Badiou proposes, is sustained by local, Maoist 'experiments', moments of militant practice that would embody 'the Idea of communism'. Badiou's actual militancy, then, is presumably dedicated to such interventions in the name of this Idea.

Indeed, in *Mémoires d'outre politique* Badiou relishes in descriptions of the Maoist militancy of his youth in the 'Red Years' of the 1970s. In one such sequence, he narrates the occupation of the Chausson car factory, in which the UCFml aligned itself with the more militant, anti-union faction of workers, the so-called 'Left Workers' [*gauche ouvrière*]. Following the police occupation of the factory,

---

8 Badiou 2015, § IV.

In the night of Sunday to Monday, a striking and very tense standoff occurred in the factory: the police inside, with the management and staff, the striking workers outside. Around 3 AM, a squadron of police attempted to escape. The workers' anger exploded, and the police squadron, bombarded by stones, broke up and abandoned their attempt. It was a moment of intense joy, one that united the workers and Maoist militants. ... By Tuesday, slowly, tortuously, there occurred movement toward a limited compromise: the management, which was in fact quite scared, agreed to give 160 francs to everyone, and promised that 250 francs [per worker] would also be distributed in November. There thus followed a return to work.[9]

While Badiou's narration of such struggles is bracing, the disparity between the Maoist militants' rhetoric and the actual terms of such struggles is glaring. In sharp contrast to Badiou's grandiose rhetoric of the Idea of communism, in Badiou's *Mémoires*, these local and singular 'fragments of truth' have a surprisingly limited 'communist' weight and bearing.

It is not only the actual, necessarily compromised results of such struggles that marks this disparity; the very terms of the demands of the Left workers and UCFml are unexpectedly modest, given the latter's militant rhetoric and putatively anti-capitalist and communist position. In the case of the Chausson struggle, three points were at stake for the UCFml, in Badiou's retrospective telling: 1. 'That the worker be respected in his work'; 2. '[Rejection] of hierarchy in its most grievous forms', including arbitrary individual salary increases and bogus 'qualifications' demanded for work reassignments; and, above all 3. 'A forty-hour workweek without salary decrease'.[10]

Now, it's obviously laudable to struggle for workers' and immigrant rights, as did the UCFml. Badiou, however, presents the militancy of the UCFml as if it were the now-forgotten cutting edge of communist, anti-capitalist struggle, when instead, his memoir arguably reveals just how much French Maoism was of a piece with what Moishe Postone disparaged four decades ago as 'tra-

---

9 Badiou 2023, p. 304.
10 Other militant sequences of the UCFml articulated similarly modest demands. In July 1975, Badiou recounts that the UCFml articulated a 'programme for the [immigrant] workers' dormitories [*foyers*]' that demanded 1. A fixed rate for rooms 2. Recognition of the workers' status as residents [*locataires*] 3. Freedom of assembly 4. Freedom to receive visitors 5. Replacement of racist overseers [*gérants*] with *concierges* 6. Improvement of hygiene and security 7. Availability of larger apartments for workers to house their families'. Badiou 2023, p. 338.

ditional Marxism': the fight for the Ricardian redistribution of wealth within an unchanged, unexamined, and ill-comprehended capitalist social form by 'Marxists' of all stripes.[11]

Among the most surprising examples in Badiou's memoir of this profound theoretical obliviousness to the nature of capitalism is his commentary on the third demand of the Chausson workers for a 40-hour workweek: 'A guaranteed forty-hour workweek without salary decrease. This is the median proposal we [the UCFml] supported. The question of salary must be separated from that of work time'. I was astounded to read, in 2023, Badiou's next two sentences, a still-enthusiastic and approving explanation of the significance of this position: 'The UCFml militants explained [to the workers] that this more or less amounted to saying that one had abolished capitalism! The bosses make their own profit from surplus value, work time extorted invisibly and without pay from the workers'.[12]

Leaving aside the condescending tone of the passage, how is it possible for an avowedly anti-capitalist, Marxist philosopher so thoroughly grounded in theory, to believe today – a half century after the *Reading Capital* project (in which, of course, Badiou himself played no role, having left the ENS in 1961 for the army and then Reims), after the *Neue Marx-Lektüre*, after the critiques of Postone, of Robert Kurz's *Wertkritik*, after the contributions of the International Symposium on Marxist Theory – that the firm would not simply go out of business or relocate in search of cheaper labour power were they unable to realise a profit with this 40-hour workweek? That the ongoing class struggle over the workweek and wages is not entirely integral to the laws of tendencies of capitalism (and thus analysed by Marx smack in the middle of Volume I of *Capital*, as Chapter 10, 'The Working Day')? That capitalism is a matter of free choice from which a handful of workers could simply opt out, rather than an all-encompassing social form? That both these workers and the UCFml militants instructing them, having successfully negotiated their 40-hour workweek and thus 'abolished capitalism', would not continue to require cash in hand to purchase their bundle of life necessities, necessities otherwise unavailable because they have been universally commodified in the capitalist social form? I could go on.

My point is plain and simple, though perhaps far-reaching in its implications for how we think about theoretical practice today. Between the lofty theory

---

11   On 'traditional Marxism', see Postone 1993, pp. 44–8.
12   'Les militants UCFml expliqueront que cela revient quasiment à dire qu'on abolit le capitalisme! C'est en effet sur la plus-value, donc un temps de travail extorqué gratuitement et invisiblement aux ouvriers, que le patronat fait son bénéfice propre'. Badiou 2023, p. 302.

of Badiou's Idea of communism and both hollow UCFml claims to have transcended capitalism and the modest, benevolent practice of UCFml militancy, lies an abyss: the unexplored Dark Continent that is Marx's theoretical practice. In the previous chapter, I constructed a palimpsest of Marx's critique drawn from the manifest content of Badiou's agnostic logic of worlds. In the absence of actual engagement with and working through of that critique at any point in Badiou's vast oeuvre, however, theory and practice alike are distorted: reduced to acting out the causality of a social form, the nature of which one is unaware, practice remains limited to the histrionic throwing of stones – granite or conceptual – at the imaginary villains of capitalist misdeeds, whether evil Wall Street bankers or 'a handful of billionaires',[13] the self-proclaimed subjects of anti-capitalism struggle on, secure in their faith, as was Lukács a century before, that 'Capitalism, after a fight of barely a century, has with great difficulty won a round. In the end, it will be defeated by a knockout'.[14]

As the capitalist social form increasingly destroys not just human lives and well-being, but planetary survivability for the majority of living species, we discover that it was Marx himself who refused all facile ideas of 'communist' or 'Marxist' practice, and instead remained faithful to the imperative of an ever-developing, relentlessly transformed theoretical practice.[15] There is no royal road to overcoming the capitalist social form, and as its global subjects, we are condemned to working through and ever more adequately conceptualising its nature, if future generations are to live on to escape its contingent, historically limited, but nonetheless implacable dynamic. What other, more incisive forms of practice might arise from this more adequate theoretical practice is a question, as Zhou Enlai famously said of the French Revolution and Commune, that it is too soon to answer definitively.

---

13 Badiou 2023, p. 317.
14 Badiou 2023, p. 318.
15 See Saito 2017; Anderson 2010; and Musto 2020.

References

Abazari, Arash 2019, 'Marx's Conception of Dialectical Contradiction in [the] Commodity', *The Hegel Bulletin*, 42, no. 2: 180–200.

Adorno, Theodor 2002, *Introduction to Sociology*, Stanford: Stanford University Press.

Adorno, Theodor, and Max Horkheimer 2002, *Dialectic of Enlightenment: Philosophical Fragments*, Stanford: Stanford University Press.

Alexis, Jacques Stephen 1955, *Compère général soleil*, Paris: Éditions Gallimard.

Althusser, Louis 1963, 'Annexe: Monisme et "acte social total" (A propos de l'article de G. Mury)', *La Pensée*, 110 (August): 43–6.

Althusser, Louis 1969, 'Lenine et la philosophie' in *Bulletin de la société française de la philosophie* 4:127–181. – 1972, *Éléments d'autocritique*, Paris: Hachette.

Althusser, Louis 1974, *Éléments d'autocritique*, Paris: Hachette.

Althusser, Louis 1976, *Essays in Self-Criticism*, London: NLB.

Althusser, Louis 1990, *Philosophy and the Spontaneous Philosophy of the Scientists*, London: Verso.

Althusser, Louis 1993, *Ecrits sur la psychanalyse*, Paris: Stock.

Althusser, Louis 1993, *The Future Lasts Forever: A Memoir*, translated by Richard Veasey, New York: New Press.

Althusser, Louis 1994, *Ecrits philosophiques et politiques*, edited by François Matheron, Paris: Stock/IMEC.

Althusser, Louis 1996 [1965], *Lire le Capital*, Paris: PUF.

Althusser, Louis 1997, 'The Only Materialist Tradition, Part I: Spinoza', in *The New Spinoza, edited by Warren Montag and Ted Stolze*, Minneapolis: University of Minnesota Press, pp. 3–20.

Althusser, Louis 1998a, 'Avant-propos du livre de G. Duménil', in *Solitude de Machiavel*, Paris: PUF.

Althusser, Louis 1998b, *Lettres à Franca (1961–1973)*, edited by François Matheron, Paris: Stock/IMEC.

Althusser, Louis 2001, *Lenin and Philosophy and Other Essays*, New York: Monthly Review Press.

Althusser, Louis 2003, *The Humanist Controversy and Other Writings*, London: Verso.

Althusser, Louis 2005, *For Marx*, London: Verso.

Althusser, Louis 2006, *Philosophy of the Encounter: Later Writings, 1978–1987*, translated by G.M. Goshgarian, New York: Verso.

Althusser, Louis 2012, *Philosophy and the Spontaneous Philosophy of the Scientists*, London: Verso.

Althusser, Louis 2014, *The Spectre of Hegel*, London: Verso.

Althusser, Louis 2015, *Être marxiste en philosophie*, Paris: PUF.

Althusser, Louis 2016, *Les vaches noires: Interview imaginaire*, Paris: PUF.

Althusser, Louis, Jacques Rancière, Pierre Macherey, Roger Establet, and Etienne Balibar 2015, *Reading Capital: The Complete Edition*, translated by Ben Brewster and David Fernbach, New York: Verso.

Anderson, Kevin B. 2010, *Marx at the Margins*, Chicago: University of Chicago Press.

Anderson, Perry 1980, *Arguments within English Marxism*, London: New Left Books.

Aristotle 1960, *Posterior Analytics*, Cambridge MA: Harvard University Press.

Arthur, Chris 2002, *The New Dialectic and Marx's Capital*, Leiden: Brill.

Arthur, Chris 2009, 'Contradiction and Abstraction: A Reply to Finelli', *Historical Materialism*, 17: 170–82.

Arthur, Chris 2022, *The Spectre of Capital: Idea and Reality*, Leiden: Brill.

Badiou, Alain 1990, *Le Nombre et les Nombres*, Paris: Editions du Seuil.

Badiou, Alain 1998, *Court traité d'ontologie transitoire*, Paris: Seuil.

Badiou, Alain 2005 [1988], *Being and Event*, London: Continuum.

Badiou, Alain 2006, *Briefings on Existence: A Short Treatise on Transitory Ontology*, translated by Norman Madarasz, Albany: State University of New York Press.

Badiou, Alain 2007 [1968], *The Concept of Model: An Introduction to the Materialist Epistemology of Mathematics*, Melbourne: Re.Press.

Badiou, Alain 2008 [1990], *Number and Numbers*, translated by Robin Mackay, Cambridge: Polity.

Badiou, Alain 2009 [2006], *Logics of Worlds. Being and Event, 2*, translated by Alberto Toscano, London: Continuum.

Badiou, Alain 2010 [2008], *Communist Hypothesis*, Brooklyn: Verso.

Badiou, Alain 2012, 'Mark and Lack: On Zero', in *Concept and Form, Volume 1: Key Texts from the Cahiers pour l'Analyse*, edited by Peter Hallward and Knox Peden, New York: Verso.

Badiou, Alain 2013a, *Being and Event*, translated by Oliver Feltham, London: Bloomsbury.

Badiou, Alain 2013b, *Le Séminaire. Lacan: L'antiphilosophie 3, 1994–1995*, Paris: Fayard.

Badiou, Alain 2013c, *Plato's Republic: A Dialogue in Sixteen Chapters*, translated by Susan Spitzer and Kenneth Reinhard, New York: Columbia University Press.

Badiou, Alain 2015, *À la recherche du réel perdu*, Paris: Fayard.

Badiou, Alain 2017, 'The Althusserian Definition of "Theory"', in *The Concept in Crisis: Reading Capital Today*, edited by Nick Nesbitt, Durham, NC: Duke University Press.

Badiou, Alain 2018a, *Lacan: Anti-philosophy 3*, translated by Kenneth Reinhard and Susan Spitzer, New York: Columbia University Press.

Badiou, Alain 2018b, *L'immanence des vérités: L'être et l'événement, 3*, Paris: Fayard.

Badiou, Alain 2019a, *Happiness*, translated by A.J. Bartlett and Justin Clemens, London: Bloomsbury.

Badiou, Alain 2019b, *Sometimes, We Are Eternal*, Lyon: Suture.

Badiou, Alain 2023, *Mémoires d'outre-politique (1937–1985)*, Paris: Flammarion.
Baki, Burhannudin 2014, *Badiou's* Being and Event *and the Mathematics of Set Theory*, London: Bloomsbury Academic.
Balibar, Etienne 1991, *Ecrits pour Althusser*, Paris: Eds. La Découverte.
Balibar, Etienne 2012, 'La Science du "Capital"', in *Le centenaire du 'Capital'*, Paris: Hermann.
Balibar, Etienne 2014 [1993], *La philosophie de Marx*, Paris: La Découverte.
Balibar, Etienne 2015a, *Violence and Civility*, translated by G.M. Goshgarian, New York: Columbia University Press.
Balibar, Etienne 2015b, 'L'objet d'Althusser', in *Politique et philosophie dans l'oeuvre de Louis Althusser*, edited by Sylvain Lazarus, Paris: PUF, pp. 81–116.
Balibar, Etienne 2018, 'Lire Lire le Capital : Préface pour une edition hongroise de "Lire le Capital"', available at http://revueperiode.net/lire-lire-le-capital/#identifier_0_6491.
Balibar, Etienne 2023, 'Hegel, Marx, Pashukanis and the Idea of Abstract Right as a Bourgeois Form', in *Institution: Critical Histories of Law*, edited by Cooper Francis and Daniel Gottlieb, London: CRMEP Books, pp. 74–100.
Banaji, Jairus 2015 [1979], 'From the Commodity to Capital: Hegel's Dialectic in Marx's *Capital*', in *Value: The Representation of Labour in Capital*, edited by Diane Elson, New York: Verso, pp. 14–45.
Barbour, Charles 2023, 'The Logic Question: Marx, Trendelenburg, and the Critique of Hegel.' *Historical Materiallism* 1–30.
Béguin, Victor 2021, 'Le caractère fétiche du concept. Marx face au discours hégélien, entre heritage et critique', *Les Études philosophiques*, 4: 105–23.
Bellofiore, Riccardo 2002, '"Transformation" and the Monetary Circuit: Marx as Monetary Theorist of Production', in *The Culmination of Capital: Essays on Volume III of Marx's* Capital, edited by Martha Campbell and Geert Reuten, New York: Palgrave, pp. 102–27.
Bellofiore, Riccardo 2009, 'A Ghost Turning into a Vampire: The Concept of Capital and Living Labour', in Bellofiore and Fineschi (eds) 2009.
Bellofiore, Riccardo 2013, 'The *Grundrisse* after *Capital*, or How to Re-read Marx Backwards', in *In Marx's Laboratory: Critical Interpretations of the* Grundrisse, edited by Riccardo Bellofiore, Guido Starosta, and Peter D. Thomas, Leiden: Brill, pp. 17–42.
Bellofiore, Riccardo 2014, 'Lost in Translation? Once Again on the Marx-Hegel Connection', in *Marx's* Capital *and Hegel's* Logic, edited by Fred Moseley and Tony Smith, Leiden: Brill.
Bellofiore, Riccardo 2018, 'Forever Young? Marx's Critique of Political Economy After 200 Years', *PSL Quarterly Review*, 71, no. 287: 353–88.
Bellofiore, Riccardo 2023, 'Crossroads: Recollections of my Marxian Encounters with Anwar Shaikh and Duncan Foley.' *New School Economic Review*, 12: 1–13.

Bellofiore, Riccardo, Guido Starosta, and Peter D. Thomas (eds) 2013, *In Marx's Laboratory: Critical Interpretations of the* Grundrisse, Leiden: Brill.

Bellofiore, Riccardo, and Massimiliano Tomba 2014, 'The "Fragment on Machines" and the *Grundrisse*: The Workerist Reading in Question', in *Beyond Marx: Theorising Global Labour Relations of the Twenty-First Century*, edited by Marcel van der Linden and Karl Heinz Roth, Boston: Brill, pp. 345–68.

Bellofiore, Riccardo, and Roberto Fineschi (eds) 2009, *Re-reading Marx: New Perspectives After the Critical Edition*, London: Palgrave.

Bhaskar, Roy 1983, "Dialectic" in Tom Bottomore (ed.) 1983, *Dictionary of Marxist Thought*, Cambridge, MA: Harvard University Press.

Bianchi, Bernardo 2018, 'Marx's Reading of Spinoza: On the Alleged Influence of Spinoza on Marx', *Historical Materialism*, 26, no. 4: 35–58.

Bidet, Jacques 2005, 'The Dialectician's Interpretation of Capital', *Historical Materialism*, 13, no. 2: 121–46.

Bidet, Jacques 2009 [1985], *Exploring Marx's Capital: Philosophical, Economic, and Political Aspects*, Chicago: Haymarket.

Bischoff, Joachim, and Christoph Lieber 2008, 'The Concept of Value in Modern Economy: On the Relationship between Money and Capital in *Grundrisse*', in *Karl Marx's Grundrisse: Foundations of the Critique of Political Economy 150 Years Later*, New York: Routledge, pp. 33–47.

Bolzano, Bernard 1804, *Beiträge zu einer begründeteren Darstellung der Mathematik*.

Bolzano, Bernard 1950 [1851], *Paradoxes of the Infinite*, New York: Routledge.

Bolzano, Bernard 1978, *Grundlegung der Logik: Ausgewählte Paragraphen aus der Wissenshaftlehre, band I und II*. Friedrich Kambartel, ed. Hamburg: Felix Meiner Verlag.

Bolzano, Bernard 2010, *Premiers écrits: Philosophie, logique mathématique*, Paris: Vrin.

Bolzano, Bernard 2011, *Théorie de la science, I–II*, Paris: Gallimard.

Bolzano, Bernard 2014, *Theory of Science*, Oxford: Oxford University Press.

Bordignon, Michela 2022, 'Hegel's Logic as a System of Illegitimate Totalities', in *Hegel's Encyclopedic System*, edited by Sebastian Stein and Joshua Wretzel, New York: Routledge, pp. 115–32.

Bottomore, Tom (ed.) 1983, *A Dictionary of Marxist Thought*, Cambridge, MA: Harvard University Press.

Bouveresse, Jacques, IMEC 20 ALT 51.7.

Brown, Nathan 2021, *Rationalist Empiricism: A Theory of Speculative Critique*, New York: Fordham University Press.

Brunschvig, Léon 1912, *Les étapes de la philosophie mathématique*, Paris: PUF.

Bruschi, Fabio 2021, *Le matérialisme politique de Louis Althusser*, Paris: Editions Mimésis.

Caffentizis, G. (2013), 'From the *Grundrisse* to *Capital* and Beyond: Then and Now', in

In Marx's Laboratory: Critical Interpretations of the Grundrisse, edited by Riccardo Bellofiore, Guido Starosta, and Peter D. Thomas, Leiden: Brill, pp. 265–83.

Caligaris, Gastón, and Guido Starosta 2014, 'Which "Rational Kernel"? Which "Mystical Shell"? A Contribution to the Debate on the Connection between Hegel's *Logic* and Marx's *Capital*', in Moseley and Smith 2014.

Cassin, Barbara et al. 2014, *Dictionary of Untranslatables: A Philosophical Lexicon*, Princeton: Princeton University Press.

Cassou-Noguès, Pierre 2017, *Un laboratoire philosophique: Cavaillès et l'épistémologie en France*, Paris: Vrin.

Cavaillès, Jean 1994, *Oeuvres complètes de Philosophie des sciences*, Paris: Hermann.

Cavaillès, Jean 2008, *Sur la logique et la théorie de la science*, Paris: Vrin.

Cavaillès, Jean 2021 [1942], *On Logic and the Philosophy of Science*, translated by Robin Mackay and Knox Peden, New York: Sequence Press.

Clarke, Simon, Terry Lovell, et al. (eds) 1980, *One-Dimensional Marxism: Althusser and the Politics of Culture*, London: Allison & Busby.

Cole, Andrew 2014, *The Birth of Theory*, Chicago: University of Chicago Press.

Colletti, Lucio 1969, *Il Marxismo e Hegel*, Rome-Bari: Laterza.

Cutler, Antony, and Michael Gane 1973, 'Statement: On the Question of Philosophy – for a Theory of Theoretical Practice', *Theoretical Practice*, 7–8: 37–50.

David, Pascal, 2014, "Dasein," in Barbara Cassin et al. 2014, *Dictionary of Untranslatables: A Philosophical Lexicon*, Princeton: Princeton University Press: 194–200.

Descombes, Vincent 1980, *Modern French Philosophy*, Cambridge: Cambridge University Press.

Diefenbach, Katja, Sara R. Farris, Gal Kirn, and Peter D. Thomas (eds) 2013, *Encountering Althusser: Politics and Materialism in Contemporary Radical Thought*, London: Bloomsbury.

Dunayevskaya, Raya 2000 [1958], *Marxism and Freedom: From 1776 until Today*, New York: Humanity Books.

Dussel, Enrique 1985, *La producción teórica de Marx. Un comentario a los 'Grundrisse'*, Mexico City: Siglo XXI.

Dussel, Enrique 2008, 'The Discovery of the Category of Surplus Value', in *Karl Marx's Grundrisse: Foundations of the Critique of Political Economy 150 Years Later*, New York: Routledge, pp. 67–78.

Elliott, Gregory 1987, *Althusser: The Detour of Theory*, New York: Verso.

Estop, Juan Domingo Sanchez 2021, *Althusser et Spinoza: Détours et retours*, Bruxelles: Editions de l'Université de Bruxelles.

Fallon, Jacques 1993, 'Compte rendu: André Lalande, *Vocabulaire technique et critique de la philosophie*', *Revue philosophique de Louvain*, 91: 512.

Feltham, Oliver 2020, 'One or Many Ontologies? Badiou's Arguments for His Thesis "Mathematics is Ontology"', *Filozofski vestnik*, XLI, no. 2: 37–56.

Fetscher, Iring 2008, 'Emancipated Individuals in an Emancipated Society: Marx's Sketch of Post-capitalist Society in the *Grundrisse*', in *Karl Marx's* Grundrisse: *Foundations of the Critique of Political Economy 150 Years Later*, New York: Routledge, pp. 107–19.

Fineschi, Roberto 2013, 'The Four Levels of Abstraction of Marx's Concept of "Capital". Or, Can We Consider the *Grundrisse* the Most Advanced Version of Marx's Theory of Capital?' in *In Marx's Laboratory: Critical Interpretations of the* Grundrisse, edited by Riccardo Bellofiore, Guido Starosta, and Peter D. Thomas, Leiden: Brill, pp. 71–100.

Fineschi, Roberto 2014, 'On Hegel's Methodological Legacy in Marx', in Moseley and Smith 2014.

Fischbach, Franck 2005, *La production des hommes: Marx avec Spinoza*, Paris: PUF.

Fluss, Harrison 2016, 'The Spector of Spinoza: The Legacy of the Pantheism Controversy in Hegel's Thought', PhD Dissertation, Stony Brook University.

Fluss, Harrison 2022, 'Dialectics', in *The Sage Handbook of Marxism*, edited by Beverley Skeggs, Sara R. Farris, Alberto Toscano, and Svenja Bromberg, Thousand Oaks, CA: Sage.

Foucault, Michel, and Gilles Deleuze 1977, 'Intellectuals and Power', in *Language, Counter-Memory, Practice: Selected Essays and Interviews by Michel Foucault*, Ithaca: Cornell University Press, pp. 205–17.

Frege, Gottlob 1980, *Foundations of Arithmetic: A Logico-mathematical Enquiry into the Concept of Number*, translated by J.L. Austin, Evanston: Northwestern University Press.

Frim, Landon, and Harrison Fluss 2018, 'Substance Abuse: Spinoza contra Deleuze', *Epoché: A Journal for the History of Philosophy*, 23, no. 1: 191–217.

Frim, Landon, and Harrison Fluss 2022, 'Reason is Red: Why Marxism Needs Philosophy', *Spectre*, 29 August, https://spectrejournal.com/reason-is-red/?fbclid=IwAR0K Ay8xA2Z8Fu2wzZtUySZ8y4j5ES9THjME2Q9n_u_K7ZuyDfqXVBN65FE

Goldstein, Rebecca 2013, *Incompleteness: The Proof and Paradox of Kurt Gödel*, New York: W.W. Norton.

Goshgarian, G.M. 2006, 'Introduction', in *Philosophy of the Encounter: Later Writings, 1978–1987*, by Louis Althusser, New York: Verso.

Hallward, Peter 2003, *Badiou: A Subject to Truth*, Minneapolis: University of Minnesota Press.

Hallward, Peter, and Knox Peden (eds) 2012, *Concept and Form, Volumes I–II*, New York: Verso.

Hegel, G.W.F. 2010a, *Encyclopedia of the Philosophical Sciences in Outline. Part I: Logic*, Cambridge: Cambridge University Press.

Hegel, G.W.F. 2010b, *The Science of Logic*, translated by George di Giovanni, Cambridge: Cambridge University Press.

Heinrich, Michael 2009, 'Reconstruction or Deconstruction? Methodological Controversies about Value and Capital, and New Insights from the Critical Edition', in *Re-reading Marx: New Perspectives After the Critical Edition*, edited by Riccardo Bellofiore and Roberto Fineschi, London: Palgrave.

Heinrich, Michael 2012, *An Introduction to the Three Volumes of Karl Marx's 'Capital'*, translated by Alexander Locascio, New York: Monthly Review Press.

Heinrich, Michael 2013, 'The "Fragment on Machines": A Marxian Misconception in the *Grundrisse* and its Overcoming in *Capital*', in *In Marx's Laboratory: Critical Interpretations of the* Grundrisse, edited by Riccardo Bellofiore, Guido Starosta, and Peter D. Thomas, Leiden: Brill, pp. 197–212.

Heinrich, Michael 2019, *Karl Marx and the Birth of Modern Society*, New York: Monthly Review Press.

Heinrich, Michael 2020, 'Marx and the Birth of Modern Society: An Interview with Michael Heinrich', *Journal of the History of Ideas Blog*, 25 November, https://www.jhiblog.org/2020/11/25/marx-and-the-birth-of-modern-society/?fbclid=IwARovPe O3Ldp_5y9YooLfNKBUv7uzmLZfRYn5Ig6bdKLAJZGME63MdV2Lap4.

Heinrich, Michael 2021, *How to Read Marx's* Capital, translated by Alexander Locascio, New York: Monthly Review Press.

Heinrich, Michael 2022 [1999], *Die Wissenschaft vom Wert: Die Marxsche Kritik der politischen Ökonomie zwischen wissenschaftlicher Revolution und klassicher Tradition*, Münster: Verlag Westfälisches Dampfboot.

Heinrich, Michael 2023, *La Scienza del Valore: La Critica Marxiana Dell'Economia Politica tra Rivoluzione Scientifica e Tradizione Classica* [*Die Wissenschaft vom Wert. Die Marxsche Kritik der politischen Ökonomie zwischen wissenschaftlicher Revolution und klassicher Tradition*], edited by Riccardo Bellofiore and Stefano Breda, translated by Stefano Breda, Rome: PGreco Edizioni.

Huhn, Wilson 2022, *The Five Types of Legal Argument*, Durham, NC: Carolina Academic Press.

Hussain, Athar 1972, 'Marx's "Notes on Adolph Wagner": An Introduction', *Theoretical Practice*, 5: 18–34.

Husserl, Edmund 2001 [1900], *Philosophical Investigations*, New York: Routledge.

Iñigo Carrera, Juan 2003, *El Capital: Razón Histórica, Sujeto Revolucionario y Conciencia*, Buenos Aires: Ediciones Cooperitivas.

Iñigo Carrera, Juan 2013, 'Method: From the *Grundrisse* to *Capital*', in *In Marx's Laboratory: Critical Interpretations of the* Grundrisse, edited by Riccardo Bellofiore, Guido Starosta, and Peter D. Thomas, Leiden: Brill, pp. 43–70.

Jameson, Fredric 2014, *Representing Capital: A Reading of Volume One*, New York: Verso.

Jappe, Anselm 2013, 'Sohn-Rethel and the Origin of "Real Abstraction": A Critique of Production or a Critique of Circulation', *Historical Materialism*, 21, no. 1: 3–14.

Kant, Immanuel 1998, *Critique of Pure Reason*, edited by Paul Guyer, translated by Allen Wood, Cambridge: Cambridge University Press.

Kaplan, E. Ann, and Michael Sprinker (eds) 1993, *The Althusserian Legacy*, London: Verso.

Kautsky, Karl 1887, *Karl Marx Oekonomische Lehren: Gemeinverständlich dargestellt und erläutert*, Stuttgart: Dietz.

Kojève, Alexandre 1980 [1947], *Introduction à la lecture de Hegel*, Paris: Gallimard.

Kurz, Robert 2016, *The Substance of Capital*, London: Chronos.

Labelle, Gilles 2020, 'Marx, lecteur d'Épicure', *Cahiers société*, 2: 151–70.

Lacan, Jacques 1991, *The Ego in Freud's Theory and in the Technique of Psychoanalysis, 1954–1955. The Seminar of Jacques Lacan, Book II*, translated by Sylvana Tomaselli, New York: W.W. Norton.

Lacan, Jacques 2016, *Anxiety, The Seminar of Jacques Lacan, Book X*, Cambridge: Polity.

Lalande, André 2010 [1923], *Vocabulaire technique et critique de la philosophie*, Paris: PUF.

Lange, Elena Louisa 2016, 'The Critique of Political Economy and the "New Dialectic": Marx, Hegel, and the Problem of Christopher J. Arthur's "Homology Thesis"', *Crisis and Critique*, 3, no. 3: 235–72.

Lange, Elena Louisa 2018a, 'Capital', in *The Bloomsbury Companion to Marx*, edited by Jeff Diamanti, Andrew Pendakis, and Imre Szeman, London: Bloomsbury.

Lange, Elena Louisa 2018b, *Value Without Fetish: Uno Kozo's Theory of Pure Capitalism in Light of Marx's Critique of Political Economy*, Leiden: Brill.

Lange, Elena Louisa 2019a, 'Form Analysis and Critique: Marx's Social Labour Theory of Value', in *Capitalism: Concept, Idea, Image. Aspects of Marx's* Capital *Today*, edited by Peter Osborne, Eric Alliez, and Eric-John Russell, London: CRMEP Books, pp. 21–35.

Lange, Elena Louisa 2019b, 'Money versus Value?' *Historical Materialism*, 28, no. 1: 1–34.

Laplanche, Jean, and Jean-Bertrand Pontalis 2018, *Language of Psychoanalysis*, New York: Routledge.

Lapointe, Sandra 2008, *Qu'est-ce que l'analyse?* Paris: Vrin.

Lapointe, Sandra 2011, *Bolzano's Theoretical Philosophy*, New York: Palgrave.

Lasowski, Aliocha 2016, *Althusser et nous*. Paris: PUF.

Laz, Jacques 1993, *Bolzano, critique de Kant*, Paris: Vrin.

Lazarus, Sylvain (ed.) 2015, *Politique et philosophie dans l'oeuvre de Louis Althusser*, Paris: PUF.

Lecourt, Dominique 1975, *Marxism and Epistemology: Bachelard, Canguilhem, and Foucault*, translated by Ben Brewster, New York: NLB.

Lesjak, Carolyn 2021, 'Dialectics', in *The Bloomsbury Companion to Marx*, edited by Jeff Diamanti, Andrew Pendakis, and Imre Szeman, London: Bloomsbury.

Levine, Norman 2009, 'Hegelian Continuities in Marx', *Critique*, 37, no. 3: 345–70.

Levine, Norman 2012, *Marx's Discourse with Hegel*, Basingstoke: Palgrave Macmillan.

Lietz, Barbara, and Winfried Schwarz 2023, 'Value, Exchange, and Heinrich's "New

Reading of Marx": Remarks on Marx's Value-Theory, 1867–72', *Historical Materialism*, 1–29.

Lordon, Frédéric 2010, *Capitalisme, désir, et servitude: Marx et Spinoza*, Paris: La fabrique.

Lukács, Georg 1972, *History and Class Consciousness: Studies in Marxist Dialectics*, Cambridge, MA: MIT Press.

Macherey, Pierre 1992, *Avec Spinoza*, Paris: PUF.

Macherey, Pierre 1999, 'En matérialiste', in *Histoires de dinosaure: Faire de la philosophie (1967–1997)*, Paris: PUF.

Macherey, Pierre 1998, *In a Materialist Way*: Selected Essays, Warren Montag (ed.), New York: Verso.

Macherey, Pierre 1997, *Introduction à l'Ethique de Spinoza: La réalité mentale* (2), Paris: PUF.

Macherey, Pierre 1998, *Introduction à l'Ethique de Spinoza: La première partie, la nature des choses* (1), Paris: PUF.

Macherey, Pierre 1997–2001, *Introduction à l'Ethique de Spinoza*, 5 vols, Paris: PUF.

Macherey, Pierre 1999, *Histoires de dinosaure : faire de la philosophie 1965–1997*, Paris: PUF.

Macherey, Pierre 2006, *A Theory of Literary Production*, translated by Geoffrey Wall, New York: Routledge.

Macherey, Pierre 2012, 'Lire *Le Capital*', in *Le centenaire du 'Capital'*, Paris: Hermann.

Macherey, Pierre 2011 [1979], *Hegel or Spinoza*, Minneapolis: University of Minnesota Press.

Macherey, Pierre 2021, 'Hegel or Spinoza: Return to a Journey', *Crisis and Critique*, 8, no. 1: 159–69.

Marx, Karl 1879, 'Notes on Adolph Wagner', retrieved from: https://www.marxists.org/archive/marx/works/1881/01/wagner.htm

Marx, Karl 1973, *Grundrisse: Foundations of the Critique of Political Economy (Rough Draft)*, translated by Martin Nicolaus, London: Penguin.

Marx, Karl 1975, MEGA² I/1, *Karl Marx Werke, Artikel Literarische Versuche bis März 1843*, Berlin: Dietz Verlag.

Marx, Karl 1975a, *Early Writings*, Rodney Livingstone, trans. New York: Penguin.

Marx, Karl 1976, *Capital: A Critique of Political Economy, Volume One*, translated by Ben Fowkes, London: Penguin.

Marx, Karl 1976b, MEGA² IV/1, *Karl Marx Friedrich Engels Exzerpte und Notizen bis 1824*, Berlin: Dietz Verlag.

Marx, Karl 1981, *Capital: A Critique of Political Economy, Volume Three*, translated by David Fernbach, New York: Penguin.

Marx, Karl 1982, MEGA² I/2, *Karl Marx Werke, Artikel, Entwürfe, März 1843 bis August 1844*. Berlin: Dietz Verlag.

Marx, Karl 1983, MEGA² II/5, *Karl Marx, Das Kapital: Kritik Der Politischen Ökonomie. Erster Band, Hamburg 1867*, Berlin: Dietz Verlag.
Marx, Karl 1987, MEGA² II/6, *Karl Marx, Das Kapital: Kritik Der Politischen Ökonomie. Erster Band, Hamburg 1872*, Berlin: Dietz Verlag.
Marx, Karl 1989, MEGA² II/7, *Le Capital, Paris, 1872–1875*, Berlin: Dietz Verlag.
Marx, Karl 1991, MEGA² II/10, *Karl Marx, Das Kapital: Kritik Der Politischen Ökonomie. Erster Band, Hamburg 1890*, Berlin: Dietz Verlag.
Marx, Karl 1996, *Later Political Writings*, translated by Terrell Carver, Cambridge: Cambridge University Press.
Marx, Karl 2008, 'Historical Materialism in Forms which Precede Capitalist Production', in *Karl Marx's* Grundrisse: *Foundations of the Critique of Political Economy 150 Years Later*, edited by Marcello Musto, London: Routledge, pp. 79–92.
Marx, Karl, and Friedrich Engels 1986, *Manifesto of the Communist Party*, edited by Terrell Carver, Cambridge: Cambridge University Press.
Matheron, Alexandre 1977, 'Le *Traité Théologico-Politique* vu par le jeune Marx', in *Cahiers Spinoza*, 1 (Summer): 159–212.
Matthys, Jean 2023, *Althusser lecteur de Spinoza: Genèse et enjeux d'une éthico-politique de la théorie*, Sesto S. Giovanni: Editions Mimésis.
Mattick, Paul 2019, *Theory as Critique: Essays on 'Capital'*, Chicago, Haymarket.
Matysik, Tracie 2023, *When Spinoza Met Marx: Experiments in Nonhumanist Activity*, Chicago: University of Chicago Press.
McIvor, Martin 2008, 'The Young Marx and German Idealism: Revisiting the Doctoral Dissertation', *Journal of the Philosophy of History*, 46, no. 3: 395–419.
McNulty, Tracy 2009, 'Demanding the Impossible: Desire and Social Change', *Differences*, 20, no. 1: 1–39.
Meaney, Mark 2015, 'Capital Breeds: Interest-bearing Capital as Purely Abstract Form', in *Marx's* Capital *and Hegel's* Logic, edited by Fred Moseley and Tony Smith, Chicago: Haymarket.
Montag, Warren 2013, *Althusser and His Contemporaries*, Durham, NC: Duke University Press.
Montag, Warren 1998, 'Editor's Introduction', in *In a Materialist Way: Selected Essays*, by Pierre Macherey, New York: Verso.
Montag, Warren 1999, *Bodies, Masses, Power: Spinoza and His Contemporaries*, New York: Verso.
Morfino, Vittorio 2015, *Plural Temporality: Transindividuality and the Aleatory between Spinoza and Althusser*, Chicago: Haymarket.
Morfino, Vittorio 2022, 'Althusser's Spinozism: A Philosophy for the Future?', *Journal of Spinoza Studies*, 1, no. 1, https://jss.rug.nl/article/view/38522.
Morfino, Vittorio 2023, 'Una nota su Heinrich e Althusser', in *La Scienza del Valore: La Critica Marxiana Dell'Economia Politica tra Rivoluzione Scientifica e Tradizione Clas-*

sica, by Michael Heinrich, edited by Riccardo Bellofiore and Stefano Breda, translated by Stefano Breda, Rome: PGreco.

Moseley, Fred (ed.) 2005, *Marx's Theory of Money: Modern Appraisals*, New York: Palgrave Macmillan.

Moseley, Fred (ed.) 2013, 'The Whole and the Parts: The Early Development of Marx's Theory of the Distribution of Surplus-Value in the *Grundrisse*', in *In Marx's Laboratory: Critical Interpretations of the* Grundrisse, edited by Riccardo Bellofiore, Guido Starosta, and Peter D. Thomas, Leiden: Brill, pp. 285–302.

Moseley, Fred (ed.) 2016, 'Editor's Introduction', in *Marx's Manuscripts of 1864–65*, Chicago: Haymarket.

Moseley, Fred (ed.) 2017, *Money and Totality: A Macro-Monetary Interpretation of Marx's Logic in 'Capital' and the End of the 'Transformation Problem'*, Chicago: Haymarket.

Moseley, Fred 2023, *Marx's Theory of Value in Chapter 1 of* Capital: *A Critique of Heinrich's Value-Form Interpretation*, Basingstoke: Palgrave Macmillan.

Moseley, Fred, and Tony Smith (eds) 2015, *Marx's* Capital *and Hegel's* Logic: *A Reexamination*, Chicago: Haymarket.

Müller-Doohm, Stefan 2004, *Adorno: A Biography*, Cambridge: Polity.

Murray, Patrick 2002, 'The Illusion of the Economic: The Trinity Formula and the "Religion of Everyday Life"', in *The Culmination of Capital: Essays on Volume III of Marx's Capital*, edited by Martha Campbell and Geert Reuten, New York: Palgrave.

Murray, Patrick 2013, 'Unavoidable Crises: Reflections on Backhaus and the Development of Marx's Value-Form Theory in the *Grundrisse*', in *In Marx's Laboratory: Critical Interpretations of the* Grundrisse, edited by Riccardo Bellofiore, Guido Starosta, and Peter D. Thomas, Leiden: Brill, pp. 121–48.

Murray, Patrick 2017, *The Mismeasure of Wealth: Essays on Marx and Social Form*, Chicago: Haymarket.

Mury, Gilbert 1963, 'Matérialisme et hyperempirisme', *La Pensée*, 108 (April): 38–51.

Musto, Marcello 2008a, 'History, Production, and Method in the 1857 "Introduction"', in *Karl Marx's* Grundrisse: *Foundations of the Critique of Political Economy 150 Years Later*, New York: Routledge, pp. 3–32.

Musto, Marcello 2020, *Last Years of Karl Marx*, Stanford: Stanford University Press.

Negri, Antonio 1985, *Marx au-delà de Marx*, Paris: L'Harmattan.

Nesbitt, Nick 2017, *The Concept in Crisis*: Reading Capital *Today*, Durham, NC: Duke University Press.

Nesbitt, Nick 2019, 'Marx's *Grundrisse*: An Inquiry into the Categorial Structure of Capitalism', in *The Bloomsbury Companion to Marx*, edited by Andrew Pendakis and Imre Szeman, London: Bloomsbury, pp. 41–56.

Nesbitt, Nick 2020, 'The Concept of the Commodity: Badiou and Marx, 1968/1989', in

Revolutions for the Future: May 68 and the Prague Spring, edited by Jana Berankova, Michael Hauser, and Nick Nesbitt, Lyon: Suture, pp. 122–39.

Nesbitt, Nick 2021, 'Bolzano's Badiou', *Filozofski Vestnik*, 41, no. 2.

Nesbitt, Nick 2022, *The Price of Slavery: Capitalism and Revolution in the Caribbean*, Charlottesville: University of Virginia Press.

Norris, Christopher 1991, *Spinoza and the Origins of Modern Critical Theory*, Oxford: Blackwell.

Oittinen, Vesa 2022, 'Soviet Spinoza: introduction', *Studies in East European Thought*, March, 2022.

Peden, Knox 2014, *Spinoza contra Phenomenology: French Rationalism from Cavaillès to Deleuze*, Stanford: Stanford University Press.

Post, Charles 2012, *The American Road to Capitalism*, Chicago: Haymarket.

Postone, Moishe 1993, *Time, Labor, and Social Domination: A Reinterpretation of Marx's Critical Theory*, Cambridge: Cambridge University Press.

Read, Jason 2007, 'The Order and Connection of Ideas: Theoretical Practice in Macherey's Turn to Spinoza', *Rethinking Marxism*, 19, no. 4.

Reuten, Geert 2014, 'An Outline of the Systematic-Dialectical Method: Scientific and Political Significance', in *Marx's* Capital *and Hegel's* Logic, edited by Fred Moseley and Tony Smith, Leiden: Brill.

Roudinesco, Elisabeth 1995, *Lacan*, New York: Columbia University Press.

Rosdolsky, Roman 1992 [1968], *The Making of Marx's 'Capital'*, London: Pluto Press.

Rubel, Maximilien 1977, 'Marx à la rencontre de Spinoza', *Cahiers Spinoza*, 1 (Summer): 7–28.

Rusnock, Paul, and Jan Šebestík 2019, *Bernard Bolzano: His Life and Work*, Oxford: Oxford University Press.

Saito, Kohei 2017, *Karl Marx's Ecosocialism*, New York: Monthly Review Press.

Schülein, Johannes-Georg 2022, 'On the Status of Nature in Hegel's Encyclopedic System', in *Hegel's Encyclopedic System*, edited by Sebastian Stein and Joshua Wretzel, New York: Routledge.

Šebestík, Jan 1986, 'La classe universelle et l'auto-appartenance chez Bernard Bolzano', *Eleutheria: Mathematical Journal of the Seminar P. Zernos*.

Sinaceur, Houya Benis 2013, *Cavaillès*, Paris: Les Belles Lettres.

Smith, Adam 1999, *The Wealth of Nations*, New York: Penguin.

Smith, Steven B. 1984, *Reading Althusser: An Essay on Structural Marxism*, Ithaca, NY: Cornell University Press.

Smith, Tony 2013, 'The "General Intellect" in the *Grundrisse* and Beyond', in *In Marx's Laboratory: Critical Interpretations of the* Grundrisse, edited by Riccardo Bellofiore, Guido Starosta, and Peter D. Thomas, Leiden: Brill, pp. 213–32.

Smith, Tony 2014, 'Hegel, Marx, and the Comprehension of Capitalism', in *Marx's* Capital *and Hegel's* Logic: *A Reexamination*, edited by Fred Moseley and Tony Smith, Leiden: Brill.

Sohn-Rethel, Alfred 2021, *Intellectual and Manual Labour: A Critique of Epistemology*, Chicago: Haymarket.

Sotiris, Panagiotis 2013, 'Rethinking Aleatory Materialism', in *Encountering Althusser: Politics and Materialism in Contemporary Radical Thought*, edited by Katja Diefenbach, Sara R. Farris, Gal Kirn, and Peter Thomas, London: Bloomsbury.

Sotiris, Panagiotis 2021, *A Philosophy for Communism: Rethinking Althusser*, Chicago: Haymarket.

Sotiris, Panagiotis n.d., 'The Strange Fate of British Althusserianism: The *Theoretical Practice* Group', unpublished manuscript.

Spinoza, Baruch 1988, *Éthique: edition bilingue Latin-Français*, Bernard Pautrat, editor and translator, Paris: Editions du Seuil.

Spinoza, Baruch 2002, *Complete Works*, translated by Samuel Shirley, Indianapolis: Hackett Publishing.

Spinoza, Baruch 2023, *Œuvres completes*, Bernard Pautrat, editor, Paris: Gallimard, Editions de la Pléiade.

Starosta, Guido 2013, 'The System of Machinery and Determinations of Revolutionary Subjectivity in the *Grundrisse* and *Capital*', in *In Marx's Laboratory: Critical Interpretations of the* Grundrisse, edited by Riccardo Bellofiore, Guido Starosta, and Peter D. Thomas, Leiden: Brill, pp. 233–64.

Stein, Sebastian, and Joshua Wretzel (eds) 2022, *Hegel's Encyclopedic System*, New York: Routledge.

Suchting, W.A. 1985, 'Marx, Hegel, and Contradiction', *Philosophy of the Social Sciences*, 15, no. 4.

Theoretical Practice [journal] 1971, 'Editorial', *Theoretical Practice*, 3–4 (Autumn): 1–9.

Thomas, Paul 2008, *Marxism and Scientific Socialism: From Engels to Althusser*, New York: Routledge.

Thomas, Peter D. 2002, 'Philosophical Strategies: Althusser and Spinoza', *Historical Materialism*, 10, no. 3: 71–113.

Thomas, Peter D. 2013, 'Althusser's Last Encounter', in *Encountering Althusser: Politics and Materialism in Contemporary Radical Thought*, edited by Katja Diefenbach, Sara R. Farris, Gal Kirn, and Peter D. Thomas, London: Bloomsbury.

Thompson, E.P. 1987, *Poverty of Theory*, New York: Monthly Review Press.

Tomich, Dale 2016, 'Introduction to the Second Edition: The Capitalist World-Economy as a Small Island', in *Slavery in the Circuit of Sugar: Martinique and the World Economy 1830–1848*, Albany: SUNY Press.

Toscano, Alberto 2008, 'The Open Secret of Real Abstraction', *Rethinking Marxism*, 20, no. 2: 273–87.

Toscano, Alberto 2014, 'Materialism without Matter: Abstraction, Absence, and Social Form', *Textual Practice*, 28, no. 7: 1221–40.

Tosel, André 2008, 'Pour une étude systématique du rapport de Marx à Spinoza: Remarques et hypotheses', in *Spinoza au XIXe siècle*, Paris: Editions de la Sorbonne, pp. 127–47.

Trendelenburg, Adolf 1840, *Logische Untersuchungen*. Berlin: Gustav Bethge, 2 vols.

Uchida, Hiroshi 2016 [1988], *Marx's Grundrisse and Hegel's Logic*, New York: Routledge.

Van der Linden, Marcel, and Gerald Hubman (eds) 2019, *Marx's Capital: An Unfinishable Project?* Chicago: Haymarket.

Van Ree, E. 2000, 'Stalin as a Marxist Philosopher', *Studies in Eastern European Thought*, 52: 259–308.

Vargas, Yves 2008, 'L'horreur dialectique (description d'un itinéraire)', in *Althusser: Une lecture de Marx*, Paris: PUF.

Wark, McKenzie 2019, *Capital is Dead: Is This Something Worse?* New York: Verso.

Williams, Caroline 2013, 'Althusser and Spinoza: The Enigma of the Subject', in *Encountering Althusser: Politics and Materialism in Contemporary Radical Thought*, edited by Katja Diefenbach, Sara R. Farris, Gal Kirn, and Peter Thomas, London: Bloomsbury, pp. 157–8.

Williams, Eric 1994, *Capitalism and Slavery*, Chapel Hill: University of North Carolina Press.

Wood, Ellen Meiksins 2002 [1999], *The Origin of Capitalism: A Longer View*, London: Verso.

Yakhot, Yehoshua 2012 [1981], *The Suppression of Philosophy in the USSR*, Oak Park: Mehring.

Young, Robert J.C. 2017, 'Rereading the Symptomatic Reading', in Nesbitt 2017, pp. 35–48.

Index

Abazari, Arash   109, 150–51, 153–54, 156, 164
Adorno, Theodor   9, 180, 232
Akselrod, Liubov   131
Alexis, Jacques Stephen   VIII
Althusser, Louis   IX–XVIII, 1–36, 38–63, 65,
  67–70, 72–81, 84–100, 102–04, 107–113,
  115, 121, 124, 127, 129–31, 134, 137–38, 141,
  156–57, 161–65, 175–78, 190, 209, 211–15,
  222, 224, 238, 239, 243, 261–62
  apodictic analysis (a. dialectic, a. demonstration, a. structure)   XII, XIII, XV,
    XVII, 2, 3, 6–7, 13, 14, 15, 17, 19, 23, 28, 31,
    32, 33, 38, 39, 61
  class struggle in theory   7, 8, 11, 17, 19, 21,
    38, 47, 59
  critique of empiricism (rejection of e.)
    35–36, 38, 58, 65, 68, 209, 212, 261
  nominalist deficiency (n. materialism, n.
    knowledge)   23, 24, 86, 87, 88, 239
  overdetermination   23, 56
  symptomatic reading   XI, 5, 8, 39, 75, 95
  theoreticism ('theoreticist' position)   IX,
    XV, XVI, 5, 6, 7–8, 17, 20, 32, 47, 57–58,
    60
Anderson, Kevin B.   266
Anderson, Perry   5, 58
Aristide, Jean-Bertrand   XIV
Aristotle   24, 27, 32, 35–36, 45, 113, 158, 159,
  171, 179, 192, 220, 243–46
Aron, Raymond   33
Arthur, Chris   XII, 1, 6, 15, 39, 72, 111, 114–15,
  120–28, 133–35, 137–49, 156, 162, 163,
  165, 177, 257, 268, 274

Bachelard, Gaston   32, 33, 70
Backhaus, Hans-Georg   41
Badiou, Alain   X, XII, XIII, XV, XVII–XVIII,
  2, 12, 14, 20, 21, 23, 25, 27, 30, 40, 46, 49,
  55, 56, 60, 61, 80, 89–95, 98–100, 111, 118,
  119, 155, 209–53, 256–58, 260, 262–66
  axiomatic thought (a. philosophy, a.
    materialism)   XVII, 61, 209, 215, 217,
    224, 227, 229, 231
  generic materialism   217, 231
  Idea of Communism   20, 232, 241, 263–
    64, 266

logic of the world (l. of capitalism)   121,
  233, 234, 249, 257, 258, 260
ontological (logical) materialism   209,
  210, 215, 216–217, 223–27
Balibar, Étienne   IX, XII, 2, 7, 9, 10, 19–21, 25,
  30, 56, 62, 75–77, 80, 127, 138, 191, 222,
  261, 262
Banaji, Jairus   108
Barbour, Charles   158–60, 192
Barthes, Roland   70
Bastiat, Frédéric Claude   32
Bauer, Bruno   158
Béguin, Victor   22
Bellofiore, Riccardo   114, 115, 123, 127, 140, 141,
  146, 147, 167, 179, 180, 181, 258
Bhaskar, Roy   26
Bianchi, Bernardo   192–194
Bidet, Jacques   1, 30, 98, 102, 103, 105, 108,
  124, 125, 127, 146–147, 165, 239
Bolzano, Bernard   XVII, 19, 24, 53, 111, 179,
  217–224, 245
Bordignon, Michela   117–19
Borges, Jorge Luis   68
Bottomore, Tom   122
bourgeois (petty b., b. thought, b. society)
  11, 122, 211, 230
Bouveresse, Jacques   18, 19, 218
Brentel, Helmut   150
Breton, Stanislas   47, 48, 55, 58, 76
Brown, Nathan   32
Brunschvicg, Léon   246
Bruschi, Fabio   7

Caligaris, Gastón   174
Cangiani, Michele   X
Canguilhem, Georges   72
Cantor, Georg   218, 245
commodification   VII, VIII, IX, XI–XII, XV,
  XVI, 5, 13, 14, 15, 26, 29, 30, 31, 32, 34, 40,
  46, 97, 99, 101–02, 109, 111, 121, 123, 124,
  125, 126, 135, 137, 142, 143, 144, 145, 151,
  162, 174, 175, 177, 181, 207, 208, 211–12,
  213, 215, 227–28, 229, 230, 231–32, 234,
  235, 236, 237, 240, 241, 242–43, 245, 247,
  249, 250–52, 253, 254–55, 257, 258, 260,
  265–66

capitalist accumulation (a. of commodities)   VIII, 14, 104, 141, 144, 161, 174, 175, 191, 232, 254, 258
capitalist mode of production   VIII, 12, 31, 63, 84, 103, 109, 128, 134, 141, 144, 145, 151, 162, 174, 224, 229, 254
  critique of c.   20, 210, 213, 227
  development of c.   110, 121, 122
  industrial c.   15, 121
  posthuman c.   227, 228, 242
  primitive accumulation   VIII, 15, 30, 97, 101, 102, 104, 145
Carrera, Juan Iñigo   29, 211
Cassin, Barbara   X, 128, 179
Cassou-Noguès, Pierre   33
Cavaillès, Jean   18, 32, 33, 70, 111, 133, 210, 217, 219, 220, 224, 239
class struggle   7–8, 10–11, 12, 17, 19, 31, 38, 47, 59, 141, 142–143, 265
class exploitation   12–13, 14
Cole, Andrew   26
commodity (nature of c., c. production)   VIII, IX, XVI, 12, 31, 46, 63, 64–66, 101, 103, 104, 108–09, 112, 119, 122, 125, 126, 128, 133–34, 137, 138, 142, 144, 146, 147, 148, 149–58, 161–62, 165, 167, 168–75, 179–86, 189, 198–99, 200, 229, 231, 232, 249–57, 258–60
  c. fetishism   XVI, 30, 98, 232, 258
  c.-based society   98, 251
commodification   VII, VIII–IX, 46, 97, 139, 162, 175, 215, 229, 230, 233, 256
communism   VIII, IX, 151, 208, 209, 231, 236, 240, 245
contradiction (*Widerspruch*)   XII, XVII, 2, 16, 22, 23, 26, 30, 42, 65, 72, 75, 101, 103, 104, 108, 109, 110, 111–12, 113, 119, 120, 125, 127, 133, 134, 135, 138–39, 146, 149, 150–58, 161, 162, 164, 165, 168, 170, 171, 172–73, 174, 180, 189, 190, 193, 197, 199, 202, 204, 230, 231, 238–39
Cutler, Antony   8

Darimon, Alfred   32
Deborin, Abram   26, 129, 131
Defoe, Daniel   68

Deleuze, Gilles   74, 87, 129, 213
Democritus   84, 192, 195, 196
Derrida, Jacques   72
Desanti, Jacques   59, 217, 260
Descartes, René   45, 46, 53, 85, 90, 107, 166
Descombes, Vincent   7
dialectics   XII, 2, 22, 23–27, 50, 68, 121, 137, 159, 139, 238
Diefenbach, Katja   X
Dietzgen, Joseph   24, 110
Dilthey, Wilhelm   72
Dragstedt, Albert   153, 155
Dukas, Paul   233
Duménil, Gérard   18, 162
Duroux, Yves   56

Elliott, Gregory   5, 7, 50, 58, 271
Engels, Friedrich   5, 12–14, 24, 26, 31, 41, 58, 76, 99, 121, 135, 136, 140, 154, 196, 205
Epicurus   192, 195–197
Establet, Roger   62
Estop, Juan Domingo Sánchez   XVIII, 10, 11, 38, 39, 42, 43, 47, 50, 51, 55–57

Fallon, Jacques   27
Farris, Sara R.   X
Feuerbach, Ludwig Andreas   192, 237, 260
Fineschi, Roberto   114, 152
Fischbach, Franck   192
Fluss, Harrison   23, 24–26, 129, 130
Forster, Edward Seymour   27
Foucault, Michel   213
Fowkes, Ben   175, 194
Frege, Gottlob   155, 217, 218, 221, 223, 224, 228, 244, 245
Freud, Sigmund   XIV, 56, 238
Frim, Landon   129, 130
Fulka, Josef   XII

Gabler, Georg Andreas   191
Gane, Michael   8
Garaudy, Roger   9, 32, 49–51
Geroult, Martial   83
Goshgarian, G.M.   7, 8, 58
Gracq, Julien   233

INDEX 283

Haeckel, Ernst   50
Hallward, Peter   213, 220
Hegel, G.W.F.   XII, XVII, 6, 21–26, 29, 30, 39,
    41, 43, 50, 51, 60–62, 68, 80, 90, 92, 101,
    107, 108, 110–19, 121–26, 130, 137, 138,
    141, 145, 149–53, 155, 159, 160, 162, 163,
    165, 173, 174, 176, 178, 179, 186, 189–93,
    195, 196, 212, 222, 223, 238, 243, 246,
    260
  Absolute Subject   XIV, 109
  Aufhebung   XVII, 65, 67, 100, 101, 103, 164,
    167, 190
  Hegelian negative dialectics   2, 68, 238
  Reflexionsbestimmungen   XVII, 41, 149,
    150, 151, 156, 157, 160, 164
Heinrich, Michael   1, 5, 12, 14, 17, 27, 32, 41,
    64, 65, 102, 107, 119–21, 124, 136, 137, 142,
    150, 153–56, 158, 161, 164, 165, 167–71,
    175–92, 231, 250–52
Hemming, Laurence   XVI
Hubman, Gerald   99
Huhn, Wilson   191
Hume, David   28
Hussain, Athar   IX
Husserl, Edmund   72, 111, 218

ideology (theory of i., i. critique)   10, 22,
    30, 50, 70, 77, 80, 97, 98, 99, 211, 214,
    216
Iñigo Carrera, Juan   29, 211

Jacobi, Carl Gustav Jacob   25
Jameson, Fredric   104
Jappe, Anselm   180
Jelles, Jarig   193

Kant, Immanuel   18, 92, 111, 219, 223, 226,
    243, 246, 248
Kaplan, E. Ann   X
Kautsky, Karl   12, 177–78
Kirn, Gal   X
Kojève, Alexandre   103, 238
Kosík, Karel   114
Koyré, Alexandre   239
Kugelmann, Ludwig   110, 154
Kurz, Robert   176, 265

Labelle, Gilles   195
labour   XVI, 15, 35, 64, 73, 104, 105, 138, 142,
    145, 146, 147, 155, 167, 168, 169, 180–89,
    198, 199, 245, 251, 252, 255, 256
  abstract labour   13, 64, 67, 104, 124, 165,
    167, 168, 169, 176, 186, 235, 241, 251, 252,
    255, 258, 259, 260
  labour power   VIII, IX, XVI, 13, 30, 97,
    101, 105, 109, 126, 138, 140, 147, 148, 199,
    201–02, 204, 205, 212, 227, 228, 249, 262,
    265
  labour theory of value   VIII, IX, 200, 243,
    258
Lacan, Jacques   XIII, XIV, 50, 56, 135, 136,
    218, 222–23, 235–42
Lalande, André   X, 27, 31, 32, 46, 49, 111, 134,
    172, 178, 179, 229, 230
Lange, Elena Louisa   124
Laplanche, Jean   47, 50, 210
Lapointe, Sandra   205, 217
Lasowski, Aliocha   63
Lassalle, Ferdinand   23
Laz, Jacques   218–221, 223
Lazarus, Sylvain   263
Lenin, Vladimir Ilyich   23, 40, 68, 85, 87, 129
Lesjak, Carolyn   26
Levine, Norman   108, 115, 195
Lévi-Strauss, Claude   72, 73, 80, 87, 213–15,
    227
Libera, Alain de   179
Lietz, Barbara   176, 177
Linden, Marcel van der   99
Lordon, Frédéric   192
Louverture, Toussaint   233
Lucretius Carus, Titus   75, 84
Lukács, Georg   10, 114, 115, 122–23, 128, 133,
    135, 266
Luxemburg, Rosa   115, 122

Macherey, Pierre   XII–XIII, XV, XVII, 1–4, 6,
    16, 18, 20–21, 23–25, 27, 28, 30, 34–40,
    42–43, 45, 46, 48, 53–56, 58–85, 87–93,
    95–96, 99–104, 106–10, 112–15, 120, 121,
    123–34, 138, 148–49, 158, 162–64, 166,
    173, 193, 202–04, 206–07, 222, 223, 230,
    238, 262
  literary (textual) production (p. of the
    text)   70, 74, 77
  materialist analysis   68, 75, 76, 80–81,
    101, 104, 106, 110
Madonia, Franca   XIII

Marx, Karl VII–XVIII, 1–24, 26–36, 38–43, 46, 47, 49, 50–53, 56, 60–69, 75–79, 84, 87, 96–115, 119–28, 130, 132–213, 215, 216, 222, 226–41, 243–46, 249–62, 265, 266
   additive synthetic (dialectical) method XVII, 163, 172
   critique of political economy VII, XI, XV, XVI, 11, 12, 14, 16, 31, 33, 35, 63, 65, 99, 137, 143, 178, 192, 203, 208, 210, 227, 230, 231, 232, 235, 236, 243, 245, 260, 262
   process (method) of exposition 28, 42, 61, 67, 68, 107, 108, 111, 113, 115, 120, 121, 145, 148, 157, 164, 189, 190, 197
   social form VII–XII, XIV, XV, XVI, XVII–XVIII, 1, 3, 4, 5, 8, 9, 11, 13–16, 29, 30, 32, 35, 39, 42, 44, 45, 46, 56, 59, 61, 63, 76, 87, 97, 100, 101, 104, 106, 107, 109, 110–111, 115, 120, 121, 122, 124, 126, 131, 133–134, 139, 141, 143, 145, 147, 151, 161, 167, 174. 175, 177–178, 184, 190, 197, 209, 210, 212, 217, 222, 227, 230–31, 234, 235–36, 241, 242–43, 245, 247, 249, 251–52, 253–260, 265–66
   thought-concrete (*Gedankenkonkretum*) 17, 34, 40, 60, 69, 78, 89, 102, 103, 177, 178, 180, 200, 211, 234
Maspero, François 1
Matheron, Alexandre 192
Matheron, François 9
Matthys, Jean XI, 2, 6–8, 10, 40, 42–45, 49, 50, 56, 89, 94
Mattick, Paul 259
Matysik, Tracie 50, 192
McIvor, Martin 195
McNulty, Tracy XIII, XIV, 136
Meiksins Wood, Ellen VIII, 102
Michel, Natasha 263
monism XI, XIV, XV, 44, 48, 49–56, 59, 89, 129, 130, 135
Montag, Warren 55, 68, 71–74, 81, 87, 127, 131
Morfino, Vittorio XIII, 1, 3, 4, 74, 75, 80, 84
Moseley, Fred 6, 80, 105, 106, 114, 120, 134–136, 139, 140, 156, 167, 169, 171, 176, 177, 179–88, 200, 201, 254, 257
Müller-Doohm, Stefan 9
Murray, Patrick IX, 26, 103, 114, 140, 200, 251, 252, 277
Mury, Gilbert 49, 51–55
Musto, Marcello 13, 15, 31, 32, 231, 266

Navarro, Fernanda 49
Nesbitt, Nick VIII, X, XI, 32, 39, 102, 105, 179, 198, 201, 211, 218

Oittinen, Vesa 26, 129
Oldenburg, Henry 164
opposition (*Gegensatz*) 65, 152, 153, 157–58, 159, 160, 172, 175, 193

Peden, Knox 83, 213
Plato 244
Plekhanov, Georgi Valentinovich XIV, 49, 50, 52, 54, 59, 121, 129
Poincaré, Henri 246
political epistemology IX, XII, 2, 3, 7, 8, 202, 206
Pontalis, Jean-Bertrand 47, 50, 210
Postone, Moishe 245, 246, 264, 265
proletariat 10, 30, 102–103, 122, 236, 237
Proust, Marcel 124

Rancière, Jacques 6, 20, 21, 62, 222
Read, Jason 84
real object 8, 9, 29, 34, 38, 40–41, 42, 56, 57, 58, 69, 90, 91, 93, 111, 214, 259, 261
Ree, Erik Van 50
reflections of determination (*Reflexionsbestimmungen*) XVII, 41, 149, 150, 156, 157, 160, 164
Reichelt, Helmut 41
Reinhard, Kenneth 268
Reuten, Geert XII, 114, 121, 122, 137, 141, 156
Ricardo, David 32, 35, 63, 251
Ricœur, Paul 48
Rimbaud, Arthur 323
Robert, Hubert 233
Robespierre, Maximilien XIV
Rosdolsky, Roman 125
Roudinesco, Elisabeth XIII, 238
Rousseau, Jean-Jacques 233
Roy, Joseph 66, 154, 189, 205
Rubel, Maximilien 192, 194, 195, 197
Rubin, Isaak Illich 76
Rusnock, Paul 218, 220
Russell, Bertrand 118, 119, 224, 225, 245, 248

Saito, Kohei 266
Sartre, Jean-Paul 233
Schmidt, Günther 192

INDEX

Schoenberg, Arnold 233
Schwarz, Winfried 176, 177
Šebestík, Jan 218, 220
Shulyatikov, Vladimir 50
Smith, Adam 29, 30, 32, 35, 63, 69, 211, 212
Smith, Tony XII, 6, 30, 80, 114, 115, 156, 257
Sohn-Rethel, Alfred X, 76, 180
Sotiris, Panagiotis IX, 8, 12, 20, 56
Spinoza, Baruch XI–XV, XVII, 2–4, 6–9, 12, 13, 16, 17, 20, 21, 24–26, 28, 29, 31, 33–38, 40–50, 53–62, 68, 69, 71, 73–75, 79–96, 98–102, 105–06, 109–13, 115, 116, 124, 127–35, 140, 143, 148–49, 158, 161, 162, 164, 166, 173, 179, 181, 189, 192–95, 197–99, 202, 203, 205, 206, 208, 215, 216, 222, 230, 238, 239, 262
  attribute of extension 34, 46, 60, 81, 82, 94, 95, 96, 110, 181
  attribute of thought XIII, XVI, 3, 6, 16, 29, 34, 38, 57, 66, 77, 81, 88, 94, 96, 105, 110, 162, 166, 196, 259, 261
  common notions 3, 42, 57, 87, 96–97, 98, 103, 132, 197, 202, 203, 206–07
  substance X, XI, XIV, XV, XVI, 3, 4, 6, 13, 18–25, 40, 43–52, 54–61, 64, 67, 81–82, 84, 85, 88–93, 97, 98, 101, 104, 105, 109–10, 113, 124, 129–34, 143, 148, 156, 159, 161–162, 165, 167, 176, 177, 179, 180–85, 193, 212, 227, 241, 249, 251, 252–53, 255, 258, 259–60
Stalin, Joseph Vissarionovich 50–52, 54, 59
Starosta, Guido 174
Stein, Sebastian 115

Thompson, Edward Palmer 5, 57, 58
Tolstoy, Lev Nikolayevich 68
Toscano, Alberto 76, 180
Tosel, André 192, 193
totality (*Totalität*) XI–XII, XIV–XV, XVII, 3, 4, 14, 26, 42, 45, 50, 52, 55, 59, 68–69, 71–72, 74–76, 78, 80, 82, 85, 88, 90, 93, 95, 100, 108, 113–41, 143, 147, 152, 156, 163–64, 166, 189, 193, 225, 226, 243, 245, 246, 248, 249
Trendelenburg, Adolf 158–60, 192
Trotsky, Leon 129

Valéry, Paul 233
value (nature or substance of v., v.-form – *Wertform*, v.-objectivity, v.-relationship) VIII, XVI, XVIII, 12–13, 14, 18, 21, 22, 34, 35, 36, 63, 64, 66, 67, 76, 97, 100, 102, 103, 104, 105, 109, 120, 122, 124, 126, 133, 134, 136, 138, 139, 141, 148, 150, 151, 153–56, 157–58, 164–65, 167–73, 174–77, 179–89, 191, 192, 198–201, 204, 205, 212, 230–31, 232, 235, 236, 241, 243, 245–46, 249, 251–53, 254–60
  exchange-value 13, 63, 64, 65, 66, 103, 108, 112, 133, 134, 151, 152, 153–54, 157, 158, 161–62, 164–65, 172, 173, 176, 179–80, 182, 188, 189, 228–29, 249–53, 254–56, 257, 258, 259
  surplus value IX, XVI, 13, 30, 42, 46, 64, 65, 66, 103, 104, 105, 106, 109, 111, 119, 124, 125, 126, 134–35, 140, 143, 144, 146–147, 148, 151, 165, 179, 184, 197, 198, 199, 200, 201, 204, 227, 239, 251, 257, 265
  use-value 64, 65, 67, 100, 103, 108, 112, 134, 138, 151, 152, 153–54, 157–58, 161–62, 164, 167, 169, 171, 172, 173, 179, 183, 185, 189, 226, 228–29, 249–50, 256
Vargas, Yves 50
Verne, Jules 68

Wagner, Adolph IX, 185, 231, 254
Wark, Mackenzie 7
Williams, Eric 56
Wittgenstein, Ludwig 235
Wood, Ellen Meiksins VIII, IX, 102
Wretzel, Joshua 115

Yakhot, Yehoshua 128, 129, 131

Zasulich, Vera 15

www.ingramcontent.com/pod-product-compliance
Lightning Source LLC
Chambersburg PA
CBHW070612030426
42337CB00020B/3771